Artificial Neural Systems Handbook

Volume II

Artificial Neural Systems Handbook
Volume II

Edited by **Sophia Nelson**

LANRYE
INTERNATIONAL

New Jersey

Published by Clanrye International,
55 Van Reypen Street,
Jersey City, NJ 07306, USA
www.clanryeinternational.com

Artificial Neural Systems Handbook: Volume II
Edited by Sophia Nelson

International Standard Book Number: 978-1-63240-071-0 (Hardback)

This book contains information obtained from authentic and highly regarded sources. Copyright for all individual chapters remain with the respective authors as indicated. A wide variety of references are listed. Permission and sources are indicated; for detailed attributions, please refer to the permissions page. Reasonable efforts have been made to publish reliable data and information, but the authors, editors and publisher cannot assume any responsibility for the validity of all materials or the consequences of their use.

The publisher's policy is to use permanent paper from mills that operate a sustainable forestry policy. Furthermore, the publisher ensures that the text paper and cover boards used have met acceptable environmental accreditation standards.

Trademark Notice: Registered trademark of products or corporate names are used only for explanation and identification without intent to infringe.

Printed in the United States of America.

Contents

Preface

The easiest way to define a neural network would be the following- It is a computing system or network which consists of simple and highly interconnected processing elements. These processing elements process information and data through their dynamic state response to external inputs and stimuli. In computer science and in fields related to it, artificial neural systems or networks usually refer to models that are inspired by a living organism's central nervous system, focussing on the brain. It is a system that is capable of pattern recognition as well as machine learning. This field does not use traditional programming. Instead it involves the creation of huge parallel networks and the training and programming of those networks towards solving specific problems. There are other machine learning systems as well and like those systems neural networks are often used to solve a huge variety of tasks which are difficult to solve using common and ordinary rule based programming, including processes like speech recognition and computer vision. These are biologically inspired methods of computing and are often believed to be the next major advancement in the computing industry. These have major ramifications in our daily lives and thus skilled technicians and researchers are of course required.

This book is an attempt to compile and collate all available research on artificial neural systems under one aegis. I am grateful to those who put their hard work, effort and expertise into these research projects as well as those who were supportive in this endeavour.

Editor

An Optimal Implementation on FPGA of a Hopfield Neural Network

W. Mansour,[1] R. Ayoubi,[2] H. Ziade,[3] R. Velazco,[1] and W. EL Falou[3, 4]

[1] *TIMA Laboratory, 46 avenue Félix Viallet, 38031 Grenoble, France*
[2] *Department of Computer Engineering, University of Balamand, Tripoli, Lebanon*
[3] *Electrical and Electronics Department, Faculty of Engineering I, Lebanese University, El Arz Street, El Kobbe, Tripoli, Lebanon*
[4] *Lebanese French University of Technology and Applied Sciences, Tripoli, Lebanon*

Correspondence should be addressed to W. EL Falou, wafalou99@hotmail.com

Academic Editor: Paolo Del Giudice

The associative Hopfield memory is a form of recurrent Artificial Neural Network (ANN) that can be used in applications such as pattern recognition, noise removal, information retrieval, and combinatorial optimization problems. This paper presents the implementation of the Hopfield Neural Network (HNN) parallel architecture on a SRAM-based FPGA. The main advantage of the proposed implementation is its high performance and cost effectiveness: it requires $O(1)$ multiplications and $O(\log N)$ additions, whereas most others require $O(N)$ multiplications and $O(N)$ additions.

1. Introduction

Artificial Neural Networks (ANN's) have become a subject of very dynamic and extensive research [1–4]. One important factor is the progress in VLSI technology, which makes easier the implementation and testing of ANNs in ways not available in the past. Indeed, the improvement of VLSI technology makes feasible the implementation of massively parallel systems with thousands of processors. Another important factor is the resurging of ANNs as a powerful paradigm for complex classification and pattern recognition applications.

There are many publications in the literature concerning the implementation of Hopfield Neural Network (HNN) in FPGAs (Field Programmable Gates Arrays). In [2] an implementation of HNN on Xilinx VirtexE is used for block truncation coding for image/video compression. Reference [4] describes an implementation of HNN on FPGA (Virtex-4LX160) for the identification of symmetrically structured DNA motifs in Alpha Data, which has better performance than the same algorithms implemented in C++ on a IBM X260 Server. In another work [1] is studied the implementation of an associative memory neural network (AMNN) using reconfigurable hardware devices such as FPGA and its applications in image pattern recognition systems. In

reference [5], the authors use a modified rule training (simultaneous perturbation learning rule) for HNN and showe its implementation in an FPGA.

The basic *associative memory* paradigm can be defined as the storage of a set of patterns in such a way that if a new pattern X is presented, the response is a pattern among the stored patterns which closely resembles X. This implies that it is possible to recall the complete pattern even if only part of it is available. This powerful concept can be utilized in many applications such as pattern recognition, image reconstruction from a partial image, noise removal, and information retrieval. The Hopfield Neural Network, a very interesting model of ANNs which was discovered by Hopfield in the 80's [6], can be used as an associative memory and as a solver of combinatorial optimization problems.

HNN consists basically of a number, usually large, of simple processing units (neurons) with small local memory per neuron. These neurons are interconnected via the so-called synapses. Thus, highly parallel computing systems with simple processing elements and point-to-point communication are typical target architectures for efficiently implementing ANNs.

Several mapping schemes have been reported to implement neural network algorithms on parallel architectures.

Examples can be found in [7–17]. In this paper, an implementation of HNN into an SRAM-based FPGA is shown.

In Section 2, the theoretical aspects related to the studied HNN are presented. Section 3 describes the implementation of the HNN according to our approach. Section 4 shows the results of the simulations performed using the ModelSim Simulation tool. In Section 5 our implementation is compared with previous work. The conclusions and planned future researches are discussed in Section 6.

2. Description of the Proposed Algorithm

Hopfield Neural Networks are recurrent artificial neural networks. In this type of ANN, the processing elements are the neurons and every output of each neuron is connected to the input of all other neurons via synaptic weights. All weights are calculated using the Hebbian rule defined as follows:

$$\text{if } i \neq j \quad w_{ij} = \sum_{p=0}^{r} x_i^P x_j^P,$$

$$\text{if } i = j \quad w_{ij} = 0,$$

(1)

where $0 < i, j < N + 1$, $X^P = \{x_1^P, x_2^P, \ldots, x_N^P\}$, and $x_i^P \in \{-1, 1\}$; P is number of bits in pattern X and r is number of patterns set.

To provide an efficient design, with less hardware and much faster than existing state-of-the-art designs, we assume that the input patterns, "$a[i]$", are binary numbers. Then we apply 2 to come up with new input patterns, and we continue the iterations until the new input patterns are exactly equal to the old ones

$$a_i[t] = f(h_i[t]) = f\left(\sum_j w_{ij} a_j[t-1]\right).$$

(2)

This equation proposes the following computation steps which are performed for $1 \leq j \leq N$.

Step 1. Distribute $a_j[t-1]$ to all elements of column j in the weight matrix $W[t]$.

Step 2. Multiply $a_j[t-1]$ and W_{ij}.

Step 3. Sum the result of the above multiplication along each row of W to compute the weighted sums $h_i[t]$.

Step 4. Apply the activation function $f(h_i[t])$.

Repeat the above steps except that the distribution of $a_j[t-1]$ in Step 1 should be done to all elements of row j instead of column j. This is possible because the weight matrix is symmetric.

Each of Steps 2 and 4 can be performed concurrently in all active Processing Elements (PEs), and therefore, each operation will be performed in parallel taking only one cycle. Figure 1 shows how the multiplications of Step 2 are done in parallel for four nodes HNN. Each node (represented by a circle) corresponds to a PE and is numbered based on the index of the weight (e.g., PE23 corresponds to W_{23}).

Considering Step 3, the summations will be performed as follows: each odd PE will add the previous result to its even neighbor and store the result in its even PE. That is, $\text{PE}_{ij} \leftarrow \text{PE}_{ij} + \text{PE}_{i(j+1)}$, where j takes on even values. Then, each PE that is distant of a multiple of four will add its result to the PE two positions apart; that is, $\text{PE}_{ij} \leftarrow \text{PE}_{ij} + \text{PE}_{i(j+2)}$, where j is multiple of four. In step k, each PE that is distant of a multiple of 2^k apart will add its result to the PE 2^{k-1} positions apart to the right; that is, $\text{PE}_{ij} \leftarrow \text{PE}_{ij} + \text{PE}_{i(j+2^{k-1})}$, where j is multiple of 2^k. In this way, for each row the weighted sum $(h_i[t]/1 \leq i \leq N)$ will be computed and stored in each PE of column 0 in $\log N$ steps. The case for the next iteration is similar to the previous case except that the addition of the PEs previous results is performed columnwise instead of rowwise. The process of alternating between rowwise and columnwise summation from iteration to another is repeated until the HNN converges to a solution. The summation method is illustrated in Figure 2 for a row of 8 neurons. Notice that after $\log N$ summation steps each PE in column 1 will have the corresponding weighted sum. As shown, after three summation steps (i.e., $\log N$ steps), the final sum is stored in the PE_{i1} of the corresponding row. A detailed description of the algorithm can be found in [7, 8].

3. Implementation on an FPGA

Considering that the HNN follows two phases in order to effectively complete the work, learning and recognition phases are to be implemented.

3.1. Learning Architecture. The HNN must learn all the combinations that will be stored. The learning process will be executed serially for each of the combinations, thus, for N combinations N clock cycles are needed to finish this process.

An HNN of N-nodes requires N^2 learning units to be capable of calculating the $N \times N$ weight matrix calculated using the Hebbian rule given in (1). Following the same equation, the weight W_{ij} can be calculated by multiplying a_i by a_j and then summing the result with the previously saved weight. Since our inputs are binary, and the learning is bipolar $\{-1, 1\}$, the result of the multiplication should be $1(0 \times 001)$ if a_i is equal to a_j and $-1(0 \times \text{FFF})$ otherwise. Then the adder will add either -1 or 1 to the previously saved weight (Figure 3).

The fact that the weight matrix is symmetric with all W_{ii}'s equal to zero will allow to implement a learning scheme that requires only $(N^2/2) - N$ learning units.

3.2. Recognition Architecture. Two types of cells are used for the implementation of the recognition phase of the proposed algorithm. The first one, the Serial Node (SN), is responsible for both the multiplication of the weights by the input patterns and the addition of two serial data. It is important to note that SNs are used only in Step 1. The second one, called Master Node (MN), is used in the second step to provide the

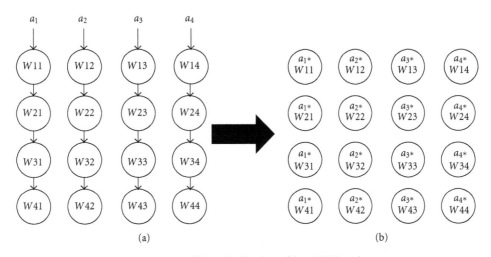

FIGURE 1: Parallel multiplication of four HNN nodes.

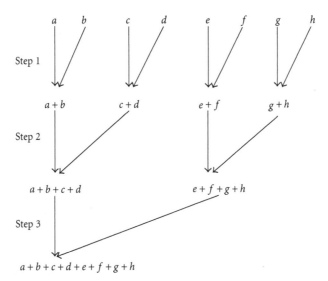

FIGURE 2: Addition of 8 cells.

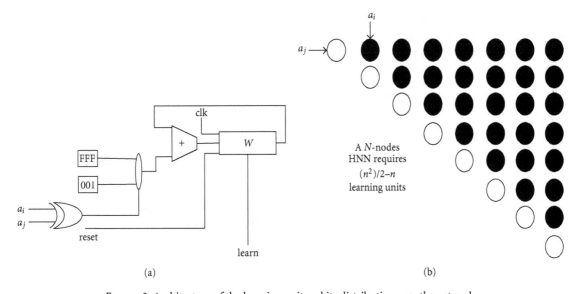

FIGURE 3: Architecture of the learning unit and its distribution over the network.

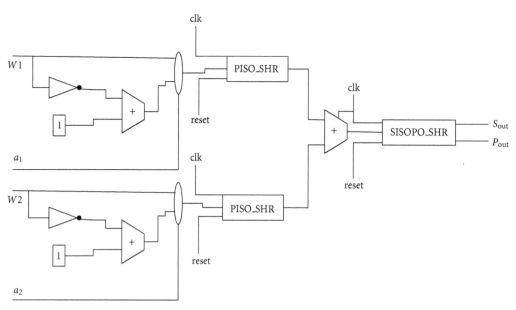

FIGURE 4: Architecture of the serial node (SN).

addition of two consecutive SNs, and in subsequent steps to provide the addition of two consecutive master cells.

To deal with larger networks, this chain of cells can be increased in a modular way. This would be done at the cost of adding extra hardware and using more cycles to obtain the final result. Each time the number of cells in a row increases by two, one master cell should be added.

3.2.1. The Serial Node (SN). Before going into the implementation details, it is worth mentioning that in order to avoid overflows the calculated weights are stored in 12-bit registers even though each weight can fit in smaller register. This is true even for large size networks. For instance, in the case of a network of 100 patterns, the range of the weights would be between -100 and $+100$. Therefore, using 12-bit registers should be more than enough to avoid overflows.

Owing that a_i are binary inputs and the calculated weights are coded with 12 bits, outputs of the learning unit and the multiplication task can be performed via a multiplexer that selects either the weight or its 2's complement. The first task of SN is to multiply the input pattern by the weight. The result is saved in a 12-bit parallel-in serial-out shift register (PISO_SHR). Then the serial output of this shift register will be added to another serial data. At the end, the result of this addition is saved in a serial-in serial-out parallel-out shift register (SISOPO_SHR) as shown in Figure 4.

3.2.2. The Master Node (MN). Since HNNs are supposed to be implemented on large networks, in Step 1 one MN should be used for every pair of adjacent SNs, while in subsequent steps another MN is used for every pair of adjacent master nodes.

As shown in Figure 5, the basic task of MN is to add two one bit inputs and store the result in a SISOPO_SHR similar to the one used in SNs.

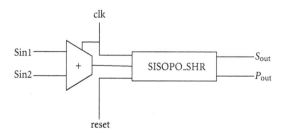

FIGURE 5: Architecture of the master node.

3.2.3. One Row Architecture. For the calculation of a row consisting of N nodes, SNs are always used in the first step while in all the other steps we use the MN. Figures 6 and 7 illustrate rows of four and eight nodes, respectively. Note that P_{out} outputs of cells other than master node are not used. Therefore they are unconnected. This is not a serious issue because the synthesis tools will optimize them away.

3.2.4. The Last Iteration. In order to stop the process one should wait until the previous input patterns are exactly equal to the new ones. The initial input patterns are used only in the first iteration whereas the recalculated patterns should be used in the following ones. This work is done by a state machine that reads the output of the network, checks it, calculates the new input patterns, and sends them to the network until the stopping condition is satisfied. Figure 8 presents an 8×8 mesh connected to the state machine (SM).

4. Simulation Results

The simulation was performed in many steps to ensure the correctness of the design. First of all, a simulation of the learning process has been done to train a 32-node HNN on three patterns: 0 x 10287C82, 0 x 243C2424, and 0 x

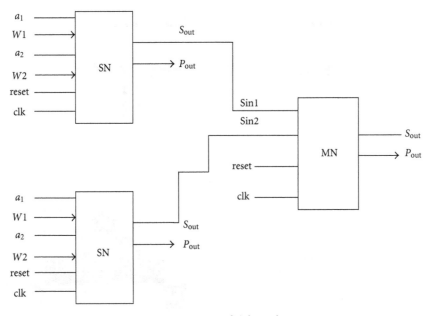

FIGURE 6: A row of eight nodes.

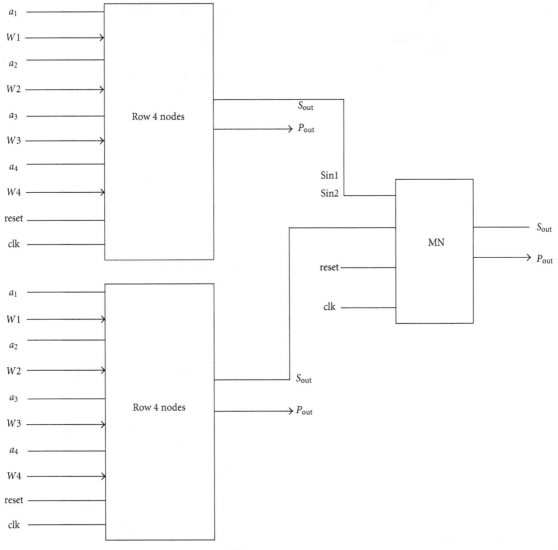

FIGURE 7: A row of four nodes.

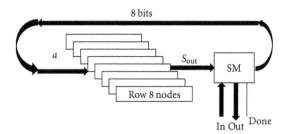

FIGURE 8: 8 × 8 mesh architecture.

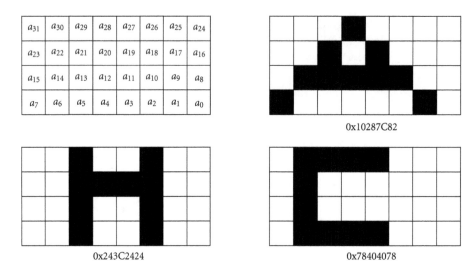

0x10287C82

0x243C2424   0x78404078

FIGURE 9: 4 × 8 patterns and the three training sets; black = 1, white = 0.

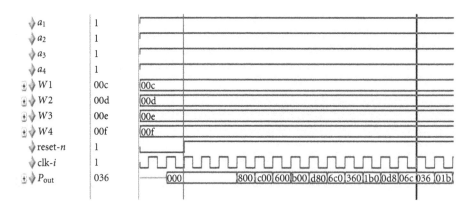

FIGURE 10: Simulation of a HNN's row of four nodes (the result 0 x 36 is the sum of the weights and it's done after 13 cycles).

78404078 (see Figure 9). The Ws correspond to the weights of one row consisting of 384 bits that is sixteen 12-bit each. The result is compared with another obtained by a training software implemented in C# to ensure the correctness of the design.

Figures 10 and 11 show the results of the simulation of a row of 4 nodes and 8 nodes, respectively. One can notice that a row that is twice larger takes two more cycles (serial adder + P_{out} register). The result of W_i is stored in P_{out} register.

After performing the training of the system, a simulation of the overall HNN 32 nodes network ("simmn32") was performed. "sys_o" is the output pattern after a "done" signal is set, while "na" is the next input pattern and the "reset_n_o" is the reset signal of the next MN. Figure 12 shows the simulation of the HNN with correct input patterns. In addition to that, the simulation given in Figure 13, performed with faulty input patterns, shows that the system converges to the expected pattern after two iterations.

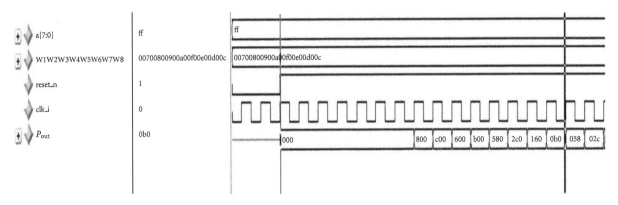

FIGURE 11: Simulation of a HNN's raw of eight nodes (the result 0 x 58 is the sum of the weights and it is done after 15 = 13 + 2 cycles).

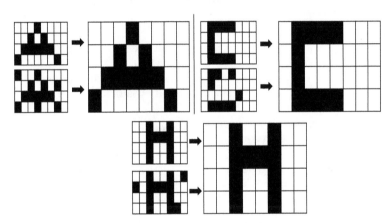

FIGURE 12: Real data example; good and disturbed inputs versus outputs.

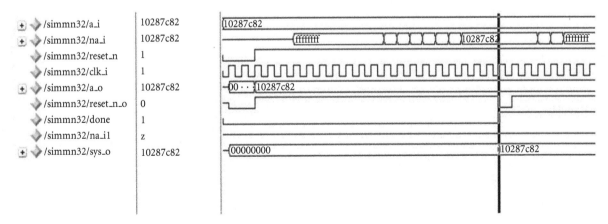

FIGURE 13: Simulation of 32-nodes HNN.

From Figures 12, 13, and 14, it can be seen that for both input patterns (values 0 x 10287C82 and 0 x 24BC2426), the HNN converges to patterns 0 x 10287C82 and 0 x 243C2424 memorized in the network. Thus, disturbed, missing, and correct patterns can be recovered correctly.

5. Performance and Comparison with Previous Work

From the simulation results presented in the previous section it can be clearly shown that a HNN of four nodes will only

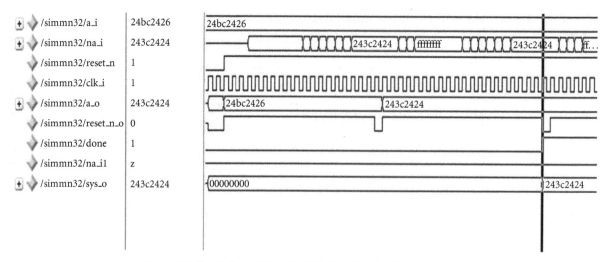

FIGURE 14: Simulation of 32 nodes HNN for disturbed input patterns.

take 13 cycles. A network of eight nodes will take $13 + 2 = 15$ cycles and in general a network of N nodes (N power of 2) takes $13 + 2 \times \log_2(N/4)$.

Many techniques for mapping ANNs onto parallel architectures have been proposed in the literature. Many of these techniques have been implemented on general-purpose parallel machines. Others were implemented on FPGA architectures.

A comparison with previous work relating general-purpose parallel machines shows the performance superiority of our implementation over known implementations on planar architectures. Most known implementations [11, 13, 14, 16, 17] require $O(N)$ time complexity, whereas the proposed implementation requires $O(\log N)$ time complexity. Implementations on nonplanar architectures, such as hypercube, show a minor performance gain over our design at the cost of much more complex interconnection network [10, 15]. This nonplanar architecture, when implemented on FPGA, requires a complex interconnectivity, which leads to more hardware resources and a lower time performance. This in turn could offset any performance gain.

Several FPGA implementations of ANNs have been reported in the literature [1–5]. Of special interest is the FPGA design proposed by Leiner et al. [1], because it implements the same Hopfield neural model. Both implementations targeted the same FPGA device, which is a Spartan2 chip the XC2S200. The implementation by Leiner et al. takes $O(N)$ multiplication and summation steps. Therefore, our implementation shows a higher performance. Moreover, we were able to achieve a clock rate of more than 157.604 MHz in contrast to a 50 MHz by Leiner et al.

6. Conclusions and Future Work

The implementation of an efficient algorithm for mapping into an FPGA the operation of the Hopfield associative memory was presented in detail. The time complexity is of order $O(\log N)$, which is better than any known algorithm on planar architecture and achieves the same performance

of higher degree architecture such as hypercubes without the added cost.

Future work will explore a similar design of an HNN including fault tolerance.

References

[1] B. J. Leiner, V. Q. Lorena, T. M. Cesar, and M. V. Lorenzo, "Hardware architecture for FPGA implementation of a neural network and its application in images processing," in *Proceedings of the 5th Meeting of the Electronics, Robotics and Automotive Mechanics Conference (CERMA '08)*, pp. 405–410, October 2008.

[2] S. Saif, H. M. Abbas, S. M. Nassar, and A. A. Wahdan, "An FPGA implementation of a hopfield optimized block truncation coding," in *Proceedings of the 6th International Workshop on System on Chip for Real Time Applications (IWSOC '06)*, pp. 169–172, December 2006.

[3] S. Saif, H. M. Abbas, S. M. Nassar, and A. A. Wahdan, "An FPGA implementation of a neural optimization of block truncation coding for image/video compression," *Microprocessors and Microsystems*, vol. 31, no. 8, pp. 477–486, 2007.

[4] M. Stepanova and F. Lin, "A hopfield neural classifier and its FPGA implementation for identification of symmetrically structured DNA motifs," *Journal of VLSI Signal Processing*, vol. 48, no. 3, pp. 239–254, 2007.

[5] Y. Maeda and Y. Fukuda, "FPGA implementation of pulse density hopfield neural network," in *Proceedings of the International Joint Conference on Neural Networks*, Orlando, Fla, USA, August 2007.

[6] J. J. Hopfield, "Neurons with graded response have collective computational properties like those of two-state neurons," *Proceedings of the National Academy of Sciences of the United States of America*, vol. 79, 1982.

[7] R. A. Ayoubi and M. A. Bayoumi, "An efficient implementation of multi-layer perceptron on mesh architecture," in *Proceedings of the IEEE International Symposium on Circuits and Systems (ISCAS '02)*, vol. 2, pp. 109–112, May 2002.

[8] R. A. Ayoubi, H. A. Ziade, and M. A. Bayoumi, "Hopfield associative memory on mesh," in *Proceedings of the IEEE International Symposium on Cirquits and Systems*, pp. 800–803, May 2004.

[9] J. Hwang and S. Kung, "Parallel algorithms/architectures neural networks," *Journal of VLSI Signal Processing*, 1982.

[10] K. Kim and V. K. P. Kumar, "Efficient implementation of neural networks on hypercube SIMD arrays," in *Proceedings of the International Joint Conference on Neural Networks*, vol. 2, pp. 614–617, Washington, DC, USA, 1989.

[11] Y. Kim, M. J. Noh, T. D. Han, and S. D. Kim, "Mapping of neutral networks onto the memory processor integrated architecture," *Neutral Networks*, no. 11, pp. 1083–1098, 1988.

[12] S. Y. Kung, "Parallel architectures for artificial neural nets," in *Proceedings of the International Conference on Systolic Arrays*, vol. 1, pp. 163–174, San Diego, DC, Calif, USA, 1988.

[13] S. Y. Kung and J. N. Hwang, "A unified systolic architecture for artificial neural networks," *Journal of Parallel and Distributed Computing*, vol. 6, no. 2, pp. 358–387, 1989.

[14] W. M. Lin, V. K. Prasanna, and K. W. Przytula, "Algorithmic mapping of neural network models onto parallel SIMD machines," *IEEE Transactions on Computers*, vol. 40, no. 12, pp. 1390–1401, 1991.

[15] Q. M. Malluhi, M. A. Bayoumi, and T. R. N. Rao, "Efficient mapping of ANNs on hypercube massively parallel machines," *IEEE Transactions on Computers*, vol. 44, no. 6, pp. 769–779, 1995.

[16] S. Shams and J. L. Gaudiot, "Implementing regularly structured neural networks on the DREAM Machine," *IEEE Transactions on Neural Networks*, vol. 6, no. 2, pp. 407–421, 1995.

[17] S. Shams and K. W. Przytula, "Mapping of neural networks onto programmable parallel machines," in *Proceedings of the IEEE International Symposium on Circuits and Systems*, pp. 2613–2617, New Orleans, La, USA, May 1990.

2

Cross-Validation, Bootstrap, and Support Vector Machines

Masaaki Tsujitani[1,2] and Yusuke Tanaka[1,2]

[1] Division of Informatics and Computer Sciences, Graduate School of Engineering, Osaka Electro-Communication University, Osaka 572-8530, Japan
[2] Biometrics Department, Statistics Analysis Division, EPS Co., Ltd., 3-4-30 Miyahara, Yodogawa-ku, Osaka 532-0003, Japan

Correspondence should be addressed to Masaaki Tsujitani, ekaaf900@ricv.zaq.ne.jp

Academic Editor: Tomasz G. Smolinski

This paper considers the applications of resampling methods to support vector machines (SVMs). We take into account the leaving-one-out cross-validation (CV) when determining the optimum tuning parameters and bootstrapping the deviance in order to summarize the measure of goodness-of-fit in SVMs. The leaving-one-out CV is also adapted in order to provide estimates of the bias of the excess error in a prediction rule constructed with training samples. We analyze the data from a mackerel-egg survey and a liver-disease study.

1. Introduction

In recent years, support vector machines (SVMs) have been intensively studied and applied to practical problems in many fields of science and engineering [1–3]. SVMs have many merits that distinguish them from many other machine learning algorithms, including the nonexistence of local minima, the speed of calculation, and the use of only two tuning parameters. There are at least two reasons to use a leaving-one-out cross-validation (CV) [4]. First, the criterion based on the method is demonstrated to be favorable when determining the tuning parameters. Second, the method can estimate the bias of the excess error in prediction. No standard procedures exist by which to assess the overall goodness-of-fit of the model based on SVM. By introducing the maximum likelihood principle, the deviance allows us to test the goodness-of-fit of the model. Since no adequate distribution theory exists for the deviance, we provide bootstrapping on the null distribution of the deviance for the model having optimum tuning parameters for SVM with a specified significance level [5–8].

The remainder of this paper is organized as follows. In Section 2, using the leaving-one-out CV, we focus on the determination of the tuning parameters and the evaluation of the overall goodness-of-fit with the optimum tuning parameters based on bootstrapping. The leaving-one-out CV

is also adapted in order to provide estimates of the bias of the excess error in a prediction rule constructed with training samples [9]. In Section 3, the one-against-one method is used to estimate a vector of multiclass probabilities for each pair of classes and then to couple the estimates together [3, 10]. In Section 4, the methods are illustrated using mackerel-egg survey and liver-disease data. We discuss the relative merits and limitations of the methods in Section 5.

2. Support Vector Machines and Resampling Methods

2.1. Support Vector Machines.
Given n training pairs $(\mathbf{x}_1, y_1), (\mathbf{x}_2, y_2), \ldots, (\mathbf{x}_n, y_n)$, where $\mathbf{x}_i$ is an input vector and $y_i \in \{-1, +1\}$, the SVM solves the following primal problem:

$$\min_{\beta, b} \quad \frac{1}{2}\boldsymbol{\beta}^T\boldsymbol{\beta} + C\sum_{i=1}^{n}\xi_i$$

$$\text{s.t.} \quad y_i\left\{\boldsymbol{\beta}^T\phi(\mathbf{x}_i) + b\right\} \geq 1 - \xi_i, \tag{1}$$

$$\xi_i \geq 0, \quad i = 1, 2, \ldots, n,$$

where $\boldsymbol{\beta}$ is a unit vector (i.e., $\|\boldsymbol{\beta}\| = 1$), T denotes the transposition of the matrix, $K(\mathbf{x}, \mathbf{x}_i) \equiv \phi(\mathbf{x}_i)^T \phi(\mathbf{x}_i)$ is the kernel function, C is the tuning parameter denoting the tradeoff between the margin width and the training data error, and $\xi_i \geq 0$ are slack variables. For an unknown input pattern $\mathbf{x}$, we have the decision function

$$f(\mathbf{x}) = \sum_{i=1}^{n} \alpha_i y_i K(\mathbf{x}, \mathbf{x}_i) + b, \tag{2}$$

where $\{\alpha_i, i = 1, 2, \ldots, n; \alpha_i \geq 0\}$ are the Lagrange multipliers. We employ the Gaussian radial basis function as the kernel function [3, 11, 12]

$$K(\mathbf{x}, \mathbf{x}') = \exp\left(-\gamma \|\mathbf{x} - \mathbf{x}'\|^2\right), \tag{3}$$

where $\gamma > 0$ is a fixed parameter, and

$$\|\mathbf{x} - \mathbf{x}'\|^2 = \langle \mathbf{x} - \mathbf{x}', \mathbf{x} - \mathbf{x}' \rangle. \tag{4}$$

Binary classification is performed by using the decision function $f(\mathbf{x})$: the input $\mathbf{X} = (\mathbf{x}_1, \mathbf{x}_2, \ldots, \mathbf{x}_n)^T$ is assigned to the positive class if $f(\mathbf{x}) \geq 0$, and to the negative class otherwise. Platt [13] proposed one method for producing probabilistic outputs from a decision function by using logistic link function

$$p(y = +1 \mid f) = \frac{1}{1 + e^{Af+B}}, \tag{5}$$

where $f_i = f(\mathbf{x}_i)$ and y_i represent the output of the SVM and the target value for the sample, respectively [14]. This is equivalent to fitting a logistic regression model to the estimated decision values. The unknown parameters A, B in (5) can be estimated by minimizing the cross-entropy

$$\operatorname*{Min}_{A,B} \left[-\sum_{i=1}^{n} \{y_i \ln p_i + (1 - y_i) \ln(1 - p_i)\} \right], \tag{6}$$

where

$$p_i = \frac{1}{1 + e^{Af_i+B}}. \tag{7}$$

Putting

$$t_i = \frac{y_i + 1}{2} = \begin{cases} 0: & y_i = -1, \\ 1: & y_i = +1, \end{cases} \tag{8}$$

from (6), (7), and (8), we obtain

$$-\{t_i \ln p_i + (1 - y_i) \ln(1 - t_i)\}$$
$$= t_i(Af_i + B) + \ln\{1 + \exp(-Af_i - B)\}. \tag{9}$$

Lin et al. [15] observed that the problem of $\ln(0)$ never occurs for (9).

2.2. Leaving-One-Out Cross-Validation

2.2.1. CV Score. We must determine the optimum values of tuning parameters C and γ in (1) and (3), respectively. This can be done by means of the leaving-one-out CV; a by-product is that the excess error rate of incorrectly predicting the outcome is estimated.

Let the initial sample $\mathbf{X} = \{\mathbf{X}_1, \mathbf{X}_2, \ldots, \mathbf{X}_{i-1}, \mathbf{X}_i, \mathbf{X}_{i+1}, \ldots, \mathbf{X}_n\}$ with $\mathbf{X}_i = (\mathbf{x}_i, t_i)$ be independently distributed according to an unknown distribution. The leaving-one-out CV algorithm is then given as follows (see, e.g., [5]).

Step 1. From the initial sample $\mathbf{X}$, $\mathbf{X}_i$ are deleted in order to form the training sample $\mathbf{X}_{[i]} = \{\mathbf{X}_1, \mathbf{X}_2, \ldots, \mathbf{X}_{i-1}, \mathbf{X}_{i+1}, \ldots, \mathbf{X}_n\}$.

Step 2. Using each training sample, fit an SVM and predict the decision value $\hat{f}_{[i]}$ for $\mathbf{X}_i$.

Step 3. From the decision value $\hat{f}_{[i]}$, we can predict $\hat{p}_{[i]}$ for the deleted ith sample using (7) and calculate the predicted log-likelihood $t_{[i]} \ln \hat{p}_{[i]} + (1 - t_{[i]}) \ln(1 - \hat{p}_{[i]})$.

Step 4. Steps 1 to 3 are repeated for $i = 1, 2, \ldots, n$.

Step 5. The CV score (i.e., averaged predicted log-likelihood) is given by

$$\text{CV} = -2\sum_{i=1}^{n} \{t_{[i]} \ln \hat{p}_{[i]} + (1 - t_{[i]}) \ln(1 - \hat{p}_{[i]})\}. \tag{10}$$

Step 6. Carry out a grid search over tuning parameters C and γ, taking the tuning parameters with minimum CV as optimal. It should be noted that the CV score is asymptotically equivalent to AIC (akaike information criterion) and EIC (extended information criterion) [16–18].

2.2.2. Excess Error Estimation. Let the *actual error rate* be the probability of incorrectly predicting the outcome of a new observation, given a discriminant rule on initial sample $\mathbf{X}$; this is useful for performance assessment of a discriminant rule. Given a discriminant rule based on the initial sample, the error rates of discrimination are also of interest. As the same observations are used for forming and assessing the discriminant rule, this proportion of errors, called the *apparent error rate*, underestimates the actual error rate. The estimate of the error rate is seriously biased when the initial sample is small. This bias for a given discriminant rule is called the *excess error* of that rule. To correct this bias and estimate the error rates, we provide the bias correction of the apparent error rate associated with a discriminant rule, which is constructed by fitting to the training sample in the SVM.

By applying a discriminant rule to the initial sample $\mathbf{X}$, we can form the realized discriminant rule $\eta_{\mathbf{X}}$. Let $\eta_{\mathbf{X}_{[i]}}$ be the discrimination rule based on $\mathbf{X}_{[i]}$. Given a subject with $\mathbf{x}_i$, we predict the response by $\eta_{\mathbf{X}_{[i]}}(\mathbf{x}_i)$. The algorithm for leaving-one-out CV that estimates the excess error rate when fitting a SVM is given as follows [9].

Step 1. Generate the training sample $\mathbf{X}_{[i]}$, and construct the realized discrimination rule $\eta_{\mathbf{X}_{[i]}}$ based on $\mathbf{X}_{[i]}$. Then, define

$$Q\left(t_i; \eta_{\mathbf{X}_{[i]}}(\mathbf{x}_i)\right) = \begin{cases} 1: & \text{incorrect discrimination}, \\ 0: & \text{otherwise}. \end{cases} \quad (11)$$

Then leaving-one-out CV error rate is given by

$$\frac{1}{n}\sum_{i=1}^{n} Q\left(t_i; \eta_{\mathbf{X}_{[i]}}(\mathbf{x}_i)\right). \quad (12)$$

Step 2. Calculate the apparent error

$$\frac{1}{n}\sum_{i=1}^{n} Q(t_i; \eta_{\mathbf{X}}(\mathbf{x}_i)). \quad (13)$$

Step 3. The cross-validation estimator of expected excess error is

$$\hat{r}_{\mathrm{CV}} = \frac{1}{n}\sum_{i=1}^{n} Q(t_i; \eta_{\mathbf{X}}(\mathbf{x}_i)) - \frac{1}{n}\sum_{i=1}^{n} Q\left(t_i; \eta_{\mathbf{X}_{[i]}}(\mathbf{x}_i)\right). \quad (14)$$

2.3. Bootstrapping. Introducing the maximum likelihood principle into the SVM, the deviance allows us to test the goodness-of-fit of the model

$$\begin{aligned} \mathrm{Dev} &= 2\left[\ln \hat{L}_f - \ln \hat{L}_c\right] \\ &= -2\sum_{i=1}^{n} \left\{t_i \ln \hat{p}_i + (1 - t_i)\ln(1 - \hat{p}_i)\right\}, \end{aligned} \quad (15)$$

where $\ln \hat{L}_c$ denotes the maximized log likelihood under some current SVM, and the log likelihood for the saturated model $\ln \hat{L}_f$ is zero. The deviance given by (15) is, however, not even approximately a χ^2 distribution for the case in which ungrouped binary responses are available [19, 20]. The number of degrees of freedom (d.f.) required for the test for significance using the assumed χ^2 distribution for the deviance is a contentious issue. No adequate distribution theory exists for the deviance. The reason for this is somewhat technical (for details, see Section 3.8.3 in [19]). Consequently, the deviance on fitting a model to binary response data cannot be used as a summary measure of the goodness-of-fit test of the model.

Based on the above discussion, the percentile of deviance for goodness-of-fit test can in principle be calculated. However, the calculations are usually too complicated to perform analytically, so Monte Carlo method can be employed [6, 7].

Step 1. Generate B bootstrap samples $\mathbf{X}^*$ from the original sample $\mathbf{X}$. Let $\mathbf{X}_b^*$ denote the bth bootstrap sample.

Step 2. For the bootstrap sample $\mathbf{X}_b^*$, compute the deviance of (15), denoted by $\mathrm{Dev}^*(b)$.

Steps 1 and 2 are repeated independently B times, and the computed values are arranged in ascending order.

Step 3. Take the value of the jth order statistic $\mathrm{Dev}^*(b)$ of the B replications as an estimate of the quantile of order $j/(B+1)$.

Step 4. The estimate of the $100(1-\alpha)$th percentile of $\mathrm{Dev}^*(b)$ is used to test the goodness-of-fit of a model having a specified significance level $\alpha = 1 - j/(B + 1)$. The value of the deviance of (15) being greater than the estimate of the percentile indicates that the model fits poorly. Typically, the number of replication B is in the range of $50 \leq B \leq 400$.

2.4. Influential Analysis. Assessing the discrepancies between t_i and $\hat{p}_i$ at the ith observation in (15), the influence measure provides guides and suggestions that may be carefully applied to a SVM [19]. The effect of the ith observation on the deviance can be measured by computing

$$\Delta\mathrm{Dev}_{[i]} = \mathrm{Dev} - \mathrm{Dev}_{[i]}, \quad (16)$$

where $\mathrm{Dev}_{[i]}$ is the deviance with ith observation deleted. The distribution of $\Delta\mathrm{Dev}_{[i]}$ will be approximated by χ^2 with d.f. = 1 when the fitted model is correct. An index plot is a reasonable rule of thumb for graphically presenting the information contained in the values of $\Delta\mathrm{Dev}_{[i]}$. The key idea behind this plot is not to focus on a global measure of goodness-of-fit but rather on local contributions to the fit. An influential observation is one that greatly changes the results of the statistical inference when deleted from the initial sample.

Platt [13] proposed the threefold CV for estimating the decision values in (9). However, the value of $\Delta\mathrm{Dev}_{[i]}$ may be negative because three SVMs are trained on splitted three parts of training pairs $(\mathbf{x}_1, y_1), (\mathbf{x}_2, y_2), \ldots, (\mathbf{x}_n, y_n)$. Therefore, in the present paper, we train a single SVM on the training pairs in order to evaluate the decision values $f_i's$ and estimate probabilistic outputs according to [15].

3. Multiclass SVM

We consider the discriminant problem with K classes and n training pairs $(\mathbf{x}_1, \mathbf{t}_1), (\mathbf{x}_2, \mathbf{t}_2), \ldots, (\mathbf{x}_n, \mathbf{t}_n)$, where $\mathbf{x}_i$ is an input vector and $\mathbf{t}_i = (t_{i1}, t_{i2}, \ldots, t_{iK})$ [10, 21, 22]. Let $p_{ii}, p_{i2}, \ldots, p_{iK}$ denote the response probabilities, with $\sum_{k=1}^{K} p_{ik} = 1$, for multiclass classification with

$$t_{ik} = \begin{cases} 1: & \text{input vector } \mathbf{x}_i \text{ is from } k\text{th class}, \\ 0: & \text{otherwise}. \end{cases} \quad (17)$$

The log-likelihood is given by

$$\ln L = \sum_{i=1}^{n}\sum_{k=1}^{K} \left\{t_{ik}\ln(p_{ik})\right\}. \quad (18)$$

For multi-class classification, the one-against-one method (also called pairwise classification) is used to produce a vector of multi-class probabilities for each pair of classes, and then to couple the estimates together [10]. The earliest used implementation for multi-class SVM is probably the one-against-one method of [21]. This method constructs $K(K - 1)/2$ classifiers based on the training on data from the kth and lth classes of training set.

The SVM solves the primal formulation [3, 10, 23]

$$\min_{\boldsymbol{\beta}^{kl}, b^{kl}, \xi^{kl}} \quad \frac{1}{2}\left(\boldsymbol{\beta}^{kl}\right)^T \boldsymbol{\beta}^{kl} + C\sum_t \xi_t^{kl}$$

$$\text{s.t.} \quad \left(\boldsymbol{\beta}^{kl}\right)^T \phi(x_t) + b^{kl} \geq 1 - \xi_t^{kl}, \quad \text{if} \quad y_t = k,$$

$$\left(\boldsymbol{\beta}^{kl}\right)^T \phi(x_t) + b^{kl} \leq -1 + \xi_t^{kl}, \quad \text{if} \quad y_t = l, \tag{19}$$

$$\xi_t^{kl} \geq 0.$$

Given K classes of data for any $\mathbf{x}$, the goal is to estimate

$$p_k = \Pr\{t = k \mid \mathbf{x}\}, \quad k = 1, 2, \ldots, K. \tag{20}$$

We first estimate pairwise class probabilities

$$r_{kl} \approx \Pr(t = k \mid t = k \text{ or } l, \mathbf{x}), \tag{21}$$

by using

$$r_{kl} \approx \frac{1}{1 + e^{Af+B}}, \tag{22}$$

where A and B are estimated by minimizing the cross entropy using training data and the corresponding decision values f.

Hastie and Tibshirani [21] proposed minimizing the Kullback-Leibler (KL) distance between r_{kl} and $\mu_{kl} = E[r_{kl}] = p_k/(p_k + p_l)$,

$$l(\mathbf{p}) = \sum_{k \neq l} n_{kl} r_{kl} \ln\left(\frac{r_{kl}}{\mu_{kl}}\right)$$

$$= \sum_{k<l} n_{kl} \left\{ r_{kl} \ln\left(\frac{r_{kl}}{\mu_{kl}}\right) + (1 - r_{kl}) \ln\left(\frac{1 - r_{kl}}{1 - \mu_{kl}}\right) \right\}, \tag{23}$$

where $r_{lk} = 1 - r_{kl}$ and n_{kl} is the number of training data in the kth and lth classes.

Wu et al. [10] propose the second approach to obtain p_k from all these r_{kl}'s by optimizing

$$\min \quad \frac{1}{2} \sum_{k=1}^K \sum_{k:k \neq l} \left(r_{kl} p_i - r_{kl} p_j \right)^2 \tag{24}$$

$$\text{s.t.} \quad \sum_{k=1}^K p_k = 0, \quad p_k \geq 0.$$

Thus, we can adopt the leaving-one-out CV similar to the method in Section 2.2.

Step 1. From the initial sample $\mathbf{X}$, $\mathbf{X}_i$ are deleted in order to form the training sample $\mathbf{X}_{[i]} = \{\mathbf{X}_1, \mathbf{X}_2, \ldots, \mathbf{X}_{i-1}, \mathbf{X}_{i+1}, \ldots, \mathbf{X}_n\}$.

Step 2. Using each training sample, fit a SVM in order to estimate $r_{kl[i]}$ by (22), and predict $(\hat{p}_{[i1]}, \hat{p}_{[i2]}, \ldots, \hat{p}_{[iK]})$ for the deleted ith sample $\mathbf{X}_{[i]}$.

Step 3. Steps 1 and 2 are repeated for $i = 1, 2, \ldots, n$.

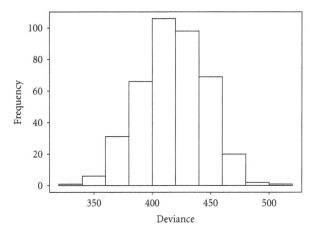

FIGURE 1: Histogram of the bootstrapped Dev*(b) for mackerel-egg survey data.

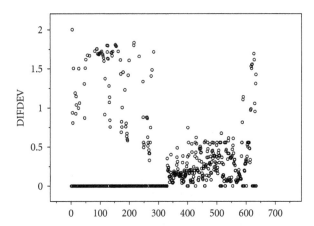

FIGURE 2: DIFDEV for mackerel-egg survey data.

Step 4. The CV score is given by

$$\text{CV} = \sum_{i=1}^n \sum_{k=1}^K \left\{ t_{[ik]} \ln\left(\hat{p}_{[ik]}\right) \right\}. \tag{25}$$

Step 5. Tuning parameters with minimum CV can be determined as optimal by carrying out a grid search over C and γ.

4. Examples

4.1. Mackerel-Egg Survey Data. We consider data consisting of 634 observations from a 1992 mackerel egg survey [24]. There are the following predictors of egg abundance: the location (longitude and latitude) at which samples were taken, depth of the ocean, distance from the 200 m seabed contour, and, finally, water temperature at a depth of 20 m. We first fit a SVM. In the same manner as described in [11], we determine tuning parameters C and γ. The optimum values of the tuning parameters are $(C, \gamma) = (28, 0.09)$. The bootstrap estimator of the percentile for the deviance is Dev*(b) = 444.31. A comparison with the deviance Dev = 443.132 from (15) suggests that the SVM fits the

TABLE 1: Error rates for mackerel-egg survey data.

Model	Apparent error rate	Leaving-one-out CV error rate
SVM	0.159	0.167
GAM	0.158	0.175
Neural network with three hidden units	0.153	0.181
Fisher's linear discriminant	0.180	0.185
Logistic discriminant	0.192	0.196

TABLE 2: Error rates for liver disease data.

Model	Training sample Apparent error	Leaving-one-out CV error	Test sample
SVM	0.085	0.209	0.292
Fisher's linear discriminant	0.366	0.360	0.340
Multinomial logistic discriminant	0.229	0.196	0.323

data fairly well. For reference purposes, the histogram of the bootstrapped Dev$^*(b)$ for $B = 400$ is provided in Figure 1.

We can estimate the apparent errors rate of incorrectly predicting outcome and leaving-one-out CV error rates for several models as shown in Table 1. The smoothing parameters in generalized additive models (GAM) [24] and the number of hidden units in a neural network in Table 1 are determined using the leaving-one-out CV. From Table 1, the leaving-one-out CV error rate for the SVM is the smallest among all models, but the apparent error rate is the smallest for the neural network. The CV scores are 477.04, 509.44, and 541.61 for the SVM, logistic discriminant, and neural network, respectively. This implies that the SVM is the best among these three models from the point of view of CV. Figure 2 shows the index plot of $\Delta\text{Dev}_{[i]}$, which indicates that no. 399 and no. 601 are influential observations at the 0.01% level of significance.

4.2. Liver Disease Data. We apply the proposed method to laboratory data collected from 218 patients with liver disorders [25–27]. Four liver diseases were observed: acute viral hepatitis (57 patients), persistent chronic hepatitis (44 patients), aggressive chronic hepatitis (40 patients), and postnecrotic cirrhosis (77 patients). The covariates consist of four liver enzymes: aspartate aminotransferase (AST), alanine aminotransferase (ALT), glutamate dehydrogenase (GIDH), and ornithine carbamyltransferase (OCT). For each (C, γ) pair, the CV performance is measured by training 70% and testing the other 30% of the data. Then, we train the whole training set by using the pair $(C, \gamma) = (93, 0.20)$, which achieves the minimum CV score (=187.93) and predicts the test set. The apparent and leaving-one-out CV error rates for traing and test samples for several models as shown in Table 2. As shown, the apparent error rate for SVM of

training sample and the error rate for SVM of test sample are the smallest among all models, but the leaving-one-out CV error rate for SVM of training sample is larger than that of the multinomial logistic discriminant model.

5. Concluding Remarks

We considered the application of resampling methods to SVMs. Statistical inference based on the likelihood approach for SVMs was discussed, and the leaving-one-out CV was suggested for determining the tuning of parameters and for estimating the bias of the excess error in prediction. Bootstrapping is used to focus on the evaluation of the overall goodness-of-fit with the optimum tuning parameters. Data from a mackerel-egg survey and a liver-disease study are used to evaluate the resampling methods.

There is one broad limitation to our approach: the SVM assumed the independence of the predictor variables. More generally, it may be preferable to visualize interactions between predictor variables. The smoothing spline ANOVA models [28] can provide an excellent means for handling data of mutually exclusive groups and a set of predictor variables. We expect that flexible methods for a discriminant model using machine learning theory [1], such as penalized smoothing splines, will be very useful in these real-world contexts.

References

[1] C. M. Bishop, *Pattern Regression and Machine Learning*, Springer, New York, NY, USA, 2006.

[2] N. Cristianini and J. Shawe-Tylor, *An Introduction to Support Vector Machines and Other Kernel-Based Learning Method*, Cambridge University Press, Cambridge, UK, 2000.

[3] C.-W. Hsu, C.-C. Chung, and C.-J. Lin, "A practical guide to support vector classification," 2009, http://www.csie.ntu.edu.tw/~cjlin/papers/guide/guide.pdf.

[4] P. Zhang, "Model selection via multifold cross validation," *Annals of Statistics*, vol. 21, pp. 299–313, 1993.

[5] B. Efron and R .J. Tibshirani, *An Introduction to the Bootstrap*, Chapman & Hall, New York, NY, USA, 1993.

[6] M. Tsujitani and T. Koshimizu, "Neural discriminant analysis," *IEEE Transactions on Neural Networks*, vol. 11, no. 6, pp. 1394–1401, 2000.

[7] M. Tsujitani and M. Aoki, "Neural regression model, resampling and diagnosis," *Systems and Computers in Japan*, vol. 37, no. 6, pp. 13–20, 2006.

[8] M. Tsujitani and M. Sakon, "Analysis of survival data having time-dependent covariates," *IEEE Transactions on Neural Networks*, vol. 20, no. 3, pp. 389–394, 2009.

[9] G. Gong, "Cross-validation, the jackknife, and the bootstrap: excess error estimation in forward logistic regression," *Journal of the American Statistical Association*, vol. 81, pp. 108–113, 1986.

[10] T.-F. Wu, C.-J. Lin, and R. C. Weng, "Probability estimates for multi-class classification by pairwise coupling," *Journal of Machine Learning Research*, vol. 5, pp. 975–1005, 2004.

[11] C. W. Hs and C. J. Lin, "A comparison of methods for multi-class support vector machines," *IEEE Transactions on Neural Networks*, vol. 13, pp. 415–425, 2002.

[12] C.-C. Chang and C.-J. Lin, "LIBSVM: a library for support vector machines," 2001, http://www.csie.ntu.edu.tw/~cjlin/libsvm.

[13] J. Platt, "Probabilistic outputs for support vector machines and comparison to regularized likelihood methods," in *Advances in Large Margin Classifiers*, A. Smola, P. Bartlett, B. Schölkopf, and D. Schuurmans, Eds., MIT Press, Cambridge, Mass, USA, 2000.

[14] A. Karatzoglou, D. Meyer, and K. Hornik, "Support vector machines in R," *Journal of Statistical Software*, vol. 15, no. 9, pp. 1–28, 2006.

[15] H. T. Lin, C. J. Lin, and R. C. Weng, "A note on Platt's probabilistic outputs for support vector machines," *Machine Learning*, vol. 68, no. 3, pp. 267–276, 2007.

[16] H. Akaike, "Information theory and an extension of the maximum likelihood principle," in *Proceedings of the 2nd International Symposium on Information Theory*, B. N. Petrov and F. Csaki, Eds., pp. 267–281, Akademia Kaido, Budapest, Hungary, 1973.

[17] M. Ishiguro, Y. Sakamoto, and G. Kitagawa, "Bootstrapping log likelihood and EIC, an extension of AIC," *Annals of the Institute of Statistical Mathematics*, vol. 49, no. 3, pp. 411–434, 1996.

[18] R. Shibata, "Bootstrap estimate of Kullback-Leibler information for model selection," *Statistica Sinica*, vol. 7, no. 2, pp. 375–394, 1997.

[19] D. Collett, *Modeling Binary Data*, Chapman & Hall, New York, NY, USA, 2nd edition, 2003.

[20] J. M. Landwehr, D. Pregibon, and A. C. Shoemaker, "Graphical methods for assessing logistic regression models," *Journal of the American Statistical Association*, vol. 79, pp. 61–71, 1984.

[21] T. J. Hastie and R. J. Tibshirani, "Classification by pairwise coupling," *Annals of Statistics*, vol. 26, no. 2, pp. 451–471, 1998.

[22] E. J. Bredensteiner and K. P. Bennett, "Multicategory classification by support vector machines," *Computational Optimization and Applications*, vol. 12, pp. 53–79, 1999.

[23] C. W. Hsu and C. J. Lin, "A formal analysis of stopping criteria of decomposition methods for support vector machines," *IEEE Transactions on Neural Networks*, vol. 13, no. 5, pp. 1045–1052, 2002.

[24] S. N. Wood, *Generalized Additive Models an Introduction with R*, Chapman & Hall, New York, NY, USA, 2006.

[25] A. Albert, *Multivariate Interpretation of Clinical Laboratory Data*, Marcel Dekker, New York, NY, USA, 1992..

[26] A. Albert and E. Lesaffre, "Multiple group logistic discrimination," *Computers and Mathematics with Applications*, vol. 12, no. 2, pp. 209–224, 1986.

[27] E. Lesaffre and A. Albert, "Multiple-group logistic regression diagnosis," *Computers and Mathematics with Applications*, vol. 38, pp. 425–440, 1989.

[28] Y. Wang, G. Wahba, C. Gu, R. Klein, and B. Klein, "Using smoothing spline anova to examine the relation of risk factors to the incidence and progression of diabetic retinopathy," *Statistics in Medicine*, vol. 16, no. 12, pp. 1357–1376, 1997.

3

Adaptive Neurofuzzy Inference System-Based Pollution Severity Prediction of Polymeric Insulators in Power Transmission Lines

C. Muniraj[1] and S. Chandrasekar[2]

[1] *Department of Electrical Engineering, K. S. Rangasamy College of Technology, Tiruchengode 637 215, India*
[2] *Department of Electrical Engineering, SonaPERT R&D Centre, Sona College of Technology, Salem 636 005, India*

Correspondence should be addressed to C. Muniraj, c.muniraj@gmail.com

Academic Editor: Christian Mayr

This paper presents the prediction of pollution severity of the polymeric insulators used in power transmission lines using adaptive neurofuzzy inference system (ANFIS) model. In this work, laboratory-based pollution performance tests were carried out on 11 kV silicone rubber polymeric insulator under AC voltage at different pollution levels with sodium chloride as a contaminant. Leakage current was measured during the laboratory tests. Time domain and frequency domain characteristics of leakage current, such as mean value, maximum value, standard deviation, and total harmonics distortion (THD), have been extracted, which jointly describe the pollution severity of the polymeric insulator surface. Leakage current characteristics are used as the inputs of ANFIS model. The pollution severity index "equivalent salt deposit density" (ESDD) is used as the output of the proposed model. Results of the research can give sufficient prewarning time before pollution flashover and help in the condition based maintenance (CBM) chart preparation.

1. Introduction

In a power system, outdoor insulators play an important role in maintaining the reliability of the system. Ceramic insulators are widely used in power transmission and distribution lines for a long time. In recent times, polymeric insulators are mostly preferred because of their superior insulation performance, in terms of contamination endurance compared with conventional ceramic insulators [1, 2]. When these insulators are installed near industrial, agricultural, or coastal areas, airborne particles are deposited on these insulators, and the pollution builds up gradually, which result in the flow of leakage current (LC) during wet weather conditions such as dew, fog, or drizzle. The LC density is nonuniform, and in some areas sufficient heat is developed leading to the formation of dry bands. Voltage redistribution along the insulator causes high electric field intensity across dry bands leading to the formation of partial arcs. When the surface resistance is sufficiently low, these partial discharges will elongate along the insulator profile which may eventually cause the insulator flashover. Pollution flashover along power line insulator has been a long-standing problem

for the security and reliability of power transmission line. Considering the recent developments in extra high voltage power transmission in India, it is imperative to predict the pollution severity of insulator surface before pollution flashovers occur and to provide an early warning for the operators. It is important to point out that the failure at any single point of the transmission network can bring down the entire system. Recent reports [3, 4] on grid disturbance in India indicate the loss of five thousand million rupees and 97% of interconnected generation on 2nd January 2001. Similar disturbances of lesser magnitudes were also observed during the period of December 2002 and 2005, Febuary and December 2006, January/Febuary 2007 and March 2008. One of the major causes identified was the pollution/contamination-induced flashovers. These events have amply portrayed that the performance of overhead transmission line string insulators and those used in outdoor substations are critical factors which govern the reliability of power delivery systems.

Quantities recommended to express pollution severity are the equivalent salt deposit density (ESDD), the leakage current, the air pollution measurements, and the nonsoluble

Adaptive Neurofuzzy Inference System-Based Pollution Severity Prediction of Polymeric Insulators in Power Transmission Lines

17

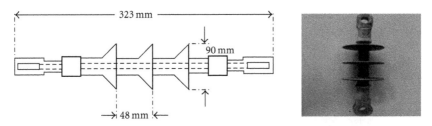

FIGURE 1: Photo and dimensions of the 11 kV composite insulator.

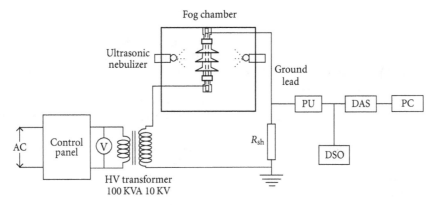

FIGURE 2: Schematic diagram of the experimental setup.

deposit density (NSDD) [5]. It has been verified that the leakage current affected by the operating voltage, temperature, and humidity can provide more comprehensive description about the state of the polluted insulators than other methods.

Suda [6] studied the LC waveforms and frequency characteristics of an artificially polluted cap and pin type insulator and classified the transition of LC waveforms into six stages in order to predict the flashover. Reddy and Nagabhushana [7] studied the leakage current behavior on artificially polluted ceramic insulator surface and derived the relationship between the surface resistance and leakage current. Sarathi and Chandrasekar [8] have shown that application of moving average technique for the trend analysis of leakage current signal could be useful to predict the surface condition of outdoor polymeric insulators. Chandrsekar and Kalaivanan [9] have investigated the harmonic content in polluted porcelain insulator and concluded that the harmonic content analysis is the effective diagnosis tool for outdoor insulators.

Neural networks have been intensively studied in the past decades. Cline et al. [10], Kontargyri et al. [11], and Saleh Al Alawi et al. [12] have implemented the neural network to predict the insulator flashover. Ahmad et al. [13] have successfully implemented the ANN model to predict the ESDD for contaminated porcelain insulators, but in this work, meteorological data like rainfall, wind velocity and so forth. are considered as the input to ANN model, which will vary according to the area and climate. Li et al. [14] have studied the time domain parameter of leakage current and give these parameters as input to ANN to predict the ESDD value. Considering the above facts, it is important to predict the pollution severity of

the transmission line insulators taking into account both time and frequency domain characteristics of LC. In ANN, the number of learning steps is high, and also the learning phase has intensive calculations. For complex problems, it may require days or weeks to train the network. The trained ANN can respond only if the input parameters are within training limits (minimum value to maximum value). Suppose that the inputs slightly deviate from the training limits, it may not give accurate results. The pollution problem in the outdoor insulator is very fuzzy due to external environmental factors, so the inputs selected to train the network and inputs given in real-time implementation may be slightly varying. So a new network model needs to be developed to overcome the drawbacks of simple artificial neural network model [11–14], and ANFIS-based model will be most suitable for prediction of ESDD values of power transmission line insulators. Having known all this, present paper focuses on prediction of pollution severity (ESDD value) on the surface of polymer insulators by using an adaptive neurofuzzy inference system (ANFIS).

2. Experimental Setup and Data Collection

A 11 kV silicone rubber insulator was used for the contamination experiments. Figure 1 shows the overall dimension of a 11 kV silicone rubber insulator used in this study. Figure 2 shows the schematic diagram of the experimental setup, where PU is protection unit, DSO is digital storage oscilloscope, DAS is data acquisition system, and PC is personal computer. The test insulator was suspended vertically inside the fog chamber (1.5 m × 1.5 m × 1.5 m). The test voltage was 11 kVrms, 50 Hz. Pollution tests were conducted as per

TABLE 1: Leakage current time and frequency domain features.

ESDD (mg/cm^2) [o/p of model]	Leakage current features [input to model]			
	Mean value (I_{em}), mA	Maximum value (I_{emax}), mA	Standard deviation (σ)	Total harmonic distortion (THD)%
0.01	0.039	0.13	0.0495	78.56
0.06	0.047	0.14	0.0583	54.35
0.08	0.286	2.07	0.3892	37.34
0.12	1.428	4.11	2.0302	24.34
0.25	2.160	4.24	3.6160	12.23

IEC 60507 clean fog test procedure [15]. Before tests, the insulator surfaces were cleaned by washing with isopropylic alcohol and rinsing with distilled water, in order to remove any trace of dirt and grease. To reproduce saline pollution typical of coastal areas, a contamination layer consisting of NaCl and 40 g of kaolin mixed with 1 litre of deionized water was applied to the surface of insulator. The concentration of NaCl salt was varied to give Equivalent salt deposit density (ESDD) in mg/cm^2. Four ultrasonic nebulizers were used to maintain the required relative humidity level inside the fog chamber. Relative humidity inside the fog chamber was measured using a wall-mounted hygrotherm instrument.

2.1. Leakage Current Measurement. The leakage current was measured through a series resistance in the ground lead. A high sampling rate data acquisition system (National Instruments, 1.25 MSa/sec) was used in the present study. In this study, all the signals were captured at a sampling rate of 5 kHz, and the data was stored in PC for further processing. Laboratory tests were carried out in silicone rubber insulator at different pollution levels varying from 0.01 ESDD to 0.25 ESDD, at a constant 100% relative humidity conditions. 50 leakage current signals were recorded at each ESDD level. The mean, maximum, standard deviation, and total harmonic distortion (THD) were calculated based on the formulas as follows:

$$I_{em} = \frac{\left(\sum_{i=1}^{N} I_e(i)\right)}{N},$$

$$I_{emax} = \max(I_{em}(i)),$$

$$\sigma = \sqrt{\frac{\sum_{i=1}^{N} (I_e(i) - I_{em})^2}{N}},$$

$$\text{THD} = \frac{\sqrt{\sum_{h=2}^{\infty} I_{h,rms}^2}}{I_{rms}} \times 100\%,$$

$$I_{rms} = \sqrt{\sum_{h=1}^{\infty} I_{h,rms}^2},$$

(1)

where N is the total number of sampling points in the test time; $I_e(i)$ is the leakage current value in one sampling period; I_{em} is the mean value of leakage current in the test

time; I_{emax} is the maximum value of leakage current in the test time; σ is the standard deviation of leakage current in the test time. The total data set 250 (50 × 5) is divided into three parts as training, validation, and testing. Training sets varied from 60 to 180 sets. The remaining 70 data sets are divided into 40 for validation and 30 for testing the model. The one set of recorded leakage current signal is shown in Figure 3, and its features are tabulated in Table 1.

The present work has been carried out in the high voltage pollution testing laboratory. However, the proposed methodology can be applied at selected highly polluted areas, and suitable leakage current sensors will be installed in the composite insulators. The acquired leakage current signals from all such sensors on towers will be transmitted to central data logging system in substation. The data logging system will be connected with a high-end configuration computer, which will process the data continuously and simultaneously for all insulators and features are extracted and given to the ANFIS model. This is not a simple task, and it probably requires an expensive infrastructure. The laboratory-based measurement leakage current signal was verified with real-time leakage current signal in literature work [16].

3. Performance Measure

Assessment of the performance of ANFIS model is done by optimal values of Root mean square error (RMSE), coefficient of determination (R^2), and correlation coefficient (r).

Root Mean Square Error (RMSE). The formula for RMSE is

$$\text{RMSE} = \left(\frac{\sum_{k=1}^{n} (X_{obs} - X_{est})^2}{n}\right)^{1/2},$$

(2)

where n is number of data points, X_{obs} is observed value X_{est}, and estimated value.

Correlation Coefficient (r). Correlation coefficient is a measure of strength and direction of a linear relationship between two random variables. In this work, Pearson's product moment correlation coefficient, denoted by r, has been adopted to determine the value of correlation efficient between two signals. If a series of n measurements of X and Y are written as x_i and y_i where $i = 1, 2, \ldots, n$, then the

Adaptive Neurofuzzy Inference System-Based Pollution Severity Prediction of Polymeric Insulators in Power
Transmission Lines

19

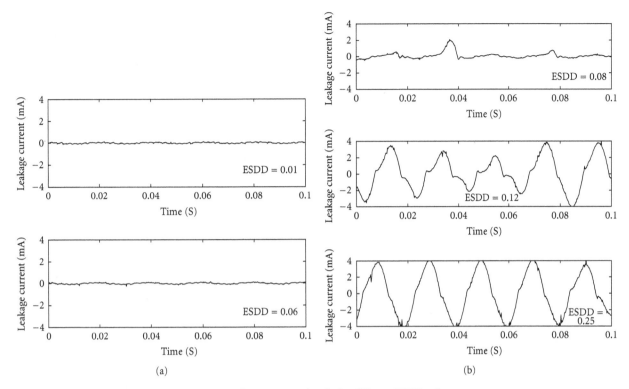

FIGURE 3: Leakage current signals for different ESDD values.

Pearson product-moment correlation coefficient to estimate the correlation of X and Y is written as

$$r_{xy} = \frac{\sum_{i=1}^{n}(x_i - \bar{x})(y_i - \bar{y})}{(n-1)S_x S_y}, \tag{3}$$

where x and y are the sample means of X_{obs} and X_{est}, S_x and S_y are the sample standard deviations of X_{obs} and X_{est}. The value of correlation coefficient is between -1 and $+1$ which measures the degree to which two signals are linearly related. If there is perfect linear relationship with positive slope between the two signals, then the correlation coefficient will be $+1$. If there is a perfect linear relationship with negative slope between the two signals, then the correlation coefficient will be -1. Correlation coefficient of 0 indicates that there is no linear relationship between the signals.

Coefficient of Determination (R^2). There are different definitions of R^2. In the case of linear regression,

$$R^2 = 1 - \frac{\sum_{i=1}^{n}(X_{\text{obs}} - X_{\text{est}})^2}{\sum_{i=1}^{n}(X_{\text{obs}} - \overline{X}_{\text{obs}})^2}. \tag{4}$$

4. Back Propagation Neural Network

Artificial neural networks are highly parallel, adaptive learning system that can learn a task by generalizing from case studies of the tasks. If a problem can be posed as an input-output mapping problem, an ANN can be used as a black box that learns the mapping from input-output examples from known cases of task. In the present work, ANN has

TABLE 2: Back propagation neural network specifications.

No. of inputs	4
No. of neurons in hidden layer	11
No. of neurons in output layer	1
Learning rate (η)	0.01
No. of iterations	2500
No. of training sets	180
No. of test input sets	70
Convergence criteria	0.001

been applied to the problem of predicting the pollution severity of polymeric insulators. Among the various ANN architectures available in the literature, the multilayer feed-forward network with back propagation learning algorithm has been used for the present study because of its simple approach and good generalization capability [17, 18]. The details of the optimized neural network used in the present study are shown in Table 2.

The convergence property and accuracy of the learning process for the BNN are significantly dependent on the scaling of the input-output data set. Hence, before training BPNN, the normalization of input-output data should be carried out. So their input values are normalized to 1 based on the following:

$$\bar{y}_i = \frac{(y_i - y_{\min})}{(y_{\max} - y_{\min})}. \tag{5}$$

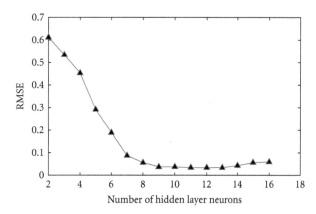

FIGURE 4: RMSE evaluation for different hidden layer neurons.

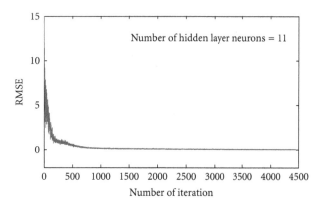

FIGURE 5: RMSE evaluation for different number of iteration.

The important factors influencing the performance of the neural network are the number of processing elements in the hidden layer and the number of iterations. Figure 4 shows the root mean square error value obtained with the different number of hidden layer neurons. It clearly indicates that the root mean square error value obtained with 11 hidden layer neurons was the minimum. As the number of hidden layer neurons increases, the neural network takes more time to learn. To obtain an optimum value for the number of iterations, the mean square error value of the network has been evaluated by maintaining the value of learning rate to be 0.01 with 11 hidden layer neurons. Figure 5 shows the performance of the network for different iteration numbers. It clearly indicates that during training the present network reaches the convergence criteria near 3000 iterations. It indicates that 3000 iterations are sufficient for the successful training of the optimized neural network.

5. Adaptive Neurofuzzy Inference System

A unique approach in neurofuzzy system is the adaptive neurofuzzy inference system (ANFIS), which has been proven better performance in modeling nonlinear function [19]. The ANFIS models possess human-like expertise within a particular domain which adapts itself and learns to do better in changing environment condition [20]. An ANFIS

aims at automatically generating unknown fuzzy rules from a given input and output data sets [21]. Figure 6 shows a typical architecture of ANFIS.

Notice that in Figure 6, each circle shows a fixed node, whereas every square indicates an adaptive node. So the rule base system has two if-then rules of Takagi-Sugeno's type as:

Rule i : if x is A_i and y is B_i, then $f_i = p_i x + q_i y + r_i$, $i = 1, 2$.

Layer 1. Each node i in this layer is an adaptive node and outputs of these nodes are given by

$$O_{1,i} = \mu A_i(x), \quad \text{for } i = 1, 2, \text{ or}$$
$$O_{1,i} = \mu B_{i-2}(y), \quad \text{for } i = 3, 4, \quad (6)$$

where $\mu A_i(x)$ and $\mu B_{i-2}(y)$ are membership functions that determine the degree to which the given x and y satisfy the quantifiers A_i and B_{i-2}. In this work, the membership function for A can be any appropriate parameterized membership function, such as the generalized bell function

$$\mu A(x) = \frac{1}{1 + |(x - c_i)/a_i|^{2b}}, \quad (7)$$

where $\{a_i, b_i, c_i\}$ is the parameter set. As the values of these parameters change, the bell-shaped function varies accordingly. Parameters in this layer are referred to as *premise parameters*.

Layer 2. In this layer, each node is a fixed node labeled Π that determines the firing strength of related rule, whose output is the product of all the incoming signals

$$O_{2,i} = \omega_i = \mu A_i(x)\mu B_i(y), \quad i = 1, 2. \quad (8)$$

Layer 3. In this layer, every node is a circle node labeled N, which computes the ratio of firing strength of each rule to the sum of all of them; the so-called normalized firing strength.

$$O_{3,i} = \bar{\omega}_i = \frac{\omega_i}{\omega_1 + \omega_2}, \quad i = 1, 2. \quad (9)$$

Layer 4. The output of each adaptive node in this layer is

$$O_{4,i} = \bar{\omega}_i f_i = \bar{\omega}_i (p_i x + q_i y + r_i), \quad (10)$$

where $\bar{\omega}_i$ is a normalized firing strength from layer 3 and $\{p_i, q_i, r_i\}$ are called as *consequence parameters*.

Layer 5. Final layer, the single node in this layer is a fixed node labeled Σ, which computes the overall output as the summation of all incoming signals,

$$\text{overall output} = O_{5,i} = \sum_i \bar{\omega}_i f_i = \frac{\sum_i \omega_i f_i}{\sum_i \omega_i}. \quad (11)$$

Thus, an adaptive network has been constructed. The proposed ANFIS-based pollution severity system is based upon Jang's ANFIS [19], which is a fuzzy inference system

Adaptive Neurofuzzy Inference System-Based Pollution Severity Prediction of Polymeric Insulators in Power Transmission Lines

21

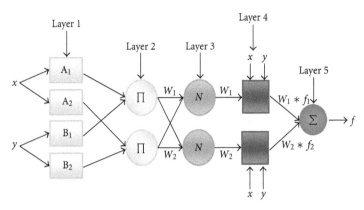

FIGURE 6: Architecture of typical ANFIS.

TABLE 3: Two passes in the hybrid learning procedure for ANFIS.

	Forward pass	Backward pass
Premise parameters	Fixed	Gradient descent
Consequent parameters	Least squares estimate	Fixed
Signals	Node output	Error rates

TABLE 4: Summary of general specifications of the used architecture.

Adaptive FIS type	Adaptive architecture	Algorithmic learning structure	Partition of spaces	Required initial knowledge	Structural change	Extracted knowledge type
ANFIS	Multilayer feed-forward network	Hybrid: supervised (gradient descent)	Adaptive fuzzy grid	Numerical data	No	If-then fuzzy rules

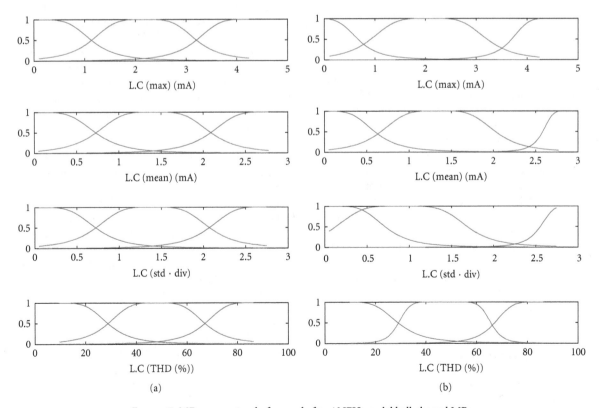

FIGURE 7: MFs parameters before and after ANFIS model bell-shaped MFs.

TABLE 5: Statistical indices for performance assessment of the different types of ANFIS models.

Type of Mf	No. of MF	RMSE		RMSE	R^2	r
		Training	Validation		Testing	
Trimf	2	0.007213	0.01282	0.00689	0.945	0.8462
	3	0.005301	0.01155	0.00683	0.967	0.9167
	4	0.003438	0.01485	0.02847	0.875	0.8413
	5	0.001705	0.00602	0.00282	0.974	0.9122
gaussmf	2	0.014395	0.00962	0.01609	0.962	0.8642
	3	0.016005	0.01687	0.01742	0.879	0.8932
	4	0.002167	0.00141	0.00031	0.999	0.9812
	5	0.009562	0.01225	0.00934	0.979	0.9232
gbellmf	2	0.009173	0.01072	0.01048	0.899	0.8652
	3	**0.001831**	**0.00513**	**0.00323**	**0.998**	**0.9945**
	4	**0.001245**	**0.00496**	**0.00289**	**0.999**	**0.9952**
	5	0.003399	0.01258	0.00894	0.969	0.9171

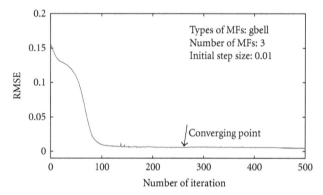

FIGURE 8: RMSE evaluation of different no. of integration for ANFIS model.

implemented on the architecture of a five-layer feed-forward network. Using a hybrid learning procedure, the ANFIS model can construct an input-output mapping based on both human knowledge (in the form of if-then rules) and input-output data observations. In the hybrid learning algorithm, in the forward pass, the functional signals go forward till layer 4, and the consequent parameters are identified by the least squares estimate. In the backward pass, the error rates propagate backward and the premise parameters are updated by the gradient descent. The consequent parameters thus identified are optimal (in the consequent parameter space) under the condition that the premise parameters are fixed. Accordingly, the hybrid approach is much faster than the strict gradient descent. Table 3 summarizes the activities in each pass. A summary of the general specifications including the learning algorithm, required initial knowledge, domain partitioning, rule structuring, and extracted knowledge type are given in Table 4.

6. Results and Discussion

In this study, automatic pollution prediction system was developed based on the leakage current feature measurement. The time and frequency domain feature of leakage current were extracted from the laboratory testing, and these data were given as inputs to train the ANFIS. Initially, the system was developed with different types of membership functions (MFs) like triangular-shaped built-in membership function (trimf), Gaussian curve built-in membership function (gaussmf), and generalized bell-shaped built-in membership function (gbellmf); each MF was tested with different linguist variables (2 [HIGH LOW]3[HIGH MEDIUM LOW] 4[HIGH MEDIUM LOW VERY LOW] 5[VERY HIGH HIGH MEDIUM LOW VERY LOW) to each input. The ANFIS model was trained by hybrid learning algorithm. Figure 7 illustrates the gbellmf membership functions before and after training. The std and mean inputs boundaries were adapted well, and max, THD inputs boundaries were slightly adapted, because the initial assignment of these boundaries was very close to actual input data. Figure 8 shows the training error curves with initial step size equal to 0.01. The converging criterion was obtained at 250th iteration. The performance of each model was tested by performance-measured coefficients. The detailed simulated results obtained by the developed ANFIS model for predicting the ESDD value of the polymer insulator were tabulated in Table 5.

According to Table 5, generalized bell-shaped (gbell) with 3 or 4 MFs is the best architecture model to predict the pollution severity of the polymeric power line insulators, because it gives lowest RMSE value during the training, validation process and lowest RMSE, highest R^2, and r during the testing process. Even though two architecture models are fit for this problem, 3 MFs architecture model was selected, because it has been trained with less time compared with the 4 MFs architecture model. The final performance of any model strictly depends on the number of training data sets, and initially different architecture ANFIS model was trained with 180 training data sets for getting best fit architecture model, then the training data sets vary from 60 to 180 sets to train the best fit model (gbell, 3 MFs) in order to get optimal training data sets to train the model.

The performance of the ANFIS model was compared with back propagation neural network (BNN) model. The same input training and testing data sets were applied to BNN model, and the performance measurement indices were

Adaptive Neurofuzzy Inference System-Based Pollution Severity Prediction of Polymeric Insulators in Power Transmission Lines

23

TABLE 6: Comparative performance assessment of models.

Models	Performance measures		
	RMSE	R^2	r
BNN	0.02524	0.943	0.9732
ANFIS	0.00323	0.998	0.9945

tabulated in Table 6. According to Table 6, ANFIS model gives more accurate results than BNN. The output of ANFIS-based model was mostly matching the tested values, because it gives lowest RMSE [0.00323], highest R^2[0.998], and r[0.9945] compared to BNN model. This was because of the highly nonlinear mapping capability and self-adaptive nature of the fine tuning of the MFs of ANFIS. After the initial training step of the ANFIS model, which was the optimization of the consequence parameters, the system adapts such that the pollution severity index value (ESDD) predicting was significantly close to the actually tested values of the polymer insulators. The RMSE to predict the ESDD values based on neural network is 0.02524 at developed BNN model and 0.035 at literature work [14], which was recently a published work with the same kind of input feature used to train the BNN model. Considering the above test results, the ANFIS model would give better accuracy than BNN models.

The accurate prediction of pollution severity index [ESDD] of polymeric insulator in power transmission line is automated by ANFIS model by on-line training. Actually, the pollution flashover may take place once the pollution severity index reaches it critical value. If the ANFIS model predicts the ESDD value prior to critical value, then the operator will get a warning instruction to wash the particular polluted polymeric insulator in the transmission tower to avoid the pollution flashover.

7. Conclusion

A methodology for the prediction of the pollution severity of polymeric insulators using ANFIS model was presented. The ANFIS model was designed based on the time and frequency domain characteristics of the polymeric insulator leakage currents. The performance of the developed model was justified by root mean square error, coefficient of determination (R^2), and correlation coefficient (r). The respective results are quite satisfactory and superior compared to BNN model. The new prediction model helps to automate the process of identification surface condition of the polymeric insulator, installed near industrial and agricultural or coastal areas. Hence, the present model could be used to predict the pollution severity of polymeric insulator and, therefore, can be used to establish condition-based maintenance practices.

Acknowledgment

Authors would like to thank All India Council for Technical Education (AICTE), NewDelhi for providing financial support under Research Promotion Scheme to carry out this experimental work.

References

[1] J. S. T. Looms, *Insulators for High Voltages*, IEE Series, 1990.

[2] R. S. Gorur, E. A. Cherney, and J. T. Burnham, *Outdoor Insulators*, Ravi S. Gorur, Phoenix, Ariz, USA, 1999.

[3] R. Dass, "Grid disturbance in India on 2nd January 2001," *Electra*, no. 196, pp. 6–15, 2001.

[4] "CEA enquiry committee report of Grid incident of Northern region," 2007.

[5] S. Kumagai and N. Yoshimura, "Leakage current characterization for estimating the conditions of ceramic and polymeric insulating surfaces," *IEEE Transactions on Dielectrics and Electrical Insulation*, vol. 11, no. 4, pp. 681–690, 2004.

[6] T. Suda, "Frequency characteristics of leakage current waveforms of an artificially polluted suspension insulator," *IEEE Transactions on Dielectrics and Electrical Insulation*, vol. 8, no. 4, pp. 705–709, 2001.

[7] B. S. Reddy and G. R. Nagabhushana, "Study of leakage current behaviour on artificially polluted surface of ceramic insulator," *Plasma Science and Technology*, vol. 5, no. 4, pp. 1921–1926, 2003.

[8] R. Sarathi and S. Chandrasekar, "Diagnostic study of the surface condition of the insulation structure using wavelet transform and neural networks," *Electric Power Systems Research*, vol. 68, no. 2, pp. 137–147, 2004.

[9] S. Chandrasekar and C. Kalaivanan, "Investigations on harmonic contents of leakage current of porcelain insulator under polluted conditions," in *Proceedings of the Fifteenth National Power Systems Conference (NPSC)*, pp. 340–344, 2008.

[10] P. Cline, W. Lannes, and G. Richards, "Use of pollution monitors with a neural network to predict insulator flashover," *Electric Power Systems Research*, vol. 42, no. 1, pp. 27–33, 1997.

[11] V. T. Kontargyri, A. A. Gialketsi, G. J. Tsekouras, I. F. Gonos, and I. A. Stathopulos, "Design of an artificial neural network for the estimation of the flashover voltage on insulators," *Electric Power Systems Research*, vol. 77, no. 12, pp. 1532–1540, 2007.

[12] S. Al Alawi, M. A. Salam, A. A. Maqrashi, and H. Ahmad, "Prediction of flashover voltage of contaminated insulator using artificial neural networks," *Electric Power Components and Systems*, vol. 34, no. 8, pp. 831–840, 2006.

[13] S. A. Ahmad, P. S. Ghosh, S. S. Ahmed, and S. A.-K Aljunid, "Assessment of ESDD on high voltage insulators using artificial neural network," *Electic Power Systems Research*, vol. 72, pp. 131–136, 2004.

[14] J. Li, C. Sun, W. Sima, Q. Yang, and J. Hu, "Contamination level prediction of insulators based on the characteristics of leakage current," *IEEE Transactions on Power Delivery*, vol. 25, no. 1, Article ID 5345710, pp. 417–424, 2010.

[15] IEC 60507, "Artificial pollution tests on high voltage insulators to be used on AC systems," 1991.

[16] S. C. Oliveira, E. Fontana, and F. J. D. M. de Melo Cavalcanti, "Leakage current activity on glass-type insulators of overhead transmission lines in the ortheast region of Brazil," *IEEE Transactions on Power Delivery*, vol. 24, no. 2, pp. 822–827, 2009.

[17] S. Haykin, *Neural Networks: A comprehensive Foundation*, Prentice Hall, New York, NY, USA, 2nd edition, 1999.

[18] B. Yegnanarayana, *Artificial Neural Networks*, Prentice Hall of India, 1999.

[19] J. S. R. Jang, "Adaptive-network-based fuzzy inference system," *IEEE Transactions on Systems, Man and Cybernetics*, vol. 23, no. 3, pp. 665–685, 1993.

[20] C. P. Kurian, J. George, I. J. Bhat, and R. S. Aithal, "ANFIS model for the time series prediction of interior daylight illuminance," *Artificial Intelligence & Machine Learning Journal*, vol. 6, pp. 35–40, 2006.

[21] J.-S. R. Jang, C.-T. Sun, and E. Mizutani, *Neuro-Fuzzy and Soft Computing: A Computational Approach to Learning and Machine Intelligence*, Prentice Hall of India, 2006.

4

Navigation Behaviors Based on Fuzzy ArtMap Neural Networks for Intelligent Autonomous Vehicles

Amine Chohra[1] and Ouahiba Azouaoui[2]

[1] Images, Signals, and Intelligent Systems Laboratory (LISSI/EA 3956), Paris-East University (UPEC), avenue Pierre Point, 77127 Lieusaint, France
[2] Autonomous Robotic Systems (ARS), Development Center of Advanced Technologies (CDTA), Cité 20 Août 1956, BP 17 Baba Hassen, 16303 Algiers, Algeria

Correspondence should be addressed to Amine Chohra, chohra@u-pec.fr

Academic Editor: Songcan Chen

The use of hybrid intelligent systems (HISs) is necessary to bring the behavior of intelligent autonomous vehicles (IAVs) near the human one in recognition, learning, adaptation, generalization, decision making, and action. First, the necessity of HIS and some navigation approaches based on fuzzy ArtMap neural networks (FAMNNs) are discussed. Indeed, such approaches can provide IAV with *more autonomy, intelligence,* and *real-time* processing capabilities. Second, an FAMNN-based navigation approach is suggested. Indeed, this approach must provide vehicles with capability, after *supervised fast stable* learning: simplified fuzzy ArtMap (SFAM), to recognize both target-location and obstacle-avoidance situations using FAMNN1 and FAMNN2, respectively. Afterwards, the decision making and action consist of two association stages, carried out by *reinforcement* trial and error learning, and their coordination using NN3. Then, NN3 allows to decide among the five (05) actions to move towards $30°$, $60°$, $90°$, $120°$, and $150°$. Third, simulation results display the ability of the FAMNN-based approach to provide IAV with *intelligent behaviors* allowing to *intelligently* navigate in partially structured environments. Finally, a discussion, dealing with the suggested approach and how its *robustness* would be if implemented on real vehicle, is given.

1. Introduction

The recent developments in autonomy requirements, intelligent components, multirobot systems, computational tools, and massively parallel computers have made intelligent autonomous vehicles (IAVs) very used in many terrestrial, underwater, and spatial applications [1–6]. In fact, IAV designers search to create dynamic systems able to navigate and achieve intelligent behaviors like human in real dynamic environments, where conditions are laborious.

To reach their targets while avoiding possibly encountered obstacles, in dynamic environments, IAV must have particularly the capability to achieve target-localization, obstacle-avoidance, decision-making, and action behaviors. More, current IAV requirements with regard to these behaviors are *real time, autonomy,* and *intelligence*. Thus, to acquire these behaviors while answering IAV requirements, IAV must be endowed with recognition, learning, adapta-

tion, generalization, decision making, and action with real-time processing capabilities. To achieve this goal, classical approaches have been replaced by current ones on the basis of new computational tools which are far more effective in the design and development of intelligent dynamic systems than the predicate-logic-based methods of traditional artificial intelligence. These tools derive from a collection of methodologies known as *soft computing* which can deal with uncertain, imprecise, and inexact data. These technologies have been experiencing extremely rapid growth in the spatial, underwater, and terrestrial applications, where they have been shown to be very effective in solving real-world problems [6–9]. In fact, the essence of *soft computing* is aimed at an accomodation with the imprecision of the real world. Thus, the guiding principle of *soft computing* is to exploit the tolerance for imprecision, uncertainty, and partial truth in order to achieve tractability, *robustness*, low solution cost, and better rapport with reality. These capabilities are required for IAV to adapt to dynamic environments and then to accomplish a wide variety of intelligent behaviors under environmental constraints particularly the target-localization, obstacle-avoidance, decision-making, and action behaviors.

Thus, several navigation approaches for IAV have been developed using *soft computing* to achieve intelligent behaviors. Particularly, the fuzzy logic (FL), neural networks (NNs), and adaptive resonance theory (ART) have been used separately or in different combinations as hybrid intelligent systems (HISs) [1, 10–22].

This paper deals with the *planning* and *intelligent control* of IAV in *partially structured environments*. The aim of this work is to suggest an HIS-based navigation approach able to provide these vehicles with *more autonomy, intelligence,* and *real-time* processing capabilities. First, the necessity of HIS for IAV and some navigation approaches based on fuzzy ArtMap neural networks (FAMNNs) are discussed. Second, an FAMNN-based navigation approach is suggested. This approach has been developed in [20] for only three (03) possible movements of vehicles, while in the suggested approach, this number is increased to five (05) possible movements. Third, simulation results of IAV navigation based on the FAMNN approach are presented and discussed. Finally, a discussion, dealing with the suggested approach and how its *robustness* would be if implemented on real vehicle, is given.

2. HIS- and FAMNN-Based Navigation

Recent research on IAV has pointed out a promising direction for future research in mobile robotics where *real time, autonomy,* and *intelligence* have received considerably more attention than, for instance, optimality and completeness. Many navigation approaches have dropped the assumption that perfect environment knowledge is available. They have also dropped the explicit knowledge representation for an implicit one on the basis of acquisition of *intelligent behaviors* that enable the vehicle to interact effectively with its environment [2]. Consequently, IAV are facing with less predictable and more complex environments; they have to orient themselves, explore their environments autonomously, recover from failures, and perform whole families of tasks in real time. More, if vehicles lack initial knowledge about themselves and their environments, *learning* and *adaptation* become then inevitable to replace missing or incorrect environment knowledge by experimentation, observation, and *generalization*. Thus, in order to reach a goal, learning and adaptation of vehicles rely on the interaction with their environment to extract information [3].

Thus, the most of the navigation approaches currently developed are based on the acquisition, by *learning* and *adaptation*, of different behaviors necessary for an intelligent navigation (i.e., navigation with intelligent behaviors) such as target localization, target tracking, obstacle avoidance, and object recognition. One of the more recent trends in the *intelligent control* research for IAV leading to intelligent

behaviors is the use of different combinations of *soft computing* technologies in HIS [7–9, 23].

Werbos [7] asserted that the relation between NN and FL is basically *complementary* rather than equivalent or competitive. In addition, HIS have been recently recognized to improve the learning, adaptation, and generalization capabilities related to variations in environments, where information is qualitative, inaccurate, uncertain, or incomplete [23]. Thus, many attempts have been made to combine FL and NN in order to achieve better performance in the learning, adaptation, generalization, decision-making, and action capabilities. Such a fusion into an integrated system will have the advantages of both NN (e.g., learning and optimization abilities) and FL (e.g., adaptation abilities and capability to cope with uncertainty). Two main combinations result from this fusion: the fuzzy neural networks (FNNs) [14, 22, 24, 25] and FAMNN [12, 17, 19, 20, 26–29]. In classification problems, FAMNN take advantage over FNN by their *fast* and *stable* learning, while the FNN trained with the gradient back-propagation learning is less faster and presents the well-known convergence problem to get stuck in local minima.

Several FAMNN-based navigation approaches have been developed. The navigation approach developed in [12] uses FAMNN to perform a perceptual space classification for the obstacle-avoidance behavior. FAMNN have been also used in a motion planning controller for path following to recognize camera images [17] and to learn a qualitative positioning of an indoor mobile robot equipped with ultrasonic sensors [19]. In these approaches, FAMNN have been used for their generalization capability, robustness, and fast and stable learning. FAMNN architecture achieves a synthesis of FL and ART-NN by exploiting a close formal similarity between the computations of fuzzy subsethood and ART category choice, resonance, and learning. This architecture performs a min-max learning rule that conjointly minimizes predictive error and maximizes code compression or generalization. This is achieved by a match traking process that increases the ART vigilance parameter ρ by the minimum amount needed to correct a predictive error.

By another way, ultrasonic sensors, infrared sensors, and camera images are very used for IAV obstacle-avoidance behavior, but their signals are often noisy giving incorrect data. FAMNN approaches with their inherent features of adaptivity and high fault and noise tolerance handle this problem making these approaches *robust*.

Thus, the use of HIS combining NN, FL, and ART in FAMNN is necessary to bring IAV behavior near the human one in recognition, learning, adaptation, generalization, decision making, and action.

3. FAMNN-Based Navigation Approach

To navigate in partially structured environments, IAV must reach their targets without collisions with possibly encountered obstacles; that is, they must have the capability to achive target-localization and obstacle-avoidance behaviors. In this approach, these two behaviors are acquired by the *supervised fast stable* learning: the simplified fuzzy ArtMap (SFAM) using FAMNN pattern classifiers. Target localization is based on FAMNN1 classifier which must recognize six (06) target-location situations, after learning, from data obtained by computing distance and orientation of vehicle-target using a temperature field strategy. Obstacle avoidance is based on FAMNN2 classifier which must recognize thirty (30) obstacle-avoidance situations, after learning, from ultrasonic sensor data giving vehicle-obstacle distances. Afterwards, the decision making and action consist of two association stages, carried out by *reinforcement* trial and error learning, and their coordination using an NN3 allowing then to decide the appropriate action.

3.1. Vehicles and Sensors.

The vehicle movements are possible in five (05) directions; that is, five (05) possible actions A_i ($i = 1,\ldots,5$) are defined as actions to move towards 30°, 60°, 90°, 120°, and 150°, respectively, as shown in Figure 1. They are expressed by the action vector $\mathbf{A} = [A_1,\ldots,A_i,\ldots,A_5]$. To detect possibly encountered obstacles, five (05) ultrasonic sensors (US) are necessary to get distances (vehicle obstacle) covering the area from 15° to 165°: US_1 from 15° to 45°, US_2 from 45° to 75°, US_3 from 75° to 105°, US_4 from 105° to 135°, and US_5 from 135° to 165°, as shown in Figure 1.

3.2. Partially Structured Environments

3.2.1. Target-Location Situations.

To localize and reach targets, the temperature field strategy defined in [21, 30] is used leading to model the vehicle environment in six (06) areas corresponding to all target locations called target location situations as shown in Figure 2. These situations are defined with six (06) classes $T_1,\ldots,T_{j1},\ldots,T_6$, where ($j1 = 1,\ldots,6$).

3.2.2. Obstacle-Avoidance Situations.

Currently, most obstacle-avoidance approaches, in mobile robotics, are inspired from observations of human navigation behavior. Indeed, human navigators do not need to calculate the exact coordinates of their positions while navigating in environments (roads, hallways, etc.). The road-following or the hallway-following behavior exhibited by humans is a reactive behavior that is learned through experience. Given a goal, human navigators can focus attention on particular stimuli in their visual input and extract meaningful information very quickly. Extra information may be extracted from the scene during reactive behavior; this information (e.g., approaching an intersection) will usually be stored away and may be retrieved subsequently for higher level reasoning.

In partially structured environments, these observations have led to obstacle-avoidance approaches on the basis of the learning and adaptation. Such environments could be factories, passenger stations, harbors, and airports with static and dynamic obstacles. In fact, human perceives the spatial situations in such environments as topological situations: rooms, corridors, right turns, left turn, junctions, and so forth. Consequently, trying to capture the human obstacle-avoidance behavior in such environments, several

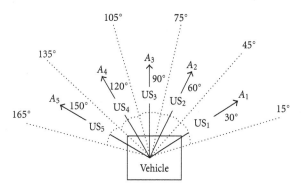

FIGURE 1: Vehicle and its sensors.

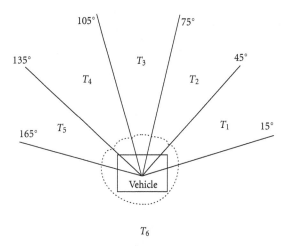

FIGURE 2: Target-location situations $\mathbf{T} = [T_1,\ldots,T_{j1},\ldots,T_6]$.

approaches based on a recognition of topological situations have been developed [10, 21, 30–33].

Thus, IAV should have the capability of recognizing spatial obstacle-avoidance situations of partially structured environments and maneuvering through these situations on the basis of their own judgement to enable themselves to navigate from one point of space to a destination without collision with static obstacles. Such obstacle-avoidance behavior is acquired using *soft computing*-based pattern classifiers under *supervised* learning and adaptation paradigms which allow to recognize topological situations from sensor data giving vehicle-obstacle distances.

(a) Description of Possibly Encountered Obstacles. Partially structured environments are dynamic with static, intelligent dynamic, and nonintelligent dynamic obstacles. In reality, static obstacles for example, Obs1,..., and Obs4 in Figure 3(a), where Veh: vehicle, Obs: obstacle, and Tar: target, of different shapes represent walls, pillars, machines, desks, tables, chairs, and so forth. The intelligent dynamic obstacles (e.g., Veh1 with regard to Veh2 and conversely in Figure 3(a)) represent in reality IAV controlled by the same suggested FAMNN-based navigation approach, where each one considers the others as obstacles. The nonintelligent dynamic obstacles, oscillating horizontally (e.g., Obs5 in Figure 3(a)), or vertically (e.g., Obs6 in Figure 3(a)) between

two fixed points, represent in reality preprogrammed, teleguided, or guided vehicles.

(b) Possibly Encountered Obstacles Structured in Topological Situations. The possible vehicle movements lead us to structure possibly encountered obstacles in thirty (30) topological situations called obstacle-avoidance situations as shown in Figure 3(b), where the directions shown correspond to those where obstacles exist. These situations are defined with thirty (30) classes $O_1, \ldots, O_{j2}, \ldots, O_{30}$, where $(j2 = 1, \ldots, 30)$.

3.3. FAMNN-Based Navigation System

During the navigation, each vehicle must built an implicit internal map (i.e., target, obstacles, and free spaces), allowing the recognition of both-target location and obstacle-avoidance situations. Then, it decides the appropriate action from two association stages and their coordination [20, 21, 30]. To achieve this, the FAMNN-based navigation system presented below is used where the only known data are the initial and final (i.e., target) positions of the vehicle.

3.3.1. System Structure. The system structure allowing to develop the suggested approach is built of three phases as shown in Figure 4. During the Phase 1, the vehicle learns to recognize target-location situations T_{j1} using FAMNN1 classifier, while it learns to recognize obstacle-avoidance situations O_{j2} using FAMNN2 classifier during the Phase 2. The Phase 3 decides the appropriate action A_i from two association stages and their coordination using NN3.

3.3.2. FAMNN Classifiers. They are networks which decide if one or several output nodes are required to represent a particular category. Indeed, these networks grow to represent the problem as it sees fit instead of being told by the network designer to function within the confines of some static architectures. In this paper, SFAM learning, which is a *supervised fast stable* learning, is used as detailed in [34]. It is specialized for pattern classification which can learn every single training pattern in only a handful of training iterations, starts with no connection weights but grows in size to suit the problem and contains only one user-selectable parameter.

Phase 1 (Target Localization). It is based on FAMNN1 classifier which must recognize, after learning, each target-location situation T_{j1}. FAMNN1 is trained (see Section 4.1) from data obtained by computing distance and orientation of the vehicle-target using a temperature field strategy [21, 30]. In each step, this temperature field is defined in the vehicle environment, and the vehicle task is therefore to localize its target corresponding to the unique maximum temperature of this field that is, the situation T_{j1} where the target is localized. Temperatures in the neighborhood of the vehicle are defined with a temperature field vector $\mathbf{X}_T = [t_{30}, t_{60}, t_{90}, t_{120}, t_{150}]$, where $t_{30}, t_{60}, t_{90}, t_{120},$ and t_{150} are the temperatures in the directions 30°, 60°, 90°, 120°, and 150°, respectively. These temperatures are computed using sine

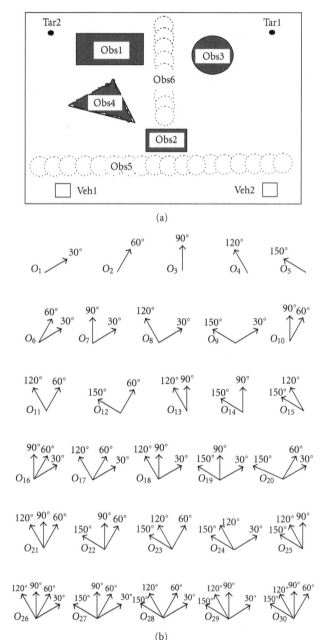

(a)

(b)

FIGURE 3: Partially structured environments: (a) Possibly encountered obstacles, and (b) obstacle-avoidance situations $\mathbf{O} = [O_1, \ldots, O_{j2}, \ldots, O_{30}]$ where directions shown, in each situation, correspond to those where obstacles exist.

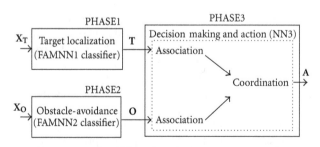

FIGURE 4: FAMNN based navigation system synopsis.

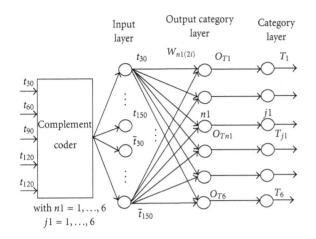

FIGURE 5: Architecture of FAMNN1 classifier (target-location situations).

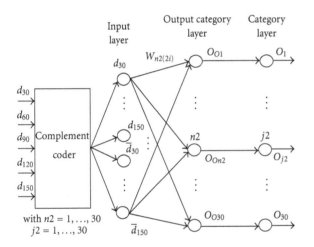

FIGURE 6: Architecture of FAMNN2 classifier (obstacle-avoidance situations).

and cosine functions as detailed in [21]. These components, normalized within the range 0 and 1, constitute the input vector $\mathbf{X_T}$ of FAMNN1 shown in Figure 5.

After learning, for each input vector $\mathbf{X_T}$, FAMNN1 provides the vehicle with capability to decide its target localization, recognizing the target location-situation T_{j1} expressed by the highly activated output T_{j1}.

Phase 2 (Obstacle Avoidance). It is based on FAMNN2 Classifier which must recognize, after learning, each obstacle-avoidance situation O_{j2}. FAMNN2 is trained (see Section 4.1) from ultrasonic sensor data obtained from the environment giving vehicle-obstacle distances. These distances are defined, in each step, in the vehicle neighborhood with a distance vector $\mathbf{X_O} = [d_{30}, d_{60}, d_{90}, d_{120}, d_{150}]$, where $d_{30}, d_{60}, d_{90}, d_{120},$ and d_{150} are the distances in the directions 30°, 60°, 90°, 120°, and 150°, respectively. These components, normalized within the range 0 and 1, constitute the input vector $\mathbf{X_O}$ of FAMNN2 shown in Figure 6.

After learning, for each input vector $\mathbf{X_O}$, FAMNN2 provides the vehicle with capability to decide its obstacle avoidance, recognizing the obstacle-avoidance situation O_{j2} expressed by the highly activated output O_{j2}.

Note that for both FAMNN1 and FAMNN2, the category proliferation is prevented by the normalization of the input vectors at the preprocessing stage and the choice of the baseline of the vigilance parameter ρ.

Phase 3 (Decision Making and Action). In this phase, two association stages between each behavior and the favorable actions and their coordination are carried out by a multilayer feedforward network NN3. Then, NN3, allowing to decide the appropriate action among the five (05) possible actions, is built of two layers as shown in Figure 7. The five (05) outputs of the output layer are obtained by (1), where N_i is a random distribution variable over $[0, \beta]$ and β is a constant

$$A_i = g\left(\sum_{j1} T_{j1} U_{ij1} + \sum_{j2} O_{j2} V_{ij2}\right) N_i, \tag{1}$$

with

$$g(x) = \begin{cases} x & \text{if } x > 0, \\ 0 & \text{otherwise.} \end{cases} \tag{2}$$

(a) Association Stages. Both situations T_{j1} and O_{j2} are associated separately in two independent stages, by *reinforcement* trial and error learning, with the favorable actions. The association between a situation and an action is usually carried out with the use of a signal provided by an outside process (e.g., a supervisor), giving the desired response. To achieve the correct association, the desired response is acquired through *reinforcement* trial and error learning. Learning, in this case, is guided only by a feedback process, that is, guided by a signal P provided by the supervisor. This signal causes a reinforcement of the association between a given situation and a favorable action if this latter leads to a favorable consequence to the vehicle; if not, the signal P provokes a dissociation. For this learning, the updating of weights U_{ij1} and V_{ij2}, in the two association stages, is achieved by (3) given for weights M_{ij} [21, 30] with τ time constant and α constant ($\alpha > 0$)

$$M_{ij}(t) = -\alpha e^{-(A_i C_j/\tau)\cdot t} + (\alpha - P). \tag{3}$$

(i) *Target-Localization Association:* Target-location situations are associated with favorable actions in an obstacle-free environment (i.e., $\mathbf{O} = 0$), (see Section 4.1). Favorable actions are defined, for each situation T_{j1}, by the human expert (supervisor providing P_1) which has traduced this fact with the vector $\mathbf{Z} = [Z_1, Z_2, Z_3, Z_4, Z_5]$, where each Z_i component is determined with regard to each possible action A_i. If $Z_i = 1$, then A_i is a favorable action, while if $Z_i = 0$, then A_i is an unfavorable action. For each situation T_{j1}, only favorable actions are represented in Figure 8.

(ii) *Obstacle-Avoidance Association:* Obstacle-avoidance situations are associated with favorable actions without considering the temperature field (i.e., $\mathbf{T} = 0$), (see Section 4.1). Favorable actions are defined, for each situation O_{j2}, by data sensors from the environment (supervisor providing P_2). In each situation O_{j2}, favorable actions are those corresponding to directions where no obstacle is detected (no collision), while unfavorable actions are those corresponding to directions where an obstacle is detected (collision). For instance, in situation O_{23} shown in Figure 3(b): only A_1 and A_3 are considered as favorable actions while A_2, A_4, and A_5 are considered as unfavorable actions.

(b) Coordination. This coordination must provide the vehicle with the capability to fulfill, in the same time, the two intelligent behaviors (target localization and obstacle avoidance) giving the appropriate action. To ensure the coordination of two association stages (see Section 4.1), actions A_i are computed by (1).

After learning of the two association stages and their coordination, NN3 provides the vehicle with capability to decide the appropriate action expressed by the highly activated output A_i.

4. Simulation Results

In this section, at first, the simulated learning (training) environments and training processes of FAMNN1, FAMNN2, and NN3 are described. Second, the simulated FAMNN-based navigation approach is described and simulation results are presented. Thus, the vehicles, ultrasonic sensors, and partially structured environments are simulated.

4.1. Training of FAMNN1, FAMNN2, and NN3

4.1.1. Training of FAMNN1. This training is achieved in the learning (training) environment shown in Figure 9(a). The vehicle moves along the paths $(1,\ldots,10)$ in an obstacle-free environment, where the target is positioned in the environment center. This allows the vehicle to be in different positions and orientations, and consequently, the target will be in different locations with regard to the vehicle. Then, each particular position and orientation corresponds to one training example for a particular target-location situation T_{j1}. Thus, training examples are defined by randomly selecting twenty four (24) positions and orientations (patterns). After only one (01) epoch, FAMNN1 sprouted $n_1 = 6$ output nodes shown in Figure 5, to arrive at the desired result, with learning rate $\eta_1 = 1.0$, $\alpha_1 = 0.0000001$, the baseline of the vigilance $\rho_1 = 0.4$, and $\varepsilon_1 = 0.0001$. Note that during the training, FAMNN learn every training example presented, either by incorporating it into an existing output node or creating a new output node for it.

4.1.2. Training of FAMNN2. The vehicle is simulated in a given position and orientation in the learning (training)

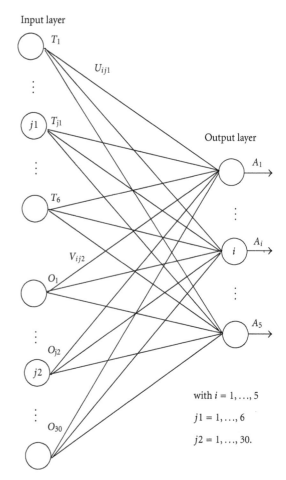

FIGURE 7: Architecture of NN3 (decision making and action).

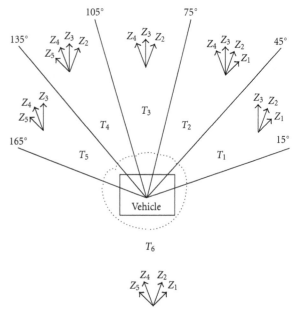

FIGURE 8: Representation of favorable actions: for each $\mathbf{T}_{j1}$ situation, where only components $\mathbf{Z}_i = 1$ of $\mathbf{Z} = [\mathbf{Z}_1, \mathbf{Z}_2, \mathbf{Z}_3, \mathbf{Z}_4, \mathbf{Z}_5]$ corresponding to favorable actions are represented.

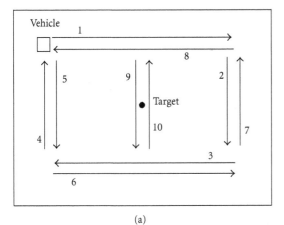

(a)

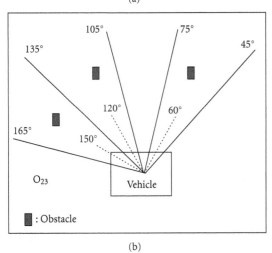

(b)

Figure 9: Learning (training) environments: (a) Target-location situations T_{j1}—the vehicle moves along the paths $(1,\ldots,10)$ represented by arrows where the target is located in the environment center, and (b) obstacle-avoidance situations O_{j2}—the vehicle is simulated in a given position and orientation, where the simulated configuration of obstacles corresponds to one training example for an obstacle-avoidance situation e.g., the obstacle-avoidance situation O_{23}.

environment, where a configuration of obstacles is simulated corresponding to one training example of a particular obstacle-avoidance situation O_{j2} (e.g., the situation O_{23} shown in Figure 9(b)). Thus, training examples are defined by randomly selecting one hundred fifty (150) positions (patterns). After only one (01) epoch, FAMNN2 sprouted $n_2 = 30$ output nodes shown in Figure 6, to arrive at the desired result, with learning rate $\eta_2 = 1.0$, $\alpha_2 = 0.0000001$, the baseline of the vigilance $\rho_2 = 0.25$, and $\varepsilon_2 = 0.0001$.

4.1.3. Training of NN3. This training is achieved with the training of two association stages and their coordination; see [21] for more details.

(a) Target-Localization Association. In this stage, the updating weights is achieved by (3), where $M_{ij} = U_{ij1}, C_j = T_{j1}$, and $(j1 = 1,\ldots,6)$ and P defined in (4). The training to

obtain U_{ij1} is achieved in an obstacle-free environment (i.e., $\mathbf{O} = 0$). Thus, the training set consists of six (06) examples using FAMNN1 outputs as NN3 inputs; see Figure 7

$$P = \begin{cases} P_1 & \text{if } Z_i = 0, \\ 0 & \text{if } Z_i = 1. \end{cases} \quad \text{with } P_1 > \alpha, \quad (4)$$

(b) Obstacle-Avoidance Association. The updating weights is achieved by (3), where $M_{ij} = V_{ij2}, C_j = O_{j2}$, and $(j2 = 1,\ldots,30)$ and P defined in (5). The training to obtain V_{ij2} is achieved without considering the temperature field (i.e., $\mathbf{T} = 0$). Thus, the training set consists of thirty (30) examples using FAMNN2 outputs as NN3 inputs; see Figure 7.

$$P = \begin{cases} P_2 & \text{if collision,} \\ 0 & \text{if no collision.} \end{cases} \quad \text{with } P_2 > \alpha, \quad (5)$$

Thus, U_{ij1} and V_{ij2} are adjusted to obtain the reinforced actions among favorable actions shown in Figure 10(a) and Figure 10(b), respectively. Solid circles correspond to positive weights which represent favorable actions, indicating reinforced association, where values are proportional to the area of circles and the most reinforced action is the one having the great positive weight. Hollow circles correspond to negative weights which represent dissociated actions.

(c) Coordination. The detection of the maximum temperature must be interpreted as the vehicle goal, while the generated actions by the presence of obstacles must be interpreted as the vehicle reflex. Then, actions generated by obstacle avoidance must have precedence over those generated by target localization; that is, P_1 and P_2 constants must be defined such as $P_2 > P_1$, while β and α must be coupled such as $0 < \beta < \alpha$. Thus, the used values of different constants are: $\beta = 1, \alpha = 5, P_1 = 7$, and $P_2 = 9$.

4.2. FAMNN-Based Navigation Approach

To reflect the vehicle behaviors acquired by learning and to demonstrate the *learning, adaptation,* and *generalization* capabilities of the suggested FAMNN-based navigation approach, the vehicle navigation is simulated in different static and dynamic *partially structured environments*.

Each simulated vehicle has only two known data: its initial and final (i.e., target) positions. From these data, it must reach its target while avoiding possibly encountered obstacles using the suggested FAMNN-based navigation approach. In this simulation, the vehicle controls only its heading, and consequently, when obstacles are detected, in the same time, in its five (05) movement directions, it must be stopped. Also, each nonintelligent dynamic obstacle is assumed to have a velocity inferior or equal to the vehicle one.

4.2.1. Static Obstacles. Tested in an environment containing static obstacles, as illustrated in Figure 11 (where Veh: vehicle and Tar: target), the vehicle succeeds to avoid the static obstacles and reach its target.

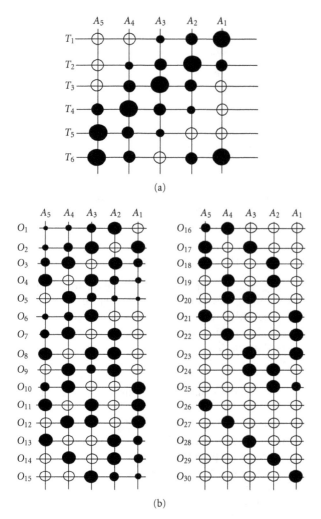

(a)

(b)

FIGURE 10: Association matrices: (a) Matrix of target localization association—solid circles correspond to positive weights which represent favorable actions, indicating reinforced association with different reinforcement degrees, where values are proportional to the area of circles and the most reinforced action is the one having the great positive weight; hollow circles correspond to negative weights which represent actions leading to a dissociation. (b) Matrix of obstacle-avoidance association—solid circles represent reinforced actions (with different reinforcement degrees) and hollow circles represent dissociated actions.

4.2.2. Intelligent Dynamic Obstacles. In the case illustrated in Figure 12, the four vehicles Veh1, Veh2, Veh3, and Veh4 try to reach their respective targets, while each one avoids the others.

4.2.3. Nonintelligent Dynamic Obstacles. In the case of two nonintelligent dynamic obstacles, oscillating vertically and horizontally between two fixed points, illustrated in Figure 13, the vehicle avoids them and reaches its target successfully.

4.2.4. Complex Environments. In the case illustrated in Figure 14, the three vehicles reach their targets without collisions with static and dynamic obstacles.

FIGURE 11: Case of static obstacles.

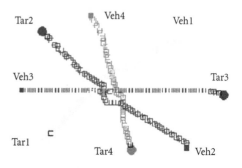

FIGURE 12: Case of intelligent dynamic obstacles.

5. Discussion and Conclusion

In this paper, the intelligent behaviors, acquired by *learning* and *adaptation*, of the target localization, obstacle avoidance, decision making, and action necessary to the navigation of IAV in partially structured environments have been suggested. Indeed, the HIS, namely, FAMNN1 and FAMNN2 under *supervised fast stable* SFAM learning have been developed to recognize the target-location situations and obstacle-avoidance situations, respectively, while the NN3 under *reinforcement* trial and error learning has been developed for the decision making and action. The simulation results illustrate not only the *learning, adaptation,* and *generalization* capabilities of both FAMNN1 and FAMNN2 classifiers, but also the *decision-making and action* capability of NN3. Nevertheless, there are a number of issues that need to be further investigation in perspective of an implementation on a real vehicle. At first, vehicle must be endowed with one or several actions to come back and a smooth trajectory generation system controlling its velocity. Also, it must be endowed also with specific sensors to detect dynamic obstacles and specific processing of data given from them.

The suggested approach in this paper presents two main advantages. The first is related to the obstacle-avoidance behavior which is deduced from the observation of the human one resulting in the principle to perceive partially structured environments as topological situations. The second is related to the performances of the FAMNN approach such as fastness and stability of learning, adaptation and generalization capabilities, fault and noise tolerance, and robustness.

The signals of sensors are often noisy, or they are defective giving incorrect data. This problem is efficiently handled by FAMNN with their inherent features of *adaptivity* and

FIGURE 13: Case of nonintelligent dynamic obstacles.

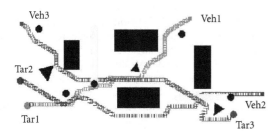

FIGURE 14: Case of a complex environment.

high fault and noise tolerance making them *robust*. Indeed, malfunctioning of one of the sensors or one of the neurons do not strongly impair the target-localization and obstacle-avoidance behaviors. This is possible because the knowledge stored in an FAMNN is distributed over many neurons and interconnections, not just a single or a few units. Consequently, concepts or mappings stored in an FAMNN have some degree of redundancy built in through this distribution of knowledge.

By another way, the incremental fuzzy ArtMap learning has proven to be fast and stable surpassing the performances of other techniques, as gradient back-propagation. In fact, a neural navigation approach has been suggested in [21]. In this neural approach, NN classifiers under gradient back-propagation learning are developed to recognize the same target-location situations and obstacle-avoidance situations presented in Figure 2 and Figure 3(b), respectively. In comparison with this neural approach, the suggested FAMNN approach presents several advantages.

One Selectable Parameter. For FAMNN, the only parameter to tune is the baseline of the vigilance ρ, while for NN, several parameters have to be tuned such as the learning rate η, number of nodes in the hidden layer, number of hidden layers, the choice of the weight initialization, and the momentum factor if used.

Fast Learning. Both FAMNN1 and FAMNN2 arrive under supervised SFAM learning to the desired result in only one (01) epoch, while in [21], NN1 and NN2 arrive under supervised gradient back-propagation learning to the desired result in fourty three (43) epochs and fifty (50) epochs, respectively.

Stable Learning. SFAM learning is stable [34, 35], while gradient back-propagation presents the well-known convergence problem to get stuck in local minima.

Number of Weights. For FAMNN1 and FAMNN2, the number of weights is $(5*2)*6 = 60$ and $(5*2)*30 = 300$, respectively; while for NN_1 and NN_2 developed in [21], the number of weights is $(5*5) + (5*6) = 55$ and $(5*15) + (15*30) = 525$. From these results, the NN take a small advantage (55 over 60) over FAMNN for a small number of classes, while the FAMNN take a great advantage (300 over 525) over NN for a great number of classes.

FPGA Implementation. An interesting alternative is to implement FAMNN1, FAMNN2, and NN3 on Xilinx's FPGA. In that case, the FPGA architectures of FAMNN1 and FAMNN2 will be simpler and will use less hardware than the NN1 and NN2 developed in [21].

Once implemented on FPGA, the suggested FAMNN-based navigation approach provides IAV with *more autonomy, intelligence,* and *real-time* processing capabilities making them *more robust* and *reliable*. Thus, they bring their target-localization, obstacle-avoidance, decision-making, and action behaviors near to that of humans in the recognition, learning, adaptation, generalization, decision making, and action.

Elsewhere, the developed simulation is simple aiming to estimate and validate the resulting quality, first of the learned target-localization and obstacle-avoidance behaviors from FAMNN1 and FAMNN2 and second of the suggested decision-making and action behavior, target-localization and obstacle-avoidance association stages acquired through reinforcement trial and error learning and learned by NN3. Of course, the final target, in future, is to implement the suggested approach on a real autonomous vehicle which could have other various sensors or complicated environments and consequently necessitate probably a refining of the number of possible actions, target-location situations, or obstacle-avoidance situations. In such case, the number of the inputs of each FAMNN will change in consequence implying a new learning of different target-location or obstacle-avoidance situations and a new learning of their associations for the decision making and action.

Concerning the repeatability of the experimental results, it is guaranteed by the capability of the learning and generalization of FAMNN1, FAMNN2, and NN3. In addition, in this simulation, the learning stability (FAMNN1 and FAMNN2) is guaranteed by the SFAM learning and by *reinforcement* trial and error learning for NN3, which are known to be stable (compared for instance to gradient back-propagation).

Note, finally, that the suggested approach demonstrate its ability in partially structured environments, with successful obstacle avoidance only face to dynamic obstacles (vehicles or nonintelligent dynamic obstacles as shown in Figure 12 and Figure 13, resp.) having the same velocity or less than the current vehicle. Thus, in the perspective of the navigation in dynamic environments with unknown or different velocities, vehicles need to be endowed with specific moving obstacle sensors, and a new dynamic obstacle classifier is needed.

An interesting alternative for future research is to extend the solutions of autonomous navigation to a set, not to just one option, and the more movement directions will bring more flexible movement capability for the vehicle. More, as the final decision part is in fact a compromise between the results of the target-localization behavior and those of the obstacle-avoidance behavior, it should be interesting to develop such decision part using an optimization method or strategy.

Another interesting alternative for future research is the lifelong vehicle learning which opens the opportunity for the transfer of learned knowledge. This knowledge could be enhanced by introducing comprehensive knowledge bases and fuzzy associative memories making IAV *more robust* and *reliable*.

References

[1] A. A. Baloch and A. M. Waxman, "Visual learning, adaptive expectations, and behavioral conditioning of the mobile robot MAVIN," *Neural Networks*, vol. 4, no. 3, pp. 271–302, 1991.

[2] S. Cherian and W. Troxell, "Intelligent behavior in machines emerging from a collection of interactive control structures," *Computational Intelligence*, vol. 11, no. 4, pp. 565–592, 1995.

[3] S. Thrun and T. M. Mitchell, "Lifelong robot learning," *Robotics and Autonomous Systems*, vol. 15, no. 1-2, pp. 25–46, 1995.

[4] A. Chohra and A. Farah, "Autonomy, behaviour, and evolution of intelligent vehicles," in *Proceedings of the International IMACS IEEE-SMC Multiconference on Computational Engineering in Systems Applications*, pp. 36–41, Lille, France, 1996.

[5] T. Fukuda et al., "Intelligent robotic system," in *Proceedings of the International IMACS IEEE-SMC Multiconference on Computational Engineering in Systems Applications*, pp. 1–10, Lille, France, 1996.

[6] O. Azouaoui and A. Chohra, "Evolution, behavior, and intelligence of Autonomous Robotic Systems (ARS)," in *Proceedings of the 3rd International IFAC Symposium on Intelligent Autonomous Vehicles (IAV '98)*, pp. 139–145, Madrid, Spain, 1998.

[7] P. J. Werbos, "Neurocontrol and fuzzy logic: connections and designs," *International Journal of Approximate Reasoning*, vol. 6, no. 2, pp. 185–219, 1992.

[8] D. W. Patterson, *Artificial Neural Networks: Theory and Applications*, Prentice-Hall, Singapore, 1996.

[9] C. L. Giles, R. Sun, and J. M. Zurada, "Guest editorial neural networks and hybrid intelligent models: foundations, theory, and applications," *IEEE Transactions on Neural Networks*, vol. 9, no. 5, pp. 721–723, 1998.

[10] M. Meng and A. C. Kak, "Mobile robot navigation using neural networks and nonmetrical environment models," *IEEE Control Systems*, vol. 13, no. 5, pp. 30–39, 1993.

[11] A. Chohra and C. Benmehrez, "Planning and intelligent control of autonomous mobile robots in partially structured environments," in *Proceedings of the International Symposium on Signal Processing, Robotics and Neural Networks*, Lille, France, 1994.

[12] A. Dubrawski and J. L. Crowley, "Self-supervised neural system for reactive navigation," in *Proceedings of the IEEE International Conference on Robotics and Automation*, pp. 2076–2081, San Diego, Calif, USA, May 1994.

[13] A. Chohra, A. Farah, and C. Benmehrez, "Neural navigation approach of an autonomous mobile robot in a partially structured environment," in *Proceedings of the International IFAC Conference on Intelligent Autonomous Vehicles*, pp. 238–243, Helsinki, Finland, 1995.

[14] I. Hiraga, T. Furuhashi, Y. Uchikawa, and S. Nakayama, "Acquisition of operator's rules for collision avoidance using fuzzy neural networks," *IEEE Transactions on Fuzzy Systems*, vol. 3, no. 3, pp. 280–287, 1995.

[15] A. Chohra, A. Farah, and C. Benmehrez, "Neuro-fuzzy navigation approach for autonomous mobile robots in partially structured environments," in *Proceedings of the International Conference on Application of Fuzzy Systems and Soft Computing*, pp. 304–313, Siegen, Germany, 1996.

[16] A. Chohra and A. Farah, "Hybrid navigation approach combining neural networks and fuzzy logic for autonomous mobile robots," in *Proceedings of the 3rd International Conference on Motion and Vibration Control*, Chiba, Japan, 1996.

[17] P. Szynkarczyk and A. Masiowski, "The fuzzy ARTMAP neural network as a controller for the mobile robot," in *Proceedings of the International Symposium on Methods and Models in Automation and Robotics*, pp. 1201–1206, Miedzyzdroje, Poland, 1996.

[18] A. Chohra, A. Farah, and M. Belloucif, "Neuro-fuzzy expert system E_S_CO_V for the obstacle avoidance of Intelligent Autonomous Vehicles (IAV)," in *Proceedings of the IEEE/RSJ International Conference on Intelligent Robot and Systems*, vol. 3, pp. 1706–1713, Grenoble, France, 1997.

[19] A. Dubrawski, "Tuning neural networks with stochastic optimization," in *Proceedings of the IEEE/RSJ International Conference on Intelligent Robot and Systems*, vol. 2, pp. 614–621, Grenoble, France, 1997.

[20] A. Chohra, "Fuzzy ArtMap neural networks (FAMNN) based navigation for intelligent autonomous vehicles (IAV) in partially structured environments," in *Proceedings of the 3rd International IFAC Symposium on Intelligent Autonomous Vehicles*, pp. 304–309, Madrid, Spain, 1998.

[21] A. Chohra, C. Benmehrez, and A. Farah, "Neural navigation approach for Intelligent Autonomous Vehicles (IAV) in partially structured environments," *Applied Intelligence*, vol. 8, no. 3, pp. 219–233, 1998.

[22] A. Chohra, A. Farah, and M. Belloucif, "Neuro-fuzzy expert system E-S-CO-V for the obstacle avoidance of intelligent autonomous vehicles (IAV)," *The International Journal of Advanced Robotic Systems*, vol. 12, no. 6, pp. 629–649, 1999.

[23] L. R. Medsker, *Hybrid Intelligent Systems*, Kluwer Academic Publishers, Dordrecht, The Netherlands, 1995.

[24] H. Ishibuchi, K. Morioka, and I. B. Turksen, "Learning by fuzzified neural networks," *International Journal of Approximate Reasoning*, vol. 13, no. 4, pp. 327–358, 1995.

[25] M. Meneganti, F. S. Saviello, and R. Tagliaferri, "Fuzzy neural networks for classification and detection of anomalies," *IEEE Transactions on Neural Networks*, vol. 9, no. 5, pp. 848–861, 1998.

[26] G. A. Carpenter, S. Grossberg, and D. B. Rosen, "Fuzzy ART: fast stable learning and categorization of analog patterns by an adaptive resonance system," *Neural Networks*, vol. 4, no. 6, pp. 759–771, 1991.

[27] G. A. Carpenter, S. Grossberg, N. Markuzon, J. H. Reynolds, and D. B. Rosen, "Fuzzy ARTMAP: a neural network architecture for incremental supervised learning of analog multidimensional maps," *IEEE Transactions on Neural Networks*, vol. 3, no. 5, pp. 698–713, 1992.

[28] C. T. Lin, C. J. Lin, and C. S. G. Lee, "Fuzzy adaptive learning control network with on-line neural learning," *Fuzzy Sets and Systems*, vol. 71, no. 1, pp. 25–45, 1995.

[29] H. M. Lee and C. S. Lai, "Supervised extended ART: a fast neural network classifier trained by combining supervised and

unsupervised learning," *Applied Intelligence*, vol. 6, no. 2, pp. 117–128, 1996.

[30] E. Sorouchyari, "Mobile robot navigation: a neural network approach," in *Proceedings of the Art du Colloque Neuromimétique*, pp. 159–175, Ecole Polytechnique de Lausanne, Lausanne, Switzerland, 1989.

[31] M. Maeda, Y. Maeda, and S. Murakami, "Fuzzy drive control of an autonomous mobile robot," *Fuzzy Sets and Systems*, vol. 39, no. 2, pp. 195–204, 1991.

[32] Y. S. Kim, I. H. Hwang, J. G. Lee, and H. Chung, "Spatial learning of an autonomous mobile robot using model-based approach," in *Proceedings of the 2nd International IFAC Conference on Intelligent Autonomous Vehicles*, pp. 250–255, Helsinki, Finland, 1995.

[33] O. Aycard, F. Charpillet, and D. Fohr, "Place learning and recognition using hidden Markov models," in *Proceedings of the IEEE/RSJ International Conference on Intelligent Robot and Systems*, pp. 1741–1746, Grenoble, France, 1997.

[34] T. Kasuba, "Simplified fuzzy ARTMAP," *AI Expert*, vol. 8, no. 11, pp. 18–25, 1993.

[35] S. Grossberg, "The link between brain learning, attention, and consciousness," *Consciousness and Cognition*, vol. 8, no. 1, pp. 1–44, 1999.

5

Oscillatory Behavior on a Three-Node Neural Network Model with Discrete and Distributed Delays

Chunhua Feng

College of Mathematics and Statistics, Guangxi Normal University, Guilin 541004, China

Correspondence should be addressed to Chunhua Feng; chfeng@mailbox.gxnu.edu.cn

Academic Editor: Songcan Chen

This paper investigates the oscillatory behavior of the solutions for a three-node neural network with discrete and distributed delays. Two theorems are provided to determine the conditions for oscillating solutions of the model. The criteria for selecting the parameters in this network are derived. Some simulation examples are presented to illustrate the effectiveness of the results.

1. Introduction

Neural networks are complex and large-scale dynamical systems. Time delay is inevitably encountered in implementation of dynamical neural networks and is frequently a source of oscillation and instability. On the one hand, information transmission from one neuron to another neuron may make the response of networks with discrete delays. On the other hand, neural networks usually have spatial extent due to the presence of a multitude of parallel pathways with a variety of axon sizes and lengths. Thus, the distributed delays in neural system need to be considered. In the past two decades, many researches have studied various neural networks with discrete and distributed delays [1–4]. In [1], Gopalsamy and Leung studied the following neural network model:

$$\frac{dx_1(t)}{dt} = -x_1(t) + a\tanh\left[x_2(t) - bx_2(t-\tau) - c\right],$$

$$\frac{dx_2(t)}{dt} = -x_2(t)$$

$$+ a\tanh\left[x_1(t) - b\int_0^\infty F(s)x_1(t-s)\,ds - c\right]. \tag{1}$$

By means of the Lyapunov functional, the authors obtained some necessary and sufficient conditions for the existence of a globally asymptotically stable equilibrium point of system (1). Ruan and Filfil [2] considered a two-neuron

network model with multiple discrete and distributed delays as follows:

$$\frac{1}{a_{10}}\frac{dx_1(t)}{dt} + x_1(t)$$

$$= F\left\{f_1 + c_{12}x_2(t-\sigma_{12})\right.$$

$$\left. + b_{11}\int_{-\infty}^t x_1(\tau)k_{11}(t-\tau)\,d\tau\right\},$$

$$\frac{1}{a_{20}}\frac{dx_2(t)}{dt} + x_2(t) \tag{2}$$

$$= F\left\{f_2 + c_{21}x_1(t-\sigma_{21})\right.$$

$$\left. + b_{22}\int_{-\infty}^t x_2(\tau)k_{22}(t-\tau)\,d\tau\right\},$$

where the delayed feedback kernel satisfies $\int_0^\infty k_{ii}(s)\,ds = $ const. and $\int_0^\infty sk_{ii}(s)\,ds < \infty$, $F(u) = (1/(1+e^{-u}))$ $(i=1,2)$. Local stability analyses are carried out for model (2). Computer simulations are performed to illustrate the obtained results. Liao et al. [3] discussed a two-neuron system with distributed delays in the frequency domain as follows:

$$\frac{dx_1(t)}{dt} = -x_1(t)$$
$$+ a_1 f \left[x_2(t) - b_2 \int_0^\infty F(r) x_2(t-r) dr - c_1 \right],$$
$$\frac{dx_2(t)}{dt} = -x_2(t)$$
$$+ a_2 f \left[x_1(t) - b_1 \int_0^\infty F(r) x_1(t-r) dr - c_2 \right],$$

$$(3)$$

where $F(r)$ is a strong kernel. For simplicity, the authors set $c_1 = c_2 = 0$. Let

$$y_1(t) = x_1(t) - b_1 \int_0^\infty F(r) x_1(t-r) dr,$$
$$y_2(t) = x_2(t) - b_2 \int_0^\infty F(r) x_2(t-r) dr.$$

$$(4)$$

Then system (3) is equivalent to the following model:

$$\frac{dy_1(t)}{dt} = -y_1(t) + a_1 f [y_2(t)]$$
$$- a_1 b_2 \int_0^\infty F(r) f [y_2(t-r)] dr,$$
$$\frac{dy_2(t)}{dt} = -y_2(t) + a_2 f [y_1(t)]$$
$$- a_2 b_1 \int_0^\infty F(r) f [y_2(t-r)] dr.$$

$$(5)$$

By applying the frequency domain approach and analyzing the characteristic equation, the Hopf bifurcation occurs when the mean delay μ exceeds a critical value. Thus, there is a family of periodic solutions bifurcates from the equilibrium point. Recently, Hajihosseini et al. [4] have investigated the following three-node network model:

$$\frac{dx_1(t)}{dt} = -x_1(t) + \tanh \left[\int_0^\infty F(r) x_2(t-r) dr \right],$$
$$\frac{dx_2(t)}{dt} = -x_2(t) + \tanh \left[\int_0^\infty F(r) x_3(t-r) dr \right],$$
$$\frac{dx_3(t)}{dt} = -x_3(t) + w_1 \tanh \left[\int_0^\infty F(r) x_1(t-r) dr \right]$$
$$+ w_2 \tanh \left[\int_0^\infty F(r) x_2(t-r) dr \right],$$

$$(6)$$

where w_1 and w_2 are parameters. The authors also make the change of variables $y_i(t) = \int_0^\infty F(r) x_i(t-r) dr$ $(i = 1, 2, 3)$ such that system (6) changes to the following:

$$\frac{dy_1(t)}{dt} = -y_1(t) + \int_0^\infty F(r) \tanh [y_2(t-r)] dr,$$
$$\frac{dy_2(t)}{dt} = -y_2(t) + \int_0^\infty F(r) \tanh [y_3(t-r)] dr,$$
$$\frac{dy_3(t)}{dt} = -y_3(t) + w_1 \int_0^\infty F(r) \tanh [y_1(t-r)] dr$$
$$+ w_2 \int_0^\infty F(r) \tanh [y_2(t-r)] dr.$$

$$(7)$$

Under the restrictive condition $|w_1 + w_2| < 1$, the Hopf bifurcation and stability of the bifurcating periodic solutions have been discussed. There are many authors who have studied the bifurcating periodic solutions for various models [5–14]. It is well known that the basic method in studying the bifurcating periodic solution for a time delay system is to discuss an algebraic equation in which the bifurcating value will be determined. Motivated by the above models we shall concern the existence of oscillating solutions for the following three-node network system with discrete and distributed delays:

$$\frac{dx_1(t)}{dt} = -a_1 x_1(t) + b_2 f [x_2(t - \tau_2)]$$
$$+ c_3 \int_0^\infty F(r) g [x_3(t-r)] dr,$$
$$\frac{dx_2(t)}{dt} = -a_2 x_2(t) + b_3 f [x_3(t - \tau_3)]$$
$$+ c_1 \int_0^\infty F(r) g [x_1(t-r)] dr,$$
$$\frac{dx_3(t)}{dt} = -a_3 x_3(t) + b_1 f [x_1(t - \tau_1)]$$
$$+ c_2 \int_0^\infty F(r) g [x_2(t-r)] dr,$$

$$(8)$$

where $F(r) = \mu^2 r e^{-\mu r}$ $(\mu > 0)$ is a strong kernel function, the passive decay rates $a_1, a_2,$ and a_3 are positive constants, b_i, c_i, and l_i $(i = 1, 2, 3)$ are constants, and delays $\tau_1, \tau_2,$ and τ_3 are nonnegative constants. It was emphasized that bifurcating approach is hard to deal with model (8), because it is very difficult to find the bifurcating parameter when $\tau_1, \tau_2,$ and τ_3 are different nonnegative constants. In order to discuss the existence of oscillating solutions for system (8) we adopt Chafee's criterion [15]. A time delay system will generate a limit cycle if the system has a unique unstable equilibrium point and bounded solutions. In other words, there exists an oscillatory solution of the model. System (8) can accord with the demands of Chafee's criterion; we refer the reader to [16, appendix].

2. Preliminaries

First we assume that the activation functions f and g both are monotone continuous bounded functions. $f, g \in C^4(R)$, $f(0) = g(0) = 0$, $uf(u) > 0$, and $ug(u) > 0$ for $u \neq 0$. For example, $f(u) = \tanh(u)$, and $g(u) = \arctan(u)$ satisfy those conditions. For the kernel function $F(r) = \mu^2 r e^{-\mu r}$ $(\mu > 0)$ we have

$$\int_0^\infty F(r)\, g\left[x_i(t-r)\right] dr$$

$$= \int_0^\infty \mu^2 r e^{-\mu r}\, g\left[x_i(t-r)\right] dr$$

$$= \int_{-\infty}^t \mu^2 (t-s) e^{-\mu(t-s)}\, g\left[x_i(s)\right] ds \tag{9}$$

$$= \mu^2 e^{-\mu t}\left(t \int_{-\infty}^t e^{\mu s}\, g\left[x_i(s)\right] ds \right.$$

$$\left. - \int_{-\infty}^t s e^{\mu s}\, g\left[x_i(s)\right] ds\right) \quad (i = 1, 2, 3).$$

From (9) we get

$$\frac{d}{dt}\left\{\int_0^\infty F(r)\, g\left[x_i(t-r)\right] dr\right\}$$

$$= -\mu \int_0^\infty F(r)\, g\left[x_i(t-r)\right] dr \tag{10}$$

$$+ \mu^2 e^{-\mu t} \int_{-\infty}^t e^{\mu s}\, g\left[x_i(s)\right] ds \quad (i = 1, 2, 3).$$

Taking the derivative on both sides of system (8) we obtain

$$\frac{dx_1^2(t)}{dt^2} = -a_1 \frac{dx_1(t)}{dt} + b_2 f'\left[x_2(t-\tau_2)\right]\frac{dx_2(t-\tau_2)}{dt}$$

$$- \mu c_3 \int_0^\infty F(r)\, g\left[x_3(t-r)\right] dr$$

$$+ c_3 \mu^2 e^{-\mu t}\int_{-\infty}^t e^{\mu s}\, g\left[x_3(s)\right] ds,$$

$$\frac{dx_2^2(t)}{dt^2} = -a_2 \frac{dx_2(t)}{dt} + b_3 f'\left[x_3(t-\tau_3)\right]\frac{dx_3(t-\tau_3)}{dt}$$

$$- \mu c_1 \int_0^\infty F(r)\, g\left[x_1(t-r)\right] dr \tag{11}$$

$$+ c_1 \mu^2 e^{-\mu t}\int_{-\infty}^t e^{\mu s}\, g\left[x_1(s)\right] ds,$$

$$\frac{dx_3^2(t)}{dt^2} = -a_3 \frac{dx_3(t)}{dt} + b_1 f'\left[x_1(t-\tau_1)\right]\frac{dx_1(t-\tau_1)}{dt}$$

$$- \mu c_2 \int_0^\infty F(r)\, g\left[x_2(t-r)\right] dr$$

$$+ c_2 \mu^2 e^{-\mu t}\int_{-\infty}^t e^{\mu s}\, g\left[x_2(s)\right] ds.$$

Set

$$- \mu c_3 \int_0^\infty F(r)\, g\left[x_3(t-r)\right] dr$$

$$= -2\mu c_3 \int_0^\infty F(r)\, g\left[x_3(t-r)\right] dr \tag{12}$$

$$+ \mu c_3 \int_0^\infty F(r)\, g\left[x_3(t-r)\right] dr,$$

so (11) can be rewritten as follows:

$$\frac{dx_1^2(t)}{dt^2} = -a_1 \frac{dx_1(t)}{dt} + b_2 f'\left[x_2(t-\tau_2)\right]\frac{dx_2(t-\tau_2)}{dt}$$

$$- 2\mu \left[\frac{dx_1(t)}{dt} + a_1 x_1(t) - b_2 f\left[x_2(t-\tau_2)\right]\right]$$

$$+ \mu c_3 \int_0^\infty F(r)\, g\left[x_3(t-r)\right] dr$$

$$+ c_3 \mu^2 e^{-\mu t}\int_{-\infty}^t e^{\mu s}\, g\left[x_3(s)\right] ds,$$

$$\frac{dx_2^2(t)}{dt^2} = -a_2 \frac{dx_2(t)}{dt} + b_3 f'\left[x_3(t-\tau_3)\right]\frac{dx_3(t-\tau_3)}{dt}$$

$$- 2\mu \left[\frac{dx_2(t)}{dt} + a_2 x_2(t) - b_3 f\left[x_3(t-\tau_3)\right]\right]$$

$$+ \mu c_1 \int_0^\infty F(r)\left[g x_1(t-r)\right] dr$$

$$+ c_1 \mu^2 e^{-\mu t}\int_{-\infty}^t e^{\mu s}\, g\left[x_1(s)\right] ds,$$

$$\frac{dx_3^2(t)}{dt^2} = -a_3 \frac{dx_3(t)}{dt} + b_1 f'\left[x_1(t-\tau_1)\right]\frac{dx_1(t-\tau_1)}{dt}$$

$$- 2\mu \left[\frac{dx_3(t)}{dt} + a_3 x_3(t) - b_1 f\left[x_1(t-\tau_1)\right]\right]$$

$$+ \mu c_2 \int_0^\infty F(r)\, g\left[x_2(t-r)\right] dr$$

$$+ c_2 \mu^2 e^{-\mu t}\int_{-\infty}^t e^{\mu s}\, g\left[x_2(s)\right] ds. \tag{13}$$

Taking the derivative again on both sides of (13) and using (10) give

$$\frac{dx_1^3(t)}{dt^3}$$

$$= -a_1 \frac{dx_1^2(t)}{dt^2} + b_2 f''\left[x_2(t-\tau_2)\right]\left(\frac{dx_2(t-\tau_2)}{dt}\right)^2$$

$$+ b_2 f'\left[x_2(t-\tau_2)\right]\frac{dx_2^2(t-\tau_2)}{dt^2} - 2\mu \frac{dx_1^2(t)}{dt^2}$$

$$- 2\mu a_1 \frac{dx_1(t)}{dt} - 2\mu b_2 f'\left[x_2(t-\tau_2)\right]\frac{dx_2(t-\tau_2)}{dt}$$

$$-\mu^2 \left(\frac{dx_1(t)}{dt} + a_1 x_1(t) - b_2 f[x_2(t-\tau_2)] \right)$$

$$+ c_3 \mu^2 g[x_3(t)],$$

$$\frac{dx_2^3(t)}{dt^3}$$

$$= -a_2 \frac{dx_2^2(t)}{dt^2} + b_3 f''[x_3(t-\tau_3)] \left(\frac{dx_3(t-\tau_3)}{dt} \right)^2$$

$$+ b_3 f'[x_3(t-\tau_3)] \frac{dx_3^2(t-\tau_3)}{dt^2} - 2\mu \frac{dx_2^2(t)}{dt^2}$$

$$- 2\mu a_2 \frac{dx_2(t)}{dt} - 2\mu b_3 f'[x_3(t-\tau_3)] \frac{dx_3(t-\tau_3)}{dt}$$

$$- \mu^2 \left(\frac{dx_2(t)}{dt} + a_2 x_2(t) - b_3 f[x_3(t-\tau_3)] \right)$$

$$+ c_1 \mu^2 g[x_1(t)],$$

$$\frac{dx_3^3(t)}{dt^3}$$

$$= -a_3 \frac{dx_3^2(t)}{dt^2} + b_1 f''[x_1(t-\tau_1)] \left(\frac{dx_1(t-\tau_1)}{dt} \right)^2$$

$$+ b_1 f'[x_1(t-\tau_1)] \frac{dx_1^2(t-\tau_1)}{dt^2} - 2\mu \frac{dx_3^2(t)}{dt^2}$$

$$- 2\mu a_3 \frac{dx_3(t)}{dt} - 2\mu b_1 f'[x_1(t-\tau_1)] \frac{dx_1(t-\tau_1)}{dt}$$

$$- \mu^2 \left(\frac{dx_3(t)}{dt} + a_3 x_3(t) - b_1 f[x_1(t-\tau_1)] \right)$$

$$+ c\mu^2 g[x_2(t)]. \tag{14}$$

Now by setting $x_4(t) = dx_1(t)/dt$, $x_5(t) = dx_2(t)/dt$, $x_6(t) = dx_3(t)/dt$, $x_7(t) = dx_1^2(t)/dt^2$, $x_8(t) = dx_2^2(t)/dt^2$, and $x_9(t) = dx_3^2(t)/dt^2$, we get the following time delay equivalent system of (8):

$$\frac{dx_1(t)}{dt} = x_4(t),$$

$$\frac{dx_2(t)}{dt} = x_5(t),$$

$$\frac{dx_3(t)}{dt} = x_6(t),$$

$$\frac{dx_4(t)}{dt} = x_7(t),$$

$$\frac{dx_5(t)}{dt} = x_8(t),$$

$$\frac{dx_6(t)}{dt} = x_9(t),$$

$$\frac{dx_7(t)}{dt} = -\mu^2 a_1 x_1(t) - \left(2\mu a_1 + \mu^2\right) x_4(t)$$

$$- (a_1 + 2\mu) x_7(t) + b_2 f''[x_2(t-\tau_2)]$$

$$\times [x_5(t-\tau_2)]^2 + b_2 f'[x_2(t-\tau_2)] x_8(t-\tau_2)$$

$$- 2\mu b_2 f'[x_2(t-\tau_2)] x_5(t-\tau_2)$$

$$+ \mu^2 b_2 f[x_2(t-\tau_2)] + c_3 \mu^2 g[x_3(t)],$$

$$\frac{dx_8(t)}{dt} = -\mu^2 a_2 x_2(t) - \left(2\mu a_2 + \mu^2\right) x_5(t)$$

$$- (a_2 + 2\mu) x_8(t) + b_3 f''[x_3(t-\tau_3)]$$

$$\times [x_6(t-\tau_3)]^2 + b_3 f'[x_3(t-\tau_3)] x_9(t-\tau_3)$$

$$- 2\mu b_3 f'[x_3(t-\tau_3)] x_6(t-\tau_3)$$

$$+ \mu^2 b_3 f[x_3(t-\tau_3)] + c_1 \mu^2 g[x_1(t)],$$

$$\frac{dx_9(t)}{dt} = -\mu^2 a_3 x_3(t) - \left(2\mu a_3 + \mu^2\right) x_6(t)$$

$$- (a_3 + 2\mu) x_9(t) + b_1 f''[x_1(t-\tau_1)]$$

$$\times [x_4(t-\tau_1)]^2 + b_1 f'[x_1(t-\tau_1)] x_7(t-\tau_1)$$

$$- 2\mu b_1 f'[x_1(t-\tau_1)] x_4(t-\tau_1)$$

$$+ \mu^2 b_1 f[x_1(t-\tau_1)] + c_2 \mu^2 g[x_2(t)]. \tag{15}$$

The linearization of system (15) around the zero point is the following:

$$\frac{dx_1(t)}{dt} = x_4(t),$$

$$\frac{dx_2(t)}{dt} = x_5(t),$$

$$\frac{dx_3(t)}{dt} = x_6(t),$$

$$\frac{dx_4(t)}{dt} = x_7(t),$$

$$\frac{dx_5(t)}{dt} = x_8(t),$$

$$\frac{dx_6(t)}{dt} = x_9(t),$$

$$\frac{dx_7(t)}{dt}$$

$$= -\mu^2 a_1 x_1(t) - \left(2\mu a_1 + \mu^2\right) x_4(t) - (a_1 + 2\mu) x_7(t)$$

$$+ b_2 f'(0) x_8 (t - \tau_2) - 2\mu b_2 f'(0) x_5 (t - \tau_2)$$

$$+ \mu^2 b_2 f'(0) x_2 (t - \tau_2) + c_3 \mu^2 g'(0) x_3 (t),$$

$$\frac{dx_8(t)}{dt}$$

$$= -\mu^2 a_2 x_2 (t) - \left(2\mu a_2 + \mu^2\right) x_5 (t) - (a_2 + 2\mu) x_8 (t)$$

$$+ b_3 f'(0) x_9 (t - \tau_3) - 2\mu b_3 f'(0) x_6 (t - \tau_3)$$

$$+ \mu^2 b_3 f'(0) x_3 (t - \tau_3) + c_1 \mu^2 g'(0) x_1 (t),$$

$$\frac{dx_9(t)}{dt}$$

$$= -\mu^2 a_3 x_3 (t) - \left(2\mu a_3 + \mu^2\right) x_6 (t) - (a_3 + 2\mu) x_9 (t)$$

$$+ b_1 f'(0) x_7 (t - \tau_1) - 2\mu b_1 f'(0) x_4 (t - \tau_1)$$

$$+ \mu^2 b_1 f'(0) x_1 (t - \tau_1) + c_2 \mu^2 g'(0) x_2 (t).$$

$$(16)$$

System (16) can be written as a matrix form:

$$\frac{dX(t)}{dt} = PX(t) + QX(t - \tilde{\tau}), \qquad (17)$$

where $X(t) = (x_1(t), x_2(t), \ldots, x_9(t))^T$, $X(t - \tilde{\tau}) = (x_1(t - \tau_1),$ $x_2(t - \tau_2), x_3(t - \tau_3), x_4(t - \tau_1), x_5(t - \tau_2), x_6(t - \tau_3), x_7(t - \tau_1),$ $x_8(t - \tau_2),$ and $x_9(t - \tau_3))^T$. So,

$$P = \begin{pmatrix} 0 & 0 & 0 & 1 & 0 & 0 & 0 & 0 & 0 \\ 0 & 0 & 0 & 0 & 1 & 0 & 0 & 0 & 0 \\ 0 & 0 & 0 & 0 & 0 & 1 & 0 & 0 & 0 \\ 0 & 0 & 0 & 0 & 0 & 0 & 1 & 0 & 0 \\ 0 & 0 & 0 & 0 & 0 & 0 & 0 & 1 & 0 \\ 0 & 0 & 0 & 0 & 0 & 0 & 0 & 0 & 1 \\ p_{71} & 0 & p_{73} & p_{74} & 0 & 0 & p_{77} & 0 & 0 \\ p_{81} & p_{82} & 0 & 0 & p_{85} & 0 & 0 & p_{88} & 0 \\ 0 & p_{92} & p_{93} & 0 & 0 & p_{96} & 0 & 0 & p_{99} \end{pmatrix},$$

$$Q = \begin{pmatrix} 0 & 0 & 0 & 0 & 0 & 0 & 0 & 0 & 0 \\ 0 & 0 & 0 & 0 & 0 & 0 & 0 & 0 & 0 \\ 0 & 0 & 0 & 0 & 0 & 0 & 0 & 0 & 0 \\ 0 & 0 & 0 & 0 & 0 & 0 & 0 & 0 & 0 \\ 0 & 0 & 0 & 0 & 0 & 0 & 0 & 0 & 0 \\ 0 & 0 & 0 & 0 & 0 & 0 & 0 & 0 & 0 \\ 0 & q_{72} & 0 & 0 & q_{75} & 0 & 0 & q_{78} & 0 \\ 0 & 0 & q_{83} & 0 & 0 & q_{86} & 0 & 0 & q_{89} \\ q_{91} & 0 & 0 & q_{94} & 0 & 0 & q_{97} & 0 & 0 \end{pmatrix},$$

$$(18)$$

where $p_{71} = -\mu^2 a_1$, $p_{73} = c_3 \mu^2 g'(0)$, $p_{74} = -(2\mu a_1 + \mu^2)$, $p_{77} = -(a_1 + 2\mu)$, $p_{81} = c_1 \mu^2 g'(0)$, $p_{82} = -\mu^2 a_2$, $p_{85} = -(2\mu a_2 + \mu^2)$, $p_{88} = -(a_2 + 2\mu)$, $p_{92} = c_2 \mu^2 g'(0)$, $p_{93} = -\mu^2 a_3$, $p_{96} = -(2\mu a_3 + \mu^2)$, $p_{99} = -(a_3 + 2\mu)$; $q_{72} = \mu^2 b_2 f'(0)$, $q_{75} = -2\mu b_2 f'(0)$, $q_{78} = b_2 f'(0)$, $q_{83} = \mu^2 b_3 f'(0)$, $q_{86} = -2\mu b_3 f'(0)$, $q_{89} = b_3 f'(0)$, $q_{91} = \mu^2 b_1 f'(0)$, $q_{94} = -2\mu b_1 f'(0)$, and $q_{97} = b_1 f'(0)$.

Lemma 1. *All solutions of system (8) are bounded.*

Proof. Since we assume that f and g both are monotone continuous bounded functions. So we have $|f(u)| \leq M$ and $|g(u)| \leq N$ (M and N are positive constants). From (8) we obtain

$$\frac{d|x_1(t)|}{dt} \leq -a_1 |x_1(t)| + A_1,$$

$$\frac{d|x_2(t)|}{dt} \leq -a_2 |x_2(t)| + A_2, \qquad (19)$$

$$\frac{d|x_3(t)|}{dt} \leq -a_3 |x_3(t)| + A_3,$$

where $A_1 = |b_2|M + |c_3|N$, $A_2 = |b_3|M + |c_1|N$, and $A_3 = |b_1| M + |c_2|N$. Thus, $|x_i(t)| \leq (A_i/a_i) + |x_i(0)|$ $(i = 1, 2, 3)$. This means that the solutions of system (8) are uniformly bounded. $\qquad \square$

Lemma 2. *Assume that the matrix*

$$B = \begin{pmatrix} -a_1 & b_2 f'(0) & c_3 g'(0) \\ c_1 g'(0) & -a_2 & b_3 f'(0) \\ b_1 f'(0) & c_2 g'(0) & -a_3 \end{pmatrix} \qquad (20)$$

is a nonsingular matrix. Then system (8) has a unique equilibrium point.

Proof. Noting that f and g both are monotone continuous bounded functions satisfying $f(0) = g(0) = 0$. Then $f(x) = f'(0)x + \alpha$, $g(x) = g'(0)x + \beta$, where α and β both are higher order infinitesimals when $x \to 0$. From (8), an equilibrium point $x^* = (x_1^*, x_2^*, x_3^*)^T$ is a solution of the following algebraic equation:

$$-a_1 x_1^* + b_2 f(x_2^*) + c_3 \int_0^\infty F(r) g(x_3^*) dr = 0,$$

$$-a_2 x_2^* + b_3 f(x_3^*) + c_1 \int_0^\infty F(r) g(x_1^*) dr = 0, \qquad (21)$$

$$-a_3 x_3^* + b_1 f(x_1^*) + c_2 \int_0^\infty F(r) g(x_2^*) dr = 0.$$

Noting that $\int_0^\infty F(r) g(x_i^*) dr = g(x_i^*) \int_0^\infty F(r) dr = g(x_i^*)$, then we have

$$-a_1 x_1^* + b_2 f'(0) x_2^* + b_2 \alpha + c_3 g'(0) x_3^* + c_3 \beta = 0,$$

$$-a_2 x_2^* + b_3 f'(0) x_3^* + b_3 \alpha + c_1 g'(0) x_1^* + c_1 \beta = 0, \qquad (22)$$

$$-a_3 x_3^* + b_1 f'(0) x_1^* + b_1 \alpha + c_2 g'(0) x_2^* + c_2 \beta = 0.$$

If $y^* = (y_1^*, y_2^*, y_3^*)^T$ is another equilibrium point of system (8), neglecting of the higher order infinitesimal, we obtain

$$-a_1 (x_1^* - y_1^*) + b_2 f'(0) (x_2^* - y_2^*) + c_3 g'(0) (x_3^* - y_3^*) = 0,$$

$$-a_2 (x_2^* - y_2^*) + b_3 f'(0) (x_3^* - y_3^*) + c_1 g'(0) (x_1^* - y_1^*) = 0,$$

$$-a_3 (x_3^* - y_3^*) + b_1 f'(0) (x_1^* - y_1^*) + c_2 g'(0) (x_2^* - y_2^*) 0. \tag{23}$$

The matrix form of (23) is follows:

$$B(x^* - y^*) = 0. \tag{24}$$

Since B is a nonsingular matrix based on the algebraic knowledge one can have $x^* - y^* = 0$ or $x^* = y^*$. This means that system (8) has a unique equilibrium point. Obviously, the unique equilibrium point exactly is zero point since $f(0) = g(0) = 0$. □

3. Oscillating Solutions Analysis

We adopt the following norms of vectors and matrices: $\|x(t)\| = \sum_{i=1}^{n} |x(t)|$, $\|P\| = \max_j \sum_{i=1}^{9} |p_{ij}|$, $\|Q\| = \max_j \sum_{i=1}^{n} |q_{ij}|$. The measure $\sigma(P)$ of the matrix P is defined by $\sigma(P) = \lim_{\theta \to 0^+} ((\|I + \theta P\| - 1)/\theta)$, which for the chosen norms reduces to $\sigma(P) = \max_{1 \le j \le 9} (p_{jj} + \sum_{i=1 i \ne j}^{9} |p_{ij}|)$.

In order to discuss the instability of equilibrium point for system (8), we consider the equivalent system (15) of (8). Note that the linearized system of (15) is (16). Obviously, if the trivial solution of (16) is unstable, it implies that the trivial solution of system (15) is unstable and thus the instability of the trivial solution of system (8). Therefore, we first have

Theorem 3. *Assume that system* (8) *has a unique equilibrium point and the determinant of matrix P is not equal to zero. Let* $\rho_1, \rho_2, \ldots, \rho_9, \varrho_1, \varrho_2, \ldots, \varrho_9$ *be the eigenvalues of the matrixes P and Q, respectively. If there is at least one* $\mathrm{Re}\rho_i > 0$ ($\mathrm{Im}\rho_i$ *may be equal to zero) or there exists one positive real eigenvalue* $\varrho_j > |\rho_j|$, *for some* $j \in \{1, 2, \ldots, 9\}$, *then the unique equilibrium point, namely, the trivial solution of system* (16) *is unstable, implying that the equivalent system* (15) *or* (8) *generates oscillating solutions.*

Proof. Since Q is a singular matrix, set $\varrho_1 = \varrho_2 = \cdots = \varrho_6 = 0$. For given value of μ, let $\rho_1, \rho_2, \ldots, \rho_9$ be the eigenvalues of the matrix P. Thus, the characteristic equation of system (16) is as follows:

$$\det \left(\lambda I_{ij} - p_{ij} - q_{ij} e^{-\lambda \tau_{ij}} \right) = 0, \tag{25}$$

where

$$I_{ij} = \begin{cases} 1 & \text{if } i = j, \\ 0 & \text{if } i \ne j, \end{cases} \qquad \tau_{ij} = \begin{cases} \tau_i & \text{if } i = j, \\ 0 & \text{if } i \ne j. \end{cases} \tag{26}$$

or

$$\prod_{i=1}^{9} \left[\lambda - \rho_i - \varrho_i e^{-\lambda \tau_i} \right] = 0. \tag{27}$$

Since there is at least one $\mathrm{Re}\rho_i > 0$, without loss of generality, set $\mathrm{Re}\rho_1 > 0$. From $\varrho_1 = 0$ we have the equation $\lambda - \rho_1 = 0$. This means that $\lambda = \rho_1$, and there is a $\mathrm{Re}\,\lambda > 0$. So, the unique equilibrium point of system (16) is unstable based on the theory of differential equation. If by corresponding some ρ_j we have $\varrho_j > |\rho_j|$ $j \in \{1, 2, \ldots, 9\}$, we pointed out that there exists positive real root for transcendental equation $\lambda - \rho_j - \varrho_j e^{-\lambda \tau_j} = 0$. Let $f(\lambda) = \lambda - \rho_j - \varrho_j e^{-\lambda \tau_j}$. Then $f(\lambda)$ is a continuous function of λ. Since $f(0) = -\rho_j - \varrho_j$, from $\varrho_j > |\rho_j|$, we know that $f(0) < 0$. Obviously, there is a suitable large $\lambda^* > 0$ such that $f(\lambda^*) = \lambda^* - \rho_j - \varrho_j e^{-\lambda^* \tau_j} > 0$ since $e^{-\lambda^* \tau_j}$ can be suitably small. Thus, by the continuity of $f(\lambda)$, there is a point, say $\overline{\lambda} \in (0, \lambda^*)$ such that $f(\overline{\lambda}) = 0$. In other words, there is a positive real eigenvalue. In this case the unique equilibrium point of system (16) is also unstable. Since all solutions of the system are bounded, on the basis of Chafee's criterion [15], system (15) generates a limit cycle, implying that there exists an oscillating solution of system (15) and therefore system (8). □

Theorem 4. *Assume that system* (8) *has a unique equilibrium point and the following inequalities hold:*

$$(\|Q\| \tau e) \exp(-|\sigma(P)| \tau) > 1,$$

$$(\|Q\| \tau^* e) \exp(-\tau^* |\sigma(P)| \tau^*) > 1, \tag{28}$$

where $\tau = \min\{\tau_1, \tau_2, \tau_3\}$ *and* $\tau^* = \max\{\tau_1, \tau_2, \tau_3\}$. *Then the unique equilibrium point, namely, the trivial solution of system* (16) *is unstable, implying that the equivalent system* (15) *or* (8) *generates oscillating solutions.*

Proof. First we consider system (16) in the case $\tau_1 = \tau_2 = \tau_3 = \tau$ and we easily get:

$$\frac{d |x_1(t)|}{dt} = |x_4(t)|,$$

$$\frac{d |x_2(t)|}{dt} = |x_5(t)|,$$

$$\frac{d |x_3(t)|}{dt} = |x_6(t)|,$$

$$\frac{d |x_4(t)|}{dt} = |x_7(t)|,$$

$$\frac{d |x_5(t)|}{dt} = |x_8(t)|,$$

$$\frac{d |x_6(t)|}{dt} = |x_9(t)|,$$

$$\frac{d |x_7(t)|}{dt} \le -\mu^2 a_1 |x_1(t)| - (2\mu a_1 + \mu^2) |x_4(t)|$$

$$- (a_1 + 2\mu) |x_7(t)| + |b_2 f'(0)| |x_8(t - \tau)|$$

$$+ |2\mu b_2 f'(0)| |x_5(t - \tau_2)|$$

$$+ |\mu^2 b_2 f'(0)| |x_2(t - \tau_2)| + |c_3 \mu^2 g'(0)| |x_3(t)|,$$

$$\frac{d\,|x_8(t)|}{dt} \leq -\mu^2 a_2\,|x_2(t)| - \left(2\mu a_2 + \mu^2\right)|x_5(t)|$$

$$- (a_2 + 2\mu)\,|x_8(t)| + \left|b_3 f'(0)\right|\left|x_9(t - \tau_3)\right|$$

$$+ \left|2\mu b_3 f'(0)\right|\left|x_6(t - \tau_3)\right|$$

$$+ \left|\mu^2 b_3 f'(0)\right|\left|x_3(t - \tau_3)\right| + \left|c_1 \mu^2 g'(0)\right|\left|x_1(t)\right|,$$

$$\frac{d\,|x_9(t)|}{dt} \leq -\mu^2 a_3\,|x_3(t)| - \left(2\mu a_3 + \mu^2\right)|x_6(t)|$$

$$- (a_3 + 2\mu)\,|x_9(t)| + \left|b_1 f'(0)\right|\left|x_7(t - \tau)\right|$$

$$+ \left|2\mu b_1 f'(0)\right|\left|x_4(t - \tau_1)\right|$$

$$+ \left|\mu^2 b_1 f'(0)\right|\left|x_1(t - \tau_1)\right| + \left|c_2 \mu^2 g'(0)\right|\left|x_2(t)\right|. \tag{29}$$

Let $(t) = \sum_{i=1}^{9} |x_i(t)|$; then for some t^*, $y(t) > 0$ ($t \geq t^*$) and we have

$$\frac{dy(t)}{dt} \leq \sigma(P)\,y(t) + \|Q\|\,y(t - \tau), \quad t \geq t^* + \tau. \tag{30}$$

Consider the scalar equation

$$\frac{dz(t)}{dt} = \sigma(P)\,z(t) + \|Q\|\,z(t - \tau), \quad t \geq t^* + \tau \tag{31}$$

with $y(s) = z(s)$ and $s \in [t^*, t^* + \tau]$. According to the comparison theorem of differential equation, one can obtain

$$y(t) \leq z(t), \quad t \geq t^* + \tau. \tag{32}$$

We claim that the trivial solution of (31) is unstable. Suppose that this is not true; then the characteristic equation associated with (31) given by

$$\lambda = \sigma(P) + \|Q\|\,e^{-\lambda \tau} \tag{33}$$

will have a real negative root say λ^* such that $\lambda^* = \sigma(P) + \|Q\|e^{-\lambda^* \tau}$, where $e^{-\lambda^* \tau} = e^{|\lambda^* \tau|}$.

So we get

$$\left|\lambda^*\right| \geq \|Q\|\,e^{|\lambda^* \tau|} - |\sigma(P)|. \tag{34}$$

Thus

$$1 \geq \frac{\|Q\|\,e^{|\lambda^* \tau|}}{|\lambda^*| + |\sigma(P)|}$$

$$= \frac{\|Q\|\,\tau\exp\left(-|\sigma(P)|\,\tau\right)\exp\left(|\lambda^*|\,\tau + |\sigma(P)\,\tau|\right)}{|\lambda^*|\,\tau + |\sigma(P)\,\tau|}. \tag{35}$$

Based on the formula $e^x \geq ex$ $(x > 0)$, from (35), we have

$$1 \geq \left(\|Q\|\,\tau e\right)\exp\left(-|\sigma(P)|\,\tau\right). \tag{36}$$

$\square$

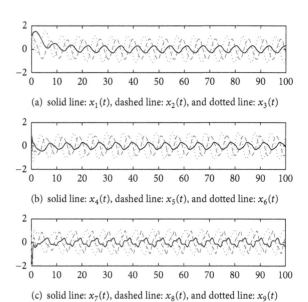

(a) solid line: $x_1(t)$, dashed line: $x_2(t)$, and dotted line: $x_3(t)$

(b) solid line: $x_4(t)$, dashed line: $x_5(t)$, and dotted line: $x_6(t)$

(c) solid line: $x_7(t)$, dashed line: $x_8(t)$, and dotted line: $x_9(t)$

FIGURE 1: Oscillatory behavior of the solutions: $mu = 3.5$, delays: (0.5, 0.6, and 0.7), and activation functions: $f(u) = g(u) = \tanh(u)$.

Inequality (36) contradicts the first inequality of (28). Therefore, our claim regarding the instability of the trivial solution is valid. Similarly, consider system (16) in the case $\tau_1 = \tau_2 = \tau_3 = \tau^*$; we know that the trivial solution is unstable if the second inequality of (28) holds. Note that $\tau \leq \tau_i \leq \tau^*$ ($i = 1, 2, 3$). So, the trivial solution of (16) is unstable when condition (28) holds, implying that the trivial solution of (15) is unstable. According to Chafee's criterion, system (15) generates a limit cycle, suggesting that there is an oscillating solution of system (15) and therefore system (8).

4. Computer Simulations

We use the equivalent system (15) of (8) for computer simulation. In Figure 1 both activation functions $f(u)$ and $g(u)$ are taken $\tanh(u)$. Thus, $f'(u) = g'(u) = 4/(e^u + e^{-u})^2 = 1 - (\tanh(u))^2$, $f''(u) = g''(u) = 2(\tanh(u))^3 - 2\tanh(u)$, and $f'(0) = g'(0) = 1$. We select $\mu = 5.5$, $a_1 = 0.48$, $a_2 = 0.65$, $a_3 = 0.78$, $b_1 = 0.6$, $b_2 = 0.8$, $b_3 = 0.9$, $c_1 = -0.8$, and $c_2 = -1.8$, $c_3 = 0.4$. Then the eigenvalues of matrix P are $-5.8250 \pm 1.8620i$, $-1.7568 \pm 2.5151i$, -0.0000, $-0.4840, -5.3568, -5.6392$, and -8.2087 and the eigenvalues of matrix Q are $-0.3780 \pm 0.6547i$, 0.7560, and $0, 0, 0, 0, 0, 0$. Note that the eigenvalue 0.7560 of matrix Q is larger than $|-0.4840| = 0.4840$. Based on Theorem 3, the trivial solution of system (15) is unstable. The system generates an oscillating solution. In order to compare the effect of the time delays, we change the delays from (0.2, 0.3, and 0.4) to (1, 1.5, and 2), while keeping the other parameters as shown in Figure 1. We see that the oscillatory amplitude and frequency both are changed (see Figure 2). In Figure 3, we keep the parameter values the same as Figure 2, the activation function $g(u) = \tanh(u)$, and change the activation function $f(u) = \arctan(u)$. Then $f'(u) = 1/(1 + u^2)$ and $f''(u) = -2u/(1 +$

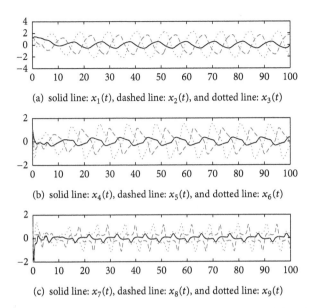

(a) solid line: $x_1(t)$, dashed line: $x_2(t)$, and dotted line: $x_3(t)$

(b) solid line: $x_4(t)$, dashed line: $x_5(t)$, and dotted line: $x_6(t)$

(c) solid line: $x_7(t)$, dashed line: $x_8(t)$, and dotted line: $x_9(t)$

FIGURE 2: Oscillatory behavior of the solutions: $mu = 5.5$, delays: (1, 1.5, and 2), and activation functions: $f(u) = g(u) = \tanh(u)$.

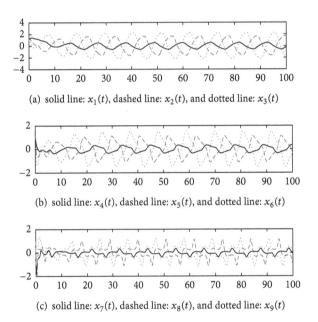

(a) solid line: $x_1(t)$, dashed line: $x_2(t)$, and dotted line: $x_3(t)$

(b) solid line: $x_4(t)$, dashed line: $x_5(t)$, and dotted line: $x_6(t)$

(c) solid line: $x_7(t)$, dashed line: $x_8(t)$, and dotted line: $x_9(t)$

FIGURE 3: Oscillatory behavior of the solutions: $mu = 5.5$, delays: (1, 1.5, and 2), and activation functions: $f(u) = \arctan(u)$, $g(u) = \tanh(u)$.

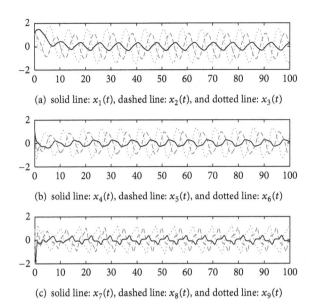

(a) solid line: $x_1(t)$, dashed line: $x_2(t)$, and dotted line: $x_3(t)$

(b) solid line: $x_4(t)$, dashed line: $x_5(t)$, and dotted line: $x_6(t)$

(c) solid line: $x_7(t)$, dashed line: $x_8(t)$, and dotted line: $x_9(t)$

FIGURE 4: Oscillatory behavior of the solutions: $mu = 3.5$, delays: (0.5, 0.6, and 0.7), and activation functions: $f(u) = 1/(1+\exp(-2u))$, $g(u) = (\exp(-2u) - 1)/(1 + \exp(-2u))$.

$u^2)^2$. We see that the graph is changed slightly in comparison with Figure 2. In Figure 4, we set the activation function $f(u) = 1/(1 + e^{-2u})$ and $g(u) = (e^{-2u} - 1)/(1 + e^{-2u})$. Then $f'(u) = 2e^{-2u}/(1 + e^{-2u})^2$, $g'(u) = -4e^{-2u}/(1 + e^{-2u})^2$, $f''(u) = 4e^{-2u}(2e^{-2u} - 1)/(1 + e^{-2u})^3$, and $g''(u) = 8e^{-2u}(1 - e^{-2u})/(1 + e^{-2u})^3$. Thus $f'(0) = 1/2$ and $g'(0) = -1$. Note that $f(0) = 1/2 \neq 0$ and $g(0) = -1/2 \neq 0$. When we select the parameters as follows: $\mu = 3.5$, $a_1 = 0.18$, $a_2 = 0.15$, $a_3 = 0.19$, $b_1 = 0.05$, $b_2 = 0.08$, $b_3 = 0.12$, $c_1 = -0.6$,

and $c_2 = 0.8$, $c_3 = 0.5$, time delays are (0.5, 0.6, and 0.7). The oscillatory solutions also appeared. This means that the restrictive condition $f(0) = g(0) = 0$, $uf(u) > 0$, and $ug(u) > 0$ for $u \neq 0$ is only for convenience of the proof.

5. Conclusion

This paper discusses the oscillatory behavior of the solutions for a three-node network model with discrete and distributed delays. Two theorems are provided to ensure the existence of oscillating solutions for the model. Computer simulations suggested that our theorems are only sufficient conditions. How to find a necessary condition is still an open problem.

Conflict of Interests

The author declares that there is no conflict of interests regarding the publication of this paper.

Acknowledgment

This work is supported by Grant no. 11361010 from NNFS of China to Chunhua Feng.

References

[1] K. Gopalsamy and I. K. C. Leung, "Convergence under dynamical thresholds with delays," *IEEE Transactions on Neural Networks*, vol. 8, no. 2, pp. 341–348, 1997.

[2] S. Ruan and R. S. Filfil, "Dynamics of a two-neuron system with discrete and distributed delays," *Physica D*, vol. 191, no. 3-4, pp. 323–342, 2004.

[3] X. Liao, S. Li, and G. Chen, "Bifurcation analysis on a two-neuron system with distributed delays in the frequency domain," *Neural Networks*, vol. 17, no. 4, pp. 545–561, 2004.

[4] A. Hajihosseini, G. R. Lamooki, B. Beheshti, and F. Maleki, "The Hopf bifurcation analysis on a time-delayed recurrent neural network in the frequency domain," *Neurocomputing*, vol. 73, pp. 991–1005, 2010.

[5] T. Y. Cai, H. G. Zhang, and F. H. Yang, "Simplified frequency meth-od for stability and bifurcation of delayed neural networks in ring structure," *Neurocomputing*, vol. 121, pp. 416–422, 2013.

[6] R. M. Sebdani and S. Farjami, "Bifurcations and chaos in a discrete-time-delayed Hopfield neural network with ring structures and different internal delays," *Neurocomputing*, vol. 99, pp. 154–162, 2013.

[7] C. Huang, L. Huang, J. Feng, M. Nai, and Y. He, "Hopf bifurcation analysis for a two-neuron network with four delays," *Chaos, Solitons and Fractals*, vol. 34, no. 3, pp. 795–812, 2007.

[8] Y. T. Ding, W. H. Jiang, and P. Yu, "Bifurcation analysis in a recurrent neural network model with delays," *Communications in Nonlinear Science and Numerical Simulation*, vol. 18, pp. 351–372, 2013.

[9] S. Guo, Y. Chen, and J. Wu, "Two-parameter bifurcations in a network of two neurons with multiple delays," *Journal of Differential Equations*, vol. 244, no. 2, pp. 444–486, 2008.

[10] Y. Huang and X. Yang, "Hyperchaos and bifurcation in a new class of four-dimensional Hopfield neural networks," *Neurocomputing*, vol. 69, no. 13-15, pp. 1787–1795, 2006.

[11] C. Sun, M. Han, and X. Pang, "Global Hopf bifurcation analysis on a BAM neural network with delays," *Physics Letters A*, vol. 360, no. 6, pp. 689–695, 2007.

[12] H. Zhao, L. Wang, and C. Ma, "Hopf bifurcation and stability analysis on discrete-time Hopfield neural network with delay," *Nonlinear Analysis: Real World Applications*, vol. 9, no. 1, pp. 103–113, 2008.

[13] I. Ncube, "Stability switching and Hopf bifurcation in a multiple-delayed neural network with distributed delay," *Journal of Mathematical Analysis and Applications*, vol. 407, pp. 141–146, 2013.

[14] T. Dong and X. F. Liao, "Hopf-Pitchfork bifurcation in a simplified BAM neural network model with multiple delays," *Journal of Computational and Applied Mathematics*, vol. 253, pp. 222–234, 2013.

[15] N. Chafee, "A bifurcation problem for a functional differential equation of finitely retarded type," *Journal of Mathematical Analysis and Applications*, vol. 35, no. 2, pp. 312–348, 1971.

[16] C. Feng and R. Plamondon, "An oscillatory criterion for a time delayed neural ring network model," *Neural Networks*, vol. 29-30, pp. 70–79, 2012.

6

Soft Topographic Maps for Clustering and Classifying Bacteria Using Housekeeping Genes

Massimo La Rosa, Riccardo Rizzo, and Alfonso Urso

ICAR-CNR, Consiglio Nazionale delle Ricerche, Viale delle Scienze, Ed.11, 90128 Palermo, Italy

Correspondence should be addressed to Riccardo Rizzo, ricrizzo@pa.icar.cnr.it

Academic Editor: Tomasz G. Smolinski

The Self-Organizing Map (SOM) algorithm is widely used for building topographic maps of data represented in a vectorial space, but it does not operate with dissimilarity data. Soft Topographic Map (STM) algorithm is an extension of SOM to arbitrary distance measures, and it creates a map using a set of units, organized in a rectangular lattice, defining data neighbourhood relationships. In the last years, a new standard for identifying bacteria using genotypic information began to be developed. In this new approach, phylogenetic relationships of bacteria could be determined by comparing a stable part of the bacteria genetic code, the so-called "housekeeping genes." The goal of this work is to build a topographic representation of bacteria clusters, by means of self-organizing maps, starting from genotypic features regarding housekeeping genes.

1. Introduction

Microbial identification is a fundamental topic for the study of infectious diseases, and new approaches in the analysis of bacterial isolates, for identification purposes, are currently under development. The classical method to identify bacterial isolates is based on the comparison of morphologic and phenotypic characteristics to those described as type or typical strains. On the other hand, recent trends focus on the analysis of bacteria genotype, taking into account the "housekeeping" genes, representing a very stable part of DNA. One of the most used genes, that in many studies has proven to be especially suitable for taxonomic and identification goals (see Section 2), is the 16S rRNA gene. Employing genotypic features allows to obtain a classification for rare or poorly described bacteria, to classify organisms with an unusual phenotype in a well-defined taxon, and to find misclassification that can lead to the discovery and description of new pathogens.

In this work, we present a method to make a topographic representation of bacteria clusters and to visualize the relations among them. This topographic map is obtained considering a single gene of bacteria genome, the 16S rRNA gene. Since the definition of a vector space to represent nucleotide sequences is not reliable and well structured, the information provided by the gene sequences is in the form of a pairwise dissimilarity matrix. We computed such a matrix in terms of string distances by means of well understood and theoretically sound techniques commonly used in genomics, and, in order to produce the topographic representation, we adopted a modified version of Self-Organizing Map that is able to work with input dataset expressed in terms of dissimilarity distances.

2. Background

The job of putting scientific names to microbial isolates, namely the bacteria identification, is within the practice of clinical microbiology. The aim is to give insight into the etiological agent causing an infectious disease, in order to find possible effective antimicrobial therapy. The traditional method for performing this task is dependent on the comparison of an accurate morphologic and phenotypic description of type strains or typical strains with the accurate morphologic and phenotypic description of the isolate to be identified. Microbiologists used standard references such as Bergey's Manual of Systematic Bacteriology [1]. In the 1980s, a new standard for identifying bacteria began to be developed by Woese et al. [2]. It was shown that phylogenetic relationships of bacteria could be determined considering genotypic methods by comparing a stable part of the genetic code. The identification of bacteria based on genotypic methods is generally more accurate than the traditional identification on the basis of phenotypic characteristics. The preferred genetic technique that has emerged is based on the comparison of the bacterial 16S rRNA gene sequence, and, in recent years, several attempts to reorganize actual bacteria taxonomy have been carried out by adopting 16S rRNA gene sequences.

Authors in [1] focused on the study of bacteria belonging to the prokaryotic phyla and adopted the Principal Component Analysis method [3] on matrices of evolutionary distances. Authors in [4–6] carried out an analysis of 16S rRNA gene sequences to classify bacteria with atypical phenotype: they proposed that two bacterial isolates would belong to different species if the dissimilarity in the 16S rRNA gene sequences between them was more than 1% and less than 3%. Clustering approaches for DNA sequences were carried out by [7, 8]: the authors considered human endogenous retrovirus sequences and a distance matrix based on the FASTA similarity scores [9]; then they adopted Median SOM [10], an extension of the Self-Organizing Map (SOM) [11], to nonvectorial data.

As the authors said, the Median SOM has a better convergence if the patterns are roughly ordered. This is not an issue for the Soft Topographic Map and the Deterministic Annealing approach. The Median SOM was also used to cluster protein sequences from SWISS-PROT database in [12]. Authors in [13] proposed a protein sequence clustering method based on the Optic algorithm [14]. In [15], a technique to find functional genomic clusters in RNA expression data by computing the entropy of gene expression patterns and the mutual information between RNA expression patterns for each pair of genes is described. INPARANOID [16] is another related approach that performs a clustering based on BLAST [17] scores to find orthologs and inparalogs in two species. The use of maps for organization of biological data was also used in [18], where a map of gammaproteobacteria is reported; the obtained map is based on a reorganization of the dissimilarity matrix, and some of the results can be obtained with the approach proposed in this work.

Topological representations are not restricted, however, only to biological data, but they can be adopted, for instance, with video and audio data [19], as well.

The proposed work represents an extended version of our preliminary results presented in [20].

3. Methods

3.1. Sequence Alignment and Evolutionary Distance.
Sequence alignment is a well-known bioinformatics technique useful to compare genomic sequences, even of different length, between two different species. In our system, we used two of the most popular alignment algorithms: ClustalW [21], implementing a multiple alignment among all sequences at the same time; Needleman and Wunsch [22], that provide a pairwise alignment, that is the best alignment configuration between two sequences.

Once aligned, it is possible to compute a distance between two homologous sequences. In bioinformatics domain, there are many types of distances, usually called "evolutionary distance"; these distances differ from each other on the basis of their a priori assumptions.

The simplest kind of distance is the number of substitutions per site, defined as

$$p = \frac{\text{number of different nucleotides}}{\text{total number of compared nucleotides}}. \tag{1}$$

The number of substitutions observed is often smaller than the number of substitutions that have actually taken place. This is due to many genetic phenomena such as multiple substitutions on the same site (*multiple hits*), convergent substitutions or retromutations. For these reasons, a series of stochastic methods has been introduced in order to obtain a better estimate of evolutionary distances. In our study, we considered the method proposed by [23], whose a priori assumptions are

(1) all sites evolve in an independent manner;

(2) all sites can change with the same probability;

(3) all kinds of substitution are equally probable;

(4) substitution speed is constant over time.

According to [23], the evolutionary distance d between two nucleotide sequences is equal to

$$d = -\frac{3}{4} \ln\left(1 - \frac{4}{3}p\right), \tag{2}$$

where p is the number of substitutions per site (1).

3.2. Soft Topographic Map Algorithm.
A widely used algorithm for topographic maps is the Kohonen's Self-Organizing Map (SOM) algorithm [11], but it does not operate with dissimilarity data. The SOM network builds a projection from an input space to a lattice (usually 2D) of neurons, visualized as a 2D map. Each neuron is a pointer to a position in the input space and is a tile on the map. The input patterns are distributed on the map because they are associated to the nearest neuron in the input space: that neuron is usually referred to as the best-matching unit (bmu). SOM networks are trained using the unsupervised learning paradigm: the label of input patterns, if present, will not be considered during training phase.

The SOM is widely used to project input data into a low-dimensional space [24, 25].

Many studies on the SOM algorithm have been carried after the original paper: according to Luttrell's work [26], the generation of topographic maps can be interpreted as an optimization problem based on the minimization of a cost function. This cost function represents an energy function, and it takes its minimum when each data point is mapped to the best matching neuron, thus providing the optimal set of parameters for the map.

An algorithm based on this formulation of the problem was developed by Graepel et al. [27, 28] and provides an extension of SOM to arbitrary distance measures. This algorithm is called Soft Topographic Map (STM) and creates a map using a set of units (neurons or models) organized in a rectangular lattice that defines their neighborhood relationships. STM is able to work with data whose features are expressed in terms of dissimilarity measures among each other. Algorithm full description, along with theoretical and practical details, can be read in [27].

4. Implementation

The Soft Topographic Map algorithm described in this paper needs some tuning; in this section, we give all the necessary information for a fruitful use of the algorithm.

4.1. Dataset. The main purpose of our work is to demonstrate that STM algorithm can be applied to a biological dataset in order to obtain a topographic map useful to visualize clusters of bacteria belonging to the same order, according to actual taxonomy. Biological dataset is composed of 16S rRNA gene sequences. Each sequence is a text string containing only four types of characters: "A," "C," "G," "T" corresponding to the four DNA nucleotides. Information content of the dataset is expressed in terms of a dissimilarity measure, computed according to (2). According to the actual taxonomy [1], we focused our attention on a class containing some of the most common and dangerous bacteria related to human pathologies: Gammaproteobacteria, belonging to the Proteobacteria phylum. In Table 1, a brief description of the experimental dataset is shown: the dataset is composed of 147 type strains, and the resulting 16S gene sequences were downloaded from NCBI public nucleotide database, GenBank [29], in FASTA format [30].

4.2. Parameters Setup. A Soft Topographic Map is an array of many neural units where patterns to classify are associated to these units at the end of the training phase. In order to speed up processing time, we applied a slightly tuned version of the Soft Topographic Map algorithm: neighborhood functions associated to each neuron have been set to zero if they referred to neurons outside a previously chosen radius in the grid. The radius has been put to 1/3 of the map dimensions. As for the other parameters of the algorithm, we put the annealing increasing factor $\eta = 1.1$ and threshold convergence $\epsilon = 10^{-5}$, as suggested by [27]. After several tests we chose, as a good compromise between processing time and clustering quality, the final value of inverse temperature equal to 10 times the initial value, leading as a consequence to 25 learning epochs; finally, we put the width of neighborhood functions σ to 0.5.

The maps have been drawn using a gray-level scale to represent the distances between the units: the color between two near occupied cells, both horizontally and vertically, is proportional to the average distance of the patterns being in those neurons. To be more precise, empty cells are filled with a gray level proportional to the mean distance among

the four closest occupied neurons, along the vertical and horizontal axes referred to that empty cell. Gray scale is calibrated so that bright values denote proximity and dark values represent distance. Two sample maps and the distance scale are shown in Figure 1.

4.3. Map Evaluation Criteria. In order to select the map dimension, it is useful to evaluate the evolution of the clustering process with regard to map size. To this end, it is possible to compare the number of neural units and the number of patterns defining the following ratio:

$$K = \frac{\text{number of pattern to classify}}{\text{number of neural units}}. \qquad (3)$$

If $K \geq 1$, then each neural unit can have many input patterns so that each neural unit can be considered as a cluster. In this case, the focus is on the use of all neural units, and the ones that are not used are often referred to as "dead units".

If $K < 1$, then the single neural unit cannot be a cluster center and the cluster is constituted by many neural units separated by a set of dead units. The maps with $K \geq 1$ are sometimes called KNN-SOM, while the ones with $K < 1$ are visualized with a technique called U-Matrix [31].

In our implementation, we started with a ratio $K \approx 2$ (using a square 8×8 STM map) in order to understand if it was possible to identify the neural units as clusters. It was difficult to find this correspondence due to the high number of units that were associated with sequences of different order. This is highlighted in the center diagram in Figure 2, that shows the number of mixed clusters (i.e., units that have associated sequences of different orders).

Usually neural network results are determined by initial weight values. A common procedure to filter this noise is to train many networks with different initial set up. In our experiments, we used 20 different network initializations for each experiment.

For the evaluation of the quality of the mapping, several methods are reported in literature, but these methods need a metric space (a vector space) where the patterns and the units of the map are represented as vectors. For a short review on topology preservation, see [32]. In our problem, we have not a feature space where the patterns are placed, and we have only a dissimilarity matrix that reports the pattern organization.

In order to establish an evaluation criteria for the obtained maps, we noticed that the rows and the columns of the map represent a linear ordering of the patterns, order that should be present also in the dissimilarity matrix. For example, selecting a row on the map, we have a set of ordered patterns; the same patterns are used to select the corresponding subset of rows and columns of the dissimilarity matrix. These dissimilarity values can be considered as distance values and allow to order the patterns in a linear fashion. A pattern sequence can be easily obtained using the Sammon mapping technique on a linear space starting from the data of dissimilarity matrix. This sequence should be identical to the one obtained from the map; the

TABLE 1: Actual taxonomy of the bacteria dataset. We focused on Gammaproteobacteria class, which is divided into 14 orders. Each order has one or more families. Inside each family, we considered only the type strains, that is, sample species.

Gammaproteobacteria	Order name	Number of families	Number of type strains	Code numbers
□	Chromatiales	3 families	25 type strains	1–25
○	Acidithiobacillales	2 families	2 type strains	26, 27
△	Xanthomonodales	1 family	11 type strains	28–38
■	Cardiobacteriales	1 family	3 type strains	39, 40, 41
●	Thiotrichales	3 families	11 type strains	42–52
▲	Legionellales	2 families	2 type strains	53, 54
▣	Methylococcales	1 families	7 type strains	55–61
◎	Oceanospirillales	4 families	11 type strains	62–72
◉	Pseudomonadales	2 families	7 type strains	73–79
⊠	Alteromonadales	1 family	13 type strains	80–92
★	Vibrionales	1 family	3 type strains	93, 94, 95
☆	Aeromonadales	2 families	7 type strains	96–102
⊙	Enterobacteriales	1 family	39 type strains	103–141
◬	Pasteurellales	1 families	6 type strains	142–147
	14 orders	25 families	147 type strains	

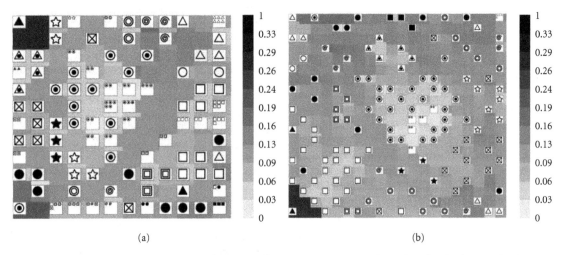

(a) (b)

FIGURE 1: 12×12 (left) and 20×20 (right) topographic maps of bacteria dataset. In the legend under the figures, the dissimilarity values corresponding to each gray level are shown. 0.33 is the max distance in our dataset, so this darkest gray level available.

two sequences can be compared using the Spearman's rank correlation coefficient [33] defined as

$$\rho = 1 - \left[\frac{6 \sum d_i^2}{n(n^2 - 1)} \right], \tag{4}$$

where d_i is the difference between each rank of corresponding values of the compared variables x and y; n is the number of pairs of values. In the above equation, we consider only the term in the square brackets because we discard the possible inversion between the pattern sequence of the map and the one of the dissimilarity matrix. Averaging all the Spearman coefficients for each column and each row, we obtain a score for a given map. All these scores, calculated for each map geometry and for initialization, are reported in the upper diagram of Figure 2 as a box plot.

Evaluating this coefficient, we can decide which geometry can be used. Maps with few neural units are discarded, because there are units with many patterns that create ties in the ordering; in fact, patterns associated with the same unit do not have any order, while very large maps present a naturally decreasing value due to the fact that the patterns are very sparse. This effect can be seen in Figure 2 on the right of the thin vertical line.

5. Results

In this Section, we present the results we obtained applying the techniques described in Section 3 to the bacteria dataset described in Section 4.

Given the dataset described above, we carried out several experiments. We obtained several maps of different

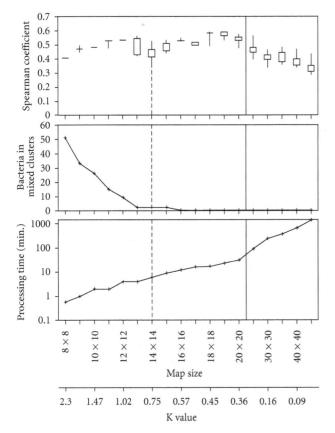

FIGURE 2: In the upper graph is the box plot graph of the Spearman coefficient. In the chart on the center, we can observe that the number of bacteria belonging to mixed clusters, that is, cells in the map labeled with bacteria of different orders, aims at decreasing as the size of maps increases. In the lower graph is the processing time in minutes (logarithmic scale).

dimensions, from 8 × 8 up to 45 × 45 neurons, and for every configuration, we trained 20 maps in order to avoid the dependence from the initial conditions.

Comparing the results provided from pairwise and multiple alignment, we saw that there are not meaningful differences in the corresponding maps, so we focused only on the evolutionary distances computed from pairwise alignment.

In Figure 1, we can see the evolution of clustering process with regard to map size: first of all, we can notice how most of the bacteria are classified according to their order in the actual taxonomy; then, we can observe that the number of bacteria belonging to mixed clusters, that is, cells in the map labeled with bacteria of different orders, aims at decreasing as the size of maps increases. We can state that small maps, according to the chart until about 10 × 10, do not provide useful results because there are too few available neurons and consequently the maps are not able to correctly discriminate among different patterns. If we look, in fact, at the charts of Figure 2, there are too many mixed clusters and high values of the Spearman coefficient. On the other side, we noticed that in very large maps (not shown in this paper), from 25 × 25 and so on, the topographic maps "lose" their

clustering properties because input patterns aim at spreading all over the grid, filling all the available space. Considering the definition of parameter K given in (3), maps with $K < 1$ and $K \gg 1$ are meaningless.

The map size and the optimal K parameter value are also a function of the method used to produce the dissimilarity matrix. For example, using Normalized Compression Distance (NCD) [34], the optimum size of the map can be different, as stated in one of our previous work about this topic [35].

One of the most interesting result is that there are some anomalies that are constant for all the tests regardless the dimension of the maps. For example, in small maps (not shown here), the "*Alterococcus agarolyticus*" (number 103 in Figure 3) bacterium of the "Enterobacteriales" order is incorrectly clustered together with bacteria of other orders, whereas, in larger maps, it is isolated in an individual cluster, usually at the border of the map and far from its homologous strains (see Figure 3). Another interesting example is given by "*Legionella pneumophila*" (number 54 in Figure 3) bacterium of "Legionellales" order: in all maps, it is located in a corner of the grid and surrounded by a dark gray area. This would suggest that these two bacteria could form new orders, not present in actual taxonomy, or at least new families. The same anomalies are confirmed by the Multidimensional Scaling and the evolutionary tree.

Since the maps provide a visualization of bacteria datasets, if there are some "anomalies", they are clearly highlighted as isolated elements standing at the border or in the corners of the map. These anomalies can suggest biologists to do further experimental trials in order to determine if, eventually, there are some misclassifications in the taxonomy. That does not mean the proposed method should mainly be used in order to perform identification or annotation of unknown bacterial species, but that the visualization is also able to detect anomalies and if there are unknown elements, to project them in the map because of unsupervised learning feature of STM algorithm (see Section 3).

The bacteria organization in the map finds some other confirmation in [18], for example, the neighborhood of Xanthomonas (33 in Figure 3), Pseudomonas (73), and Enterobacteriales (114); notice also that the position of Buchnera (106) is not in the same compact group of the other Enterobacteriales in the map center, although not so distant as depicted in [18].

Considering the evaluation of the map, reported in Figure 2, we choose in the set of the 14 × 14 maps the one that presents the absolute minimum of the Spearman coefficient before of its natural decreasing on the right side of the thin vertical line. This choice also minimizes the number of mixed clusters, as can be seen in the center diagram of Figure 2.

5.1. Comparison with Phylogenetic Tree. We compared the chosen 14 × 14 map with the phylogenetic tree referred to our dataset. In Figure 3, it is possible to notice that there are four outliers bacteria: "*Francisella tularensis*" (45), "*Legionella pneumophila*" (54), "*Alterococcus agarolyticus*" (103), and "*Buchnera aphidicola*" (106). The first three

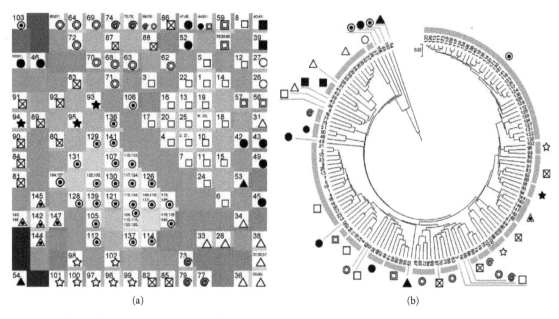

(a)   (b)

FIGURE 3: Comparison between the phylogenetic tree and the selected 14×14 map. It is possible to notice that there are four outliers bacteria: "*Francisella tularensis,*" "*Alterococcus agarolyticus,*" "*Legionella pneumophila,*" "*Buchnera aphidicola.*" The first three bacteria are clustered in the border of the map and far from their homologous strains; the remaining one lies in a single cell surrounded by a dark gray area that indicates its actual distance from its neighbors is bigger than the one shown in the map. There are other bacteria far from their homologous strains: "*Schineria larvae,*" "*Arhodomonas aquaeolei,*" "*Halothiobacillus neapolitanus,*" "*Nitrosococcus nitrosus.*" "Enterobacteriales" and "Pasteurellales" form compact group in both representations.

bacteria are positioned on the border of the map and far from their homologous strains; the remaining one lies in a single cell surrounded by a dark gray area that indicates its actual distance from its neighbors is bigger than it appears. Apart from these four elements, in the phylogenetic tree, we found other bacteria far from their order, for instance, "*Schineria larvae*" (34), "*Halothiobacillus neapolitanus*" (8), "*Nitrosococcus nitrosus*" (12), and "*Arhodomonas aquaeolei*" (3): once again these elements are at the border or in a zone on the map surrounded by a dark gray level. Although "*Schineria larvae*" (34) and "*Halothiobacillus neapolitanus*" (8) are coupled in the dendrogram, we can see in the map how they are actually far away: that happens because some pairings in the tree are forced, and, in this case, do not give useful information. "*Schineria larvae*" (34) and "*Francisella tularensis*" (45), whose actual distance is 0.1339, are close in the map, but their surrounding gray level explains their real distance, as we can also see in the phylogenetic tree.

If we consider entire orders, for example, "Enterobacteriales" and "Pasteurellales", they form compact groups both in the tree and in the map. Moreover, the "Methylococcales" order that in actual taxonomy has one family, in the map, is divided in two clusters (56, 57 and 55, 58, 59, 60, 61) as reported in the phylogenetic tree and in [18].

Our visualization method allows, then, not only to detect some singular situations, but also to understand their relative positions with regards to all the patterns in the dataset. At a first look to the phylogenetic tree, in fact, it should be possible to wrongly realize that the four outliers described above are far from all the other bacteria, but near each other. Using the map, instead, we can see how the four outliers are

completely isolated. At the same time our method provides a very simple system to immediately visualize compact orders and/or families, as previously explained.

This is clear looking at Figure 3 where the map and the tree contain the same objects but the map is far more readable.

5.2. Comparison with Multidimensional Scaling. Multidimensional Scaling (MDS) is a widely used technique for embedding a dataset, defined only in terms of pairwise distances, in an euclidean space and plotting it in a 2D (or 3D) plane [36]. For this reason, we compared our two-dimensional topographic representation with a 2D plot, obtained through MDS, of our bacteria dataset, presented in Figure 4.

First of all, we can notice that the four outliers bacteria, "*Francisella tularensis,*" "*Buchnera aphidicola,*" "*Alterococcus agarolyticus,*" "*Legionella pneumophila,*" are separated from all the other elements. Apart from this evident result, there are not many other similarities with our map nor with the phylogenetic tree. Bacteria belonging to "Pasteurellales" order, for example, forming in the previous visualizations a well-defined group, in MDS plot, stand in very distant zones without any observable relationship. There are some dislocated elements even inside "Enterobacteriales," though most of them still form a compact group in the center part of the diagram. Moreover, it is difficult to give a clue on the distance among the patterns.

In conclusion, the use of MDS plotting gives less information with respect to the ones obtained by means of topographic map and phylogenetic tree. Because of the

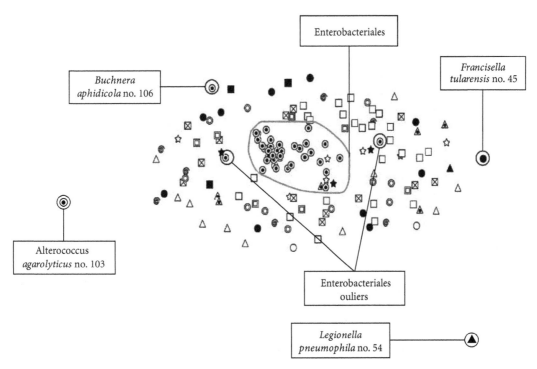

FIGURE 4: 2D representation of bacteria dataset obtained through Multidimensional Scaling. Apart from the four outliers, "*Legionella pneumophila,*" "*Alterococcus agarolyticus,*" "*Francisella tularensis,*" "*Buchnera aphidicola,*" that are separated from all the other elements, the remaining bacteria do not show meaningful similarities with the visualizations obtained through topographic map and phylogenetic tree.

distortion introduced by MDS, in fact, most of the patterns, with the exception of the four outliers, have lost their distinctive properties already discussed in the previous paragraph.

6. Conclusion

In recent trends for the definition of bacteria taxonomy, genotypical characteristics are considered very important and type strains are compared on the basis of the stable part of the genetic code. In this paper, the Soft Topographic Map algorithm has been applied to the visualization and clustering of bacteria according to their genotypic similarity. In the similarity measure, we have adopted the 16S rRNA gene sequence, as commonly used for taxonomic purposes. A characteristic of the proposed approach is that the topographic map is built from the genetic data, using the Soft Topographic Map algorithm working on proximity data, rather than using a vector space representation. The generated maps show that the proposed approach provides a clustering that generally reflects the current taxonomy with some singular cases. Moreover, the results depend on the size of the maps, since small and large maps, with regards to the number of input patterns, do not give meaningful information. The size of the maps should be chosen so that the ratio between input elements and neurons is $K \approx 1$, with a corresponding value of Spearman coefficient representing a local minimum.

The visualization of bacteria dataset through the map also allows an easy identification of cases representing some "anomalies" in input dataset. These anomalies should be further investigated because they, eventually, could represent incorrect classification or incorrect registration in the database. It also provides a compact representation, in one image, useful to visualize bacteria clusters and their mutual separation, although the evaluation of distance between clusters is still inaccurate. Furthermore our system has proved to be a valid alternative to the traditional visualizing tool used in bioinformatics, like phylogenetic trees and 2D plot obtained through MDS.

In future research activities, we intend to extend the analysis to other "housekeeping" genes and to combine different genotypical characteristics in order to obtain finer clustering and classification. We would like also to use other distance measures, eventually alignment-free, and different clustering algorithm in order to improve execution time and the quality of clustering.

References

[1] G. M. Garrity, B. A. Julia, and T. Lilburn, "The revised road map to the manual," in *Bergey's Manual of Systematic Bacteriology*, G. M. Garrity, Ed., pp. 159–187, Springer, New York, NY, USA, 204.

[2] C. R. Woese, E. Stackebrandt, T. J. Macke, and G. E. Fox, "A phylogenetic definition of the major eubacterial taxa," *Systematic and Applied Microbiology*, vol. 6, no. 2, pp. 143–151, 1985.

[3] I. T. Joliffe, *Principal Component Analysis*, Springer, New York, NY, USA, 1986.

[4] J. E. Clarridge, "Impact of 16S rRNA gene sequence analysis for identification of bacteria on clinical microbiology and infectious diseases," *Clinical Microbiology Reviews*, vol. 17, no. 4, pp. 840–862, 2004.

[5] M. Drancourt, C. Bollet, A. Carlioz, R. Martelin, J.-P. Gayral, and D. Raoult, "16S ribosomal DNA sequence analysis of a large collection of environmental and clinical unidentifiable bacterial isolates," *Journal of Clinical Microbiology*, vol. 38, pp. 3623–3630, 2000.

[6] M. Drancourt, P. Berger, and D. Raoult, "Systematic 16S rRNA gene sequencing of atypical clinical isolates identified 27 new bacterial species associated with humans," *Journal of Clinical Microbiology*, vol. 42, no. 5, pp. 2197–2202, 2004.

[7] M. Oja, P. Somervuo, S. Kaski, and T. Kohonen, "Clustering of human endogenous retrovirus sequences with median self-organizing map," in *Proceedings of the Workshop on Self-Organizing Maps (WSOM '03)*, 2003.

[8] M. Oja, G. O. Sperber, J. Blomberg, and S. Kaski, "Self-organizing map-based discovery and visualization of human endogenous retroviral sequence groups," *International Journal of Neural Systems*, vol. 15, no. 3, Article ID 163179, 2005.

[9] W. R. Pearson and D. J. Lipman, "Improved tools for biological sequence comparison," *Proceedings of the National Academy of Sciences of the United States of America*, vol. 85, no. 8, pp. 2444–2448, 1988.

[10] T. Kohonen and P. Somervuo, "How to make large self-organizing maps for nonvectorial data," *Neural Networks*, vol. 15, no. 8-9, pp. 945–952, 2002.

[11] T. Kohonen, *Self-Organizing Maps*, Springer, Berlin, Germany, 1995.

[12] P. Somervuo and T. Kohonen, "Clustering and visualization of large protein sequence databases by means of an extension of the self-organizing map," in *Proceedings of the 3rd International Conference on Discovery Science*, pp. 76–85, 2000.

[13] Y. Chen, K. D. Reilly, A. P. Sprague, and Z. Guan, "Seqoptics: a protein sequence clustering method," in *Proceedings of the 1st International Multi- Symposiums on Computer and Computational Sciences (IMSCCS'06)*, vol. 1, pp. 69–75, June 2006.

[14] M. Ankerst, M. M. Breunig, H. P. Kriegel, and J. Sander, "Optics: ordering points to identify the clustering structure," in *Proceedings of the ACM SIGMOD International Conference on Management of Data*, pp. 49–60, Philadelphia, Pa, USA, June 1999.

[15] A. J. Butte and I. S. Kohane, "Mutual information relevance networks: functional genomic clustering using pairwise entropy measurements," in *Proceedings of the Pacific Symposium on Biocomputing*, vol. 5, pp. 415–426, 2000.

[16] M. Remm, C. E. V. Storm, and E. L. L. Sonnhammer, "Automatic clustering of orthologs and in-paralogs from pairwise species comparisons," *Journal of Molecular Biology*, vol. 314, no. 5, pp. 1041–1052, 2001.

[17] S. F. Altschul, W. Gish, W. Miller, E. W. Myers, and D. J. Lipman, "Basic local alignment search tool," *Journal of Molecular Biology*, vol. 232, pp. 584–599, 1993.

[18] G. M. Garrity and T. G. Lilburn, "Self-organizing and self-correcting classifications of biological data," *Bioinformatics*, vol. 21, no. 10, pp. 2309–2314, 2005.

[19] C. Fyfe, W. Barbakh, W. C. Ooi, and H. Ko, "Topological mappings of video and audio data," *International Journal of Neural Systems*, vol. 18, no. 6, pp. 481–489, 2008.

[20] M. La Rosa, G. Di Fatta, S. Gaglio, G. M. Giammanco, R. Rizzo, and A. M. Urso, "Soft topographic map for clustering and classification of bacteria," in *Advances in Intelligent Data Analysis VII*, vol. 4723 of *Lecture Notes in Computer Science*, pp. 332–343, 2007.

[21] J. D. Thompson, D. G. Higgins, and T. J. Gibson, "CLUSTAL W: Improving the sensitivity of progressive multiple sequence alignment through sequence weighting, position-specific gap penalties and weight matrix choice," *Nucleic Acids Research*, vol. 22, no. 22, pp. 4673–4680, 1994.

[22] S. B. Needleman and C. D. Wunsch, "A general method applicable to the search for similarities in the amino acid sequence of two proteins," *Journal of Molecular Biology*, vol. 48, no. 3, pp. 443–453, 1970.

[23] T. H. Jukes and C. R. Cantor, "Evolution of protein molecules," in *Mammalian Protein Metabolism*, H. N. Munro, Ed., pp. 21–132, Academic Press, New York, NY, USA, 1969.

[24] A. N. Gorban and A. Zinovyev, "Principal manifolds and graphs in practice: from molecular biology to dynamical systems," *International Journal of Neural Systems*, vol. 20, no. 3, pp. 219–232, 2010.

[25] W. Barbakh and C. Fyfe, "Online clustering algorithms," *International Journal of Neural Systems*, vol. 18, no. 3, pp. 185–194, 2008.

[26] S. P. Luttrell, "A Bayesian analysis of self-organizing maps," *Neural Computation*, vol. 6, pp. 767–794, 1994.

[27] T. Graepel, M. Burger, and K. Obermayer, "Self-organizing maps: generalizations and new optimization techniques," *Neurocomputing*, vol. 21, no. 1–3, pp. 173–190, 1998.

[28] T. Graepel and K. Obermayer, "A stochastic self-organizing map for proximity data," *Neural Computation*, vol. 11, no. 1, pp. 139–155, 1999.

[29] GenBank, 2007, http://www.ncbi.nlm.nih.gov/entrez/query.fcgi?db=Nucleotide.

[30] Fasta, 2007, http://www.ncbi.nlm.nih.gov/blast/fasta.shtml.

[31] A. Ultsch, "Maps for the visualization of high dimensional data spaces," in *Proceedings of the Workshop on Self-Organizing Maps (WSOM '03)*, vol. 3, pp. 225–230, 2003.

[32] D. Vidaurre and J. Muruzábal, "A quick assessment of topology preservation for SOM structures," *IEEE Transactions on Neural Networks*, vol. 18, no. 5, pp. 1524–1528, 2007.

[33] E. W. Weisstein, *The CRC Concise Encyclopedia of Mathematics*, CRC Press, New York, NY, USA, 1999.

[34] M. Li, X. Chen, X. Li, B. Ma, and P. M. B. Vitanyi, "The similarity metric," *IEEE Transactions on Information Theory*, vol. 50, no. 12, pp. 3250–3264, 2004.

[35] M. La Rosa, S. Gaglio, R. Rizzo, and A. Urso, "Normalised compression distance and evolutionary distance of genomic sequences: comparison of clustering results," *International Journal of Knowledge Engineering and Soft Data Paradigms*, vol. 1, no. 4, pp. 345–362, 2009.

[36] W. S. Torgerson, "Multidimensional scaling: I. Theory and method," *Psychometrika*, vol. 17, pp. 401–419, 1952.

7

Applying Artificial Neural Networks for Face Recognition

Thai Hoang Le

Department of Computer Science, Ho Chi Minh University of Science, Ho Chi Minh City 70000, Vietnam

Correspondence should be addressed to Thai Hoang Le, lhthai@fit.hcmus.edu.vn

Academic Editor: Naoyuki Kubota

This paper introduces some novel models for all steps of a face recognition system. In the step of face detection, we propose a hybrid model combining AdaBoost and Artificial Neural Network (ABANN) to solve the process efficiently. In the next step, labeled faces detected by ABANN will be aligned by Active Shape Model and Multi Layer Perceptron. In this alignment step, we propose a new 2D local texture model based on Multi Layer Perceptron. The classifier of the model significantly improves the accuracy and the robustness of local searching on faces with expression variation and ambiguous contours. In the feature extraction step, we describe a methodology for improving the efficiency by the association of two methods: geometric feature based method and Independent Component Analysis method. In the face matching step, we apply a model combining many Neural Networks for matching geometric features of human face. The model links many Neural Networks together, so we call it Multi Artificial Neural Network. MIT + CMU database is used for evaluating our proposed methods for face detection and alignment. Finally, the experimental results of all steps on CallTech database show the feasibility of our proposed model.

1. Introduction

Face recognition is a visual pattern recognition problem. In detail, a face recognition system with the input of an arbitrary image will search in database to output people's identification in the input image. A face recognition system generally consists of four modules as depicted in Figure 1: detection, alignment, feature extraction, and matching, where localization and normalization (face detection and alignment) are processing steps before face recognition (facial feature extraction and matching) is performed [1].

Face detection segments the face areas from the background. In the case of video, the detected faces may need to be tracked using a *face tracking* component. *Face alignment* aims at achieving more accurate localization and at normalizing faces thereby, whereas face detection provides coarse estimates of the location and scale of each detected face. Facial components, such as eyes, nose, and mouth and facial outline, are located; based on the location points, the input face image is normalized with respect to geometrical properties, such as size and pose, using geometrical transforms or morphing. The face is usually further normalized with respect to photometrical properties such illumination and gray scale. After a face is normalized geometrically and photometrically, *feature extraction* is performed to provide effective information that is useful for distinguishing between faces of different persons and stable with respect to the geometrical and photometrical variations. For *face matching*, the extracted feature vector of the input face is matched against those of enrolled faces in the database; it outputs the identity of the face when a match is found with sufficient confidence or indicates an unknown face otherwise.

Artificial neural networks were successfully applied for solving signal processing problems in 20 years [2]. Researchers proposed many different models of artificial neural networks. A challenge is to identify the most appropriate neural network model which can work reliably for solving realistic problem.

This paper provides some basic neural network models and efficiently applies these models in modules of face recognition system. For *face detection module*, a three-layer feedforward artificial neural network with Tanh activation function is proposed that combines AdaBoost to detect human faces so that face detecting rate is rather high. For *face alignment module*, a multilayer perceptron (MLP)

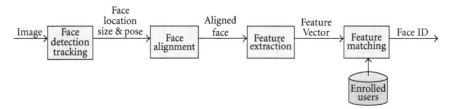

FIGURE 1: Structure of a face recognition system.

with linear function (three-layer) is proposed, and it creates 2D local texture model for the active shape model (ASM) local searching. For *feature extraction module,* a method for combination of geometric feature-based method and ICA method in facial feature extraction is proposed. For *face matching,* a model which combines many artificial neural networks applied for geometric features classification is proposed. This case study demonstrates how to solve face re cognition in the neural network paradigm. Figure 2 illustrates algorithms for the steps of the face recognition system.

The face detection and alignment steps are conducted on MIT + CMU test set [3] in order to evaluate effectively the performance. Then, the system, which is built from The proposed models, is conducted on CalTech database [4]. Experimental results show that our method performs favorably compared to state-of-the-art methods.

The paper is structured as follows: Section 2 will describe in detail the applying of AdaBoost and artificial neural network for detecting faces. Section 3 will present an ASM method with a novel local texture model, which uses multilayer perceptron (MLP) for ASM local searching. Section 4 will describe a methodology for improving the efficiency of feature extraction stage based on the association of two methods: geometric feature-based method and independent component analysis (ICA) method. Section 5 will present multiartificial neural network (MANN) and MANN application for face matching. The experimental results are presented in Section 6. Conclusions are mentioned in Section 7.

2. AdaBoost and ANN for Face Detection

The face detection processing is the first step of the face recognition system. The step will decide the performance of the system, so it is the most important step of the recognition system. To carry out its efficiently, many researchers have proposed different approaches. In general, there are four groups of face detecting methods [5]: (1) *Knowledge-based methods*; (2) *Invariant feature-based methods*; (3) *Template matching-based methods*; (4) *Machine learning-based methods*.

In this paper, we focus on only machine learning methods because they eliminate subjective thinking factors from human experience. Moreover, they only depend on training data to make final decisions. Thus, if training data is well organized and adequate, then these systems will achieve high performance without human factors.

One of the most popular and efficient learning machine-based approaches for detecting faces is AdaBoost approach [6]. Viola and Jones designed a fast, robust face detection system where AdaBoost learning is used to build nonlinear classifiers. AdaBoost is used to solve the following three fundamental problems: (1) learning effective features from a large feature set; (2) constructing weak classifiers, each of which is based on one of the selected features; (3) boosting the weak classifiers to construct a strong classifier. Viola and Jones make use of several techniques for effective computation of a large number of such features under varying scale and location which is important for real-time performance. Moreover, the cascade of strong classifiers which form cascade tree will make the computation even more efficient. Their system is the first real-time frontal-view face detector. However, their system still has some drawbacks. Since the detection results depend on weak classifiers, the detection results often have many false positives. To decrease the rate of false positives, it is compelled to increase the number of strong classifiers and Haar-like features in cascade tree, but this will cause a significant increase in the performance time, and detection rate can be decreased. Thus, to deal with the issue, we should combine AdaBoost with other machine learning techniques to achieve the same face detecting ratios but with the minimum number of false positives and the running time.

One of the popular methods having the same achievement as well is artificial neural networks (ANNs) [7]. ANN is the term on the method to solve problems by simulating neuron's activities. In detail, ANNs can be most adequately characterized as "computational models" with particular properties such as the ability to adapt or learn, to generalize, or to cluster or organize data, and which operation is based on parallel processing. However, many of the previously mentioned properties can be attributed to non-neural models. A hybrid approach combining AdaBoost and ANN is proposed to detect faces with the purpose of decreasing the performance time but still achieving the desired faces detecting rate.

Our hybrid model is named ABANN. This is the model of combining AB and ANN for detecting faces. In this model, ABs have a role to quickly reject nonface images; then ANNs continue filtering false negative images to achieve better results. The final result is face/nonface.

The selected neural network here is three-layer feed-forward neural network with back propagation algorithm. The number of input neurons T is equivalent to the length of extracted feature vector, and the number of output neurons

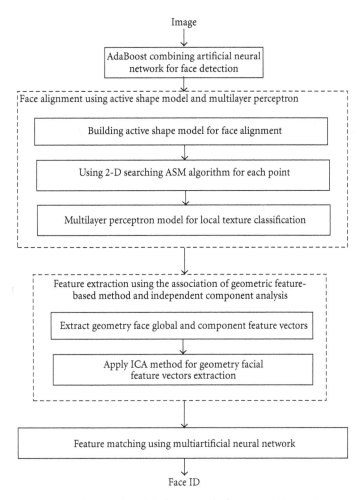

Image

AdaBoost combining artificial neural network for face detection

Face alignment using active shape model and multilayer perceptron

Building active shape model for face alignment

Using 2-D searching ASM algorithm for each point

Multilayer perceptron model for local texture classification

Feature extraction using the association of geometric feature-based method and independent component analysis

Extract geometry face global and component feature vectors

Apply ICA method for geometry facial feature vectors extraction

Feature matching using multiartificial neural network

Face ID

FIGURE 2: Proposed models for steps of a face recognition system.

is just 1 ($C = 1$), This will return *true* if the image contains a human face and *false* if it does not. The number of hidden neurons H will be selected based on the experiment; it depends on the sample database set of images.

The result image (20×20 pixels) of AB is the input of ANN. The output of the ANN is a real value between -1 (false) and $+1$ (true). The preprocessing and ANN steps are illustrated in Figure 3(b). The original image is decomposed into a pyramid of images as follows: 4 blocks 10×10 pixels, 16 blocks 5×5 pixels, and 5 overlapping blocks 20×6 pixels. Thus, the ANN will have 4 + 16 + 5 = 25 input nodes. Its goal is to find out important face features: horizontal blocks to find out mouths and eyes, square blocks to find out each of the eyes, noses, and mouths. The system uses one hidden layer with 25 nodes to represent local features that characterize faces well [7]. Its activation function is Tanh function with the learning rate $\varepsilon = 0.3$ [7].

In detail, a model of cascade of classifiers includes many strong classifiers, and ANN is combined with the strong classifiers to be a final strong classifier of the system to achieve better results in Figure 3(a). For example, AB includes 5 strong classifiers, called AB5, which will be combined with ANN, the sixth strong classifier, to be ABANN5.

The image results of the step will be the inputs of the face alignment step. The next section elaborates our proposed method.

3. Local Texture Classifiers Based on Multilayer Perceptron for Face Alignment

The face alignment is one of the important stages of the face recognition. Moreover, face alignment is also used for other face processing applications, such as face modeling and synthesis. Its objective is to localize the feature points on face images such as the contour points of eye, nose, mouth, and face (illustrated in Figure 4).

There have been many face alignment methods. Two popular face alignment methods are active shape model (ASM) and active appearance model (AAM) proposed by Cootes [8]. The two methods use a statistical model to parameterize a face shape with PCA method. However, their feature model and optimization are different. ASM algorithm has a 2-stage loop: in the first stage, given the initial labels, searching for a new position for every label point in its local region which best fits the corresponding local 1D profile texture model; in the second stage, updating the shape parameters which best fit these new label positions.

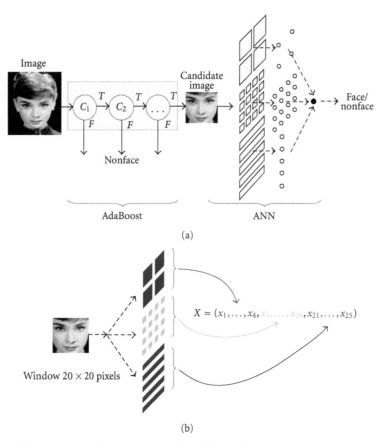

$$X = (x_1,\ldots,x_4, x_5,\ldots,x_{20}, x_{21},\ldots,x_{25})$$

(b)

FIGURE 3: (a) The process of detecting faces of ABANN and (b) input features for neural network.

FIGURE 4: Face alignment.

AAM method uses its global appearance model to directly conduct the optimization of shape parameters. Owing to the different optimization criteria, ASM performs more precisely on shape localization and is quite more robust to illumination and bad initialization. In the paper extent, we develop the classical ASM method to create a new method named MLP-ASM which has achieved better results.

Because ASM only uses a 1D profile texture feature, which is not enough to distinguish feature points from their local regions, the ASM algorithm often fell into local minima problem in the local searching stage. A few representative texture features and pattern recognition methods are proposed to reinforce the ASM local searching, for example, Gabor wavelet [9], Haar wavelet [10], Ranking-Boost [11], and FisherBoost [12]. However, an accurate local texture model to large databases is still unachieved target.

In the next subsection, we present an ASM method with a novel local texture model, which uses multilayer perceptron (MLP) for ASM local searching. MLP is very sufficient for face detecting [13].

3.1. Statistical Shape Models. A face shape can be represented by n points $\{(x_i, y_i)\}$ as a $2n$-element vector, $X = (x_1, y_1, \ldots, x_n, y_n)^T$. Given s training face images, there are s shape vectors $\{X_i\}$. Before we can perform statistical analysis on these vectors, it is important that the shapes represented are in the same coordinate frame. Figure 5 illustrates shape model.

In particular, we seek a parameterized model of the form $X = \text{Model}(b)$ (Figure 6), where b is a vector of parameters of the model. Such a model can be used to generate new vectors, X. If we can model the distribution of parameters, $p_b(b)$, we can limit them so the generated Xs are similar to those in the training set. Similarly, it should be possible to estimate $p_X(X)$ using the model.

To simplify the problem, we first wish to reduce the dimensionality of the data from $2n$ to something more manageable. An effective approach is to apply PCA to the data. The data form a cloud of points in the $2n$-D space. PCA computes the main axes of this cloud, allowing one to approximate any of the original points using a model with fewer than $2n$ parameters. The approach is as follows [1].

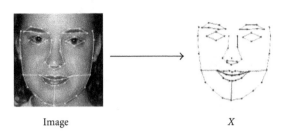

Image X

FIGURE 5: Shape model of an image.

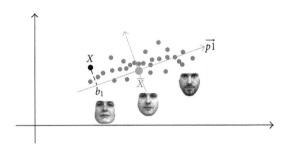

FIGURE 6: Using PCA to compute statistical shape model.

Step 1. Compute the mean of the data set

$$\overline{X} = \frac{1}{s}\sum_{i=1}^{s} X_i. \tag{1}$$

Step 2. Compute the covariance matrix of the data set

$$S = \frac{1}{s-1}\sum_{i=1}^{s}\left(X_i - \overline{X}\right)\left(X_i - \overline{X}\right)^T. \tag{2}$$

Step 3. Compute the eigenvectors, p_j, and corresponding eigenvalues, λ_j, of the data set S (sorted so $\lambda_j \geq \lambda_{j+1}$).

Step 4. We can approximate X from the training set

$$X \approx \overline{X} + P_s b_s, \tag{3}$$

where $P_s = (p_1 | p_2 | \cdots | p_t)$ (t, the number of modes, can be chosen to explain a given proportion of 98% of the variance in the training data set) and $b_s = (b_1, b_2, \ldots, b_t)$, shape model parameters, given by

$$b_s = P_s^T\left(X - \overline{X}\right), \qquad b_i \in \left\{-3\sqrt{\lambda_i} + 3\sqrt{\lambda_i}\right\}. \tag{4}$$

A real shape $\mathbf{X}$ of images can be generated by applying a suitable transformation $\mathbf{T}$ to the points X:

$$\mathbf{X} = \mathbf{T}\left(\overline{X} + P_s b_s, x_c, y_c, s_x, s_y, \theta\right). \tag{5}$$

This transformation includes a translation (x_c, y_c), a scaling (s_x, s_y), and a rotation (θ).

3.2. ASM Algorithm. Given a rough starting approximation, the parameters of an instance of a model can be modified to better fit the model to a new image. By choosing a set of

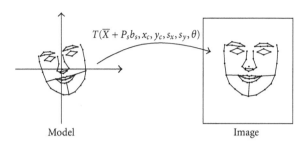

Model   Image

FIGURE 7: Transformation model into image.

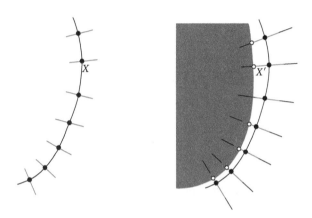

FIGURE 8: 1D profile texture model.

shape parameters, b_s, for the model, we define the shape of the object in an object-centered coordinate frame. We can create an instance X of the model in the image frame by defining the position (x_c, y_c), orientation θ, and scale (s_x, s_y) parameters. An iterative approach to improve the fit of the instance, $\mathbf{T}(\overline{X} + P_s b_s, x_c, y_c, s_x, s_y, \theta)$ (Figure 7), to an image proceeds as follows.

Step 1. Examine a region of the image around each point of X to find the best nearby match for the points X'. There are some ways to find $\underline{X}'$. A popular method, the classical texture model, will be presented in Section 3.3, then our method, the MLP local texture model, will be presented in Section 3.4.

Step 2. Repeat until convergence.
    Update the parameters $(b_s, x_c, y_c, s_x, s_y, \theta)$ to best fit to the new found points X' to minimize the sum of square distances between corresponding model and image points:

$$E\left(b_s, x_c, y_c, s_x, s_y, \theta\right) = \left| X' - T\left(\overline{X} + P_s b_s, x_c, y_c, s_x, s_y, \theta\right) \right|^2. \tag{6}$$

Substep 2.1. Fix b_s and find $(x_c, y_c, s_x, s_y, \theta)$ to minimize E.

Substep 2.2. Fix $(x_c, y_c, s_x, s_y, \theta)$ and find b_s to minimize E.

3.3. Classical Local Texture Model. The objective is to search for local match for each point (illustrated in Figure 8). The model is assumed to have The strongest edge, correlation, and statistical model of profile.

Step 1. Computing normal vector at point (x_i, y_i) and calculating tangent vector t,

$$t_x = x_{i+1} - x_{i-1}, \qquad t_y = y_{i+1} - y_{i-1}. \qquad (7)$$

Normalize tangent vector t,

$$t_x = \frac{t_x}{|t|}, \qquad t_y = \frac{t_y}{|t|}. \qquad (8)$$

Calculate normal vector n,

$$n_x = -t_y, \qquad n_y = t_x. \qquad (9)$$

Step 2. Calculate $g(k)$ by sampling along the 1D profile of point (x_i, y_i),

$$G(k) = \text{image}\left[x_i + kn_x, y_i + kn_y\right],$$
$$k \in [\dots, -2, -1, 0, 1, 2, \dots]. \qquad (10)$$

To noise images, The average orthogonal to the 1D profile.

$$g(k) = \frac{g_{kl}}{4} + \frac{g_{kc}}{2} + \frac{g_{kr}}{4}. \qquad (11)$$

Making the edges of images clear by image derivation, we can select the point at the strongest edge. However, sometimes the true point is not at the strongest edge. We use the local probability model to locate the point. For each point, we estimate the probability density function *(p.d.f)* on the 1D profile from the training data set to search for the correct point. The classical ASM method has some weak points, for example, since PCA did not consider discriminative criterions between positive samples (feature points or true points) and negative samples (nonfeature points, its neighbors), the result of local searching stage often falls into local minima (Figure 9).

To deal with the problem, distinguishing feature points from nonfeature points, which are critical to diminish the effects of local minima problem, we propose the local 2D structure model for each point, which uses MLP trained over a large training set. After training, the model can classify feature points correctly. Multilayer perceptron has been proven to be robust and efficient in face detection [2, 13].

3.4. Multilayer Perceptron Model for Local Texture Classification

3.4.1. Structure of Multilayer Perceptron [2, 13].
A multilayer perceptron (MLP) is a function

$$\hat{y} = \text{MLP}(x, W); \quad x = (x_1, x_2, \dots, x_n); \quad \hat{y}(\hat{y}_1, \hat{y}_2, \dots, \hat{y}_m), \qquad (12)$$

W is the set of parameters $\{w_{ij}^L, w_{i0}^L\}, \forall i, j, L$.
For each unit i of layer L of the MLP,
Integration:

$$s = \sum_j y_j^{L-1} w_{ij}^L + w_{i0}^L. \qquad (13)$$

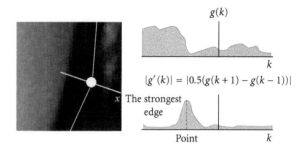

FIGURE 9: Selecting the feature point at the strongest edge.

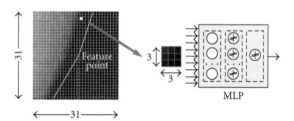

FIGURE 10: Multilayer perceptron for searching for feature points.

Transfer: $y_j^L = f(s)$, where

$$f(x) = \begin{cases} -1 & x \le -\dfrac{1}{a}, \\[2mm] a \cdot x & -\dfrac{1}{a} < x < +\dfrac{1}{a}, \\[2mm] 1 & x \ge +\dfrac{1}{a}. \end{cases} \qquad (14)$$

On the input layer $(L = 0)$: $y_j^L = x_j$.
On the output layer $(L = \mathbf{L})$: $y_j^L = \hat{y}_j$.
The MLP uses the algorithm of gradient backpropagation for training to update W.

3.4.2. Applying the Multilayer Perceptron for Searching for Feature Points.
For each feature point, we define the region of a $[-5,15] \times [-15,15]$ window centered at the feature point. Then, positive samples, feature points, are collected from image points within a $[-1,1] \times [-1,1]$ subwindow at the center, while negative samples, nonfeature points, are sampled randomly out of the sub-window within the region. Then through learning with gradient backpropagation [13], W weights of the MLP are updated, and it outputs a value which is $(+1)$ corresponding to the feature point or (-1) corresponding to the nonfeature point. Figure 10 illustrates MLP for searching for feature points.

The MLP structure for a sub-window has three layers: an input layer, a hidden layer, and an output layer. The input layer has 9 units (input values are the first-order derivation of pixels in the sub-window); the hidden layer has 9 units, and the output layer has one unit (output value $\in \{-1, 1\}$). Such that, the MLP has (9 inputs + 1 bias) $\times$ 9 + 9 + 1 bias = 100 parameters. The MLP uses the transfer function as a linear function with $a = 0.5$ (9) (this is the best fit value from our experiments over MIT + CMU database [3] and our database).

A local searching procedure will find around the current feature point to be the new feature position, see Algorithm 1.

4. The Association of Geometric Feature-Based Method and Independent Component Analysis in Facial Feature Extraction

One of the most important steps in the face recognition problem is the facial feature extraction. A good feature extraction will increase the performance of face recognition system. Various techniques have been proposed in the literature for this purpose and are mainly classified in four groups. (1) *Geometric feature-based method group*: the features are extracted by using relative positions and sizes of the important components face such as eyes, nose, mouth and other important component of face. The advantage of these methods is the concentration on important components of face such as eyes, nose, and mouth but the disadvantage is not to remain face global structure [14]. (2) *Template-based method Group*: based on a template function and appropriate energy function, this method group will extract the feature of important components of face such as eyes and mouth, or face shape. An image region is the best appropriateness with template (eyes, mouth, etc.) which will minimize the energy [15–17]. Advantages of this group method are using template and determining parameter for important components of face, but disadvantage is not to reflect face global structure. (3) *Color segmentation-based method group*: this group method is based on skin's color to isolate the face [18, 19]. (4) *Appearance-based method group*: The goal of this method group is using linear transformation and statistical methods to find the basic vectors to represent the face. Methods have been proposed in the literature for this aim such as PCA [20] and ICA [21, 22]. In detail, goal of PCA method is to reduce the number of dimensions of feature space, but still to keep principle features to minimize loss of information. PCA method uses second-order statistic (covariance matrix) in the data. However, PCA method has still disadvantages. High-order dependencies still exist in PCA analysis, for example, in tasks as face recognition, much of the important information may be contained in the high-order relationships among the image pixels, not only second order. Therefore, we need to find a method more general than PCA; ICA [23] is a satisfying method. Instead of principle component analysis, ICA uses technique-independent component analysis, an analysis technique that not only uses second-order statistic but also uses high-order statistic (kurtosis). PCA can be derived as a special case of ICA which uses Gaussian source models. In this case, the mixing matrix cannot determine. PCA is not the good method in cases of non-Gaussian source models. In particular, it has been empirically observed that many natural signals, including speech and natural images, are better described as linear combinations of sources with "super-Gaussian" distributions (kurtosis positive). In this case, ICA method is better than PCA method because (1) ICA provides a better probabilistic model of the data. (2) It uniquely

identifies the mixing matrix. (3) It finds an unnecessary orthogonal basic which may reconstruct the data better than PCA in the presence of noise such as variations lighting and expressions of face. (4) It is sensitive to high-order statistics in the data, not just to the covariance matrix.

The appearance-based method group has been found the best performer in facial feature extraction problem because it keeps the important information of face image, rejects redundant information, and reflects face global structure.

In many applications of face recognition such as identity authentication for credit card and video surveillance, accuracy of face recognition problem is the best important factor. Therefore, besides principle components, independent components of data and face global structure are kept by PCA and ICA method. Combination of these features with geometric features such as nose, eyes, and mouth in recognition will increase accuracy, confident of face recognition system.

In this section, we present architectures of ICA for face recognition and combining ICA method with geometric feature-based method (GICA) [24], then comparison of GICA method and GPCA method on CalTech database [4]. Since then, practicability of GICA method for face recognition problem is demonstrated.

4.1. Geometric-Face Global Feature Vector. Labeled faces were detected by ABANN20 (Section 2), which will be normalized in a standard size of 30×30 pixels. After standardization, the face images will be represented by vectors $x_{\text{face}} = (x_1, x_2, \ldots, x_{900})^T$.

4.2. Geometric-Face Component Feature Vectors. Section 3 presented a method to align face by MLP-ASM (multilayer perceptron—active shape model). After face alignment, we can detect image regions that contain eyes and mouth, in face images. To define face component feature vectors, we detect two image regions: (a) region 1 contains eyes, which was detected by coordinates of feature points: *left temple* and *right temple* features, *left outer top eye brow* and *left inner top eye brow* features, *right outer top eye brow* and *right inner top eye brow* features, *left eye bottom* and *right eye bottom* features; (b) region 2 contains labeled face without mouth, which was detected by coordinates of feature points: *Left Jaw* and *Right Jaw* features, *Left Outer Top Eye Brow* and *Left Inner Top Eye Brow* features, *Right Outer Top Eye Brow* and *Right Inner Top Eye Brow* features, and *Left Nose Bottom, Nose base,* and *Right Nose Bottom*. For instance in Figure 11.

After locating image regions of face image, region 1 and region 2 will be normalized in a standard size of 30×30 pixels. We have vectors that represent eyes image region: $x_{\text{eyes}} = (x_1, x_2, \ldots, x_{900})^T$, and face without mouth image region: $x_{\text{face\_no\_mouth}} = (x_1, x_2, \ldots, x_{900})^T$. These vectors are called "*Geometric-component feature vector.*"

4.3. ICA Method for Facial Feature Extraction. Independent component analysis (ICA) minimizes both second-order and higher-order dependencies in the input data and attempts to find the basis along which the data (when projected onto them) are statistically independent. Bartlett et al. [22]

Input shape X $\{(x_i, y_i)\}$
Output new shape X' $\{(x_i', y_i')\}$
   For each point (x_i, y_i) of shape X
      For each sub-window sw' centered at point (x', y')
      of the window centered at the feature point (x_i, y_i).
        (i) Computing MLP (sw', W). If the return value is $(+1)$ then point (x', y') is at the edge.
        (ii) Selecting the nearest point (x', y') to the point
           (x_i, y_i) as the new feature point (x_i', y_i').

ALGORITHM 1

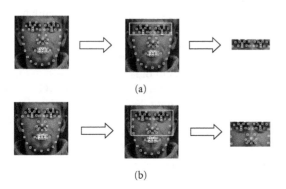

(a)

(b)

FIGURE 11: Extraction of face important components: (a) region 1 contains eyes, (b) region 2 contains labeled face without mouth.

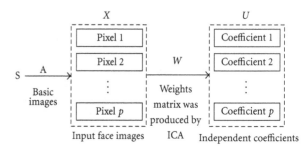

FIGURE 12: Finding coefficients whose presentation images are independent.

provided two architectures of ICA for face recognition task: architecture I statistically independent basis images, and Architecture II factorial code representation.

In a face recognition problem, our goal is to find coefficients of feature vectors to achieve the most independent in desire. Therefore, in this section, we selected architecture II of ICA method for the face representation. A number of algorithms for performing ICA have been proposed (see [25] for reviews). In this section, we apply FastICA algorithm developed by Hyvärinen and Oja [25] for our experiments.

Architecture II: Statistically Independent Coefficients. The goal in this approach is to find a set of statistically independent coefficients.

We organize the data matrix X so that the images are in columns and the pixels are in rows. Pixels i and j are independent if when moving across the entire set of images, it is not possible to predict the value taken by pixel i based on the corresponding value taken by pixel j on the same image. The goal in architecture I that uses ICA is to find a set of statistically independent basic images. Although basic images found in architecture I are approximately independent, when projecting down statistically independent basic images subspace, feature vectors of each image are not necessarily independent. Architecture II uses ICA to find a representation whose coefficients are used to represent an image in the basic images subspace being statistically independent. Each row of weight matrix W is an image A, an inverse matrix of W, which contains basic images in its columns. Statistically independent coefficients in S will be recovered in columns of U (Figure 12); each column of U

contains coefficients for combination of basic images in A to construct images of X.

Architecture II is implemented through the following steps.

Assume that we have n images; each image has p pixels. Therefore, data matrix X has an order of $p \times n$.

(1) Let R be a $p \times m$ matrix containing the first m eigenvectors of a set of n face images in its columns.

(2) Calculating a set of principle components of a set of images in X,

$$C = R^T \times X. \tag{15}$$

(3) The coefficients for linearly combining the basic images in A are determined:

$$U = W \times C. \tag{16}$$

Assume that we have a set of images for testing X_{test}, feature extraction of X_{test} is computed through the following steps: firstly, from X_{test}, we calculate a set of principle components of X_{test} by

$$C_{\text{test}} = R^T \times X_{\text{test}}. \tag{17}$$

Then, a set of feature vectors of X_{test} in the basic images space is calculated by

$$U_{\text{test}} = W \times C_{\text{test}}. \tag{18}$$

Each column of U_{test} is a feature vector corresponding with each image of X_{test}.

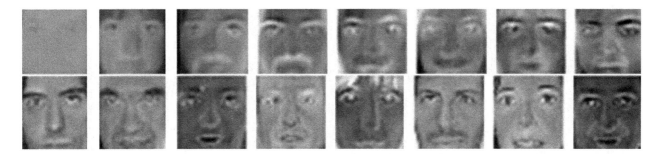

FIGURE 13: First row contains eight eigenfaces corresponding to the highest eight eigenvalues for PCA. Second row first of eight basic images for architecture II ICA.

Firstly, to face representation with ICA method, we apply PCA to project the data into an m-dimensional subspace in order to control the number of independent components made by ICA, and then ICA is applied to the eigenvectors to minimize the statistical dependence of feature vectors in the basic images space. Thus, PCA uncorrelated input data and high-order dependence will remain separated by ICA.

The first row in Figure 13 contains the eight eigenvectors (eight eigenfaces) corresponding to the eight highest eigenvalues of PCA method, and the second row includes the first of eight basic images in architecture II of ICA on CalTech database [4].

4.4. The Association of Geometric Feature-Based Method and ICA in Facial Feature Extraction.

After the processed steps of Sections 4.1 and 4.2, we get one vector which represents *geometric-face global feature vector*: $x_{\text{face}} = (x_1, x_2, \ldots, x_{900})^T$ and two vectors which repesent *Geometric-component feature vector*: $x_{\text{eyes}} = (x_1, x_2, \ldots, x_{900})^T$, $x_{\text{face\_no\_mouth}} = (x_1, x_2, \ldots, x_{900})^T$. ICA method was applied to these vectors. Therefore, we get vectors which represent component facial features and global face in ICA subspace.

In detail, vector x_{face} will be mapped into an ICA face feature subspace. Vector representing faces in the face feature subspace is $y_{\text{face}} = (y_1, y_2, \ldots, y_k)^T$, where k is dimensions in the face feature subspace; y_{face} is called "*ICA global feature vector*." Face component feature vectors $x_{\text{eyes}} = (x_1, x_2, \ldots, x_{900})^T$ and $x_{\text{face\_no\_mouth}} = (x_1, x_2, \ldots, x_{900})^T$ will be mapped into ICA component feature subspace; we have $y_{\text{eyes}} = (y_1, y_2, \ldots, y_k)^T$, $y_{\text{face\_no\_mouth}} = (y_1, y_2, \ldots, y_k)^T$. These vectors are called "*ICA component feature vector*."

The combination of these vectors will creates vector which reflects texture and geometric feature of face image. The process of feature extraction in our study was illustrated in Figure 14. y_{comb} is a feature vector of combining the geometric feature-based method and the ICA method. It will be used for face recognition step.

5. Multi-artificial Neural Network for Facial Feature Matching

5.1. Multiartificial Neural Network Applys for Pattern Classification.

Artificial neural network was successfully applied for face detection and face recognition [26]. Most of the other

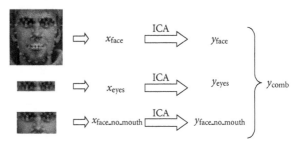

FIGURE 14: Facial feature extraction by geometric feature-based method combination with ICA method.

approaches are to apply ANN for detected face [27, 28]. We proposed the multiartificial neural network (MANN) [29] to apply for pattern and image classification. Firstly, patterns or images are projected to difference spaces. Secondly, in each of these spaces, patterns are classified into responsive class using a neural network called subneural network (SNN) of MANN. Lastly, we use MANN's global frame (GF) consisting some component neural network (CNN) to compose the classified result of all SNN.

5.1.1. The Proposal of MANN Model.

Multiartificial neural network (MANN), applying for pattern or image classification with parameters (m, n, L), has m subneural network (SNN) and a global frame (GF) consisting L component neural network (CNN). In particular, m is the number of feature vectors of image, n is the number of feature vector dimensions, and L is the number of classes.

Definition 1. SNN is a 3-layered (input, hidden, and output) neural network. SNN has n (the dimensions of feature vector) input nodes and L (the number classes) output nodes. The number of hidden nodes is experimentally determined. There are m (the number of feature vectors) SNNs in MANN model. The input of the ith SNN, symbol is SNN_i, is the feature vector of image. The output of SNN_i is the classified result based on the ith feature vector of image.

Definition 2. Global frame is the frame consisting L component neural networks which compose the output of SNN(s).

Definition 3. Collective vector kth, symbol R_k ($k = 1 \cdots L$), is vector joining the output kth of all SNNs. Collective vector

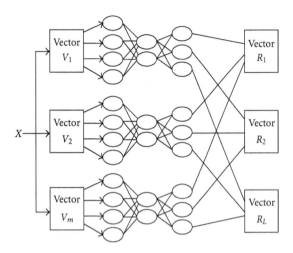

FIGURE 15: Create collective vector for CNN(s).

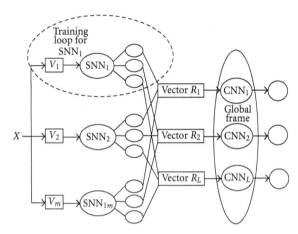

FIGURE 17: Local training for SNN$_1$.

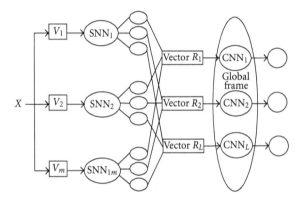

FIGURE 16: MANN with parameters (m, n, L).

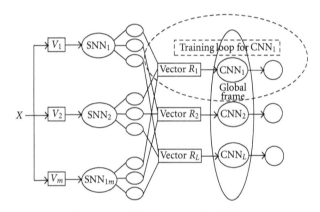

FIGURE 18: Global training for CNN$_1$.

is m-dimensional vector because there are m SNNs (see Figure 15).

Definition 4. CNN is a 3-layered (input, hidden, and output) neural network. CNN has m (the number of dimensions of collective vector) input nodes and 1 (the number classes) output nodes. The number of hidden nodes is experimentally determined. There are L CNNs. The output of the jth CNN, symbols is CNN$_j$, gives the probability of X in the jth class (see Figure 16).

5.1.2. The Process of MANN Model. The training process in MANN is separated into two phases. Phase (1) is to train SNN(s) one-by-one called local training. Phase (2) is to train CNN(s) in GF one by one called global training.

In local training phase, we will train the SNN$_1$ first. After that, we will train SNN$_2, \ldots,$ SNN$_m$ (see Figure 17).

In the global training phase, we will train the CNN$_1$ first. After that we will train CNN$_2, \ldots,$ CNN$_L$ (see Figure 18).

The classification process of pattern X using MANN is as follows: firstly, pattern X is extracted to m feature vectors. The ith feature vector is the input of SNN$_i$ classifying pattern. All the kth output of all SNNs is joined to create the kth ($k = 1 \cdots L$) collective vector, symbol R_k. R_k is the input of CNN$_k$. The output of CNN$_k$ is the kth output of MANN. It gives us

the probability of X in the kth class. If the kth output is max in all output of MANN and bigger than the threshold, we conclude pattern X in the kth class.

5.2. Face Recognition Using Multiartificial Neural Network

5.2.1. Facial Feature Extraction. After the processed steps of Section 4.4, we get *ICA global feature vector:* $y_{\text{face}} = (y_1, y_2, \ldots, y_k)^T$ and *ICA component feature vector:* $y_{\text{eyes}} = (y_1, y_2, \ldots, y_k)^T$, $y_{\text{face\_no\_mouth}} = (y_1, y_2, \ldots, y_k)^T$, where k is dimensions in the face feature subspace. Figure 19 illustrates the steps of facial feature extraction. Instead of combining these vectors to create y_{comb} (Section 4.4), we used y_{face}, y_{eyes}, and $y_{\text{face\_no\_month}}$ which are inputs of multiartificial neural network (MANN), and outputs of MANN are face identified of candidate face image.

5.2.2. Multiartificial Neural Network for Facial Feature Matching. We have conducted experiments on a CalTech database consisting of 441 labeled faces of 26 people which were detected by ABANN20 (Section 2) and face alignment by MLP_ASM (Section 3). We divide up the database into two parts. Training set contains 120 images and testing set contains 321 images. We repeated our experiments for 10

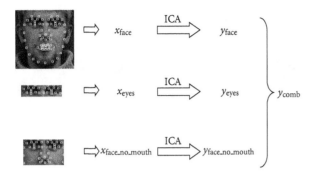

FIGURE 19: The steps of facial feature extraction.

Name	Input nodes	Hidden nodes	Output nodes	Learning rate
ANN_FACE	25	25	1	0.3

random divisions of the database, so that every image of the subject can be used for testing. The results were reported on the average performance.

A labeled face is a pattern that is featured by 3 vectors (y_{face}, y_{eyes}, and $y_{\text{face\_no\_mouth}}$) which have 100 dimensions ($k = 100$ for ICA) (Section 5.2.1). Face images need to be classified in one of the 26 people (CalTech database). So we apply MANN with parameters ($m = 3$, $n = 100$, $L = 26$) (see Figure 17) for facial feature matching.

Thus, MANN model in this case has three SNNs and one GF consisting of 26 CNNs. The ith ($i = 1 \cdots 3$) feature vector of an image will be processed by SNN_i in order to create the ($L = 26$) dimensional output vector of responsive SNN. To join all the kth ($k = 1 \cdots 26$), The element of these output vectors gets the collective vector R_k. These collective vectors are the input of CNNs. The only one output node of CNN is an output node of MANN.

Our implementation uses backpropagation neural network which has 3 layers with the transfer function that is sigmoid function [2, 30] for SNN and CNN. The number of hidden nodes of SNN_i ($i = 1 \cdots 3$) and CNN_j ($j = 1 \cdots 26$) is experimentally determined from 10 to 100 hidden nodes.

Every SNN_i has $n = 100$ (the dimensions of feature vector) input nodes and $L = 26$ (the number of classes) output nodes. The kth ($k = 1 \cdots 26$) output of the SNN_i is the probability measure which reflects whether the input image is in the kth class.

Every CNN_j has $m = 3$ (the number of feature vectors) input nodes and only one output node. Input of CNN_j is the jth output of all SNNs. It means that CNN_j composes the probability of image in the jth class appraised by all SNNs. Output of CNN_j is the jth output of MANN model. It gives the probability of image in the jth class. It is easy to see that to build MANN model, only neural network technology is used to develop our system.

6. Experimental Results and Discussion

6.1. Face Detection

6.1.1. Database for Experiments. To train the detector, a set of face and nonface training images were used. To create the face training set, we select 11000 face images from 14051 face images of FERET database [31]. With each image which is selected, we cropped the regions which contained face and

scaled to a base resolution of 20 by 20 pixels. Some typical face examples are shown in Figure 20.

The nonface subwindows used to train the detector come from 5817 images which were manually inspected and found not to contain any faces. There are about 950 million subwindows within these nonface images. Each classifier in the cascade was trained with the 11000 training faces and 5000 nonface subwindows (also of size 20 by 20 pixels). To train AdaBoost detector, we used open-source Haar training (in OpenCv library) which is created by Lienhart and Maydt [32].

We used Rowley's ANN model [7] for detecting faces presented in Table 1.

Thus, a system is implemented by the three-layer feedforward ANN with the Tanh activation function (19) and the backpropagation learning algorithm [2]. The system ran on a PC, 2.0 GHz Pentium IV processor, RAM 1 GB. We also used 11000 training faces and 5000 nonface subwindows (also of size 20 by 20 pixels) to train the ANN. It took about 8 hours to train the ANN.

$$\text{Tanh function:} f(x) = \frac{1 - e^{-x}}{1 + e^{-x}}, \quad f(x) \in [-1, 1]. \quad (19)$$

6.1.2. Experimental Results of AdaBoost-Based System. We used the model of cascade of boosted classifiers in which the number of stage classifiers is 20 and 25 stages. We tested the system on the MIT + CMU [3] test set. This database consists of 130 images with 507 labeled faces. Table 2 presents performance of AdaBoost detector.

With a 2.0 GHz Pentium IV processor, RAM 1 GB, the face detector can process a 276-by-343 pixels image in about 0.172 seconds. The scale and step size of slide window are 1.2 and 2, respectively.

6.1.3. Experimental Results of ANN-Based System. We used trained ANN model for detecting faces (Table 1). We also tested the system on the MIT + CMU [3] test set. Table 3 presents the performance of ANN.

6.1.4. Evaluations on AdaBoost and ANN. The experiments prove that AdaBoost and ANN approaches for detecting faces do not achieve good results of performance time and detecting rate yet.

AdaBoost method is one of today's fastest algorithms. However, false face detecting rate is rather high. The cascade of boosted classifier depends on weak classifiers. False images are often false negative. To solve the drawback, there are two solutions. First, we can increase the large number of stage classifiers in order to achieve the desired results. However, increasing the number of both classifiers

FIGURE 20: Example of face images used for training AdaBoost detector.

TABLE 2: Performance of detecton on MIT + CMU test set of AdaBoost detector.

Method	Number of stages	Number of Haar-like features used	Face detected	Missed faces (false rejection)	False detections	Detection rates	Average time to process an image (second)
AB20	20	1925	467	40	202	92.11%	0.179
AB25	25	2913	452	55	40	89.15%	0.202

and features too much will decrease the algorithm speed. Second, we can combine AdaBoost with other classification techniques to reject false negative images in order to increase the correctness of the system.

ANN, a strong classification technique, has been used efficiently in the problem of detecting faces. In addition, the performance time is not high. Since then, we suggest a hybrid model of AdaBoost and ANN. On the other hand, we append ANN at the final stage to create a complete hybrid system.

6.1.5. Experimental Results of Hybrid Model of AdaBoost and ANN. AdaBoost and ANN detector are trained The same as in Section 2. These experiments were done on MIT + CMU test set [3]. Table 4 presents The performance of AB ANN detector.

All ABANN20 and ABANN25 get detection rate approximate with AB20 and AB25, respectively, but with less than the number of false detection. ABANN20 gets the detection rate 91.91%; it is approximate with 92.11% of AB20 and higher detection rate of AB25. The number of false positives only is 13. It is very small in comparison with 202 of AB20 and smaller than 40 of AB25. Furthermore, the processing time to process 130 images is 24.576 seconds. It is approximate with the time of AdaBoost detector. In case of ABANN25, it gets a detection rate of 88.76%. This is equal to AB25, but the number of false positives is only 3; this is very small in comparison with 40 of AB25. The processing time of our detector for a 276×343 image is about 0.174 seconds on a P4 1.8 GHz PC.

Figure 21 presents some experimental results on MIT + CMU test set. From the achieved results and theoretical analyses presented in Section 2, we have recognized that the proposed model of associating AdaBoost with ANN is necessary and can be applied in practicality.

We have researched the two popular methods of detecting faces, AdaBoost and ANN, analyzing, and evaluating ones' advantages and disadvantages. From the study, we has recognized that AdaBoost (cascade of boosted AdaBoost) has the fastest performance time; however, the correctness rate is not

high (because detection results depend on weak classifiers or Haar-like features); it is proved by the experiments on database CalTech. ANN will reach good verifying results if it has a suitable structure; nevertheless, the detection speed is quite slow due to the complexness of ANN. Hence, in the experiments, we used simple ANN or three-layer feedforward neural network proposed by Rowley. To improve the performance and eliminate its limitations, we have proposed the hybrid model of AdaBoost and ANN (ABANN) for detecting faces. The proposed system has achieved better results of both correctness rate and performance comparing with individual models (AdaBoost or ANN) on database MIT + CMU, and the testing time is insignificant. Since then, we have reached a conclusion that our hybrid model is very efficient and has a practical meaning in the problem of detecting faces.

6.2. Face Alignments. We tested system on the MIT + CMU [3] test set. This database consists of 130 images with 507 labeled faces. We used ABANN20 (Section 2) for face detection and got 466 labeled faces (Table 4). We have conducted experiments on an MIT + CMU database consisting of 450 labeled faces which were chosen from 466 labeled faces that had been detected by ABANN20 (Section 2). They include male and female aging from young to old people, many of which are with exaggerated expressions such as smiles and closed eyes. We randomly chose 300 images for training, and the rest 150 images for testing. The face shape model is made up of 89 feature points that extract with specific groups as follows: face boundary (22 points), right eyebrow (8 points), left eyebrow (8 points), left eye (8 points), right eye (8 points), nose (13 points), and oral (22 points).

For each feature point, an MLP is trained. For comparison, classical ASM was also implemented and trained on the same training set.

6.2.1. Accuracy. The accuracy is measured with point to point error. The feature points were initialized from the face window which was detected by ABANN20 (Section 2).

TABLE 3: Performance of detecton on MIT + CMU test set of ANN detector.

Method	Face detected	Missed faces (false rejection)	False detections	Detection rates	Average time to process an image (second)
ANN [7]	476	31	17	93.89%	71.56

TABLE 4: Performance of detection on MIT + CMU test set of ABANN detector.

Name	AdaBoost structure		ANN structure	Face detected	Missed faces (false rejection)	False detections	Detection rate	Average time to process an image (second)
	Number of strong classifiers	Number of Haar-like features						
AB-ANN	20	1925	Rowley's model	466	41	13	91.91%	0.174
AB-ANN	25	2913		450	57	3	88.76%	0.195

TABLE 5: The average performance time per iteration (a two-stage process).

Algorithm	Classical ASM	MLP ASM
Time per iteration	2 ms	15 ms

TABLE 6: Percentage accuracy values on the CalTech database (%).

Method	GPCA	GICA
Recognition rate	94.70	96.57

After the alignment procedure, the errors were measured. The average errors of the 89 feature points are compared in Figure 22. The x-axis, which represents the index of feature points, is grouped by organ. It shows that our method outperforms classical ASM; especially, the improvement of our methods is mainly on feature points of mouth and contour.

6.2.2. Efficiency.

The average performance time is listed in Table 5. All the tests are carried out on a 2.0 GHz Pentium IV processor, RAM 1 GB. The classical ASM is the fastest since its computation of local texture model is very simple. Our method is a little slower but is still comparable with the classical ASM (Figure 23).

In conclusion, we proposed a robust face alignment algorithm with a local texture model (MLP ASM). Instead of modeling a local feature by 1D profile texture, our classifier is learned from its 2D profile texture patterns against its neighbor ones as a local texture model. The classifier is of a great benefit to the local searching of feature points because of its strong discriminative power. The generality and robustness of the MLP method guarantee the performance. Therefore, compared to existing ones achieving their models in relative small training sets, our method shows potential in practical applications.

6.3. Facial Feature Extraction

6.3.1. Database for Experiments.

In this section, we describe our experiments on CalTech face database.

CalTech Database. The database includes Markus Weber's 450 color images at California Institute of Technology. After using AdaBoost + ANN (ABANN20—Section 2) to detect face regions, we get 441 face images of 26 people. 441 labeled faces were aligned by MLP ASM (Section 3). After face alignment, we used 441 of these images to perform GPCA and GICA. In CalTech database, almost all images are frontal faces, and there is not a same illumination. Some images are too dark or too bright. Some images are hidden important components such as eyes. Some images have different face expressions. We divided up database into two parts. Training set contains of 120 images, and testing set contains 321 images. We repeated our experiments for ten random divisions of the database, so that every image of the subject can be used for testing. The results were reported on the average performance. CalTech database is publicly available for research aims at the URL: http://www.vision.caltech.edu/html-files/archive.html. Figure 24 shows sample images from CalTech database.

The recognizer was implemented by the neural network method. Fast artificial neural network is used in our experiment. Fast artificial neural network library (FANN), which is a free open-source neural network library, implements multilayer artificial neural networks in C language and supports for both fully connected and sparsely connected networks. FANN has been used in many studies. FANN implementation includes training step: assume that we have n classes (n different people), training with FANN will create n sets of weights. Each set of weights corresponds to each class (each person).

Testing step: the input is a person's face image (one of the n people mentioned above); this face image was tested with n sets of weights which had been created in the training step. This person belongs to a class which

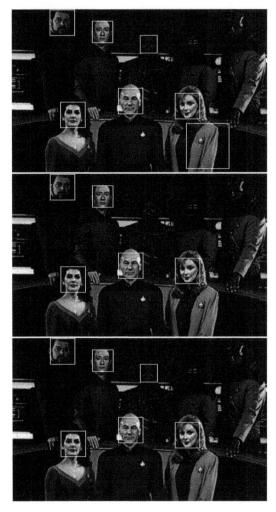

FIGURE 21: Output of our face detector on a number of test images from the MIT + CMU test set.

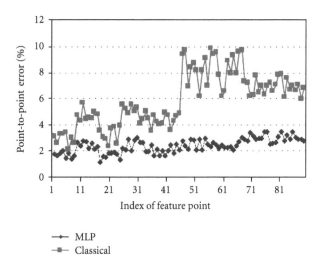

FIGURE 22: Comparison of classical ASM and MLP ASM.

TABLE 7: Percentage accuracy values on the CalTech database (%).

Method	SNN1 (y_{face})	SNN2 (y_{eyes})	SNN3 ($y_{face\_no\_mouth}$)	GICA	Average	MANN
Precision	93.25	91.11	94.75	96.57	96.84	98.91

corresponding to the set of weights makes the biggest output. FANN is publicly available for research aims at the URL: http://leenissen.dk/fann/.

6.3.2. Results on the CalTech Database. Table 6 reports the results on CalTech database of two different algorithms applied to the face recognition. The recognition rate for GICA method shows a better recognition rate.

The average number of principal components for PCA representation of *global feature vector* and *component feature vector* was 100 ($k = 100$). The average number of independent components for ICA representation of *global feature vector* and *component feature vector* was 100 ($k = 100$).

The cumulative match score versus rank curve is used to show the performance of each method (Figure 25). Here, cumulative match score and rank are the percentage accuracy that can be achieved by considering the first k biggest output (corresponds with k classes in database) of FANN. The rank is a reliability measure and is very important for video-surveillance applications in uncontrolled environments. Even in this case, the GICA method gives a sharp

improvement of the performance in comparison with GPCA method.

A technique for automatic facial feature extraction based on the geometric features of human face and ICA method is presented. With applying neural network method in the recognition step, this paper makes comparisons and evaluations about GPCA and GICA methods on CalTech database (containing 450 images). Through experiment, we notice that GICA method will have good results in cases of face input with the suitable brightness and position mentioned in Section 6.3.1. In future, we continue experiment with other face database so that it demonstrates The practicability of GICA method in face recognition system.

6.4. Recognition Results of System. We evaluated our proposed system with an MANN model with parameters ($m = 3$, $n = 100$, $L = 26$) by all steps in Section 5.2. We compare our propose MANN model with selected method (choose only one subneural network result), average combination method, and GICA (Section 4). The average experimental classified result uses SNN, average combination method, and MANN in the same image set in Table 7.

In this research, the classification result in the CalTech database shows that the proposed model MANN improves the classification result versus the selection and average combination method and GICA (y_{comb} in Section 4).

7. Conclusions

This paper presented novel models for all steps of the recognition of human faces in 2-dimensional digital images. For *face detection module*, a model to combine three-layer

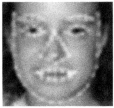 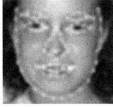 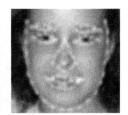

Initialization   Classical ASM   MLP ASM

FIGURE 23: Instances from experimental results.

FIGURE 24: Samples of face images from CalTech database.

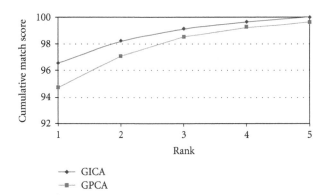

FIGURE 25: Rank curves on the CalTech database. Reported results show that the GICA method produces a more reliable system.

feedforward artificial neural network and AdaBoost was presented for detecting human faces. The experiments were done on a difficult face detection database which has been widely studied (MIT + CMU database). The results show that ABANN not only gets approximate detection rate and processing time AdaBoost detector but also minimizes false detections. ABANN had solved the drawbacks of AdaBoost and ANN detector. For *face alignment module*, an MLP-ASM model was presented; multilayer perceptron (MLP) was used as a 2D local texture model for the active shape model (ASM) local searching. Comparison of classical ASM and MLP ASM was done on MIT + CMU database which shows the feasibility of MLP ASM model. For *feature extraction module*, a method (GICA) for combination of geometric feature based method and ICA method in facial feature extraction was presented. GICA was comparable with the GPCA on the same database (CalTech database) which indicates the usefulness of GICA. For *face matching*, a model, which combines many artificial neural networks for pattern recognition (multiartificial neural network (MANN))

[29], was applied for ICA-geometric features classification. Comparison with some of the existing traditional techniques in the face recognition rate on the same database (CalTech database) shows the feasibility of MANN model.

References

[1] S. Z. Li and A. K. Jain, *Handbook of Face Recognition*, Springer, New York, NY, USA, 2004.

[2] C. Bishop, *Pattern Recognition and Machine Learning*, Springer, New York, NY, USA, 2006.

[3] CBCL Database #1, Center for Biological and Computational Learning at MIT and MIT, http://cbcl.mit.edu/software-datasets/FaceData2.html.

[4] Markus Weber, Frontal Face Database, California Institute of Technology, 1999, http://www.vision.caltech.edu/html-files/archive.html/.

[5] M. H. Yang, D. J. Kriegman, and N. Ahuja, "Detecting faces in images: a survey," *IEEE Transactions on Pattern Analysis and Machine Intelligence*, vol. 24, no. 1, pp. 34–58, 2002.

[6] P. Viola and M. Jones, "Rapid object detection using a boosted cascade of simple features," in *Proceedings of the IEEE Computer Society Conference on Computer Vision and Pattern Recognition*, pp. 511–518, December 2001.

[7] H. A. Rowley, *Neural Network Based Face Detection*, Neural network Based Face Detection, School of Computer Science, Computer Science Department, Carnegie Mellon University, Pittsburgh, Pa, USA, 1999.

[8] T. F. Cootes, "Statistical models of appearance for computer vision," http://www.isbe.man.ac.uk/~bim/refs.html/.

[9] F. Jiao, S. Li, H.-Y. Shum, and D. Schuurmans, "Face alignment using statistical models and wavelet features," in *Proceedings of the IEEE Computer Society Conference on Computer Vision and Pattern Recognition*, June 2003.

[10] F. Zuo and P. H. N. D. With, "Fast facial feature extraction using a deformable shape model with haar-wavelet based local texture attributes," in *Proceedings of the International Conference on Image Processing (ICIP '04)*, pp. 1425–1428, October 2004.

[11] S. Yan, M. Li, H. Zhang, and Q. Cheng, "Ranking prior likelihood distributions for Bayesian shape localization framework," in *Proceedings of the 8th IEEE International Conference on Computer Vision*, pp. 51–58, October 2003.

[12] J. Tu, Z. Zhang, Z. Zeng, and T. Huang, "Face localization via hierarchical CONDENSATION with Fisher Boosting feature selection," in *Proceedings of the IEEE Computer Society Conference on Computer Vision and Pattern Recognition (CVPR '04)*, pp. I719–I724, July 2004.

[13] S. Marcel, "Artificial neural network for pattern recognition: application to face detection and recognition," 2004, http://www.idiap.ch/~marcel/.

[14] T. Kawaguchi, D. Hidaka, and M. Rizon, "Detection of eyes from human faces by Hough transform and separability filter," in *Proceedings of the International Conference on Image Processing*, vol. 1, no. 2000, pp. 49–52, Vancouver, Canada, 2000.

[15] A. L. Yuille, D. S. Cohen, and P. W. Hallinan, "Feature extraction from faces using deformable template. Computer vision and pattern recognition," in *Proceedings of the IEEE Computer Society Conference*, pp. 104–109, San Diego, CA, USA, June 1989.

[16] L. Zhang, "Estimation of the mouth features using deformable templates," in *Proceedings of the International Conference on Image Processing*, vol. 3, pp. 328–331, Santa Barbara, CA, USA, October 1997.

[17] P. Kuo and J. Hannah, "An improved eye feature extraction algorithm based on deformable templates," in *Proceedings of the IEEE International Conference on Image Processing (ICIP '05)*, pp. 1206–1209, September 2005.

[18] S. L. Phung, A. Bouzerdoum, and D. Chai, "Skin segmentation using color and edge information. Signal processing and its applications," in *Proceedings of the 7th International Symposium*, vol. 1, pp. 525–528, July 2003.

[19] T. Sawangsri, V. Patanavijit, and S. Jitapunkul, "Segmentation using novel skin-color map and morphological technique," in *Proceedings of the World Academy of Science, Engineering and Technology*, vol. 2, January 2005.

[20] M. Turk and A. Pentland, "Face recognition using eigenfaces," in *Proceedings of the IEEE Conference on Computer Vision and Pattern Recognition*, pp. 586–591, 1991.

[21] B. A. Draper, K. Baek, M. S. Bartlett, and J. R. Beveridge, "Recognizing faces with PCA and ICA," *Computer Vision and Image Understanding*, vol. 91, no. 1-2, pp. 115–137, 2003.

[22] M. S. Bartlett, J. R. Movellan, and T. J. Sejnowski, "Face recognition by independent component analysis," *IEEE Transactions on Neural Networks*, vol. 13, no. 6, pp. 1450–1464, 2002.

[23] P. Comon, "Independent component analysis—a new concept?" *Signal Processing*, vol. 36, no. 3, pp. 287–314, 1994.

[24] T. T. Do and T. H. Le, "Facial feature extraction using geometric feature and independent component analysis," in *Proceedings of the Pacific Rim Knowledge Acquisition Workshop (PKAW '08)*, Hanoi, Vietnam, December 2008, (Revised Selected Papers) in Knowledge Acquisition: Approaches, Algorithms and Applications, Lecture Notes in Artificial Intelligence, Springer, Berlin, Germany, pp.231–241, 2009.

[25] A. Hyvärinen and E. Oja, "Independent component analysis: algorithms and applications," *Neural Networks*, vol. 13, no. 4-5, pp. 411–430, 2000.

[26] O. A. Uwechue and A. S. Pandya, *Human Face Recognition using Third-Order Synthetic Neural Networks*, The Springer International Series in Engineering and Computer Science, Springer, 1st edition, 1997.

[27] H. A. Rowley, S. Baluja, and T. Kanade, "Neural network-based face detection," *IEEE Transactions on Pattern Analysis and Machine Intelligence*, vol. 20, no. 1, pp. 23–38, 1998.

[28] S. Lawrence, C. L. Giles, A. C. Tsoi, and A. D. Back, "Face recognition: a convolutional neural network approach," *IEEE Transactions on Neural Networks, Special Issue on Neural Networks and Pattern Recognition*, vol. 8, no. 1, pp. 98–113, 1997.

[29] T. H. Le, N. T. D. Nguyen, and H. S. Tran, "Landscape image of regional tourism classification using neural network," in *Proceedings of the 3rd International Conference on Communications and Electronics (ICCE '10)*, Nha Trang, Vietnam, August 2010.

[30] L. H. Thai, *Building, development and application, some combination model of neural network (NN), fuzzy logic(FL) and genetics algorithm (GA)*, Ph.D. thesis, Natural Science University, HCM City, Vietnam, 2004.

[31] P. J. Phillips, H. Moon, P. J. Rauss, and S. A. Rizvi, "The FERET evaluation methodology for face-recognition algorithms," *IEEE Transactions on Pattern Analysis and Machine Intelligence*, vol. 22, no. 10, pp. 1090–1104, 2000.

[32] R. Lienhart and J. Maydt, "An extended set of Haar-like features for rapid object detection," in *Proceedings of the International Conference on Image Processing*, September 2002.

8

Hybrid Wavelet-Postfix-GP Model for Rainfall Prediction of Anand Region of India

Vipul K. Dabhi[1] and Sanjay Chaudhary[2]

[1] *Information Technology Department, Dharmsinh Desai University, Nadiad 387001, India*
[2] *IICT, Ahmedabad University, Ahmedabad 380009, India*

Correspondence should be addressed to Vipul K. Dabhi; vipul.k.dabhi@gmail.com

Academic Editor: Djamel Bouchaffra

An accurate prediction of rainfall is crucial for national economy and management of water resources. The variability of rainfall in both time and space makes the rainfall prediction a challenging task. The present work investigates the applicability of a hybrid wavelet-postfix-GP model for daily rainfall prediction of Anand region using meteorological variables. The wavelet analysis is used as a data preprocessing technique to remove the stochastic (noise) component from the original time series of each meteorological variable. The Postfix-GP, a GP variant, and ANN are then employed to develop models for rainfall using newly generated subseries of meteorological variables. The developed models are then used for rainfall prediction. The out-of-sample prediction performance of Postfix-GP and ANN models is compared using statistical measures. The results are comparable and suggest that Postfix-GP could be explored as an alternative tool for rainfall prediction.

1. Introduction

An accurate prediction of rainfall is crucial for agriculture based Indian economy. Moreover, it also helps in the prevention of flood, the management of water resources, and generating recommendations related to crop for farmers [1]. The variability of rainfall in both time and space makes the rainfall prediction a challenging task. Moreover, the meteorological parameters needed for the rainfall prediction are complex and nonlinear in nature. Practitioners have applied numerical [2, 3] and statistical [4, 5] models for the rainfall prediction. The Numerical Weather Prediction (NWP) models are deterministic models and approximate complex physical processes for weather prediction. However, the models are not useful for prediction at smaller scale due to inherent limitations of these models to initial conditions and model parameterization. Practitioners have also used autoregressive moving average (ARMA) and autoregressive integrated moving average (ARIMA) techniques for developing a model for the rainfall [6]. However, these approaches were developed based on the assumption of stationarity of the given time series and the independence of the residuals. Moreover, these approaches lack the ability to identify nonlinear patterns and irregularity in the time series.

Hence, in recent years, use of different machine learning techniques for modeling and prediction of rainfall has received much attention of practitioners [7]. Hung et al. [8] developed a neural network for 1 to 3 hours ahead forecast of rainfall for Bangkok. They used meteorological parameters (air pressure, relative humidity, wet bulb temperature, and cloudiness) and the rainfall registered at the neighbor stations as input in the neural network. They used the hydrometeorological data that covers both rainy and nonrainy periods for training the neural network. Moustris et al. [9] used a neural network approach for forecasting the monthly minimum, maximum, mean, and cumulative precipitation for the four meteorological stations of Greece. They noted that ANN was not able to predict the peaks in all cases. They suggested increasing the size of training dataset to overcome this problem [9]. Lin and Chen [10] used a neural network for forecasting typhoon rainfall. ANN is developed which takes typhoon characteristics (direction of typhoon movement, latitude and longitude of the typhoon centre, the maximum wind speed, and atmospheric pressure of the centre) and the spatial rainfall information of nearby rain gauge as inputs and gives 1 hour ahead forecast of typhoon rainfall. Practitioners applied ANN [11, 12] and approach based on chaos theory [13] for numerical model error prediction in hydrology. ANN and concepts of chaos theory are used to adjust the value of outputs produced by the numerical model.

The hydrometeorological time series can be considered as a composition of stochastic (noise or fluctuations) and structured components. The stochastic component obscures the modeling of time series. The structured component can be extracted by removing the stochastic component from a time series. Then, a deterministic model can be developed for the structured component of a time series. Practitioners have used following data preprocessing techniques for cleaning hydrological time series: wavelet analysis (WA), principal component analysis (PCA), and singular spectrum analysis (SSA). However, in recent years, the wavelet analysis has become an effective tool for analyzing nonstationary time series.

Partal and Cigizoglu [14] proposed a wavelet-ANN approach for predicting the daily precipitation of 12 meteorological stations of Turkey. They used meteorological data for precipitation prediction. Nasseri et al. [15] applied a combination of back propagation algorithm and genetic algorithm (GA) for rainfall forecasting in western suburbs of Sydney. They used GA to train and optimize feed-forward neural network. They concluded that a combined approach outperformed an approach that uses a neural network alone. A modular artificial neural network (MANN) [16] is combined with three data preprocessing techniques: moving average (MA), PCA, and SSA for prediction of two monthly and two daily precipitation series.

The symbolic regression technique can be used for developing a model (mathematical model in a symbolic form) that can explain the relationship between rainfall and meteorological parameters. The advantage of the symbolic regression technique over traditional regression techniques is that it searches for both the structure and the appropriate numeric coefficients of the model. Symbolic regression can be performed by means of genetic programming (GP) [17]. Moreover, GP approach is preferred over other approaches for symbolic regression because the approach produces an explicit mathematical expression as a solution (model) [18]. The produced model can provide an insight into the process which gives rise to the data [19]. Moreover, the interpretation of the produced model allows us to combine evolved knowledge with already existing knowledge [20, 21]. An exhaustive survey on open issues and approaches used by practitioners to deal with these issues in field of symbolic regression through GP is presented in [22]. Kisi and Shiri [23] suggested that use of GP is preferred in following situations: (i) the relationship between the relevant variables are poorly understood, (ii) determination of optimal solution is difficult, (iii) an approximate solution is acceptable, and (iv) there is a large amount of training data to be modeled.

Considering the mentioned advantages, many practitioners applied GP for rainfall prediction. GP is used in [24] to develop a model that can explain the cause and effect relationship between rainfall and runoff processes at a catchment in Singapore. Babovic and Keijzer [25] employed GP for developing rainfall-runoff models using the hydrometeorological data and the available domain knowledge. Khu et al. [26] applied GP for real-time runoff forecasting at the Orgeval catchment in France. The GP is used as an error updating strategy to accompany a rainfall-runoff model. The GP produced results are compared with those obtained using autoregression and Kalman filter. The results suggest that GP outperforms other strategies for real-time flow forecasting [26].

The objective of the present work is to explore the applicability of a hybrid wavelet-postfix-GP model for prediction of daily rainfall of Anand station of Gujarat, India, using meteorological variables. The wavelet analysis is used to decompose the original series of each meteorological variable into various discrete wavelet (DW) subseries. The decomposition is useful to identify the DW subseries which have high correlation with the original rainfall series. The effective DW subseries for each meteorological variable are added to generate a final subseries. The objective behind addition of DW subseries is to increase the correlation between the final subseries and the original rainfall series. The Postfix-GP, a GP variant, is then used to develop a model that can explain the relationship between the final subseries of meteorological variables and the original rainfall series. The Postfix-GP uses linear individual representation and stack based evaluation. This helps Postfix-GP to minimize both the memory requirement and evaluation time compared to conventional tree based representation. The evolved Postfix-GP models are then used for out-of-sample predictions. The performance of the evolved Postfix-GP model is measured using mean absolute error (MAE), mean squared error (MSE), and correlation coefficient (CC).

The rest of the paper is organized as follows. The next section presents homogeneity analysis of collected meteorological data. Section 3 presents the proposed hybrid wavelet-Postfix-GP model for rainfall prediction. Section 4 presents experimental settings. The evolved Postfix-GP model that represents rainfall as function of meteorological subseries is presented in Section 5. The section also presents comparison of the out-of-sample predictive performance of wavelet-Postfix-GP model and wavelet-ANN model. Conclusions are presented in Section 6.

2. Data and Homogeneity Analysis

Meteorological time series of Anand region for 12 years (from 1991 to 2002) were collected from Anand Agriculture University, Anand, Gujarat, India. We have used 10 years of data for training and 2 years of data for predictions. We have collected time series data for the following meteorological variables: (i) minimum temperature—T_{Min}, (ii) maximum temperature—T_{Max}, (iii) mean temperature—T_{Mean}, (iv) relative humidity—RH, (v) evaporation—EP, (vi) 1-day previous rainfall—RF_1, and (vii) 2-day previous rainfall—RF_2. The objective is to evolve a model (as a function of mentioned meteorological

TABLE 1: Result of different homogeneity tests.

Test	T_{Min}	T_{Max}	T_{Mean}	RH	EP	RF
Pettitt	0.204	0.241	0.238	0.354	0.481	0.093
SNHT	0.372	0.466	0.500	0.528	0.225	0.151
BR	0.287	0.438	0.395	0.508	0.455	0.115
VNR	0.495	0.146	0.595	0.004	0.304	0.127

variables) for daily rainfall using a hybrid wavelet-Postfix-GP approach.

Homogeneity tests are applied to detect the variability of the meteorological data. Several factors can affect the quality of meteorological data. The main sources of inhomogeneity are station relocation, changes in measurement techniques and observational procedures, and changes in instruments. Homogeneity test are useful to detect the break (shift in the mean) in the given time series. As many meteorological parameters are highly variable in time and space, most of the homogeneity tests are designed for monthly or yearly data and not for daily data. We applied the following four homogeneity tests to meteorological time series [27]: standard normal homogeneity test (SNHT), Buishand range (BR) test, Pettitt test, and von Neumann ratio (VNR) test. The null hypothesis for all the mentioned tests is the annual values X_i of the test variable X which are independent and identically distributed and series can be viewed as homogeneous [27]. The alternative hypothesis for BR test, SNHT, and Pettit test presumes that there is a break in the mean of the series and the series can be viewed as inhomogeneous. The reason for applying more than one test to check homogeneity is that these tests have different sensitivity in detecting a break. For example, the SNHT test is sensitive in detecting a break near the starting and the end of the series whereas Pettit and Buishand tests are sensitive in detecting break in the middle of the series.

The significance level is set to 1% for all tests. If the obtained P value is lower than the selected significance level, then we reject the null hypothesis. Table 1 presents the results of homogeneity tests for the annual mean values of meteorological parameters. As all the tests give values greater than 0.01, the null hypothesis cannot be rejected (time series is homogeneous). For the relative humidity, VNR test gives a P value of 0.004, less than 0.01. However, as the P values associated to the other tests are greater than 0.01, we accept the null hypothesis.

3. A Hybrid Wavelet Postfix-GP Model

The architecture that integrates discrete wavelet transform (DWT) and Postfix-GP for modeling and prediction of rainfall time series is presented in Figure 1. The architecture comprises the following main steps: (i) apply DWT on meteorological data and generate DW subseries at every level, (ii) calculate the correlation coefficient between the generated DW subseries and the original rainfall series, (iii) identify the significant DW subseries, (iv) add significant DW subseries to generate a new subseries for each meteorological variable,

(v) normalize the values of newly generated subseries in the range (0, 1), (vi) divide the normalized dataset into (a) training and (b) test dataset, (vii) evolve the model for training data using Postfix-GP, and (viii) apply the evolved model for out-of-sample rainfall prediction. The objective is to evolve a model (as a function of mentioned meteorological variables) for rainfall using a hybrid wavelet-Postfix-GP approach. In the following subsections, we discuss the wavelet transform and Postfix-GP in brief.

3.1. Wavelet Transform. The properties of irregularity in shape and compactness make wavelets an ideal tool for analysis of nonstationary signals. Fourier analysis decomposes a signal into sine and cosine waves of various frequencies whereas wavelet analysis decomposes a signal into shifted and scaled versions of the mother wavelet. The shifting (delaying) of the mother wavelet provides local information of the signal in time domain whereas scaling (stretching or compressing) of the mother wavelet provides local information of the signal in frequency domain [28]. The scaling and shifting operations applied to mother wavelet are used to calculate wavelet coefficients that provide correlation between the wavelet and local portion of the signal. From the calculated wavelet coefficients, we can extract two types of components: approximate coefficients and detail coefficients. The approximate coefficients represent high scale, low frequency component of the original signal whereas detail coefficients represent low scale, high frequency component.

Continuous wavelet transform (CWT) operates at every scale from that of the original signal up to some maximum scale. This distinguishes CWT from DWT (which operates at dyadic scales only). CWT is also continuous in terms of shifting: during computation, the analyzing wavelet is shifted smoothly over the full domain of signal. The results of the CWT are wavelet coefficients, which are a function of scale and position. Multiplying each coefficient by the appropriately scaled and shifted wavelet gives the constituent wavelets of the original signal.

The computation of wavelet coefficients at every scale requires large computational time. To reduce the time, it is preferred to calculate wavelet coefficients for selected subset of scales and positions. If the scales and positions are selected based on power of two (dyadic scales and positions), then the analysis will be efficient and just as accurate, named discrete wavelet transform (DWT) [29]. The process of decomposition can be iterated, with successive approximations being decomposed in turn (discarding detail coefficients), so that original signal is broken down into many lower-resolution components. This process is referred

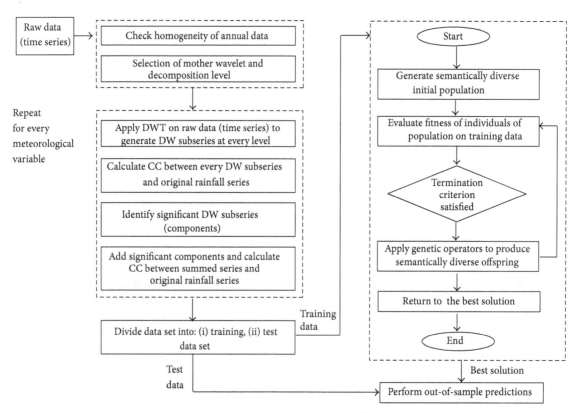

FIGURE 1: Hybrid Wavelet-Postfix-GP architecture for rainfall modeling and prediction.

as multiresolution analysis. We have selected Db4 (length-4 Daubechies) [28] wavelet as mother wavelet because this is one of the commonly used wavelets for separating fluctuations from the given time series. The smoothness of different wavelets depends on the number of vanishing moments [29]. Db4 wavelet has four vanishing moments, a smallest length wavelet with smoothness property. We have set maximum resolution level to value 10 for decomposition of every meteorological time series.

The forward discrete wavelet transform is employed to decompose original time series of every meteorological variable at different scale (maximum level n = 10). The wavelet transform produces high-pass (detail) coefficients at every level and one low-pass (approximation) coefficient. The inverse discrete wavelet transform is applied on the produced coefficients at every level to generate DW subseries, which are of the same length as the original series. Thus, we obtain $n + 1$ (n detail and one approximate) DW subseries for the original time series of every meteorological variable. The correlation coefficient between the generated DW subseries at different level and the original rainfall series is calculated. The number of DW subseries which have high correlation with the original rainfall series is identified and summed up to generate a new (final) subseries for that meteorological variable. The objective behind addition of DW subseries having high correlation with the original rainfall series is to reduce the number of variables (dimensions or inputs) and to increase the correlation between newly generated subseries and the original rainfall series. This process is repeated for every meteorological time series.

3.2. Postfix Genetic Programming.
Postfix-GP [30], a GP variant, adopts postfix notation for individual representation. Individuals represented in form of postfix strings can be easily evaluated using stack. Moreover, the individual representation without pointers assists Postfix-GP to minimize the fitness evaluation time and required memory to store the individual. Each Postfix-GP individual contains the following three attributes: MinLength, MaxLength, and ValidLength. The MinLength and MaxLength attributes define the range of syntactically valid Postfix-GP individuals. The ValidLength attribute refers to the index of the last element of an individual forming a valid postfix expression. An individual with ValidLength greater than MinLength and less than MaxLength is considered as valid [30].

Postfix-GP employs idea of Stack count, introduced by Keith and Martin [31], to find out the ValidLength of an individual. The Stack count of an element is calculated as the number of arguments pushed on the stack minus the number of arguments popped off the stack by the element. For example, the stack count value for an operand is 1, whereas it is 0 for unary operator. Furthermore, the total sum of stack count values must be 1 at the ValidLength position of an individual. A Postfix-GP individual with its syntactically valid portion and corresponding tree representation is depicted in Figure 2. It should be noted that the transformation of syntactically valid portion to a tree representation is not required for fitness calculation; it is shown for better comprehension of the reader.

Table 2 presents difference between an individual representation scheme of Postfix-GP and other evolutionary

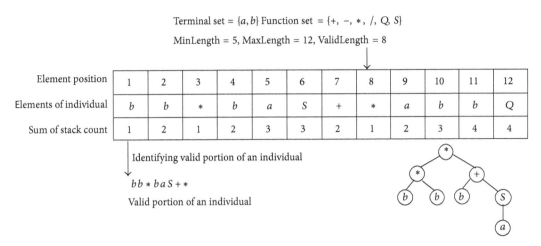

FIGURE 2: Postfix-GP individual representation.

TABLE 2: Difference between individual representation schemes of Postfix-GP and other evolutionary approaches.

Evolutionary algorithms	Genotype	Phenotype	Mapping
GA	Linear string of fixed length	Decoding genotype	Problem dependent
GP	Parse tree	Parse tree	Traversing tree
GEP	Linear string of fixed length	Parse tree	Karva notation
Postfix-GP	Linear string of fixed length	Linear string	Postfix notation

approaches, GA [32], GP [17], and gene expression programming (GEP) [33]. The standard GA represents an individual using a fixed length binary string. The individual representation scheme of GA does not permit the model structure to vary during evolutionary process. Standard GP employs a variable length, tree structure for an individual representation. The representation scheme of GP is more general and flexible than GA since it allows model structure to vary during evolution. GEP is a GP variant that represents an individual using multiple genes, where each gene represents a small subexpression. Each GEP gene is composed of two different domains—a head and a tail. GEP applies Karva notation to transform a linear representation to tree representation. Grammatical evolution (GE) [34] employs a string of integers to represent an individual (genotype). The string of integers is used to determine the sequence of production rules in context-free grammar. By following these sequences, an individual can be converted into an expression tree (phenotype). Adaptive logic programming (ALP) [35] also uses a string of integers for individual representation. However, the string of integers is used to select clauses in a logic program instead of production rules of a context-free grammar.

Postfix-GP produces initial population of individuals at random. The ValidLength of these individuals will have value in between MinLength and MaxLength. Postfix-GP employs semantic aware subtree crossover [36] to improve population diversity among individuals. The operator checks semantic equivalence [37, 38] of two subtrees, to be swapped, while performing crossover operation. Moreover, the operator

selects behaviorally different parents for generating offspring, which is useful to minimize the "no change to fitness" events [39]. Crossover of two dissimilar parents is likely to produce a change in offspring (solution) quality.

Postfix-GP extracts all subtrees of an individual having ValidLength greater than MinLength and treat the extracted subtrees as separate solutions during the evolutionary process. Postfix-GP employs one-point mutation operator, where the chosen element of an individual is interchanged with a different element of the same arity. An archive is used to store "best-so-far" found solutions, useful to exploit good solutions over a number of generations [40]. Postfix-GP uses MAE as a standardized fitness measure. However, MAE measure is not range bound. Therefore, we have normalized the fitness value of an individual between 0 and 1 using (1). The normalized fitness is referred to as an adjusted fitness of an individual and is useful to differentiate between individuals having close standardized fitness values, which may happen in generations near the end of Postfix-GP run. Postfix-GP is developed using .NET [41] framework on Windows XP operating system. Zedgraph [42], an open source graph library, is used for plotting charts.

$$\text{Adjusted Fitness} = \frac{1}{(1 + \text{Standardized Fitness})}. \quad (1)$$

4. Experimental Settings

We set a range of solution search space by specifying a minimum and maximum number of elements (nodes) that

TABLE 3: Correlation coefficient between each subseries and the original rainfall series.

Subseries	T_{Min}	T_{Max}	T_{Mean}	RH	EP	RF_1	RF_2
DW_1	−0.079	−0.029	−0.076	0.033	−0.127	−0.304	−0.013
DW_2	−0.068	−0.093	−0.103	0.110	−0.124	0.130	−0.249
DW_3	−0.060	−0.098	−0.097	0.101	−0.156	0.355	0.187
DW_4	−0.033	−0.098	−0.087	0.114	−0.177	0.302	0.258
DW_5	−0.027	−0.115	−0.094	0.132	−0.165	0.273	0.259
DW_6	−0.043	−0.053	−0.056	0.052	−0.065	0.138	0.135
DW_7	−0.030	−0.145	−0.102	0.160	−0.153	0.211	0.210
DW_8	0.230	0.117	0.211	0.225	0.025	0.251	0.250
DW_9	0.013	−0.045	−0.013	0.072	−0.044	0.081	0.081
DW_{10}	−0.016	−0.018	−0.017	0.019	−0.026	0.019	0.019
Approximate	0.018	0.004	0.014	0.034	0.008	0.044	0.044
Summed	0.230	−0.236	0.211	0.356	−0.347	0.613	0.519

a solution can have during an evolutionary run. The Min-Length and MaxLength parameters of Postfix-GP are used to attain this task. The MinLength and MaxLength parameters of Postfix-GP are set to values 10 and 40. The function set includes both arithmetic and trigonometric operators: {+, −, /, *, S, C, E, L, K, Q}, where S, C, E, L, and Q represent sine, cosine, exponential, logarithmic, and square root functions. The terminal set includes final subseries for T_{Min}, T_{Max}, T_{Mean}, RH, EP, RF_1, RF_2} and a list of constants in range [−10,...,10]. The population size and the number of generations are set to values 500 and 100. The crossover and mutation rates are set to 0.9 and 0.1. The Postfix-GP uses archive based roulette wheel selection [40]. Crossover operation is performed between parents chosen from an archive and current population

$$\text{MAE} = \frac{1}{N} \sum_{i=1}^{N} |(y_i - \widehat{y}_i)|.$$

$$\text{MSE} = \frac{1}{N} \sum_{i=1}^{N} (y_i - \widehat{y}_i)^2, \quad (2)$$

$$r = \frac{\text{cov}\left(Y, \widehat{Y}\right)}{\sigma_Y \sigma_{\widehat{Y}}},$$

We have shown the evolved Postfix-GP solutions with their mean absolute error (MAE), mean squared error (MSE), and correlation coefficient (CC). Equations in (2) are used to calculate these statistical measures, where y_i, $\widehat{y}_i$, Y, $\widehat{Y}$, and cov$(Y, \widehat{Y})$ stand for given ith observation, corresponding ith observation calculated by the evolved model, actual observed series, estimated series by the evolved model, and covariance between the observed and the estimated series. Value of r close to zero indicates no correlation between predicted and observed values. We have used MSE to measure closeness between the given set of points and those generated by the evolved solution.

5. Results

5.1. Identification of Important Components.
The discrete wavelet transform (DWT) is applied on daily time series of every meteorological variable to decompose the series into several DW subseries [14]. Each time series is decomposed up to 10 resolution levels. We have selected the resolution level of 10 because we required addressing both annual and seasonal factors. The levels DW_2, DW_3, DW_4, DW_5, DW_6, DW_7, DW_8, DW_9, and DW_{10} correspond to the temporal scale of 4, 8, 16, 32, 64, 128, 256, 512, and 1024 days. The subseries, DW_8, correspond to a temporal scale of 256 days (approximately one year). The correlation coefficient between the generated DW subseries at different levels and the original rainfall series is calculated. Table 3 presents the values of the correlation coefficient between each DW subseries and the original rainfall series. These correlation values are used to determine the effective DW components (subseries) for rainfall prediction.

According to Table 3, for minimum and mean temperature, the correlation between DW_8 subseries and the original rainfall series has high value. This reveals the fact that annual component of mean and minimum temperature subseries influences the amount of rainfall. The DW_7 subseries of maximum temperature has high correlation compared to other DW subseries. Moreover, the DW_2, DW_3, DW_4, and DW_5 subseries of maximum temperature have little high correlation compared to other DW subseries. Similarly, the DW_1, DW_2, DW_3, DW_4, DW_5, and DW_7 subseries of evaporation have high correlation compared to other DW subseries. This suggests that shorter time period components of maximum temperature and evaporation have correlation with the original rainfall series. The high correlation value is noticed for DW_8 subseries of relative humidity. Moreover, the correlation between the original rainfall and DW_2, DW_3, DW_4, DW_5, and DW_7 subseries of relative humidity is little high compared to correlation between the rainfall and remaining DW subseries of relative humidity. This suggests that both annual and shorter time period components of relative humidity have correlation with the rainfall.

TABLE 4: Selected DW components for generating final subseries.

T_{Min}	T_{Max}	T_{Mean}	RH	EP	RF_1	RF_2
DW_8	$DW_2 + DW_3 +$ $DW_4 + DW_5 +$ DW_7	DW_8	$DW_2 + DW_3 +$ $DW_4 + DW_5 +$ $DW_7 + DW_8$	$DW_1 + DW_2 +$ $DW_3 + DW_4 +$ $DW_5 + DW_7$	$DW_2 + DW_3 +$ $DW_4 + DW_5 +$ $DW_6 + DW_7 +$ DW_8	$DW_3 + DW_4 +$ $DW_5 + DW_6 +$ $DW_7 + DW_8$

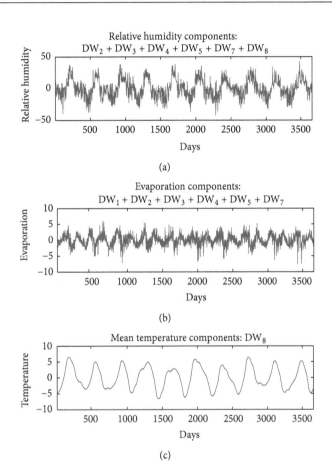

FIGURE 3: Summed subseries: (a) relative humidity, (b) evaporation, and (c) mean temperature.

The high correlation between both shorter and yearly components of relative humidity and rainfall is observed because of direct relation between these two variables. The humidity and rainfall data of the examined region show similar meteorological characteristics. The DW_3 subseries of one-day previous rainfall show high correlation with the original rainfall series. The DW_2, DW_4, DW_5, DW_6, DW_7, and DW_8 subseries also show little high correlation compared to other DW subseries. The number of DW subseries which have high correlation with the original rainfall series is identified and summed up to generate a new (final) subseries for that meteorological variable. The selected DW components for different meteorological variables are presented in Table 4. However, the selection of number of DW components (subseries) depends on the user. Partal and Cigizoglu [14] suggested that applying a threshold on correlation value would be helpful to determine the number of DW components (subseries).

Usage of each selected DW subseries as input increases the dimension of the solution search space. Moreover, it also increases the complexity of the final model. Therefore, the selected DW subseries, having high correlation with the original rainfall series, are added together to form a new (final) subseries. The final subseries are generated for every meteorological variable. The addition of selected DW components (subseries) is helpful to improve the correlation between the final subseries and the original rainfall series. For example, the DW_8 subseries of relative humidity have correlation value of 0.225. However, for the added ($DW_2 + DW_3 + DW_4 + DW_5 + DW_7 + DW_8$) subseries, the correlation value increases to 0.355.

The added subseries of the relative humidity, evaporation, and mean temperature are shown in Figure 3. The summed series of the maximum temperature, minimum temperature, and previous day rainfall are presented in Figure 4. We normalized the data of added subseries in the range (0, 1).

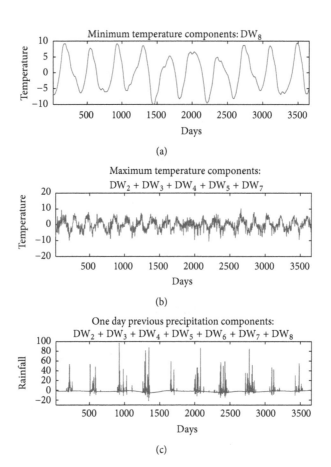

FIGURE 4: Summed subseries: (a) minimum temperature, (b) maximum temperature, and (c) 1-day previous rainfall.

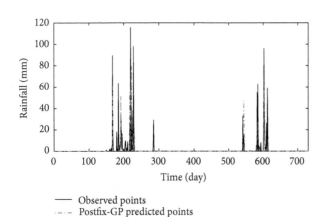

FIGURE 5: Daily rainfall prediction by Postfix-GP Model for the test period (2 years).

The data normalization assures that large value variables do not overwhelm small value variables.

5.2. Evolved Postfix-GP Solutions. The evolved Postfix-GP solution (for terminal set $\{T_{\text{Min}}, T_{\text{Max}}, T_{\text{Mean}}, \text{EP}, \text{RH}, \text{RF}_1\}$) is shown in (3). It is noted that the solution contains significant meteorological variables (evaporation, minimum temperature, relative humidity, and maximum temperature) which are useful for rainfall prediction. We got MSE = 48.2860, adjusted fitness = 0.3926, and $r = 0.7469$ for the training data

$$e^{(\cos(\cos(-10.6\,\text{EP}\,T_i))-(X_i/(\sin(\text{RF}_1\,\text{RH})*\text{RH}))+3.7292)}, \qquad (3)$$

where $X_i = \text{EP} * e^{\text{Log}_{10}(4.3\,\text{EP}+0.4941)} / (T_x + \text{RH})$.

The observed and Postfix-GP model predicted values for the testing period are presented in Figure 5. The model has predicted the general behavior of the observed rainfall data. It has accurately predicted the summer days and estimated zero rainfall for these days. However, the model performs satisfactory for estimating maximum rainfall values.

5.3. Comparison of Result Obtained by Wavelet-Postfix-GP and Wavelet-ANN Models. We have compared the performance of wavelet-Postfix-GP and wavelet-ANN models for the daily rainfall prediction. The selection of architecture (number of layers and number of nodes in each layer) and the training algorithm is important design parameters of ANN. There is

TABLE 5: Statistical measures for the best wavelet-Postfix-GP and wavelet-ANN models for different input combinations for test period.

Model inputs	Wavelet-Postfix-GP			Wavelet-ANN			
	MSE	Adj_{Fit}	R	ANN structure	MSE	Adj_{Fit}	R
$T_{\text{Min}}, T_{\text{Max}}, T_{\text{Mean}}$, EP, RH, RF_1, RF_2	49.2494	0.4002	0.6661	7, 5, 1	52.6614	0.2804	0.6919
$T_{\text{Min}}, T_{\text{Max}}, T_{\text{Mean}}$, EP, RH, RF_1	47.5766	0.4017	0.6794	6, 6, 1	50.4010	0.3545	0.7641

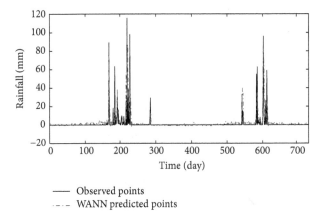

—— Observed points
.–.– WANN predicted points

FIGURE 6: Daily rainfall prediction by ANN model for the test period (2 years).

no rule available to find out the number of hidden layers and appropriate number of nodes for each hidden layer. However, practitioners [43] found that ANN with one hidden layer is complex enough to model the nonlinear properties of the hydrologic processes. We investigated different architecture with different activation functions and number of neurons for the hidden layer and selected the one which gives an optimal result. A multilayer feed-forward ANN that comprises seven nodes in the input layer, one hidden layer with five nodes, and one node in the output layer is selected for the rainfall prediction. Moreover, the input and hidden layers have an additional bias neuron. The ANN is trained with back propagation (BP) learning algorithm. We set log-sigmoid transfer function between input and hidden layers and pure linear transfer function between hidden and output layers.

Figure 6 presents the observed and wavelet-ANN model predicted rainfall values. The model has predicted the general behavior of the observed rainfall data. It is observed that wavelet-ANN model has produced negative prediction for some days having zero rainfall, which are not practically possible. Partal and Cigizoglu [14] found the similar behavior while applying ANN for predicting daily precipitation. They noted that the negative prediction problem occurred due to extrapolation ability of feed-forward back-propagation mechanism. Moreover, similar to Postfix-GP, the ANN failed in accurately predicting the peak values of rainfall during the test period.

Table 5 presents the statistical results for both wavelet-Postfix-GP and wavelet-ANN hybrid models for different input combinations for the test period. The Postfix-GP model has produced slightly better results than ANN from the MSE and fitness viewpoint. The ANN model slightly outperforms Postfix-GP in terms of correlation coefficient. The results

suggest that Postfix-GP produces comparable results and can be an alternative to ANN approach.

6. Conclusion

We applied four homogeneity tests (SNHT, BR, Pettit, and VNR) to detect the variability of the meteorological (minimum temperature, mean temperature, maximum temperature, evaporation, and relative humidity) variables recorded at Anand station. The results of homogeneity tests suggest that the time series of the meteorological variables are homogeneous. The series of every meteorological variable is decomposed up to 10 resolution level using discrete wavelet transform. The correlation coefficient between the generated DW subseries at different levels and the original rainfall series is calculated. The number of DW subseries which have correlation with the original rainfall series is identified and summed up to generate a new subseries for every meteorological variable. It is observed that both annual and shorter time period components of relative humidity have correlation with rainfall. The annual components of minimum and mean temperature show correlation with rainfall series. The newly generated meteorological subseries are regarded as inputs and the rainfall series as output.

The Postfix-GP is then employed to develop a model that can explain relationship between the inputs and the output. The developed model is then used for the rainfall prediction. The prediction performance of the evolved model was good, giving low values for MAE and MSE and high value for the correlation coefficient, suggesting that Postfix-GP is able to evolve an accurate and reliable model. The advantage of Postfix-GP over ANN is that it gives an explicit mathematical nonlinear equation that describes the relationship between inputs and output. The predictive performance of Postfix-GP and ANN models is compared. The results show that the Postfix-GP is a fair competitor of ANN approach. Moreover, the predictive performance of the evolved Postfix-GP model for the nonrainy (zero rainfall) periods and rainy (highest rainfall) periods is satisfactory as compared to ANN model, which produces negative prediction for some days of summer season. We conclude that wavelet-Postfix-GP approach obtained good quality solutions for the tested rainfall prediction series and could be explored as an alternative tool for predicting the hydrometeorological variables. Our future plan is to apply Postfix-GP for developing more accurate and reliable models using different combination of function and terminal sets.

Conflict of Interests

The authors declare that there is no conflict of interests regarding the publication of this paper.

Acknowledgments

The authors would like to acknowledge Krishi bhavan, Gandhinagar, and Anand Agricultural University, Anand, for their support in terms of meteorological data.

References

[1] V. Y. Jain, A. Sharma, S. Chaudhary, and V. K. Tyagi, "Spatial analysis for generating recommendations for agricultural crop production," in *Proceedings of the India Conference on Geospatial Technologies and Applications (ICGTA '12)*, 2012.

[2] L. R. Nayagam, R. Janardanan, and H. S. R. Mohan, "An empirical model for the seasonal prediction of southwest monsoon rainfall over Kerala, a meteorological subdivisionof India," *International Journal of Climatology*, vol. 28, no. 6, pp. 823–831, 2008.

[3] T. DelSole and J. Shukla, "Linear prediction of Indian monsoon rainfall," *Journal of Climate*, vol. 15, no. 24, pp. 3645–3658, 2002.

[4] A. R. Ganguly and R. L. Bras, "Distributed quantitative precipitation forecasting using information from radar and numerical weather prediction models," *Journal of Hydrometeorology*, vol. 4, no. 6, pp. 1168–1180, 2003.

[5] T. Diomede, S. Davolio, C. Marsigli et al., "Discharge prediction based on multi-model precipitation forecasts," *Meteorology and Atmospheric Physics*, vol. 101, no. 3-4, pp. 245–265, 2008.

[6] C. Chatfield, *The Analysis of Time Series: An Introduction*, CRC press, New York, NY, USA, 2003.

[7] V. Babovic, "Data mining in hydrology," *Hydrological Processes*, vol. 19, no. 7, pp. 1511–1515, 2005.

[8] N. Q. Hung, M. S. Babel, S. Weesakul, and N. K. Tripathi, "An artificial neural network model for rainfall forecasting in Bangkok, Thailand," *Hydrology and Earth System Sciences*, vol. 13, no. 8, pp. 1413–1425, 2009.

[9] K. P. Moustris, I. K. Larissi, P. T. Nastos, and A. G. Paliatsos, "Precipitation forecast using artificial neural networks in specific regions of Greece," *Water Resources Management*, vol. 25, no. 8, pp. 1979–1993, 2011.

[10] G.-F. Lin and L.-H. Chen, "Application of an artificial neural network to typhoon rainfall forecasting," *Hydrological Processes*, vol. 19, no. 9, pp. 1825–1837, 2005.

[11] V. Babovic, R. Cañizares, H. R. Jensen, and A. Klinting, "Neural networks as routine for error updating of numerical models," *Journal of Hydraulic Engineering*, vol. 127, no. 3, pp. 181–193, 2001.

[12] Y. Sun, V. Babovic, and E. S. Chan, "Multi-step-ahead model error prediction using time-delay neural networks combined with chaos theory," *Journal of Hydrology*, vol. 395, no. 1-2, pp. 109–116, 2010.

[13] V. Babovic, S. A. Sannasiraj, and E. S. Chan, "Error correction of a predictive ocean wave model using local model approximation," *Journal of Marine Systems*, vol. 53, no. 1–4, pp. 1–17, 2005.

[14] T. Partal and H. K. Cigizoglu, "Prediction of daily precipitation using wavelet-neural networks," *Hydrological Sciences Journal*, vol. 54, no. 2, pp. 234–246, 2009.

[15] M. Nasseri, K. Asghari, and M. J. Abedini, "Optimized scenario for rainfall forecasting using genetic algorithm coupled with artificial neural network," *Expert Systems with Applications*, vol. 35, no. 3, pp. 1415–1421, 2008.

[16] C. Wu, K. Chau, and C. Fan, "Prediction of rainfall time series using modular artificial neural networks coupled with data-preprocessing techniques," *Journal of Hydrology*, vol. 389, no. 1-2, pp. 146–167, 2010.

[17] J. R. Koza, *Genetic Programming: On the Programming of Computers by Means of Natural Selection*, MIT Press, Cambridge, Mass, USA, 1992.

[18] V. Babovic, "Introducing knowledge into learning based on genetic programming," *Journal of Hydroinformatics*, vol. 11, no. 3-4, pp. 181–193, 2009.

[19] M. Keijzer and V. Babovic, "Declarative and preferential bias in GP-based scientific discovery," *Genetic Programming and Evolvable Machines*, vol. 3, no. 1, pp. 41–79, 2002.

[20] V. Babovic and M. B. Abbott, "The evolution of equations from hydraulic data Part I: theory," *Journal of Hydraulic Research*, vol. 35, no. 3, pp. 397–430, 1997.

[21] V. Babovic and M. B. Abbott, "Evolution of equations from hydraulic data. Part II: applications," *Journal of Hydraulic Research*, vol. 35, no. 3, pp. 411–430, 1997.

[22] V. K. Dabhi and S. Chaudhary, "Empirical modeling using genetic programming: a survey of issues and approaches," *Natural Computing*, 2014.

[23] O. Kisi and J. Shiri, "Precipitation forecasting using wavelet-genetic programming and wavelet-neuro-fuzzy conjunction models," *Water Resources Management*, vol. 25, no. 13, pp. 3135–3152, 2011.

[24] S.-Y. Liong, T. R. Gautam, T. K. Soon, V. Babovic, M. Keijzer, and N. Muttil, "Genetic Programming: a new paradigm in rainfall runoff modeling," *Journal of the American Water Resources Association*, vol. 38, no. 3, pp. 705–718, 2002.

[25] V. Babovic and M. Keijzer, "Rainfall-runoff modelling based on genetic programming," *Nordic Hydrology*, vol. 33, no. 5, pp. 331–346, 2002.

[26] S. T. Khu, S.-Y. Liong, V. Babovic, H. Madsen, and N. Muttil, "Genetic programming and its application in real-time runoff forecasting," *Journal of the American Water Resources Association*, vol. 37, no. 2, pp. 439–451, 2001.

[27] J. B. Wijngaard, A. M. G. Klein Tank, and G. P. Können, "Homogeneity of 20th century European daily temperature and precipitation series," *International Journal of Climatology*, vol. 23, no. 6, pp. 679–692, 2003.

[28] I. Daubechies, *Ten Lectures on Wavelets*, vol. 61, SIAM, Philadelphia, Pa, USA, 1992.

[29] S. Mallat, "A wavelet tour of signal processing," *A Wavelet Tour of Signal Processing*, 2009.

[30] V. K. Dabhi and S. K. Vij, "Empirical modeling using symbolic regression via postfix genetic programming," in *Proceedings of the International Conference on Image Information Processing (ICIIP '11)*, pp. 1–6, November 2011.

[31] M. J. Keith and M. C. Martin, "Genetic programming in c++: implementation issues," in *Advances in Genetic Programming*, pp. 285–310, 1994.

[32] J. H. Holland, *Adaptation in Natural and Artificial Systems: An Introductory Analysis with Applications to Biology, Control and Artificial Intelligence*, MIT Press, Cambridge, Mass, USA, 1992.

[33] C. Ferreira, "Gene expression programming: a new adaptive algorithm for solving problems," *Complex Systems*, vol. 13, no. 2, pp. 87–129, 2001.

[34] M. O'Neil and C. Ryan, "Grammatical evolution," in *Grammatical Evolution*, pp. 33–47, Springer, New York, NY, USA, 2003.

[35] M. Keijzer, V. Babovic, C. Ryan, M. O'Neill, and M. Cattolico, "Adaptive logic programming," in *Proceedings of the Genetic and Evolutionary Computation Conference (GECCO '01)*, pp. 42–49, 2001.

[36] V. K. Dabhi and S. Chaudhary, "Semantic sub-tree crossover operator for postfix genetic programming," *Advances in Intelligent Systems and Computing*, vol. 201, no. 1, pp. 391–402, 2013.

[37] N. Q. Uy, N. X. Hoai, and M. O'Neill, "Semantic aware crossover for genetic programming: the case for real-valued function regression," in *Proceedings of the 12th European Conference on Genetic Programming (EuroGP '09)*, pp. 292–302, Springer, Berlin, Germany, 2009.

[38] N. Q. Uy, N. X. Hoai, M. O'Neill, R. I. McKay, and E. Galván-López, "Semantically-based crossover in genetic programming: application to real-valued symbolic regression," *Genetic Programming and Evolvable Machines*, vol. 12, no. 2, pp. 91–119, 2011.

[39] S. Gustafson, E. K. Burke, and N. Krasnogor, "On improving genetic programming for symbolic regression," in *Proceedings of the IEEE Congress on Evolutionary Computation (IEEE CEC '05)*, vol. 1, pp. 912–919, September 2005.

[40] M. Laumanns, L. Thiele, E. Zitzler, and K. Deb, "Archiving with guaranteed convergence and diversity in multi-objective optimization," in *Proceedings of the Genetic and Evolutionary Computation Conference (GECCO '02)*, pp. 439–447, Morgan Kaufmann, San Francisco, Calif, USA, 2002.

[41] Microsoft, Microsoft.net framework software development kit, 2007, http://msdn.microsoft.com/ .

[42] Zedgraph, 2008, http://sourceforge.net/projects/zedgraph/ .

[43] N. J. De Vos and T. Rientjes, "Constraints of artificial neural networks for rainfall-runoff modelling: trade-offs in hydrological state representation and model evaluation," *Hydrology and Earth System Sciences*, vol. 9, no. 1-2, pp. 111–126, 2005.

9

Exponential Stability of Periodic Solution to Wilson-Cowan Networks with Time-Varying Delays on Time Scales

Jinxiang Cai, Zhenkun Huang, and Honghua Bin

School of Science, Jimei University, Xiamen 361021, China

Correspondence should be addressed to Zhenkun Huang; hzk974226@jmu.edu.cn

Academic Editor: Songcan Chen

We present stability analysis of delayed Wilson-Cowan networks on time scales. By applying the theory of calculus on time scales, the contraction mapping principle, and Lyapunov functional, new sufficient conditions are obtained to ensure the existence and exponential stability of periodic solution to the considered system. The obtained results are general and can be applied to discrete-time or continuous-time Wilson-Cowan networks.

1. Introduction

The activity of a cortical column may be mathematically described through the model developed by Wilson and Cowan [1, 2]. Such a model consists of two nonlinear ordinary differential equations representing the interactions between two populations of neurons that are distinguished by the fact that their synapses are either excitatory or inhibitory [2]. A comprehensive paper has been done by Destexhe and Sejnowski [3] which summarized all important development and theoretical results for Wilson-Cowan networks. Its extensive applications include pattern analysis and image processing [4]. Theoretical results about the existence of asymptotic stable limit cycle and chaos have been reported in [5, 6]. Exponential stability of a unique almost periodic solution for delayed Wilson-Cowan type model has been reported in [7]. However, few investigations are fixed on the periodicity of Wilson-Cowan model [8] and it is troublesome to study the stability and periodicity for continuous and discrete system with oscillatory coefficients, respectively. Therefore, it is significant to study Wilson-Cowan networks on time scales [9, 10] which can unify the continuous and discrete situations.

Motivated by recent results [11–13], we consider the following dynamic Wilson-Cowan networks on time scale $\mathbb{T}$:

$$
\begin{aligned}
X_P^\Delta(t) &= -a_P(t) X_P(t) + \left[k_P(t) - r_P(t) X_P(t)\right] \\
&\quad \times G\left[w_P^1(t) X_P(t - \tau_P(t))\right. \\
&\qquad \left. -w_N^1(t) X_N(t - \tau_N(t)) + I_P(t)\right], \\
X_N^\Delta(t) &= -a_N(t) X_N(t) + \left[k_N(t) - r_N(t) X_N(t)\right] \\
&\quad \times G\left[w_P^2(t) X_P(t - \tau_P(t))\right. \\
&\qquad \left. -w_N^2(t) X_N(t - \tau_N(t)) + I_N(t)\right],
\end{aligned}
$$

$$(1)$$

$t \in \mathbb{T}$, where $X_P(t)$, $X_N(t)$ represent the proportion of excitatory and inhibitory neurons firing per unit time at the instant t, respectively. $a_P(t) > 0$ and $a_N(t) > 0$ represent the function of the excitatory and inhibitory neurons with natural decay over time, respectively. $r_P(t)$ and $r_N(t)$ are related to the duration of the refractory period; $k_P(t)$ and $k_N(t)$ are positive scaling coefficients. $w_P^1(t)$, $w_N^1(t)$, $w_P^2(t)$, and $w_N^2(t)$ are the strengths of connections between the populations. $I_P(t)$, $I_N(t)$ are the external inputs to the excitatory and the inhibitory populations. $G(\cdot)$ is the response function of neuronal activity. $\tau_P(t)$, $\tau_N(t)$ correspond to the transmission time-varying delays.

The main aim of this paper is to unify the discrete and continuous Wilson-Cowan networks with periodic coefficients and time-varying delays under one common framework and to obtain some generalized results to ensure the existence and exponential stability of periodic solution on time scales. The main technique is based on the theory of time scales, the contraction mapping principle, and the Lyapunov functional method.

2. Preliminaries

In this section, we give some definitions and lemmas on time scales which can be found in books [14, 15].

Definition 1. A time scale $\mathbb{T}$ is an arbitrary nonempty closed subset of the real set $\mathbb{R}$. The forward and backward jump operators $\sigma, \rho : \mathbb{T} \to \mathbb{T}$ and the graininess $\mu : \mathbb{T} \to \mathbb{R}^+$ are defined, respectively, by

$$\sigma(t) := \inf\{s \in \mathbb{T} : s > t\}, \qquad \rho(t) := \sup\{s \in \mathbb{T} : s < t\},$$
$$\mu(t) := \sigma(t) - t. \tag{2}$$

These jump operators enable us to classify the point $\{t\}$ of a time scale as right-dense, right-scattered, left-dense, or left-scattered depending on whether

$$\sigma(t) = t, \quad \sigma(t) > t, \quad \rho(t) = t, \quad \rho(t) < t, \tag{3}$$
$$\text{respectively, for any } t \in \mathbb{T}.$$

The notation $[a, b]_{\mathbb{T}}$ means that $[a, b]_{\mathbb{T}} := \{t \in \mathbb{T} : a \leq t \leq b\}$. Denote $\mathbb{T} := \{t \in \mathbb{T} : t \geq 0\}$.

Definition 2. One can say that a time scale $\mathbb{T}$ is periodic if there exists $p > 0$ such that $t \in \mathbb{T}$; then $t \pm p \in \mathbb{T}$; the smallest positive number p is called the period of the time scale.

Clearly, if $\mathbb{T}$ is a p-periodic time scale, then $\sigma(t + np) = \sigma(t) + np$ and $\mu(t + np) = \mu(t)$. So, $\mu(t)$ is a p-periodic function.

Definition 3. Let $\mathbb{T}(\neq \mathbb{R})$ be a periodic time scale with period p. One can say that the function $f : \mathbb{T} \to \mathbb{R}$ is periodic with period $\omega > 0$ if there exists a natural number n such that $\omega = np$, $f(t + \omega) = f(t)$ for all $t \in \mathbb{T}$ and ω is the smallest number such that $f(t + \omega) = f(t)$. If $\mathbb{T} = \mathbb{R}$, one can say that f is periodic with period $\omega > 0$ if ω is the smallest positive number such that $f(t + \omega) = f(t)$ for all $t \in \mathbb{R}$.

Definition 4 (Lakshmikantham and Vatsala [16]). For each $t \in \mathbb{T}$, let N be a neighborhood of t. Then, one defines the generalized derivative (or Dini derivative), $D^+u^\Delta(t)$, to mean that, given $\varepsilon > 0$, there exists a right neighborhood $N(\varepsilon) \subset N$ of t such that

$$\frac{u(\sigma(t)) - u(s)}{u(t, s)} < D^+u^\Delta(t) + \varepsilon \tag{4}$$

for each $s \in N(\varepsilon)$, $s > t$, where $\mu(t, s) = \sigma(t) - s$.

In case t is right-scattered and $u(t)$ is continuous at t, one gets

$$D^+u^\Delta(t) = \frac{u(\sigma(t)) - u(t)}{\sigma(t) - t}. \tag{5}$$

Definition 5. A function $f : \mathbb{T} \to \mathbb{R}$ is called right-dense continuous provided that it is continuous at right-dense points of $\mathbb{T}$ and the left-side limit exists (finite) at left-dense continuous functions on $\mathbb{T}$. The set of all right-dense continuous functions on $\mathbb{T}$ is defined by $C_{rd} = C_{rd}(\mathbb{T}, \mathbb{R})$.

Definition 6. A function $p : \mathbb{T} \to \mathbb{T}$ is called a regressive function if and only if $1 + p(t)\mu(t) \neq 0$.

The set of all regressive and right-dense continuous functions is denoted by $\mathscr{R}$. Let $\mathscr{R}^+ := \{p \in C_{rd} : 1 + p(t)\mu(t) > 0 \text{ for all } t \in \mathbb{T}\}$. Next, we give the definition of the exponential function and list its useful properties.

Definition 7 (Bohner and Peterson [14]). If $p \in C_{rd}$ is a regressive function, then the generalized exponential function $e_p(t, s)$ is defined by

$$e_p(t, s) = \exp\left\{\int_s^t \xi_{\mu(\tau)}(p(\tau)) \, \Delta\tau\right\}, \quad s, t \in \mathbb{T}, \tag{6}$$

with the cylinder transformation

$$\xi_h(z) = \begin{cases} \dfrac{\text{Log}(1 + hz)}{h}, & h \neq 0, \\ z, & h = 0. \end{cases} \tag{7}$$

Definition 8. The periodic solution

$$Z^*(t) = \left(X_P^*(t), X_N^*(t)\right)^\top \tag{8}$$

of (1) is said to be globally exponentially stable if there exists a positive constant ε and $N = N(\varepsilon) > 0$ such that all solutions

$$Z(t) = \left(X_P(t), X_N(t)\right)^\top \tag{9}$$

of (1) satisfy

$$|X_P(t) - X_P^*(t)| + |X_N(t) - X_N^*(t)|$$

$$\leq N(\varepsilon) e_{\ominus\varepsilon}(t, \alpha) \left(\sup_{s \in [-\tau_0, 0]_{\mathbb{T}}} |X_P(s) - X_P^*(s)|\right.$$

$$\left. + \sup_{s \in [-\tau_0, 0]_{\mathbb{T}}} |X_N(s) - X_N^*(s)|\right),$$

$$t \in \mathbb{T}. \tag{10}$$

Lemma 9 (Bohner and Peterson [15]). *If $p, q \in \mathscr{R}$, then*

(i) $e_0(t, s) \equiv 1$ and $e_p(t, t) \equiv 1$;

(ii) $e_p(\sigma(t), s) = (1 + \mu(t)p(t))e_p(t, s)$;

(iii) $1/e_p(t, s) = e_{\ominus p}(t, s)$, where $\ominus p(t) = -p(t)/(1 + \mu(t)p(t))$;

(iv) $e_p(t, s) = 1/e_p(s, t) = e_{\ominus p}(s, t)$;

(v) $e_p(t, s) e_p(s, r) = e_p(t, r)$;

(vi) $e_p(t, s) e_q(t, s) = e_{p \oplus q}(t, s)$;

(vii) $e_p(t, s)/e_q(t, s) = e_{p \ominus q}(t, s)$;

(viii) $(1/e_p(\cdot, s))^{\Delta} = -p(t)/e_p^{\sigma}(\cdot, s)$.

Lemma 10 (contraction mapping principle [17]). *If Ω is a closed subset of a Banach space X and $\mathscr{F} : \Omega \rightarrow \Omega$ is a contraction, then $\mathscr{F}$ has a unique fixed point in Ω.*

For any ω-periodic function $\mathscr{V}$ defined on $\mathbb{T}$, denote $\overline{\mathscr{V}} = \max_{t \in [0, \omega]} \mathscr{V}(t)$, $\underline{\mathscr{V}} = \min_{t \in [0, \omega]} \mathscr{V}(t)$, $\overline{|\mathscr{V}|} = \max_{t \in [0, \omega]} |\mathscr{V}(t)|$, and $\underline{|\mathscr{V}|} = \min_{t \in [0, \omega]} |\mathscr{V}(t)|$. Throughout this paper, we make the following assumptions:

(A_1) $k_P(t)$, $k_N(t)$, $r_P(t)$, $r_N(t)$, $w_P^1(t)$, $w_P^2(t)$, $w_N^1(t)$, $w_N^2(t)$, $a_P(t)$, $a_N(t)$, $\tau_P(t)$, $\tau_N(t)$, $I_P(t)$, and $I_N(t)$ are ω-periodic functions defined on $\mathbb{T}$, $-a_P(t)$, $-a_N(t) \in \mathscr{R}^+$.

(A_2) $G(\cdot) : \mathbb{R} \rightarrow \mathbb{R}$ is Lipschitz continuous; that is, $|G(u) - G(v)| \leq L|u - v|$, for all $u, v \in \mathbb{R}$, and $G(0) = 0$, $\sup_{v \in \mathbb{R}} |G(v)| \leq M$.

For simplicity, take the following denotations:

$$R = \max\left\{\overline{r_P}, \overline{r_N}\right\}, \qquad I = \max\left\{L\overline{|I_P|}, L\overline{|I_N|}\right\},$$

$$K = \max\left\{\overline{k_P}, \overline{k_N}\right\},$$

$$W = \max\left\{L\overline{w_P^1}, L\overline{w_N^1}, L\overline{w_P^2}, L\overline{w_N^2}\right\}, \tag{11}$$

$$\tau_0 = \min\left\{\underline{|\tau_P|}, \underline{|\tau_N|}\right\}.$$

Lemma 11. *Suppose (A_1) holds; then $Z(t)$ is an ω-periodic solution of (1) if and only if $Z(t)$ is the solution of the following system:*

$$X_P(t) = \frac{1}{e_{\ominus(-a_P)}(\omega, 0) - 1}$$

$$\times \int_t^{t+\omega} \frac{e_{\ominus(-a_P)}(s, t)}{1 - \mu(s) a_P(s)} \left[k_P(s) - r_P(s) X_P(s)\right]$$

$$\times G\left[w_P^1(s) X_P(s - \tau_P(s))\right.$$

$$\left. - w_N^1(s) X_N(s - \tau_N(s)) + I_P(s)\right] \Delta s,$$

$$X_N(t) = \frac{1}{e_{\ominus(-a_N)}(\omega, 0) - 1}$$

$$\times \int_t^{t+\omega} \frac{e_{\ominus(-a_N)}(s, t)}{1 - \mu(s) a_N(s)} \left[k_N(s) - r_N(s) X_N(s)\right]$$

$$\times G\left[w_P^2(s) X_P(s - \tau_P(s))\right.$$

$$\left. - w_N^2(s) X_N(s - \tau_N(s)) + I_N(s)\right] \Delta s. \tag{12}$$

Proof. Let $Z(t) = (X_P(t), X_N(t))^{\top}$ be a solution of (1); we can rewrite (1) as follows:

$$X_P^{\Delta}(t) + a_P(t) \left(X_P^{\sigma}(t) - \mu(t) X_P^{\Delta}(t)\right)$$

$$= \left[k_P(t) - r_P(t) X_P(t)\right]$$

$$\times G\left[w_P^1(t) X_P(t - \tau_P(t))\right.$$

$$\left. - w_N^1(t) X_N(t - \tau_N(t)) + I_P(t)\right],$$

$$X_N^{\Delta}(t) + a_N(t) \left(X_N^{\sigma}(t) - \mu(t) X_N^{\Delta}(t)\right) \tag{13}$$

$$= \left[k_N(t) - r_N(t) X_N(t)\right]$$

$$\times G\left[w_P^2(t) X_P(t - \tau_P(t))\right.$$

$$\left. - w_N^2(t) X_N(t - \tau_N(t)) + I_N(t)\right],$$

which leads to

$$X_P^{\Delta}(t) + \ominus(-a_P)(t) X_P^{\sigma}(t)$$

$$= \left[k_P(t) - r_P(t) X_P(t)\right]$$

$$\times G\left[w_P^1(t) X_P(t - \tau_P(t))\right.$$

$$\left. - w_N^1(t) X_N(t - \tau_N(t)) + I_P(t)\right] \frac{1}{1 - \mu(t) a_P(t)},$$

$$X_N^{\Delta}(t) + \ominus(-a_N)(t) X_N^{\sigma}(t)$$

$$= \left[k_N(t) - r_N(t) X_N(t)\right]$$

$$\times G\left[w_P^2(t) X_P(t - \tau_P(t))\right.$$

$$\left. - w_N^2(t) X_N(t - \tau_N(t)) + I_N(t)\right] \frac{1}{1 - \mu(t) a_N(t)}. \tag{14}$$

Multiplying both sides of the above equalities by $e_{\ominus(-a_P)}(t, 0)$ and $e_{\ominus(-a_N)}(t, 0)$, respectively, we have

$$\left[e_{\ominus(-a_P)}(t, 0) X_P(t)\right]^{\Delta}$$

$$= \left[k_P(t) - r_P(t) X_P(t)\right]$$

$$\times G\left[w_P^1(t) X_P(t - \tau_P(t))\right.$$

$$\left. - w_N^1(t) X_N(t - \tau_N(t)) + I_P(t)\right] e_{\ominus(-a_P)}(\sigma(t), 0),$$

$$\left[e_{\ominus(-a_N)}(t, 0) X_N(t)\right]^{\Delta}$$

$$= \left[k_N(t) - r_N(t) X_N(t)\right]$$

$$\times G\left[w_P^2(t) X_P(t - \tau_P(t))\right.$$

$$\left. - w_N^2(t) X_N(t - \tau_N(t)) + I_N(t)\right]$$

$$\times e_{\ominus(-a_N)}(\sigma(t), 0). \tag{15}$$

Integrating both sides of the above equalities from t to $t + \omega$ and using $X_P(t + \omega) = X_P(t)$ and $X_N(t + \omega) = X_N(t)$, we have

$$
X_P(t) = \int_t^{t+\omega} \Big[\big[k_P(s) - r_P(s) X_P(s) \big]
$$
$$
\times G \big[w_P^1(s) X_P(s - \tau_P(s))
$$
$$
- w_N^1(s) X_N(s - \tau_N(s)) + I_P(s) \big] \Big]
$$
$$
\times \frac{e_{\Theta(-a_P)}(\sigma(s), 0)}{e_{\Theta(-a_P)}(t + \omega, 0) - e_{\Theta(-a_P)}(t, 0)} \Delta s
$$
$$
= \int_t^{t+\omega} \Big[\big[k_P(s) - r_P(s) X_P(s) \big]
$$
$$
\times G \big[w_P^1(s) X_P(s - \tau_P(s))
$$
$$
- w_N^1(s) X_N(s - \tau_N(s)) + I_P(s) \big] \Big]
$$
$$
\times \frac{e_{\Theta(-a_P)}(\sigma(s), t)}{e_{\Theta(-a_P)}(t + \omega, t) - 1} \Delta s,
$$
$$
X_N(t) = \int_t^{t+\omega} \Big[\big[k_N(s) - r_N(s) X_N(s) \big]
$$
$$
\times G \big[w_P^2(s) X_P(s - \tau_P(s))
$$
$$
- w_N^2(s) X_N(s - \tau_N(s)) + I_N(s) \big] \Big]
$$
$$
\times \frac{e_{\Theta(-a_N)}(\sigma(s), 0)}{e_{\Theta(-a_N)}(t + \omega, 0) - e_{\Theta(-a_N)}(t, 0)} \Delta s
$$
$$
= \int_t^{t+\omega} \Big[\big[k_N(s) - r_N(s) X_N(s) \big]
$$
$$
\times G \big[w_P^2(s) X_P(s - \tau_P(s))
$$
$$
- w_N^2(s) X_N(s - \tau_N(s)) + I_N(s) \big] \Big]
$$
$$
\times \frac{e_{\Theta(-a_N)}(\sigma(s), t)}{e_{\Theta(-a_N)}(t + \omega, t) - 1} \Delta s. \tag{16}
$$

Since

$$
\frac{e_{\Theta(-a_P)}(s, t)}{1 - \mu(s) a_P(s)} = e_{\Theta(-a_P)}(\sigma(s), t),
$$
$$
\frac{e_{\Theta(-a_N)}(s, t)}{1 - \mu(s) a_N(s)} = e_{\Theta(-a_N)}(\sigma(s), t) \tag{17}
$$

and $a_P(t + \omega) = a_P(t)$, $a_N(t + \omega) = a_N(t)$, we obtain that

$$
X_P(t) = \frac{1}{e_{\Theta(-a_P)}(\omega, 0) - 1}
$$
$$
\times \int_t^{t+\omega} \frac{e_{\Theta(-a_P)}(s, t)}{1 - \mu(s) a_P(s)} \big[k_P(s) - r_P(s) X_P(s) \big]
$$
$$
\times G \big[w_P^1(s) X_P(s - \tau_P(s))
$$
$$
- w_N^1(s) X_N(s - \tau_N(s)) + I_P(s) \big] \Delta s,
$$

$$
X_N(t) = \frac{1}{e_{\Theta(-a_N)}(\omega, 0) - 1}
$$
$$
\times \int_t^{t+\omega} \frac{e_{\Theta(-a_N)}(s, t)}{1 - \mu(s) a_N(s)} \big[k_N(s) - r_N(s) X_N(s) \big]
$$
$$
\times G \big[w_P^2(s) X_P(s - \tau_P(s))
$$
$$
- w_N^2(s) X_N(s - \tau_N(s)) + I_N(s) \big] \Delta s. \tag{18}
$$

The proof is completed. $\qquad\square$

3. Main Results

In this section, we prove the existence and uniqueness of the periodic solution to (1).

Theorem 12. *Suppose* (A_1)-(A_2) *hold and* $\max\{\alpha, W\} < 1$. *Then* (1) *has a unique* ω-*periodic solution, where*

$$
\alpha_1 := \frac{\omega \exp\left(\int_0^\omega \left| \xi_{\mu(\tau)} \ominus (-a_P(\tau)) \right| \Delta\tau \right) (K + R\beta + RM/W)}{\left| e_{\Theta(-a_P)}(\omega, 0) - 1 \right| \left(1 - \overline{a_P}\, \overline{\mu} \right)},
$$

$$
\alpha_2 := \frac{\omega \exp\left(\int_0^\omega \left| \xi_{\mu(\tau)} \ominus (-a_N(\tau)) \right| \Delta\tau \right) (K + R\beta + RM/W)}{\left| e_{\Theta(-a_N)}(\omega, 0) - 1 \right| \left(1 - \overline{a_P}\, \overline{\mu} \right)}, \tag{19}
$$

and $\alpha := \max\{\alpha_1, \alpha_2\}$.

Proof. Let $\mathbb{X} = \{Z(t) = (z_P(t), z_N(t)) \mid Z \in C_{rd}(\mathbb{T}, \mathbb{R}^2), Z(t + \omega) = Z(t)\}$ with the norm $\|Z\| = \sup_{t \in \mathbb{T}}\{|z_P(t)| + |z_N(t)|\}$; then $\mathbb{X}$ is a Banach space [14]. Define

$$
\mathscr{F} : \mathbb{X} \longrightarrow \mathbb{X}, \quad (\mathscr{F}Z)(t) = \left((\mathscr{F}Z)_P(t), (\mathscr{F}Z)_N(t) \right), \tag{20}
$$

where $Z(t) = (z_P(t), z_N(t)) \in \mathbb{X}$ and

$$
(\mathscr{F}Z)_P(t) = \frac{1}{e_{\Theta(-a_P)}(\omega, 0) - 1}
$$
$$
\times \int_t^{t+\omega} \frac{e_{\Theta(-a_P)}(s, t)}{1 - \mu(s) a_P(s)} \big[k_P(s) - r_P(s) z_P(s) \big]
$$
$$
\times G \big[w_P^1(s) z_P(s - \tau_P(s))
$$
$$
- w_N^1(s) z_N(s - \tau_N(s)) + I_P(s) \big] \Delta s,
$$

$$
(\mathscr{F}Z)_N(t) = \frac{1}{e_{\Theta(-a_N)}(\omega, 0) - 1}
$$
$$
\times \int_t^{t+\omega} \frac{e_{\Theta(-a_N)}(s, t)}{1 - \mu(s) a_N(s)} \big[k_N(s) - r_N(s) z_N(s) \big]
$$
$$
\times G \big[w_P^2(s) z_P(s - \tau_P(s))
$$
$$
- w_N^2(s) z_N(s - \tau_N(s)) + I_N(s) \big] \Delta s \tag{21}
$$

for $t \in \mathbb{T}$. Note that

$$e_{\Theta(-a_P)}(s,t) = e^{\int_t^s \xi_{\mu(\tau)}(\Theta(-a_P)(\tau))\Delta\tau}$$

$$\leq e^{\int_t^{t+\omega} |\xi_{\mu(\tau)}(\Theta(-a_P)(\tau))|\Delta\tau} \qquad (22)$$

$$= e^{\int_0^\omega |\xi_{\mu(\tau)}(\Theta(-a_P)(\tau))|\Delta\tau}.$$

Let $\Omega = \{Z(t) \mid Z \in \mathbb{X}, \|Z\| \leq I/(1-W)\}$ and $\beta := I/(1-W)$. Obviously, Ω is a closed nonempty subset of $\mathbb{X}$. Firstly, we prove that the mapping $\mathscr{F}$ maps Ω into itself. In fact, for any $Z(t) \in \Omega$, we have

$$\left|(\mathscr{F}Z)_P(t)\right|$$

$$= \left| \frac{1}{e_{\Theta(-a_P)}(\omega,0) - 1} \right.$$

$$\times \int_t^{t+\omega} \frac{e_{\Theta(-a_P)}(s,t)}{1 - \mu(s)a_P(s)} [k_P(s) - r_P(s)z_P(s)]$$

$$\times G\left[w_P^1(s)z_P(s - \tau_P(s))\right.$$

$$\left. -w_N^1(s)z_N(s - \tau_N(s)) + I_P(s)\right] \Delta s \Bigg|$$

$$\leq \frac{\exp\left(\int_0^\omega \left|\xi_{\mu(\tau)}(\Theta(-a_P)(\tau))\right|\Delta\tau\right)}{\left|e_{\Theta(-a_P)}(\omega,0) - 1\right|(1 - \overline{a_P}\,\overline{\mu})}$$

$$\times \int_t^{t+\omega} \Big| [k_P(s) - r_P(s)z_P(s)]$$

$$\times G\left[w_P^1(s)z_P(s - \tau_P(s))\right.$$

$$\left. -w_N^1(s)z_N(s - \tau_N(s)) + I_P(s)\right] \Delta s \Big|$$

$$\leq \frac{\exp\left(\int_0^\omega \left|\xi_{\mu(\tau)}(\Theta(-a_P)(\tau))\right|\Delta\tau\right)(K + R\beta)}{\left|e_{\Theta(-a_P)}(\omega,0) - 1\right|(1 - \overline{a_P}\,\overline{\mu})}$$

$$\times \int_t^{t+\omega} \left|[Wz_P(s - \tau_P(s)) + Wz_N(s - \tau_N(s)) + I]\right| \Delta s$$

$$\leq \alpha_1\left(I + W\sup_{t \in \mathbb{T}}(|z_P(t)| + |z_N(t)|)\right). \qquad (23)$$

Similarly, we have

$$\left|(\mathscr{F}Z)_N(t)\right|$$

$$= \left| \frac{1}{e_{\Theta(-a_N)}(\omega,0) - 1} \right.$$

$$\times \int_t^{t+\omega} \frac{e_{\Theta(-a_N)}(s,t)}{1 - \mu(s)a_N(s)} [k_N(s) - r_N(s)z_P(s)]$$

$$\times G\left[w_P^2(s)z_N(s - \tau_P(s))\right.$$

$$\left. -w_N^2(s)z_N(s - \tau_N(s)) + I_N(s)\right] \Delta s \Bigg|$$

$$\leq \alpha_2\left(I + W\sup_{t \in \mathbb{T}}(|z_P(t)| + |z_N(t)|)\right). \qquad (24)$$

It follows from (23) and (24) that

$$\|\mathscr{F}Z\| \leq \alpha I + \alpha W\|Z\| \leq \frac{I}{1 - W}. \qquad (25)$$

Hence, $\mathscr{F}Z \in \Omega$.

Next, we prove that $\mathscr{F}$ is a contraction mapping. For any $Z(t) = (z_P(t), z_N(t)) \in \Omega$, $Z'(t) = (z_P'(t), z_N'(t)) \in \Omega$, we have

$$\left|(\mathscr{F}Z)_P(t) - (\mathscr{F}Z')_P(t)\right|$$

$$= \left| \frac{1}{e_{\Theta(-a_P)}(\omega,0) - 1} \right.$$

$$\times \int_t^{t+\omega} \frac{e_{\Theta(-a_P)}(s,t)}{1 - \mu(s)a_P(s)} [k_P(s) - r_P(s)z_P(s)]$$

$$\times G\left[w_P^1(s)z_P(s - \tau_P(s))\right.$$

$$\left. -w_N^1(s)z_N(s - \tau_N(s)) + I_P(s)\right] \Delta s$$

$$- \frac{1}{e_{\Theta(-a_P)}(\omega,0) - 1}$$

$$\times \int_t^{t+\omega} \frac{e_{\Theta(-a_P)}(s,t)}{1 - \mu(s)a_P(s)} [k_P(s) - r_P(s)z_P'(s)]$$

$$\times G\left[w_P^1(s)z_P'(s - \tau_P(s))\right.$$

$$\left. -w_N^1(s)z_N'(s - \tau_N(s)) + I_P(s)\right] \Delta s \Bigg|$$

$$\leq \frac{\exp\left(\int_0^\omega \left|\xi_{\mu(\tau)}(\Theta(-a_P)(\tau))\right|\Delta\tau\right)(KW + RW\beta + RM)}{\left|e_{\Theta(-a_P)}(\omega,0) - 1\right|(1 - \overline{a_P\mu})}$$

$$\times \int_t^{t+\omega} \Big|z_P(s - \tau_P(s)) - z_P'(s - \tau_P(s)) + z_N(s - \tau_N(s))$$

$$-z_N'(s - \tau_N(s))\Big| \Delta s$$

$$\leq \alpha_1 W\sup_{t \in \mathbb{T}}\left[|z_P(t) - z_P'(t)| + |z_N(t) - z_N'(t)|\right]. \qquad (26)$$

Similarly, we have

$$\left|(\mathscr{F}Z)_N(t) - (\mathscr{F}Z')_N(t)\right|$$

$$= \left| \frac{1}{e_{\Theta(-a_N)}(\omega,0) - 1} \right.$$

$$\times \int_t^{t+\omega} \frac{e_{\Theta(-a_N)}(s,t)}{1 - \mu(s)a_N(s)} [k_N(s) - r_N(s)z_N(s)]$$

$$\times G\left[w_P^2(s)z_P(s - \tau_P(s))\right.$$

$$\left. -w_N^2(s)z_N(s - \tau_N(s)) + I_N(s)\right] \Delta s$$

$$-\frac{1}{e_{\Theta(-a_N)}(\omega, 0) - 1}$$

$$\times \int_t^{t+\omega} \frac{e_{\Theta(-a_N)}(s,t)}{1 - \mu(s) a_N(s)} \left[k_N(s) - r_N(s) z_N'(s) \right]$$

$$\times G \left[w_P^2(s) z_P'(s - \tau_P(s)) \right.$$

$$\left. - w_N^2(s) z_N'(s - \tau_N(s)) + I_N(s) \right] \Delta s \Big|$$

$$\le \alpha_2 W \sup_{t \in \mathbb{T}} \left[\left| z_P(t) - z_P'(t) \right| + \left| z_N(t) - z_N'(t) \right| \right].$$

$$(27)$$

From (26) and (27), we can get

$$\left\| (\mathscr{F} Z) - \left(\mathscr{F} Z' \right) \right\| \le \alpha W \left\| Z - Z' \right\|. \qquad (28)$$

Note that $\alpha W < 1$. Thus, $\mathscr{F}$ is a contraction mapping. By the fixed point theorem in the Banach space, $\mathscr{F}$ possesses a unique fixed point. The proof is completed. $\qquad \square$

Theorem 13. *Under the conditions of Theorem 12, suppose further the following.*

(A_3) *There exist some constants $\epsilon > 0$, $\xi > 0$, $\xi' > 0$ such that*

$$\left(1 + \frac{\xi'}{\xi} \right) \frac{(1 + \epsilon \mu(t + \tau_0))(K + R\beta) W}{(\underline{a_P} - RM)(1 + \epsilon \mu(t)) - \epsilon} e_\epsilon(t + \tau_0, t) < 1,$$

$$\left(1 + \frac{\xi}{\xi'} \right) \frac{(1 + \epsilon \mu(t + \tau_0))(K + R\beta) W}{(\underline{a_N} - RM)(1 + \epsilon \mu(t)) - \epsilon} e_\epsilon(t + \tau_0, t) < 1;$$

$$(29)$$

then the periodic solution of (1) is globally exponentially stable.

Proof. It follows from Theorem 12 that (1) has an ω-periodic solution $Z^* = (X_P^*(t), X_N^*(t))^\top$.

Let $Z(t) = (X_P(t), X_N(t))^\top$ be any solution of (1); then we have

$$(X_P(t) - X_P^*(t))^\Delta$$

$$= -a_P(t) (X_P(t) - X_P^*(t))$$

$$+ k_P(t) G \left[w_P^1(t) X_P(t - \tau_P(t)) \right.$$

$$\left. - w_N^1(t) X_N(t - \tau_N(t)) + I_P(t) \right]$$

$$- k_P(t) G \left[w_P^1(t) X_P^*(t - \tau_P(t)) \right.$$

$$\left. - w_N^1(t) X_N^*(t - \tau_N(t)) + I_P(t) \right]$$

$$- r_P(t) X_P(t) G \left[w_P^1(t) X_P(t - \tau_P(t)) \right.$$

$$\left. - w_N^1(t) X_N(t - \tau_N(t)) + I_P(t) \right]$$

$$+ r_P(t) X_P^*(t) G \left[w_P^1(t) X_P^*(t - \tau_P(t)) \right.$$

$$\left. - w_N^1(t) X_N^*(t - \tau_N(t)) + I_P(t) \right],$$

$$(X_N(t) - X_N^*(t))^\Delta$$

$$= -a_N(t) (X_N(t) - X_N^*(t))$$

$$+ k_N(t) G \left[w_P^2(t) X_P(t - \tau_P(t)) \right.$$

$$\left. - w_N^2(t) X_N(t - \tau_N(t)) + I_N(t) \right]$$

$$- k_N(t) G \left[w_P^2(t) X_P^*(t - \tau_P(t)) \right.$$

$$\left. - w_N^2(t) X_N^*(t - \tau_N(t)) + I_N(t) \right]$$

$$- r_N(t) X_N(t) G \left[w_P^2(t) X_P(t - \tau_P(t)) \right.$$

$$\left. - w_N^2(t) X_N(t - \tau_N(t)) + I_N(t) \right]$$

$$+ r_N(t) X_N^*(t) G \left[w_P^2(t) X_P^*(t - \tau_P(t)) \right.$$

$$\left. - w_N^2(t) X_N^*(t - \tau_N(t)) + I_N(t) \right],$$

$$(30)$$

which leads to

$$D^+ |X_P(t) - X_P^*(t)|^\Delta$$

$$\le - \left(\underline{a_P} - RM \right) |X_P(t) - X_P^*(t)| + (K + R\beta) W$$

$$\times \left(|X_P(t - \tau_0) - X_P^*(t - \tau_0)| \right.$$

$$\left. + |X_N(t - \tau_0) - X_N^*(t - \tau_0)| \right),$$

$$D^+ |X_N(t) - X_N^*(t)|^\Delta$$

$$\le - \left(\underline{a_N} - RM \right) |X_N(t) - X_N^*(t)| + (K + R\beta) W$$

$$\times \left(|X_P(t - \tau_0) - X_P^*(t - \tau_0)| \right.$$

$$\left. + |X_N(t - \tau_0) - X_N^*(t - \tau_0)| \right).$$

$$(31)$$

For any $\alpha \in [-\tau_0, 0]_{\mathbb{T}}$, construct the Lyapunov functional $V(t) = V_1(t) + V_2(t) + V_3(t) + V_4(t)$, where

$$V_1(t) = \xi e_\epsilon(t, \alpha) |X_P(t) - X_P^*(t)|,$$

$$V_3(t) = \xi' e_\epsilon(t, \alpha) |X_N(t) - X_N^*(t)|,$$

$$V_2(t) = \xi \int_{t-\tau_0}^t (1 + \epsilon \mu(s + \tau_0)) e_\epsilon(s + \tau_0, \alpha)(K + R\beta) W$$

$$\times (|X_P(s) - X_P^*(s)| + |X_N(s) - X_N^*(s)|) \Delta s,$$

$$V_4(t) = \xi' \int_{t-\tau_0}^t (1 + \epsilon \mu(s + \tau_0)) e_\epsilon(s + \tau_0, \alpha)(K + R\beta) W$$

$$\times (|X_P(s) - X_P^*(s)| + |X_N(s) - X_N^*(s)|) \Delta s.$$

$$(32)$$

Calculating $D^+V(t)^\Delta$ along (1), we can get

$$D^+V_1(t)^\Delta\Big|_{(1)}$$

$$\leq \xi\left[\epsilon e_\epsilon(t,\alpha)\left|X_P(t)-X_P^*(t)\right|\right.$$

$$\left.+e_\epsilon(\sigma(t),\alpha)D^+\left|X_P(t)-X_P^*(t)\right|^\Delta\right]$$

$$\leq \xi\left\{\epsilon e_\epsilon(t,\alpha)\left|X_P(t)-X_P^*(t)\right|+e_\epsilon(\sigma(t),\alpha)\right.$$

$$\times\left[-\left(\underline{a_P}-RM\right)\left|X_P(t)-X_P^*(t)\right|+(K+R\beta)W\right.$$

$$\times\left(\left|X_P(t-\tau_0)-X_P^*(t-\tau_0)\right|\right.$$

$$\left.\left.\left.+\left|X_N(t-\tau_0)-X_N^*(t-\tau_0)\right|\right)\right]\right\}$$

$$=\xi\left[\epsilon-\left(\underline{a_P}-RM\right)(1+\epsilon\mu(t))\right]e_\epsilon(t,\alpha)\left|X_P(t)-X_P^*(t)\right|$$

$$+\xi(1+\epsilon\mu(t))e_\epsilon(t,\alpha)(K+R\beta)W$$

$$\times\left(\left|X_P(t-\tau_0)-X_P^*(t-\tau_0)\right|\right.$$

$$\left.+\left|X_N(t-\tau_0)-X_N^*(t-\tau_0)\right|\right),$$

$$D^+V_2(t)^\Delta\Big|_{(1)}$$

$$\leq \xi(1+\epsilon\mu(t+\tau_0))e_\epsilon(t+\tau_0,\alpha)(K+R\beta)W$$

$$\times\left(\left|X_P(t)-X_P^*(t)\right|+\left|X_N(t)-X_N^*(t)\right|\right)$$

$$-\xi(1+\epsilon\mu(t))e_\epsilon(t,\alpha)(K+R\beta)W$$

$$\times\left(\left|X_P(t-\tau_0)-X_P^*(t-\tau_0)\right|\right.$$

$$\left.+\left|X_N(t-\tau_0)-X_N^*(t-\tau_0)\right|\right),$$

$$(33)$$

which leads to

$$D^+\left(V_1(t)+V_2(t)\right)^\Delta\Big|_{(1)}$$

$$\leq \xi\left[\epsilon-\left(\underline{a_P}-RM\right)(1+\epsilon\mu(t))\right]$$

$$\times e_\epsilon(t,\alpha)\left|X_P(t)-X_P^*(t)\right|$$

$$+\xi(1+\epsilon\mu(t+\tau_0))e_\epsilon(t+\tau_0,\alpha)(K+R\beta)W \qquad(34)$$

$$\times\left(\left|X_P(t)-X_P^*(t)\right|\right)$$

$$+\xi(1+\epsilon\mu(t+\tau_0))e_\epsilon(t+\tau_0,\alpha)(K+R\beta)W$$

$$\times\left(\left|X_N(t)-X_N^*(t)\right|\right).$$

Note that

$$D^+V_3(t)^\Delta\Big|_{(1)}$$

$$\leq \xi'\left[\epsilon-\left(\underline{a_N}-RM\right)(1+\epsilon\mu(t))\right]e_\epsilon(t,\alpha)$$

$$\times\left|X_N(t)-X_N^*(t)\right|+\xi'(1+\epsilon\mu(t))e_\epsilon(t,\alpha)(K+R\beta)$$

$$\times W\times\left(\left|X_P(t-\tau_0)-X_P^*(t-\tau_0)\right|\right.$$

$$\left.+\left|X_N(t-\tau_0)-X_N^*(t-\tau_0)\right|\right),$$

$$D^+V_4(t)^\Delta\Big|_{(1)}$$

$$\leq \xi'(1+\epsilon\mu(t+\tau_0))e_\epsilon(t+\tau_0,\alpha)(K+R\beta)W$$

$$\times\left(\left|X_P(t)-X_P^*(t)\right|+\left|X_N(t)-X_N^*(t)\right|\right)$$

$$-\xi'(1+\epsilon\mu(t))e_\epsilon(t,\alpha)(K+R\beta)W$$

$$\times\left(\left|X_P(t-\tau_0)-X_P^*(t-\tau_0)\right|\right.$$

$$\left.+\left|X_N(t-\tau_0)-X_N^*(t-\tau_0)\right|\right).$$

$$(35)$$

We have

$$D^+\left(V_3(t)+V_4(t)\right)^\Delta\Big|_{(1)}$$

$$\leq \xi'\left[\epsilon-\left(\underline{a_N}-RM\right)(1+\epsilon\mu(t))\right]$$

$$\times e_\epsilon(t,\alpha)\left|X_N(t)-X_N^*(t)\right|$$

$$+\xi'(1+\epsilon\mu(t+\tau_0))e_\epsilon(t+\tau_0,\alpha)(K+R\beta)W$$

$$\times\left(\left|X_N(t)-X_N^*(t)\right|\right)+\xi'(1+\epsilon\mu(t+\tau_0))$$

$$\times e_\epsilon(t+\tau_0,\alpha)(K+R\beta)W\left(\left|X_P(t)-X_P^*(t)\right|\right).$$

$$(36)$$

From (34) and (36), we can get

$$D^+V(t)^\Delta\Big|_{(1)}$$

$$\leq\left\{\xi\left[\epsilon-\left(\underline{a_P}-RM\right)(1+\epsilon\mu(t))\right]\right.$$

$$\left.+\left(\xi+\xi'\right)(1+\epsilon\mu(t+\tau_0))e_\epsilon(t+\tau_0,t)(K+\beta R)W\right\}$$

$$\times e_\epsilon(t,\alpha)\left|X_P(t)-X_P^*(t)\right|$$

$$+\left\{\xi'\left[\epsilon-\left(\underline{a_N}-RM\right)(1+\epsilon\mu(t))\right]+\left(\xi+\xi'\right)\right.$$

$$\left.\times(1+\epsilon\mu(t+\tau_0))e_\epsilon(t+\tau_0,t)(K+\beta R)W\right\}$$

$$\times e_\epsilon(t,\alpha)\left|X_N(t)-X_N^*(t)\right|.$$

$$(37)$$

By assumption (A_3), it follows that $V(t)\leq V(0)$ for $t\in\mathbb{T}^+$. On the other hand, we have

$$V(0)\leq\left[\xi e_\epsilon(0,\alpha)+\left(\xi+\xi'\right)\right.$$

$$\left.\times\int_{-\tau_0}^0(1+\epsilon\mu(s+\tau_0))e_\epsilon(s+\tau_0,\alpha)(K+\beta R)W\Delta s\right]$$

$$\times\sup_{s\in[-\tau_0,0]_\mathbb{T}}\left|X_P(s)-X_P^*(s)\right|$$

$$+ \left[\xi' e_\epsilon (0, \alpha) + \left(\xi + \xi' \right) \right.$$

$$\left. \times \int_{-\tau_0}^0 \left(1 + \epsilon \mu (s + \tau_0) \right) e_\epsilon (s + \tau_0, \alpha) (K + \beta R) W \Delta s \right]$$

$$\times \sup_{s \in [-\tau_0, 0]_{\mathbb{T}}} |X_N (s) - X_N^* (s)|$$

$$= \Gamma (\epsilon) \left(\sup_{s \in [-\tau_0, 0]_{\mathbb{T}}} |X_P (s) - X_P^* (s)| \right.$$

$$\left. + \sup_{s \in [-\tau_0, 0]_{\mathbb{T}}} |X_N (s) - X_N^* (s)| \right),$$

$$(38)$$

where $\Gamma (\epsilon) = \max\{\Delta_1, \Delta_2\}$,

$$\Delta_1 = \xi e_\epsilon (0, \alpha) + \left(\xi + \xi' \right)$$

$$\times \int_{-\tau_0}^0 \left(1 + \epsilon \mu (s + \tau_0) \right) e_\epsilon (s + \tau_0, \alpha) (K + \beta R) W \Delta s,$$

$$\Delta_2 = \xi' e_\epsilon (0, \alpha) + \left(\xi + \xi' \right)$$

$$\times \int_{-\tau_0}^0 \left(1 + \epsilon \mu (s + \tau_0) \right) e_\epsilon (s + \tau_0, \alpha) (K + \beta R) W \Delta s.$$

$$(39)$$

It is obvious that

$$\xi e_\epsilon (t, \alpha) |X_P (t) - X_P^* (t)| + \xi' e_\epsilon (t, \alpha) |X_N (t) - X_N^* (t)|$$

$$\leq V (t) \leq V (0),$$

$$(40)$$

which means that

$$\min \left\{ \xi, \xi' \right\} e_\epsilon (t, \alpha) \left(|X_P (t) - X_P^* (t)| + |X_N (t) - X_N^* (t)| \right)$$

$$\leq V (0).$$

$$(41)$$

Thus, we finally get

$$|X_P (t) - X_P^* (t)| + |X_N (t) - X_N^* (t)|$$

$$\leq \frac{\Gamma (\epsilon) e_{\ominus \epsilon} (t, \alpha)}{\min \left\{ \xi, \xi' \right\}} \times \left(\sup_{s \in [-\tau_0, 0]_{\mathbb{T}}} |X_P (s) - X_P^* (s)| \right.$$

$$\left. + \sup_{s \in [-\tau_0, 0]_{\mathbb{T}}} |X_N (s) - X_N^* (s)| \right).$$

$$(42)$$

Therefore, the unique periodic solution of (1) is globally exponentially stable. The proof is completed. □

4. Examples

In this section, two numerical examples are shown to verify the effectiveness of the result obtained in the previous section.

Consider the following Wilson-Cowan neural network with delays on time scale $\mathbb{T}$:

$$X_P^\Delta (t)$$

$$= -a_P (t) X_P (t) + [k_P (t) - r_P (t) X_P (t)]$$

$$\times G \left[w_P^1 (t) X_P (t - 2) - w_N^1 (t) X_N (t - 1) + I_P (t) \right],$$

$$X_N^\Delta (t)$$

$$= -a_N (t) X_N (t) + [k_N (t) - r_N (t) X_N (t)]$$

$$\times G \left[w_P^2 (t) X_P (t - 2) - w_N^2 (t) X_N (t - 1) + I_N (t) \right].$$

$$(43)$$

Case 1. Consider $\mathbb{T} = \mathbb{R}$. Take $(a_P(t), a_N(t))^\top = (2+\sin(t), 2+\cos(t))^\top$. Obviously, $\underline{a_P} = \underline{a_N} = 1$,

$$\frac{\exp \left(\int_0^{2\pi} a_P (s) \, ds \right)}{\exp \left(\int_0^{2\pi} a_P (s) \, ds \right) - 1} = \frac{e^{4\pi}}{e^{4\pi} - 1},$$

$$\frac{\exp \left(\int_0^{2\pi} a_N (s) \, ds \right)}{\exp \left(\int_0^{2\pi} a_N (s) \, ds \right) - 1} = \frac{e^{4\pi}}{e^{4\pi} - 1}.$$

$$(44)$$

Take $(I_P(t), I_N(t))^\top = (-1 + \sin(t), \cos(t))^\top$, $k_P(t) = k_N(t) = r_P(t) = r_N(t) = 0.01$, $w_P^1(t) = w_N^1(t) = w_P^2(t) = w_N^2(t) = 0.1$, and $G(x) = (1/2)(|x + 1| - |x - 1|)$. We have $L = 1$. Let $\xi = 1$, $\xi' = 2$. One can easily verify that

$$\alpha_1 = \omega \left(K + R\beta + \frac{RM}{W} \right) \frac{\exp \left(\int_0^{2\pi} a_P (s) \, ds \right)}{\exp \left(\int_0^{2\pi} a_P (s) \, ds \right) - 1}$$

$$\approx 0.831 < 1,$$

$$\alpha_2 = \omega \left(K + R\beta + \frac{RM}{W} \right) \frac{\exp \left(\int_0^{2\pi} a_N (s) \, ds \right)}{\exp \left(\int_0^{2\pi} a_N (s) \, ds \right) - 1}$$

$$(45)$$

$$\approx 0.831 < 1,$$

$$-\xi \left(\underline{a_P} - RM \right) + \left(\xi + \xi' \right) (K + \beta R) W \approx -0.980 < 0,$$

$$-\xi' \left(\underline{a_N} - RM \right) + \left(\xi + \xi' \right) (K + \beta R) W \approx -1.970 < 0.$$

It follows from Theorems 12 and 13 that (43) has a unique 2π-periodic solution which is globally exponentially stable (see Figure 1).

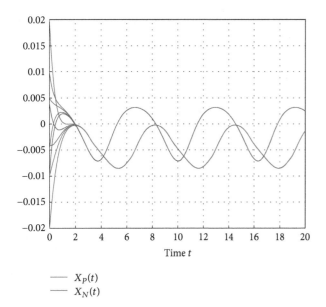

FIGURE 1: Globally exponentially stable periodic solution of (43).

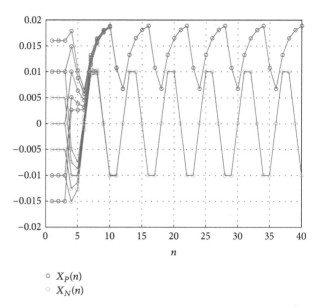

FIGURE 2: Globally exponentially stable periodic solution of (46).

Case 2. Consider $\mathbb{T} = \mathbb{Z}$. Equation (43) reduces to the following difference equation:

$$X_P(n+1) - X_P(n)$$
$$= -a_P(n)X_P(n) + [k_P(n) - r_P(n)X_P(n)]$$
$$\times G[w_P^1(n)X_P(n-2)$$
$$- w_N^1(n)X_N(n-1) + I_P(n)],$$

$$X_N(n+1) - X_N(n)$$
$$= -a_N(n)X_N(n) + [k_N(n) - r_N(n)X_N(n)]$$
$$\times G[w_P^2(n)X_P(n-2) - w_N^2(n)X_N(n-1) + I_N(n)],$$

$$(46)$$

for $n \in \mathbb{Z}_0^+$. Take $(a_P(n), a_N(n))^\top = (1/2, 1/2)^\top$. Obviously, $\underline{a_P} = \underline{a_N} = 1/2$, $\overline{a_P} = \overline{a_N} = 1/2$, $(I_P(t), I_N(t))^\top = (1 + \sin(n\pi/3), \cos(n\pi/3))^\top$, $k_P(t) = k_N(t) = r_P(t) = r_N(t) = 0.01$, $w_P^1(t) = w_N^1(t) = w_P^2(t) = w_N^2(t) = 0.1$, and $G(x) = (1/2)(|x + 1| - |x - 1|)$. We have $L = 1$. Let $\xi = 1$, $\xi' = 2$. If $\mathbb{T} = \mathbb{Z}$, $(\mu(t) = 1)$, choosing $\omega = 6$, by simple calculation, we have

$$\alpha_1$$
$$= \left(K + R\beta + \frac{RM}{W}\right)$$
$$\times \frac{\omega \left|1 - \prod_{k=1}^{\omega-1}(1 - a_P(k))\right| \exp\left(\sum_{k=0}^{\omega-1} |\text{Log}(1 - a_P(k))|\right)}{\left|\prod_{k=1}^{\omega-1}(1 - a_P(k))\right|(1 - \overline{a_P})}$$
$$\approx 0.015 < 1,$$

$$\alpha_2$$
$$= \left(K + R\beta + \frac{RM}{W}\right)$$
$$\times \frac{\omega \left|1 - \prod_{k=1}^{\omega-1}(1 - a_N(k))\right| \exp\left(\sum_{k=0}^{\omega-1} |\text{Log}(1 - a_N(k))|\right)}{\left|\prod_{k=1}^{\omega-1}(1 - a_N(k))\right|(1 - \overline{a_N})}$$
$$\approx 0.015 < 1,$$

$$-\xi\left(\underline{a_P} - RM\right) + \left(\xi + \xi'\right)(K + \beta R)W \approx -0.480 < 0,$$

$$-\xi'\left(\underline{a_N} - RM\right) + \left(\xi + \xi'\right)(K + \beta R)W \approx -0.970 < 0.$$
$$(47)$$

It follows from Theorems 12 and 13 that (46) has a unique 6-periodic solution which is globally exponentially stable (see Figure 2).

5. Conclusion Remarks

In this paper, we studied the stability of delayed Wilson-Cowan networks on periodic time scales and obtained some more generalized results to ensure the existence, uniqueness, and global exponential stability of the periodic solution. These results can give a significant insight into the complex dynamical structure of Wilson-Cowan type model. The conditions are easily checked in practice by simple algebraic methods.

Conflict of Interests

The authors declare that there is no conflict of interests regarding the publication of this paper.

Acknowledgments

This research was supported by the National Natural Science Foundation of China (11101187 and 11361010), the Foundation for Young Professors of Jimei University, the Excellent Youth Foundation of Fujian Province (2012J06001 and NCETFJ JA11144), and the Foundation of Fujian Higher Education (JA10184 and JA11154).

References

[1] H. R. Wilson and J. D. Cowan, "Excitatory and inhibitory interactions in localized populations of model neurons," *Biophysical Journal*, vol. 12, no. 1, pp. 1–24, 1972.

[2] H. R. Wilson and J. D. Cowan, "A mathematical theory of the functional dynamics of cortical and thalamic nervous tissue," *Kybernetik*, vol. 13, no. 2, pp. 55–80, 1973.

[3] A. Destexhe and T. J. Sejnowski, "The Wilson-Cowan model, 36 years later," *Biological Cybernetics*, vol. 101, no. 1, pp. 1–2, 2009.

[4] K. Mantere, J. Parkkinen, T. Jaaskelainen, and M. M. Gupta, "Wilson-Cowan neural-network model in image processing," *Journal of Mathematical Imaging and Vision*, vol. 2, no. 2-3, pp. 251–259, 1992.

[5] C. van Vreeswijk and H. Sompolinsky, "Chaos in neuronal networks with balanced excitatory and inhibitory activity," *Science*, vol. 274, no. 5293, pp. 1724–1726, 1996.

[6] L. H. A. Monteiro, M. A. Bussab, and J. G. Berlinck, "Analytical results on a Wilson-Cowan neuronal network modified model," *Journal of Theoretical Biology*, vol. 219, no. 1, pp. 83–91, 2002.

[7] S. Xie and Z. Huang, "Almost periodic solution for Wilson-Cowan type model with time-varying delays," *Discrete Dynamics in Nature and Society*, vol. 2013, Article ID 683091, 7 pages, 2013.

[8] V. W. Noonburg, D. Benardete, and B. Pollina, "A periodically forced Wilson-Cowan system," *SIAM Journal on Applied Mathematics*, vol. 63, no. 5, pp. 1585–1603, 2003.

[9] S. Hilger, "Analynis on measure chains-a unified approach to continuous and discrete calculus," *Results in Mathematics*, vol. 18, pp. 18–56, 1990.

[10] S. Hilger, "Differential and difference calculus—unified!," *Nonlinear Analysis: Theory, Methods & Applications*, vol. 30, no. 5, pp. 2683–2694, 1997.

[11] A. Chen and F. Chen, "Periodic solution to BAM neural network with delays on time scales," *Neurocomputing*, vol. 73, no. 1-3, pp. 274–282, 2009.

[12] Y. Li, X. Chen, and L. Zhao, "Stability and existence of periodic solutions to delayed Cohen-Grossberg BAM neural networks with impulses on time scales," *Neurocomputing*, vol. 72, no. 7-9, pp. 1621–1630, 2009.

[13] Z. Huang, Y. N. Raffoul, and C. Cheng, "Scale-limited activating sets and multiperiodicity for threshold-linear networks on time scales," *IEEE Transactions on Cybernetics*, vol. 44, no. 4, pp. 488–499, 2014.

[14] M. Bohner and A. Peterson, *Dynamic Equations on Time Scales: An Introduction with Applications*, Birkhäuser, Boston, Mass, USA, 2001.

[15] M. Bohner and A. Peterson, *Advance in Dynamic Equations on Time Scales*, Birkhäuser, Boston, Mass, USA, 2003.

[16] V. Lakshmikantham and A. S. Vatsala, "Hybrid systems on time scales," *Journal of Computational and Applied Mathematics*, vol. 141, no. 1-2, pp. 227–235, 2002.

[17] A. Ruffing and M. Simon, "Corresponding Banach spaces on time scales," *Journal of Computational and Applied Mathematics*, vol. 179, no. 1-2, pp. 313–326, 2005.

10

Intelligent Control for USV Based on Improved Elman Neural Network with TSK Fuzzy

Shang-Jen Chuang, Chiung-Hsing Chen, Chih-Ming Hong, and Guan-Yu Chen

Department of Electronic Communication Engineering, National Kaohsiung Marine University, Kaohsiung 81157, Taiwan

Correspondence should be addressed to Chih-Ming Hong; d943010014@student.nsysu.edu.tw

Academic Editor: António Dourado Pereira Correia

In recent years, based on the rising of global personal safety demand and human resource cost considerations, development of unmanned vehicles to replace manpower requirement to perform high-risk operations is increasing. In order to acquire useful resources under the marine environment, a large boat as an unmanned surface vehicle (USV) was implemented. The USV is equipped with automatic navigation features and a complete substitute artificial manipulation. This USV system for exploring the marine environment has more carrying capacity and that measurement system can also be self-designed through a modular approach in accordance with the needs for various types of environmental conditions. The investigation work becomes more flexible. A catamaran hull is adopted as automatic navigation test with CompactRIO embedded system. Through GPS and direction sensor we not only can know the current location of the boat, but also can calculate the distance with a predetermined position and the angle difference immediately. In this paper, the design of automatic navigation is calculated in accordance with improved Elman neural network (ENN) algorithms. Takagi-Sugeno-Kang (TSK) fuzzy and improved ENN control are applied to adjust required power and steering, which allows the hull to move straight forward to a predetermined target position. The route will be free from outside influence and realize automatic navigation purpose.

1. Introduction

During WWII, there were reported records of unmanned vessels for reducing the damages of vessels as well as injuries and fatality of human. Using small torpedos or larger-sized unmanned ships for collecting information [1], global positioning system (GPS) brings high efficiency through the use of low-cost, unmanned design. There is no need for the concern of pilot's safety in using unmanned vehicles for marine environmental survey.

Vessels for marine environmental survey are usually equipped with USV system. It allows heavier loading capacity. In addition, the design of vessels can be modularized. There is better flexibility for adjustment according to the needs from various types of environments and investigations.

The effective control range of many USV systems varies from 50 meters to 30 kilometers [2, 3], mainly restrained by the wireless transceiver modules. In order to increase the effective working range of USV, a design of unmanned vessels would be necessary. To allow USV systems to be autonavigating and to replace manual operation completely, the autonavigation system is the most needed task for every unmanned carrier.

The Elman neural network (ENN) was first proposed for speech processing. Generally, the ENN can be considered as a special kind of feed-forward neural network with additional memory neurons and local feedback. Because of the context neurons and local recurrent connections between the context layer and the hidden layer, it has certain dynamic advantages over static neural network, such as multilayer perceptrons and radial-basis function networks. It also makes ENN very suitable to be applied in the neurocontrol field. However, the typical ENN cannot approximate high-order dynamic systems closely, and its convergence speed is usually slow and not suitable for time-critical applications. Several kinds of modified ENNs were proposed to overcome such issues

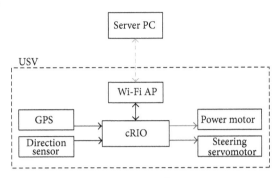

FIGURE 1: System architecture.

to improve the dynamic characteristics and convergence speed of the original ENN [4, 5]. Compared with BP neural network, ENN has many advantages: faster convergence speed, less training iteration, stronger robustness, no local minimum, and so forth. On the other hand, the method of fuzzy inference proposed by Sugeno and Kang [6], which is known as the Takagi-Sugeno-Kang (TSK) model in fuzzy systems literature, has been one of the major topics in theoretical studies and practical applications of fuzzy modeling and control. The basic idea of this method is to decompose the input space into fuzzy regions and to approximate the system in every region by a simple model. The overall fuzzy model is thus considered as a combination of interconnected subsystems with simpler models.

2. Research Methods

The designed vehicle's overall system architecture includes a high precision programmable controller-cRIO as main core, a global satellite positioning receiver developing module (GPS receiver module), a direction sensor, a steering servomotor, and power motor, which are all shown in Figure 1.

2.1. Unmanned Surface Vehicle. The main body of USV in this paper is a catamaran-type boat which was designed and built by students and teacher of Department of Naval Architecture and Ocean Engineering, National Kaohsiung Marine University. This catamaran is 5.27 meters long, 1.74 meters wide, and 1.17 meters high, and the electric motor to drive the power can carry 5~6 passengers.

Using a catamaran design as an USV has the following main features:

(1) sea wave balance performance is better;

(2) low-speed navigation and rotation of the catamaran are better;

(3) it has a flat usable space and is easier to allocate required instruments to conduct measurement work.

The designed USV provides more flexible space to install various equipment (e.g., water quality monitoring meter, fish finder machine, anemometer, wind direction sensor module, etc.), to establish marine environmental data collection. A large solar panel installed on top of the hull can strengthen sailing range.

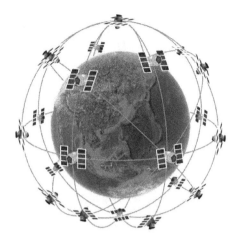

FIGURE 2: Global positioning system [7].

FIGURE 3: GPS receiver.

2.2. Global Positioning System. Global positioning system (GPS) is a combination of satellites and wireless communication technology as shown in Figure 2. GPS is a globalization and all-purpose system which has many important features, like all-weather function, being easy to operate, high economic efficiency of navigation positioning, and timing systems. Its advantages include all-weather function free from any interference, global coverage up to 98%, three-dimensional fixed constant speed precision, time-saving, high efficiency, widely used, versatile, and mobile positioning [10].

In this paper, the GPS receiver used (Figure 3) to receive GPS satellite signals is manufactured by ICP DAS Company, model GT-321R. Using RS-232 serial port, protocol setting as 4800 bps baud rate and 8-N-1 format. The four messages to retrieve mainly including longitude, latitude, speed and time, so NMEA information output format (GPRMC) message was chosen as the designed USV position information in the marine environment and sailing speed.

2.3. Direction Sensor. Direction sensor is called the electronic compass (e-compass), the most suitable range for the Earth's magnetic field detection. DC static magnetic field can be detected; it can detect the magnetic field strength and direction. Earth's magnetic field strength of 0.5 to 0.6 gauss can be simplified as shown in Figure 4 of bipolar magnetic field, which is equivalent along centre of the earth.

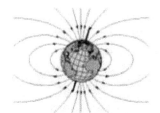

Figure 4: Earth's magnetic field.

Figure 5: Direction sensor [8].

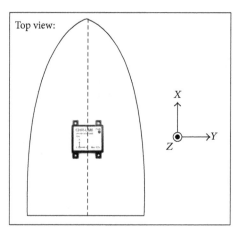

Figure 6: Installation diagram of direction sensor.

Electronic compass pointing along the local magnetic field determines the direction, the direction of the local magnetic north usually. Because the magnetic north and true north are not the same, so the magnetic north and true north are not usually together. The local magnetic variation is called magnetic declination (declination angle). It is a simple description of the magnetic north and geographic north difference between the angles, expressed as easterly or westerly direction.

Electronic compass which suffered all kinds of interference can be broadly divided into two categories.

(1) Hard Iron Interference. Fixed-intensity magnetic interferences, such as sensor surrounding the original electronic parts, such as speakers, microphones, batteries, panels, and metal shield, will release a fixed magnetic force to influence the electronic compass of reading. Calibration must be done to zero.

(2) Soft Iron Interference. It will change the intensity and direction or can distort the magnetic field lines of interfering substances, such as battery electricity consumption changes in the user's environment; surrounding the original electronic parts of interference depends on precision quasi-level specifications to determine the need for correction [11].

The UM6 ultraminiature orientation sensor measuring orientation in all three dimensions at 500 Hz using a combination of rate gyros, accelerometers, and magnetic sensors was applied to monitor sailing direction as shown in Figure 5. The direction sensor was mounted on designed USV and was along with the direction of the boat as shown in Figure 6. Hence, the Earth's magnetic field and USV sailing direction will be identical.

2.4. Controller Core System. Thinking of sea environment, we must pay more attentions to choose a more reliable computer as the unmanned vehicle controller, and the selected controller's capability must meet the basic requirements for the processing speed and vibrations from outside interference. And it must withstand higher temperature ranges. Due to the fact that the complexity of autopilot operation is very high, and the wave on sea level is greater, the calculation ability and processing speed of central controller must be considered.

National instruments' CompactRIO (cRIO) is quite applicable to the previous requirements. The selected cRIO is a programmable automation controller (programmable automation controller, PAC), a low-cost, reconfigurable control, and acquisition system for the need for efficient performance and reliability applications is designed. The system is done through a small, rugged, industrial-grade hot-swappable input and output (input/output) module, not only cRIO to have industrial-grade architecture, but also can be placed in the factory or under inclement environment ensure that the system the reliability [12].

In this system, due to the need of external input for receiving control commands,

(1) RS-232 serial transmission (GPS receivers, direction sensors, and left turn servomotor),

(2) DO digital signal output (status display),

(3) AO analog output (power output of the motor for control),

selected interface card must comply with the previous specifications. Three module adapter cards in this optional module for national Instruments' CompactRIO are, respectively, NI-9870, NI-9403, and NI-9263. Each module card into NI-9074 chassis has been shown in Figure 7.

2.5. Steering Mechanism. In this paper, a small boat which can afford 5~6 passengers and has outboard rudder with DC motor as power is adopted as USV main body. In order to achieve unmanned automatic navigation function, a mechanical device must be driven on the steering wheel to take control of sailing direction. Therefore, in this paper Mitsubishi

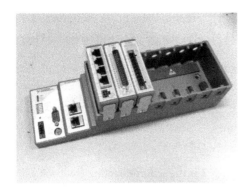

FIGURE 7: cRIO hardware platform.

FIGURE 8: MR-J2S-10A servomotor [9].

MR-J2S-10A servomotor is used to drive, as shown in Figure 8. A servomotor with high precision position control and baud rate of 9600 bps via an RS-232 serial port by way of torque and speed control is adopted in this design.

3. Architecture and Research Method

There are three layers in the system architecture, as shown in Figure 9. The first layer is the user's application interface of the console. It is for perception of voyage information or delivery of mission commands. The second layer is the linking layer for interconnection. This is for data transmission between the two ends, via wireless network stations. The third layer is the system layer—the core of this unmanned autonavigation system. It controls the steering and dynamic of the whole body through precise calculation.

Chi-Chin harbor is the site where testing of autonavigation in this experiment was conducted. The test vessel is a double-hull boat, designed by the department of naval architecture and ocean engineering, and is equipped with a brushless outboard motor as the engine of the vessel. The primary sensing instruments used in the test are GPS and orientation sensor, and cRIO-9074 is used for calculation and justification of the automatic navigation system to control the steering and power-output of the outboard motor. GPS of the autonavigation system is installed on top of the vessel, as

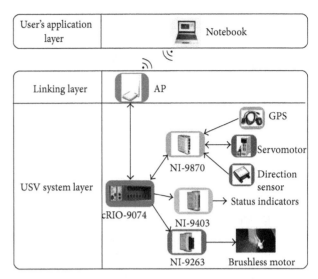

FIGURE 9: Architecture of the unmanned automatic system.

FIGURE 10: Illustration of layout of equipment.

shown in Figure 10. The orientation sensors are installed in front of the cockpit, in line with the orientation of the vessel body.

4. Design of Control Algorithm Based on Improved ENN with TSK Fuzzy

In order to design the automatic navigation control system without sea wave inferences, a lot of efforts are used to design the fuzzy and neural network control. Hence, fuzzy control process proceeds to the amount of control requirement [13, 14]. Intelligent control of nonlinear systems capable of handling and uncertainty, especially in the comparison of PID and fuzzy control, using the fastest design of neural network control, even in the output control can improve accuracy [15], so in this fuzzy neural network control theory will be used as an automatic navigation system control.

4.1. Improved Elman Neural Network (ENN) Controller. The architecture of the proposed improved ENN including

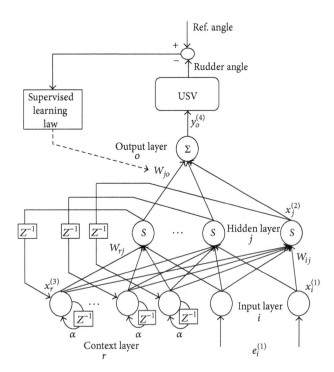

FIGURE 11: Architecture of the improved ENN.

the input layer, the hidden layer, the context layer, and the output layer with two input nodes, nine hidden nodes, and one output node is shown in Figure 11, where the control law is defined as rudder angle, and the two ENN inputs are $e_1^{(1)}$ and $e_2^{(1)}$ with $e_1^{(1)} = e(k)$ and $e_2^{(1)} = ce(k) = e(k) - e(k-1)$, the change of error. For the kth sampling instant, the error can be expressed as angular deviation $e(k) = \theta_r^*(k) - \theta_r(k)$.

The proposed ENN [4, 5] takes the feedback into account, and better learning efficiency can be obtained. Moreover, to make the neurons sensitive to the history of input data, self-connections of the context nodes and output feedback node are added. So the proposed ENN has the ability to deal with nonlinear problems and can effectively improve the convergence precision and reduce the learning time. The signal propagation and the basic function in each layer are introduced below.

Layer 1: Input Layer. In the input layer, the node is defined by

$$net_i^{(1)} = e_i^{(1)}(k),$$
$$x_i^{(1)}(k) = f_i^{(1)}\left(net_i^{(1)}(k)\right) = net_i^{(1)}, \quad i = 1, 2, \tag{1}$$

where k represents the kth iteration; $e_i^{(1)}(k)$ and $x_i^{(1)}(k)$ are the input and the output of the layer.

Layer 2: Hidden Layer. In the hidden layer, the node is defined by

$$net_j^{(2)} = \sum_i W_{ij} \times x_i^{(1)}(k) + \sum_r W_{rj} \times x_r^{(3)}(k),$$
$$x_j^{(2)}(k) = \frac{1}{1 + \exp\left(-net_j^{(2)}\right)}, \quad j = 1, 2, \ldots, 9, \tag{2}$$

where $x_i^{(1)}$, $x_r^{(3)}$ are input and $x_j^{(2)}(k)$ is output of the hidden layer. $x_r^{(3)}(k)$ is also the output of the context layer; W_{ij} and W_{rj} are the connecting weights of input neurons to hidden neurons and context neurons to hidden neurons, respectively.

Layer 3: Context Layer. In the context layer, the node input and output are represented as

$$x_r^{(3)}(k) = \alpha x_r^{(3)}(k-1) + x_j^{(2)}(k-1), \tag{3}$$

where $0 \le \alpha < 1$ is the self-connecting feedback gain.

Layer 4: Output Layer. In the output layer, the node input and output are represented as

$$y_o^{(4)}(k) = f_o^{(4)}\left(net_o^{(4)}(k)\right) = net_o^{(4)}(k),$$
$$net_o^{(4)}(k) = \sum_j W_{jo} \times x_j^{(2)}(k), \tag{4}$$

where W_{jo} is the connecting weight of hidden neurons to output neurons and $y_o^{(4)}(k)$ is the output of the improved ENN and also the control law of the proposed controller.

4.2. Online Supervised Learning and Training Process. Once the improved ENN has been initialized, supervised learning is used to train this system based on gradient descent theory. The derivation is the same as that of the backpropagation (BP) algorithm. It is employed to adjust the parameters of the ENN by using the training patterns. By recursive application of the chain rule, the error term for each layer is first calculated. The adaptation of weights to the corresponding layer is then given. The purpose of supervised learning is to minimize the energy function E expressed as [16]

$$E = \frac{1}{2}\left(\theta_r^* - \theta_r\right)^2 = \frac{1}{2}e_L^2, \tag{5}$$

where θ_r^* and θ_r represent the angle output reference and actual angle output of the USV, respectively, and e_L denotes the tracking error. The learning algorithm is described below.

Layer 4: Update Weight W_{jo}. The error term to be propagated is given by

$$\delta_o = -\frac{\partial E}{\partial net_o^{(4)}} = \left[-\frac{\partial E}{\partial y_o^{(4)}}\frac{\partial y_o^{(4)}}{\partial net_o^{(4)}}\right]. \tag{6}$$

Then the weight w_j is adjusted by the amount

$$\Delta W_{jo} = -\frac{\partial E}{\partial W_{jo}} = \left[-\frac{\partial E}{\partial y_o^{(4)}}\frac{\partial y_o^{(4)}}{\partial net_o^{(4)}}\right]\left(\frac{\partial net_o^{(4)}}{\partial W_{jo}}\right) = \delta_o x_j^{(2)} \tag{7}$$

and updated by

$$W_{jo}(k+1) = W_{jo}(k) + \eta_1 \Delta W_{jo}, \tag{8}$$

where η_1 is the learning rate.

Layer 3: Update Weight W_{rj}. By using the chain rule, the update law of W_{rj} is

$$\Delta W_{rj} = -\frac{\partial E}{\partial W_{rj}} = \left[-\frac{\partial E}{\partial y_o^{(4)}} \frac{\partial y_o^{(4)}}{\partial \text{net}_o^{(4)}} \right] \left(\frac{\partial \text{net}_o^{(4)}}{\partial x_j^{(2)}} \frac{\partial x_j^{(2)}}{\partial W_{rj}} \right) \quad (9)$$

$$= \delta_o W_{jo} x_j^{(2)} \left[1 - x_j^{(2)} \right] x_r^{(3)}.$$

The connecting weight W_{rj} is updated according to

$$W_{rj}(k+1) = W_{rj}(k) + \eta_2 \Delta W_{rj}, \quad (10)$$

where η_2 is the learning rate.

Layer 2: Update Weight W_{ij}. By using the chain rule, the update law of W_{ij} is

$$\Delta W_{ij} = -\frac{\partial E}{\partial W_{ij}} = \left[-\frac{\partial E}{\partial y_o^{(4)}} \frac{\partial y_o^{(4)}}{\partial \text{net}_o^{(4)}} \right] \left(\frac{\partial \text{net}_o^{(4)}}{\partial x_j^{(2)}} \frac{\partial x_j^{(2)}}{\partial W_{ij}} \right) \quad (11)$$

$$= \delta_o W_{jo} x_j^{(2)} \left[1 - x_j^{(2)} \right] x_i^{(1)}.$$

The connecting weight W_{ij} is updated according to

$$W_{ij}(k+1) = W_{ij}(k) + \eta_3 \Delta W_{ij}, \quad (12)$$

where η_3 is the learning rate.

4.3. Takagi-Sugeno-Kang (TSK) Fuzzy Controller. Typically, a TSK fuzzy model consists of IF-THEN rules that have the following form:
R^i: if x_1 is A_1^i, x_2 is A_2^i, ..., and x_n is A_n^i, then

$$h^i = f_i\left(x_1, x_2, \dots, x_n; a^i\right) = a_o^i + a_1^i x_1 + \cdots a_n^i x_n. \quad (13)$$

For $i = 1, 2, \dots, C$, where C is the number of rules, A_j^i is the fuzzy set of the ith rule for x_j with the adjustable parameter set θ_j^i, and $a^i = (a_0^i, a_1^i, \dots, a_n^i)$ is the parameter set in the consequent part. The predicted output of the fuzzy model is inferred as [16]

$$\hat{y} = \frac{\sum_{i=1}^{C} h^i w^i}{\sum_{i=1}^{C} w^i}, \quad (14)$$

where h^i is the output of the ith rule; $w^i = \min_{j=i,i+1,\dots,n} A_j^i(\theta_j^i; x_j)$ is the ith rule's firing strength, which is obtained as the minimum of the fuzzy membership degrees of all fuzzy variables. There are many choices for the types of membership functions, such as triangular, trapezoidal, or Gaussian. In this paper, a Gaussian membership function is employed for two reasons. Firstly, a fuzzy system with Gaussian membership function has been shown to approximate any nonlinear functions on a compact set. Secondly, a multidimensional Gaussian membership function generated during the learning process can be easily decomposed into the product of 1D Gaussian membership functions. Choosing Gaussian membership function, in (16), the parameters of the premise parts

(i.e., θ_j^i) include m_{ij} and σ_{ij}, which are the center (or mean) and the width (or variance) of the Gaussian membership function of the ith rule at jth dimension, respectively. Both the premise parts (i.e., θ_j^i) and the consequent parts (i.e., a^i) in a TSK fuzzy model are required to be identified [17, 18].

The considered problem is to obtain correct distribution of fuzzy rules and its corresponding polynomial from a set of observations. The input-output pairs are $\{(x_1, y_1), (x_2, y_2), \dots, (x_N, y_N)\}$, where $x_k = k/N$ is normalization of kth subcarrier channel number; $y_k = \text{real}(\widetilde{H}_p(k))$ is the real part (or imaginary part) of the corresponding channel transfer function. We assume that those observations are obtained from an unknown function $y_k = f(x_k)$. We want to construct a TSK model that can accurately represent f in terms of input-output relationship. In order to simplify the algorithm and loose the compute burden, we fix the number of rules as $C = N/2$ and the parameters of each rule as

$$m_i = \frac{2i-1}{N}, \quad (15)$$

$$\sigma_i = \frac{2}{N}, \quad (16)$$

where m_i and σ_i are the center and width of the membership function, respectively. The fire strength of each input represents the degree x_k belonging to the corresponding rule. Since the input is one dimension, the fire strength can be calculated by

$$F^i = e^{-[(x_k - m_i)^2/\sigma_i^2]}. \quad (17)$$

Since the normalized firing strength is employed, the w^i in (14) can be defined as

$$w^i = \frac{F^i}{\sum F^i}. \quad (18)$$

Furthermore, the parameters of each rule are fixed; the only adjustable parameter of TSK model is a^i in (13). The parameter is updated by the following rule:

$$a^i(t+1) = a^i(t) + \eta \left[\hat{y}_k - y_k \right] x(k) w^i, \quad (19)$$

where $x(k)$ is input vector $[1, x_k]$, η is the learning rate, and $\hat{y}_k$ is the current output of fuzzy model calculated using (14).

Finally, the procedure of the used TSK learning algorithm is described as follows.

Step 1. Define the fuzzy rule in (15) and (16); the initial value of a^i is set to be $[1, 1]$.

Step 2. The first snapshot of all-pilot subcarriers is used to train the in a^i (13) to (19). When the error is small enough, then go to Step 3.

Step 3. Estimate the channel transfer function using (13) to (18). When the input is at pilot symbol channel, a^i is updated to trace the variation of channel. A block diagram of the TSK fuzzy controller is presented in Figure 12. The power control with a processing flowchart is shown in Figure 13.

Table 1: Test of linear acceleration.

Power (%)	Task Average speed (NM)
20	0
40	1.7
60	1.9
80	2.3
100	2.5

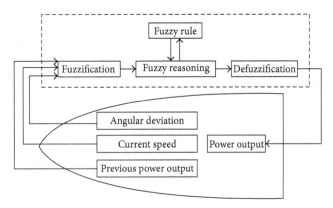

Figure 12: Block diagram of TSK fuzzy control of power output.

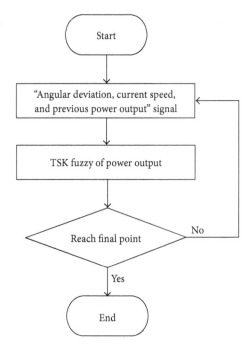

Figure 13: Flowchart of TSK fuzzy control.

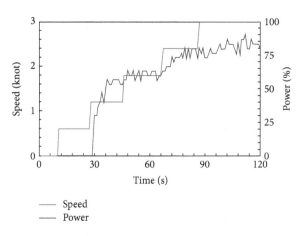

Figure 14: Test of linear acceleration.

5. Test of the Unmanned Automatic System

For obtaining the basic dynamic data of the boat, it is necessary to test the boat in driving along a straight line and in turning directions. Before the design of an unmanned autonavigation, it is required to figure out the dynamic power for controlling the speed of the boat as well as the steering characteristics and adequate turning speeds. After collection of required data, design and programming of improved ENN with TSK fuzzy control can then be preceded. The cRIO-9074 and computer are installed on the boat to record boat's relevant data. The speed data of the boat is obtained via GPS, and computer is used to control the power output.

5.1. Straight Movement. Data about the dynamic of linear acceleration is collected during the test. As illustrated in Figure 14, it is revealed that the boat's main speed range is mainly 1.8~2.5 NM/h. Due to the design of double-hulled frame and a weight of 1.3 tons, the maximum speed is no more than 3 NM/h. Moreover, even at low startup speed, initiated with 30% maneuver power, it took a bit longer time to achieve working speed.

From Table 1, it is clear that by controlling the power in the range of 50~85%, vessel per hour sailing is around 1.8~2.4 NM/h, which is more stable in movement.

5.2. Turning Radius. When testing turning movement, the main method is to test speeds in segmentation to obtain the radius for turning the boat for 360°. From our result, it is obvious that at 40% of power output, the turning of the boat is almost spinning on the spot. It reveals the better stability with the design of the double-hulled frame. Nonetheless, the

power output should be greater than 40% relatively effective performance if there is the need for moving forward while turning.

6. Experimental Results

The automatic navigation design is shown in the diagram of Figure 12; the module of improved ENN control is needed for modification of orientation if the boat is deviating from its navigated direction. In addition, for the control of power output, data about angular deviation, current speed, and previous power are required for maintaining the boat at working speed through TSK fuzzy control.

The USV automatic navigation test begins with inputs of destined navigating points, as illustrated in Figure 15, and then the information is transmitted to the cRIO-9074 system

TABLE 2: Performance of proposed control method.

Method	Tracking distance error (m)	Angular response (s)	X/Y position response (s)
Improved ENN with TSK fuzzy method	±2.5	350	600

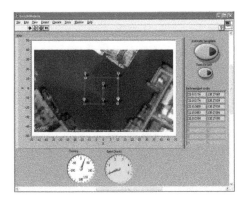

FIGURE 15: Command panel of PC sever.

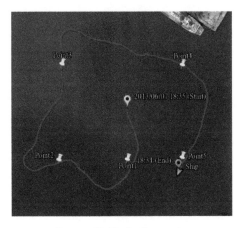

FIGURE 16: Navigation route.

on the boat. When the server presses the "automatic navigation" button, the boat begins a voyage along the destined navigating points. Data transmitted back from cRIO-9074 includes power outputs, speeds, and tracks of the boat for realization of the navigation conditions. It is obviously illustrated in Figure 16 that USV follows the destined route successfully in navigation.

Figure 17 shows the navigation data of this test trip. It reveals clearly that the boat successfully followed the design of TSK fuzzy control, to maintain the speed of moving straight forward at around 2.2 NM/h and speeds of turning at around 1.8~2 NM/h. When turning, it is demonstrated in Figure 18 that the boat declination has followed the target declination. It is also clearly illustrated that when the boat was ordered to turn at 90 seconds, it did adjust the orientation effectively

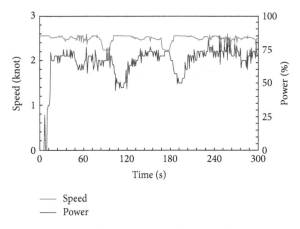

—— Speed
—— Power

FIGURE 17: Navigation data of power and speed.

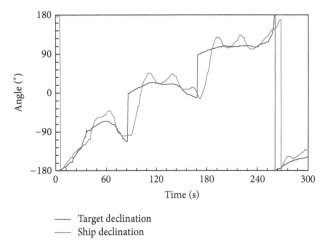

—— Target declination
—— Ship declination

FIGURE 18: Data of target declination and boat declination.

to keep on the navigated direction. The performance of proposed control method is summarized in Table 2.

7. Conclusion

This study uses a platform developed by the department of naval architecture for the autonavigation system, using GPS, orientation sensors, and cRIO-9074, as well as combining LabView and intelligent control algorithm, to reduce the cost of sensors and time of system development effectively. For the autonavigation system, there are two sets of intelligent control algorithm, designed for power output and steering of this electric double-hulled boat, to control the boat stably to travel along the navigation route.

As the wave heights in Chi-Chin harbor vary dramatically, the test results show that the double-hulled boat has pretty good stability and keeps steering control. The task of autonavigation could be easily and nicely performed.

Conflict of Interests

The authors declare that there is no conflict of interests regarding the publication of this paper.

References

[1] B. Volker, *Unmanned Surface Vehicles—A Survey*, Skibsteknisk Selskab, Copenhagen, Denmark, 2008.

[2] C. S. Huang, *An ambulate wireless control robotic arm in the application of anti-explosion [M.S. thesis]*, I-Shou University, Taiwan, 2008.

[3] H. F. Kuo, *Design and implementation of a remotely controlled robot-car with real-time image identification technique for object tracking [M.S. thesis]*, National Cheng Kung University, 2006.

[4] X. Li, G. Chen, Z. Chen, and Z. Yuan, "Chaotifying linear Elman networks," *IEEE Transactions on Neural Networks*, vol. 13, no. 5, pp. 1193–1199, 2002.

[5] F.-J. Lin and Y.-C. Hung, "FPGA-based elman neural network control system for linear ultrasonic motor," *IEEE Transactions on Ultrasonics, Ferroelectrics, and Frequency Control*, vol. 56, no. 1, pp. 101–113, 2009.

[6] M. Sugeno and G. T. Kang, "Structure identification of fuzzy model," *Fuzzy Sets and Systems*, vol. 28, no. 1, pp. 15–33, 1988.

[7] Global Positioning System, http://hep.ccic.ntnu.edu.tw/.

[8] CHR-UM6 Direction Sensors, http://www.chrobotics.com/.

[9] MR-J2S-A, http://www.two-way.com.tw/html/product/.

[10] S. H. Tsao, *Research and development of unmanned aerial vehicle control software [M.S. thesis]*, National Defense University, 2009.

[11] Acceleration Sensor and Electronic Compass Principle Introduced, http://www.seraphim.com.tw/upfiles/c_supports01328152963.pdf.

[12] NI CompactRIO, http://www.ni.com/compactrio/zht/whatis.htm.

[13] S. C. Liu, *Automatic navigation of a wheeled mobile robot using particle swarm optimization and fuzzy control [M.S. thesis]*, National Central University, 2011.

[14] Y. H. Lin, *Integrated flight path planning system and flight control system for navigation and guidance of unmanned helicopter [M.S. thesis]*, National Cheng Kung University, 2009.

[15] C. M. Hong, T. C. Ou, and K. H. Lu, "Development of intelligent MPPT control for a grid-connected hybrid power generation system," *Energy*, vol. 50, pp. 270–279, 2013.

[16] C. T. Lin and C. S. G. Lee, *Neural Fuzzy Systems*, Prentice-Hall, 1996.

[17] S. X. Yang, H. Li, M. Q.-H. Meng, and P. X. Liu, "An embedded fuzzy controller for a behavior-based mobile robot with guaranteed performance," *IEEE Transactions on Fuzzy Systems*, vol. 12, no. 4, pp. 436–446, 2004.

[18] T.-M. Wang, P.-C. Lin, H.-L. Chan, J.-C. Liao, T.-W. Sun, and T.-Y. Wu, "Energy saving of air condition using fuzzy control system over Zigbee temperature sensor," in *Proceedings of the 24th IEEE International Conference on Advanced Information Networking and Applications Workshops (WAINA '10)*, pp. 1005–1010, April 2010.

11

A Radial Basis Function Spike Model for Indirect Learning via Integrate-and-Fire Sampling and Reconstruction Techniques

X. Zhang,[1] G. Foderaro,[1] C. Henriquez,[2] A. M. J. VanDongen,[3] and S. Ferrari[1]

[1] *Laboratory for Intelligent Systems and Control (LISC), Department of Mechanical Engineering and Materials Science, Duke University, Durham, NC 27708, USA*
[2] *Department of Biomedical Engineering and Department of Computer Science, Duke University Durham, NC 27708, USA*
[3] *Program in Neuroscience & Behavioral Disorders, Duke-NUS Graduate Medical School, Singapore, Singapore*

Correspondence should be addressed to S. Ferrari, sferrari@duke.edu

Academic Editor: Olivier Bastien

This paper presents a deterministic and adaptive spike model derived from radial basis functions and a leaky integrate-and-fire sampler developed for training spiking neural networks without direct weight manipulation. Several algorithms have been proposed for training spiking neural networks through biologically-plausible learning mechanisms, such as spike-timing-dependent synaptic plasticity and Hebbian plasticity. These algorithms typically rely on the ability to update the synaptic strengths, or weights, directly, through a weight update rule in which the weight increment can be decided and implemented based on the training equations. However, in several potential applications of adaptive spiking neural networks, including neuroprosthetic devices and CMOS/memristor nanoscale neuromorphic chips, the weights cannot be manipulated directly and, instead, tend to change over time by virtue of the pre- and postsynaptic neural activity. This paper presents an indirect learning method that induces changes in the synaptic weights by modulating spike-timing-dependent plasticity by means of controlled input spike trains. In place of the weights, the algorithm manipulates the input spike trains used to stimulate the input neurons by determining a sequence of spike timings that minimize a desired objective function and, indirectly, induce the desired synaptic plasticity in the network.

1. Introduction

This paper presents a deterministic and adaptive spike model obtained from radial basis functions (RBFs) and a leaky integrate-and-fire (LIF) sampler for the purpose of training spiking neural networks (SNNs), without directly manipulating the synaptic weights. Spiking neural networks are computational models of biological neurons comprised of systems of differential equations that can reproduce some of the spike patterns and dynamics observed in real neuronal networks [1, 2]. Recently, SNNs have also been shown capable of simulating sigmoidal artificial neural networks (ANNs) and of solving small-dimensional nonlinear function approximation problems through reinforcement learning [3–5]. Like all ANN learning techniques, existing SNN training algorithms rely on the direct manipulation of the synaptic weights [4–9]. In other words, the learning

algorithms typically include a weight-update rule by which the synaptic weights are updated over several iterations, based on the reinforcement signal or network performance.

In many potential SNN applications, including neuroprosthetic devices, light-sensitive neuronal networks grown *in vitro*, and CMOS/memristor nanoscale neuromorphic chips [10], the synaptic weights cannot be updated directly by the learning algorithm. In several of these applications, the objective is to stimulate a network of biological or artificial spiking neurons to perform a complex function, such as processing an auditory signal or restoring a cognitive function. In neuroprosthetic medical implants, for example, the artificial device may consist of a microelectrode array or integrated circuit that stimulates biological neurons via spike trains. Therefore, the device is not capable of directly modifying the synaptic efficacies of the biological neurons, as do existing SNN training algorithms, but it is capable of stimulating a subset of neurons through controlled pulses of electrical current.

As another example, light-sensitive neuronal networks grown *in vitro* can be similarly stimulated through controlled light patterns that cause selected neurons to fire at precise moments in time, in an attempt to induce plasticity, while their output is being recorded in real time using a multielectrode array (MEA) [11]. In this case, a digital computer can be used to determine the desired stimulation patterns for an *in-vitro* neuronal network with random connectivity, produced by culturing dissociated cortical neurons derived from embryonic day E18 rat brain [11, 12]. As a result, the cultures may be used to verify biophysical models of the mechanisms by which biological neuronal networks execute the control and storage of information via temporal coding and learn to solve complex tasks over time. In these networks, the actual connectivity and synaptic plasticities are typically unknown and cannot be manipulated directly as required by existing SNN learning algorithms.

This paper presents a novel indirect learning approach and algorithm that assume synaptic weights cannot be updated or manipulated at any time. The learning algorithm induces changes in the SNN weights by modulating spike-timing dependent plasticity (STDP) through controlled input spike trains. The algorithm adapts the input spike trains that are used to stimulate the input neurons of the SNN and, thus, are realizable through controlled pulses of electric voltage or controlled pulses of blue light. The main difficulty to be overcome in indirect learning is that the algorithm aims at adapting pulse signals, such as square waves, in place of continuous-valued weights. While available in closed analytic form, these signals typically are represented by piece-wise continuous, multi-valued (or many-to-one), and nondifferentiable functions that are difficult to adapt or update using optimization or reinforcement-learning algorithms. Furthermore, stimulation patterns typically are generated by spike models that are stochastic, such as the Poisson spike model [5, 13–15]. Thus, even when the spike model is optimized, it does not allow for precise timing of pre- and post-synaptic firings, and as a result, may induce undesirable changes in the synaptic weights.

In this paper, a deterministic spike model that allows for precise timing of neuron firings is obtained using adaptive RBFs to model the characteristics of the spike pattern through a continuous and infinitely differentiable function that also is one to one. The RBF model is combined with an LIF sampling technique originally developed in [16, 17] for the approximate reconstruction of bandlimited functions. It is shown that, by this approach, the spike trains generated by the LIF sampler display the precise characteristics specified by the RBF model. Furthermore, this deterministic spike model can be optimized to modulate STDP through controlled input spike trains that bring about the desired SNN weight change without direct manipulation. The indirect learning approach presented in this paper is applicable both in supervised and unsupervised settings. In fact, when the desired SNN output is unknown, it can be replaced by a reinforcement signal produced by a critic SNN, as shown by the adaptive critic method reviewed in Section 3.

The paper is organized as follows. The model of spiking neural network used to derive and demonstrate the training equations is presented in Section 2. In Section 3, an adaptive critic approach is described to illustrate how the proposed indirect training methodology can be applied using reinforcement learning, for example, to model or control a dynamical plant. The novel spike model and indirect training methodology are presented in Section 4 and demonstrated on a benchmark problem involving a two-node spiking neural network. The generalized form of gradient equations for indirect training is presented in Section 5 and demonstrated through a three-node spiking neural network. These gradient equations show how the methodology can be generalized to any spiking neural network with the characteristics described in the next section.

2. Spiking Neural Network Model

2.1. Models of Neuron and Synapse. Various models of SNNs have been proposed in recent years, motivated by biological studies that have shown complex spike patterns and dynamics to be an essential component of information processing and learning in the brain. The two crucial considerations involved in determining a suitable SNN model are the range of neurocomputational behaviors the model can reproduce, and its computational efficiency [18]. As can be expected, the implementation efficiency typically increases with the number of features and behaviors that can be accurately reproduced [18], such that each model offers a tradeoff between these competing objectives. One of the computational neuron models that is most biophysically accurate is the well-known Hodgkin-Huxley (HH) model [2]. Due to its extremely low computational efficiency, however, using the HH model to simulate large networks of neurons can be computationally prohibitive [18]. Recently, bifurcation studies have been used to reduce the HH dynamics from four to two differential equations, referred to as the Izhikevich model, which are capable of reproducing a wide range of spiking patterns and behaviors with much higher efficiency than the HH model [19].

In [15], the authors proposed an indirect training method based on a Poison spike model and demonstrated it on a network of Izhikevich neurons. In this work it was found that the adaptive critic architecture described in Section 3 could be implemented without modeling the neuron response in closed form. However, the effectiveness of the approach in [15] was limited in that, due to the use of a stochastic Poison model, the Izhikevich SNN could not converge to the optimal control law. Therefore, in this paper, a new deterministic spike model is proposed and implemented by deriving the training equations in closed form, using a leaky integrate-and-fire (LIF) SNN. The LIF is the simplest model of spiking neuron. It has the advantages that it displays the highest computational efficiency and is amenable to mathematical analysis [13, 14].

The LIF membrane potential, $v(t)$, is governed by

$$C_m \frac{dv(t)}{dt} = I_{\text{leak}}(t) + I_s(t) + I_{\text{inj}}(t), \qquad (1)$$

where C_m is the membrane capacitance, $I_{leak}(t)$ is the current due to the leak of the membrane, $I_s(t)$ is the synaptic input to the neuron, and $I_{inj}(t)$ is the current injected to the neuron [20]. The leak current is defined as follow:

$$I_{leak}(t) = -\frac{C_m}{\tau_m}[v(t) - V_0], \qquad (2)$$

where V_0 is the resting potential and τ_m is the passive-membrane time constant [20]. τ_m is related to the capacitance, C_m, and the membrane resistance, R_m, of the membrane potential by $\tau_m = R_m C_m$.

The response of the membrane potential is obtained by solving the differential equation (1) analytically for $v(t)$, such that

$$v(t) = V_0 + e^{-t/\tau_m}\int_{t_0}^{t}\frac{I_{inj}(\rho)}{C_m}e^{\rho/\tau_m}d\rho, \qquad (3)$$

where ρ is a dummy variable used for integration and t_0 is the time at which the membrane potential equals V_0 [20]. Whenever the membrane potential, $v(t)$, reaches a prescribed threshold value, V_{th}, the neuron will fire. At this point, we have considered an isolated neuron that is stimulated by an external current, $I_{inj}(t)$. When the LIF neuron (1) is part of a larger network, the input current, referred to as the *synaptic current*, is generated by the activity of presynaptic neurons.

Let the synaptic current, denoted by $I_s(t)$, be modeled as the sum of the currents of *excitatory* presynaptic neurons and of *inhibitory* presynaptic neurons,

$$I_s(t) = C_m\sum_{k=1}^{N_E}a_{E,k}S_{E,k}(t) + C_m\sum_{k=1}^{N_I}a_{I,k}S_{I,k}(t), \qquad (4)$$

where the subscript E denotes inputs from *excitatory* neurons, while the subscript I denotes inputs from *inhibitory* neurons. The amplitudes, $a_{E,k} > 0$ and $a_{I,k} < 0$, represent the change in potential due to a single synaptic event and depend on the weight of the synapse. N_E and N_I are the numbers of excitatory and inhibitory current synapses, respectively. $S_{E,k}$ and $S_{I,k}$ describe the excitatory and inhibitory synaptic inputs as a series of input spikes to each synapse. The synaptic inputs are modeled as a sum of instantaneous impulse functions,

$$S_{E,k}(t) = \sum_{t_{E,k}}\delta(t - t_{E,k}), \qquad (5)$$

$$S_{I,k}(t) = \sum_{t_{I,k}}\delta(t - t_{I,k}), \qquad (6)$$

where $t_{E,k}$ and $t_{I,k}$ are the firing times of the presynaptic neurons and δ represents the Dirac delta function [21].

In addition to the above deterministic properties, there are prevalent stochastic qualities in biological neural networks caused by effects such as thermal noise and random variations in neurotransmitters. For simplicity, these effects are assumed negligible in this paper. However, the reader is referred to [15] for a technique that can be used to incorporate these effects in the above SNN model.

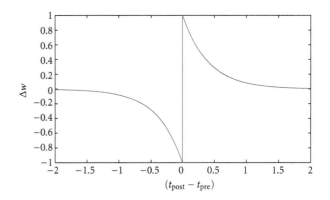

FIGURE 1: STDP term as a function of the time delay between the last spike of postsynaptic neuron and presynaptic neuron.

2.2. Model of Spike-Timing-Dependent Plasticity (STDP).

A persistent learning mechanism known as spike-timing-dependent plasticity, recently observed in biological neuronal networks, is used in this paper to model synaptic plasticity in the LIF SNN. Synaptic plasticity refers to the mechanism by which the synaptic efficacies or *strengths* between neurons are modified over time, typically as a result of the neuronal activity. These changes are known to be driven in part by the correlated activity of adjacently connected neurons. The directions and magnitudes of the changes are dependent on the relative timings of the presynaptic spike arrivals and postsynaptic firings. For simplicity, in this paper, all changes in synaptic strengths are assumed to occur solely as a result of the spike-timing-dependent plasticity mechanism. The approach presented in [5] can be used to also incorporate a model of the Hebbian plasticity.

Spike-timing-dependent plasticity (STDP) is known to modify the synaptic strengths according to the relative timing of the output and input action potentials, or spikes, of a particular neuron. If the presynaptic neuron fires shortly before the postsynaptic neuron, the strength of the connection will be increased. In contrast, if the presynaptic neuron fires after the postsynaptic neuron, the strength of the connection will be decreased, as illustrated in Figure 1. Two constants τ_+ and τ_- determine the ranges of the presynaptic to postsynaptic interspike intervals over which synaptic strengthening and weakening occur. Let the synaptic efficacy or strength be referred to as *weight* and denoted by w. A is the maximum amplitude of the change of weight due to a pair of spikes. t_{pre} and t_{post} denote firing times of the presynaptic neuron and the postsynaptic neuron, respectively. Then, for each set of neighboring spikes, the weight adjustment is given by,

$$\Delta w = Ae^{[(t_{pre}-t_{post})\tau]}, \qquad (7)$$

such that the connection weight increases when the postsynaptic spike follows the presynaptic spike and the weight decreases when the opposite occurs. The amplitude of the adjustment Δw lessens as the time between the spikes becomes larger, as is illustrated in Figure 1.

Different methods can be used to identify the spikes that give rise to the STDP mechanism. In this paper, the *nearest-spike STDP model* [22] is adopted, by which, for every spike of the presynaptic neuron, its nearest postsynaptic spike is used to calculate the timing difference in (7), regardless of whether it takes place before or after the presynaptic firing. Then, from (7), the weight change due to one of the spikes of the ith neuron is modeled by the rule

$$\Delta w_i(\Delta t_i) = \begin{cases} A_+ e^{\Delta t_i/\tau_+} & \text{if } \Delta t_i \leq 0 \\ A_- e^{-\Delta t_i/\tau_-} & \text{if } \Delta t_i > 0, \end{cases} \quad (8)$$

where

$$\Delta t_i = t_{1,i} - \operatorname*{argmin}_{t_{2,k}} |t_{1,i} - t_{2,k}|. \quad (9)$$

Δt_i is the firing time difference between the two neurons, $t_{1,i}$ is the firing time of the presynaptic neuron, and $t_{2,i}$ is the firing time of the postsynaptic neuron. The constants used in this paper are $\tau_+ = \tau_- = 20$ ms, $A_+ = 0.006$, and $A_- = 1.5A_+$, where A_+ and A_- determine the maximum amounts of synaptic modification that occur when Δt is approximately zero [21].

From (8), the firing time of the postsynaptic neuron is chosen such that the absolute firing time difference between the presynaptic neuron and the postsynaptic neuron, $|t_{1,i} - t_{2,k}|$, is minimized. Therefore, the postsynaptic spike $t_{2,k}$ that is nearest to the presynaptic firing time $t_{1,i}$ is used to calculate the firing time difference Δt_i. The value of $t_{2,k}$ that minimizes $|t_{1,i} - t_{2,k}|$ can be found by comparing the firing time difference of the two neurons. In order to obtain an indirect learning method that does not rely on the direct manipulation of the synaptic weights, in this paper, it is assumed that the weights can only be modified according to the STDP rule (8). Also, the training algorithm cannot specify any of the terms in (8) directly but can only induce the firing times in (8) by stimulating the input neurons, for example, through controlled pulses of electric voltage or blue light.

3. Adaptive Critic Architecture for Indirect Reinforcement Learning

Many approaches have been proposed to train SNNs by modifying the synaptic weights by means of reward signals or by update rules inspired by reward-driven Hebbian learning and modulation of STDP [5, 8]. However, these methods are not applicable to approaches involving biological neuronal networks (e.g., neuronal cultures grown *in vitro*), because biological synaptic efficacies cannot be manipulated directly by the training algorithm. Similarly, in nanoscale neuromorphic chips, the CMOS/memristor synaptic weights cannot be manipulated directly but may be modified via controlled programming voltages that induce a mechanism analogous to STDP, as demonstrated in [10]. This paper presents an approach for training an SNN through controlled input pulse signals (e.g., voltages or blue light) that are generated by a new deterministic and adaptive spike model presented in Section 4.1.

The derivation of the training equations used to adapt the proposed spike model and subsequent pulse signals are demonstrated in Section 4.2 using a two-node LIF SNN. It is shown that the synaptic weight can be updated by the proposed indirect training method and driven precisely to a desired value, by minimizing a function of the synaptic weight error. It follows that, using a simple chain rule, the same training equations can be used to minimize a function of the decoded SNN output error, as is typically required by supervised training. In this section, we show how the indirect training method can be used for reinforcement learning, using a critic SNN to modulate the STDP mechanisms in an action SNN with synaptic weights that cannot be manipulated directly (e.g., a biological neuronal network).

Let NN_a represent an action SNN of LIF neurons, exhibiting STDP and modeled as described in Section 2. It is assumed that the weights of the action SNN cannot be manipulated directly, and the only controls available to the learning algorithm are the training signals (Figure 2), comprised of programming voltages that can be delivered using a square wave or the Rademacher function (Section 4.1). Now, let NN_c denote a critic SNN of feedforward fully connected HH neurons. In this architecture, schematized in Figure 2, NN_a is treated as a biological network and NN_c is treated as an artificial network implemented on a computer or integrated circuit. Thus, the synaptic weights of NN_c, defined as w_{ij}, are directly adjustable, while the synaptic efficacies of NN_a can only be modified through a simulated STDP mechanism which is modulated by the input spikes from NN_c. The algorithm presented in this section trains the network by changing the values of w_{ij} inside NN_c, which are assumed to be bounded by a positive constant $w_{\max}$ such that $-w_{\max} \leq w_{ij} \leq w_{\max}$, for all i, j.

In this paper, spike frequencies are used to code continuous signals, and the leaky integrator

$$\hat{u} = \alpha \sum_{t_k \in S_i(T)} e^{\beta(t_k - t)} H(t - t_k) - \gamma \quad (10)$$

is used to decode spike trains and convert them into continuous signals as required according to the architecture in Figure 2 Where, α, β, and γ are user-specified constants, $H(\cdot)$ is the Heaviside function, and $S_i(T)$ is the set of spiking times of the output neuron. One advantage of the leaky integrator decoder is its effectiveness of filtering inevitable noise during the flight control without influencing the speed of matching the continuous value with the target function.

3.1. Adaptive Critic Recurrence Relations. Typically, adaptive critic algorithms are used to update the actor and critic weights by computing a synaptic weight increment through an optimization-based algorithm, such as backpropagation ([23], page 359). Therefore a new approach is required in order to apply adaptive critics to SNNs in which changes in the synaptic weights can occur only as a result of pre- and postsynaptic neuronal activity. The training approach presented in Section 4 can be combined with the policy and value-iteration procedures described in this section to supervise stimulation patterns in the action SNN such that the synaptic strengths, and subsequently their dynamic mappings, are adapted according to the STDP rule in (8).

Suppose the action SNN is being trained to control or model a dynamical system which obeys a nonlinear differential equation of the form

$$\dot{x}(t) = f[x(t), u(t), t], \tag{11}$$

where $x \in X \subset \mathbb{R}^n$ and $u \in U \subset \mathbb{R}^m$ denote the dynamical system state and control inputs, respectively, and $\dot{x}$ denotes the derivative of x with respect to time. The model of the dynamical system (11) may be unknown or imperfect and may be improved upon over time by a system identification (ID) algorithm. The macroscopic behavioral goals of the plant can be expressed by the value function or *cost-to-go*

$$V^\pi[x(t_k)] = \sum_{t_k=t}^{t_f-1} \mathcal{L}[x(t_k), u(t_k), x(t_k+1)], \tag{12}$$

where $u(t_k) = \pi[x(t_k)]$ is the unknown control law or dynamic mapping to be learned by the action SNN, NN_a. Then, the cost-to-go in (12) can be used to represent the future performance of the action network and dynamical system, as is accrued from the present, t_k, up to the final time, t_f, if subject to the present control law $\pi[\cdot]$. The Lagrangian $\mathcal{L}[\cdot]$ represents instantaneous behavioral goals as a function of x and u.

Since the dynamic mapping $\pi[\cdot]$ must be adapted over time through the learning algorithm and an accurate plant model may not be available, the cost-to-go typically is unknown and is learned by the critic, NN_c. Then, by Bellman's principle of optimality [24], at any time t_k the cost-to-go can be minimized online with respect to the present control law, based on the known value of $x(t_k)$ and predictions of $x(t_k + 1)$. The value of $x(t_k)$ is assumed to be fully observable from the dynamical system at any present time t_k, and $x(t_k + 1)$ is predicted or estimated from the approximation of the system's dynamics (11), based on the present values of the state and the control. In [25], Howard showed that if iterative approximations of the control law and optimal cost-to-go, denoted by π_ℓ and V_ℓ, respectively, are modified by a policy-improvement routine and a value-determination operation, respectively, they eventually converge to their optimal counterparts π^* and V^*.

The policy-improvement routine states that, given a cost-to-go function $V(\cdot, \pi_\ell)$ corresponding to a control law π_ℓ, an improved control law $\pi_{\ell+1}$ can be obtained as follows:

$$\pi_{\ell+1}[x(t_k)] = \arg\min_{u \in U} \{ \mathcal{L}[x(t_k), u(t_k), x(t_k+1)] \\ + V[x(t_{k+1}, \pi_\ell)] \}, \tag{13}$$

such that $V[x(t_k), \pi_{\ell+1}] \leq V[x(t_k), \pi_\ell]$, for any $x(t_k)$. Furthermore, the sequence of functions $C = \{\pi_\ell \mid \ell = 0, 1, 2, \ldots\}$ converges to the optimal control law π^*. The value-determination operation states that given a control

law $\pi(\cdot)$, the cost-to-go can be updated according to the following rule:

$$V_{\ell+1}[x(t_{k+1}), \pi] = \mathcal{L}[x(t_k), u(t_k), x(t_k+1)] + V_{\text{ell}}[x(t_{k+1}, \pi)], \tag{14}$$

such that the sequence of functions $V = \{V_\ell \mid \ell = 0, 1, 2, \ldots\}$ converges to V^*.

Then, at every iteration cycle ℓ of the adaptive critic algorithm, the above policy and value-iteration procedures can be used to in tandem to supervise training of the actor and critic SNN; that is,

$$u(t_k) \longleftarrow NN_a[\ell, x(t_k)] \approx \pi_\ell[x(t_k)], \tag{15}$$

$$V^\pi[x(t_k)] \longleftarrow NN_c[\ell, x(t_k), \pi] \approx V_\ell[x(t_k), \pi], \tag{16}$$

respectively where $\ell = Mk$ and M is a positive constant chosen based on the desired frequency of the updates. It can be seen that, at $\ell + 1$, the desired mappings for NN_a and NN_c, provided by (13) and (14), respectively, are based on the actor and critic outputs at ℓ, and on $x(t_{k+1})$, which can be estimated from an available dynamical system model (11). To accomplish (15) and (16), two error metrics defined as a function of the actual (decoded) actor and critic outputs and of the desired actor and critic outputs (13) and (14) must be minimized by the chosen training algorithm, as explained in the following subsection.

3.2. Action and Critic Network Training Algorithm. The action and critic networks implemented in Figure 2 differ in that while the critic network can be trained by a conventional algorithm that manipulates the synaptic weights directly (e.g., see [5, 15]), the action network must be trained by inducing weight changes indirectly through STDP (8), such that its (decoded) output $\hat{u}$ will closely match u in (15), for all $x \in X$. Since the weights within NN_a cannot be adjusted directly, they are manipulated with training signals from NN_c. Connections are made between q pairs of action/critic neurons which serve as outputs in NN_c and inputs for NN_a (Figure 2). To provide feedback signals to the critic, connections are also created between r pairs of neurons from NN_a to NN_c. The information flow through the networks is illustrated in Figure 2. Since it is not known what training signals will produce the desired results in NN_a, the critic must also be trained to match V^π in (16) for all $x \in X$ and $u \in U$.

Both updates (15) and (16) can be formulated as follows. Let $SNN[\cdot]$ denote an action or critic network comprised of multiple spiking neurons and STDP synapses. Then, as shown in (15) and (16), $SNN[\cdot]$ must represent a desired mapping between two vectors $\xi \in \mathbb{R}^p$ and $y \in \mathbb{R}^r$:

$$y(t_k) = g_\ell[\xi(t_k)] \longleftarrow SNN[\xi(t_k), W_\ell(t_k)] \triangleq \hat{y}(t_k). \tag{17}$$

The desired mapping $g_\ell : \mathbb{R}^p \to \mathbb{R}^r$ can be assumed known and stationary during every iteration cycle ℓ and is updated by the policy/value-iteration routine. Let $W_\ell(t_k) = \{w_{ij}(t_k)\}$ denote a matrix containing the SNN synaptic weights at time t_k. Then, for proper values of W_ℓ, if the SNN is provided

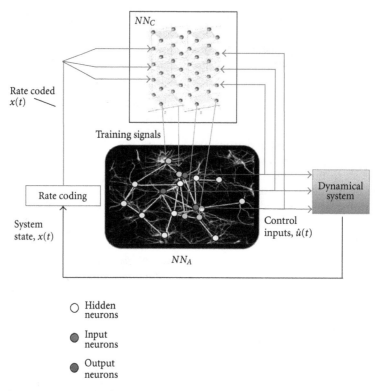

FIGURE 2: Adaptive critic architecture comprised of a critic network, NN_c, and, an action network, NN_a, to control a dynamical system.

with an observation of the input, ξ^l, encoded as n spike train sequences $X_i^l = \{\hat{t}_{i,\kappa} : \kappa = 1,\ldots,N_i^l\}$, $i = 1,\ldots,n$, over a time interval $[t_k, t_{k+\tau}]$ with the firing times at $\hat{t}_{i,\kappa}$, the decoded output of the SNN must match the output $y^l = g_e[\xi^l]$, where since $\tau \ll (t_{k+1} - t_k)$, X_i^l can be used to encode instantaneous values of ξ^l at any t_k. Then, the chosen SNN training algorithm must modify the synaptic weights such that a figure of merit representing distance is optimized at the output space of the mapping in (17).

For the critic network, NN_c, the synaptic weights are adjusted manually, using the reward-modulated Hebbian approach presented in [5, 15]. Because the target function y is known for all values of ξ, the SNN output error $(y - \hat{y})$ is also known and can be used as a feedback to the critic in the form of an imitated chemical reward, $r(t)$, that decays over time with time constant τ_c. The critic reward is modeled as

$$r(t) = \frac{[b(\hat{y}, y) + r(t - \Delta t)]e^{-(t-\hat{t}_i)}}{\tau_c}, \qquad (18)$$

where for the critic $y \in \mathbb{R}$. Therefore, the error function can be defined as $b(\hat{y}, y) = \operatorname{sgn}(y - \hat{y})$, where $\operatorname{sgn}(\cdot)$ is the signum function. Thus, the value of $b(\cdot)$ is positive when the critic's output is too low, and it is negative when the critic's output is too high.

For the action network, NN_a, the synaptic weights cannot be manipulated directly; therefore the distance between y and the (decoded) SNN's output $\hat{y}$ is minimized with respect to the parameters of the RBF spike model described in the next section. From (17), we identify (tag) two sets of

neurons referred to as input and output neurons (Figure 2), where each neuron in the set provides the response for one element of ξ and y, respectively, in the form of a spike train. It is assumed that the set of input neurons can be induced to fire on command with very high precision over a training time interval $[t_k, t_{k+\tau}]$, with $\tau < T \ll (t_{k+1} - t_k)$. The input neurons' firings could be implemented in practice by using local programming voltages with controlled pulse width and height that are easily realizable both in CMOS/memristor chips [10] and in neuronal networks grown *in vitro* [26]. In order to induce STDP in a manner that will improve the SNN representation of the mapping in (17), the programming voltages are delivered based on an optimized spiking sequence $S_i^l = \{\hat{t}_{i,\kappa} : \kappa = 1,\ldots,N_i^l\}$, $i = 1,\ldots,q$, during the ith time interval of the training algorithm, $[t_i, t_{i+1}]$.

Existing spike models [13, 14] cannot be used to generate S_i^l because they are stochastic and, as such, they do not allow for precise timing of pre- and postsynaptic firings. As a result, they may induce undesirable changes in the synaptic weights by virtue of the STDP rule (7), illustrated in Figure 1, which shows that a small difference in the arrival time of a pre- and postsynaptic spike can obtain the opposite effect in terms of the weight change Δw. Beside allowing for precise timing of neuron firings, the new deterministic spike model presented in the next section can be updated by the training algorithm, by optimizing a corresponding continuous signal modeled by a superposition of Gaussian radial basis functions (RBFs), which is characterized by a set of adjustable parameters $P = \{w_k, c_k, \beta_k \mid k = 1,\ldots,N\}$, where w_k is the height the RBF

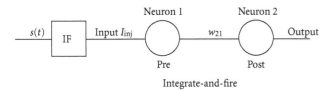

FIGURE 3: Model of two-node LIF spiking neural network.

pulse, c_k is the center of RBF pulse, β_k is the width of the RBF pulse, and N is the number of RBF pulses. As shown in the next section, the continuous RBF signal can be integrated against a suitable averaging function in a leaky integrator and then compared to a positive threshold, by means of a leaky integrate-and-fire (LIF) sampler. Subsequently, a precise pulse function with desired widths and intensity can be generated at a sequence of time instants, $\hat{t}_{i,\kappa}$, during the interval $[t_i, t_{i+1}]$, that correspond to the centers of the RBF signal specified by P. Thus, a set of optimal RBF parameters P^* used to generate S_i^l can be determined by minimizing a measure of the distance between the (decoded) SNN's output $\hat{y}$ and the desired output y, computed by the policy-improvement routine (13).

In the next section, the derivation of gradient equations that can be used to minimize the SNN's output error $(y - \hat{y})$ with respect to P is illustrated by means of a two-node LIF neural network, with STDP modeled as shown in Section 2. Let $P = \{p_{lk}\}$ denote a matrix of RBF parameters to be adjusted by the training algorithm. It can be easily shown that the minimization of an error function $E(y - \hat{y})$ with respect to the elements of P when y is a known constant can be accomplished using the gradients $\partial\hat{y}/\partial p_{lk}$, or some function thereof, based on the chosen unconstrained minimization algorithm [27]. As shown in (17), for a given input ξ^l the only SNN variables to be optimized are the synaptic weights w_{ij}. From the STDP rule (7), the weights are a function of the parameters p_{lk}, which determine the input spike sequence (or training signal) to the SNN (Figure 3). By virtue of the chain rule of differentiation, it follows that

$$\frac{\partial\hat{y}}{\partial p_{lk}} = \frac{\partial\hat{y}}{\partial w_{ij}}\frac{\partial w_{ij}}{\partial p_{lk}}. \qquad (19)$$

Since $\partial\hat{y}/\partial w_{ij}$ can be computed from the SNN model (Section 2), it follows that if a training algorithm can successfully modify the synaptic weights w_{ij} using the proposed spike model, it also can successfully modify $\hat{y}$, simply by redefining the error function. In other words, if a training algorithm can successfully train the synaptic weights of an SNN using the gradient $\partial w_{ij}/\partial p_{lk}$, it follows that it can also train the SNN using the gradient $\partial\hat{y}/\partial p_{lk}$, since the component $\partial\hat{y}/\partial w_{ij}$ is known and given by the SNN equations (1)–(5). Based on this property, the novel spike model and indirect training algorithm are illustrated by training the synaptic weight of a two-node LIF SNN to meet a desired value w^*, without direct manipulation.

4. Indirect Training Methodology

Consider the two-node LIF SNN schematized in Figure 3, modeled using the approach described in Section 2. $s(t)$ represents the input given to the LIF sampler, and $S(t)$ denotes the corresponding LIF sampler's output. Based on the approach presented in Section 3, the SNN synaptic strength w_{21}, representing the synaptic efficacy for a pre-synaptic neuron (labeled by $i = 1$) and a postsynaptic neuron (labeled by $i = 2$) cannot be modified directly by the training algorithm but can only change as a result of the STDP mechanism described in Section 2. In place of controlling w_{21}, the goal of the indirect training algorithm is to determine a spike train that can be used to stimulate the input neuron ($i = 1$) using I_{inj}, thereby inducing it to spike, such that the synaptic weight w_{21} changes from an initial (random) value to a desired value w^*.

For this purpose, we introduce a continuous spike model comprised of a superposition of Gaussian radial basis functions (RBFs):

$$s(t) = \sum_{k=1}^{N} w_k \exp\left[-\beta_k(\|t - c_k\|)^2\right], \qquad (20)$$

where w_k determines the height of the kth RBF, which will decide the constant current input I_{inj}. β_k determines the width of the kth RBF and c_k determines the center of the kth RBF, where $k = 1, \ldots, N$ and N is the number of RBFs. Thus, the set of RBF adjustable parameters is $P = \{w_k, c_k, \beta_k \mid k = 1, \ldots, N\}$. A spike train can be obtained from the continuous spike model (20) by processing s using a suitable LIF sampler that outputs a square pulse function $S(t)$ with the same heights, widths, and centers, as the RBF spike model (20).

In this two-node SNN model, there is no synaptic current sent to the first neuron because there are no presynaptic neurons connected to it. Rather, the input for the first neuron is the square pulse function provided by the output of the LIF sampler. Therefore, during one square pulse, the input, $I_{inj}(t)$, to neuron $i = 1$ can be viewed as a constant, which for our case is h, the height of the RBF. For a fixed threshold and a constant input, the time it takes for the first neuron to fire (or a spike to be generated) is

$$T = -\tau_m \ln\left[1 - \frac{\theta}{hR_m}\right] \quad (hR_m > \theta), \qquad (21)$$

where θ is the potential difference between the spike generating threshold, V_{th}, and the resting potential, V_0; that is, $\theta = V_{th} - V_0$. h is the height of input square pulse, R_m is the resistance of the membrane, and τ_m is the passive-membrane time constant [20]. Thus, from (21), the value of T can be controlled by adjusting h. We allow the first neuron to fire near the end of a square pulse by inputting a spike sequence generated by an RBF model with a suitable width and height. Then, the firing times of the first neuron can be easily adjusted by altering the centers of the RBF.

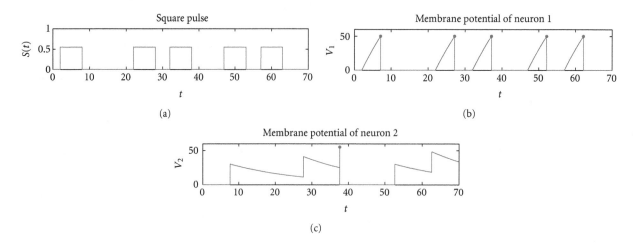

FIGURE 4: Membrane potential of the two neurons in the SNN in Figure 3.

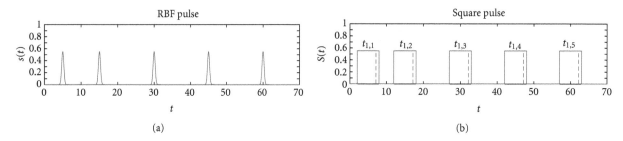

FIGURE 5: Deterministic spike model signals.

In this simple example, it is assumed that the synapse is of the excitatory type. Therefore, (4) can be written as,

$$I_s(t) = C_m a_E \sum_{k=k_0}^{k_t} \delta(t - t_{1,k} - \tau_d), \tag{22}$$

where τ_d is a known constant that represents the conduction delay of the synaptic current from neuron $i = 1$ and $t_{1,k}$ are the firing times of the first neuron. k_0 is the index of the spike of the first neuron, which occurs after the previous spike of the second neuron, and k_t is the index of the spike of the first neuron, which provokes the firing time of the second neuron. The only input to the second neuron is the synaptic current defined in (22). Therefore, substituting (22) and (2) into (1) results in the following equation for the membrane potential,

$$C_m \frac{dv(t)}{dt} = -\frac{C_m}{\tau_m}[v(t) - V_0] + C_m a_E \sum_{k=k_0}^{k_t} \delta(t - t_{1,k} - \tau_d). \tag{23}$$

Solving (23) for the membrane potential of the second neuron provides the response of neuron $i = 2$,

$$v(t) = V_0 + \sum_{k=k_0}^{k_t} a_E \exp\left[-\frac{t - t_{1,k} - \tau_d}{\tau_m}\right] H(t - t_{1,k} - \tau_d), \tag{24}$$

where $H(\cdot)$ is the Heaviside function. Whenever the membrane potential in (24) exceeds the threshold V_{th}, the second

neuron fires, and the membrane potential $v(t)$ is then set instantly equal to V_0. It follows that the firing times of the second neuron $t_{2,j}$ can be written as a function of the firing times of the first neuron,

$$t_{2,j} = (t_{1,k_t} + \tau_d) H\left\{ \sum_{k=k_0}^{k_t} a_E \exp\left[-\frac{t_{2,j} - t_{1,k} - \tau_d}{\tau_m}\right] \right.$$
$$\left. \times H\left(t_{2,j} - t_{1,k} - \tau_d\right) - (V_{\text{th}} - V_0) \right\}, \tag{25}$$

where j is the index of the firing times. In addition, the membrane potentials of the first neuron and the second neuron can be calculated using (24) and (21).

An example of the membrane potential time history for the two neurons is plotted in Figure 4, where the square pulse function S used to stimulate the first neuron is plotted along with the neurons' membrane potentials v_1 and v_2. The red dots denote the firing times and potentials for the two neurons. It can be seen from Figure 4 that, with this input, the first neuron fires five times and the second neuron fires one time. In this SNN, the input to the second neuron is given only by the synaptic current caused by the firing of the first neuron. It can be seen that only when the second and third firing times of the first neuron are very close, the membrane potential of the second neuron increases over the threshold, causing it to fire, whereas the fourth and fifth

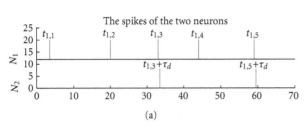

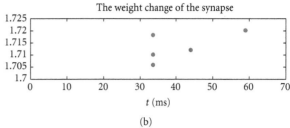

FIGURE 6: Optimized input spike train and indirect weight changes brought about by STDP.

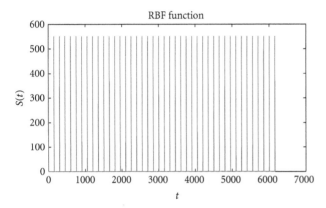

FIGURE 7: Optimized RBF spike model for the SNN in Figure 3.

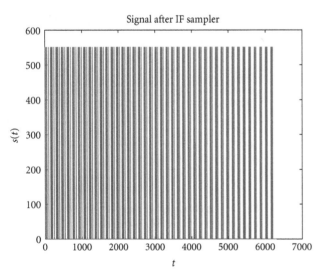

FIGURE 8: Square wave obtained by the LIF sampler, for the RBF spike model in Figure 7.

functions is adopted, which converts any continuous signal $f(t)$ into a square wave function by integrating it against an averaging function $u_{k,z}(t)$. The integrated result is compared to a positive threshold and a negative threshold, such that when either one of the two thresholds is reached, a pulse is generated at time $t_k = z$. The value of the integrator is then reset and the process repeats. In this paper, the averaging function $u_{k,z}(t)$ is chosen to be the exponential $e^{\alpha(t-z)}X_{[t_k,z]}$, where X_I is the characteristic function of I and $\alpha > 0$ is a constant that models the leakage of the integrator, as due to practical implementations [28]. Then, the LIF sampler firing condition that generates the square wave (or sequence of pulses) is

$$\pm\theta = \int_{t_k}^{t_{k+1}} f(t)e^{\alpha(t-t_{k+1})}dt \triangleq \langle f, u_k \rangle, \quad (26)$$

where t_k is the time instant of the sample, t_{k+1} is the next time instant of the sample, u_k is the averaging function, θ is the threshold value, and α is the leakage of the integrator. The output of the LIF sampler can be expressed in terms of the time instants at which the integral reaches the threshold, $\{t_0, \ldots, t_n\}$, and by the samples $q_1, \ldots, q_n$, defined as

$$q_j \triangleq \int_{t_j}^{t_{j-1}} f(x)e^{\alpha(x-t_j)}dx, \quad \text{for } 1 \le j \le n. \quad (27)$$

From (26), it follows that $|q_j| = \theta$. By adjusting the parameters of the LIF sampler, it is possible to convert the RBF signal in (20) to a square wave comprised of pulses with the same width, height, and centers as the RBFs in (20). Thus, by using the RBF spike model in (26) with suitable widths and heights, it is possible to induce the first neuron to fire shortly before the end of each pulse of the square-pulse function (also considering the refractory period of the neuron). For simplicity, in this example, it is assumed that the heights w_k and widths β_k are known positive constants of equal magnitudes for all k. Then, the centers of the RBF comprise the set of adjustable parameters, $P = \{c_k \mid k = 1, \ldots, N\}$, to be optimized. The same approach can be easily extended to a case where all of the RBF parameters are adapted.

firing times of the first neuron are too far apart to cause firing of the second neuron.

4.1. Deterministic Spike Model.
The deterministic spike model consists of a continuous RBF model in the form (20) combined with an LIF sampler that converts the RBF into a square wave function. The LIF sampler developed in [28] for the approximate reconstruction of bandlimited

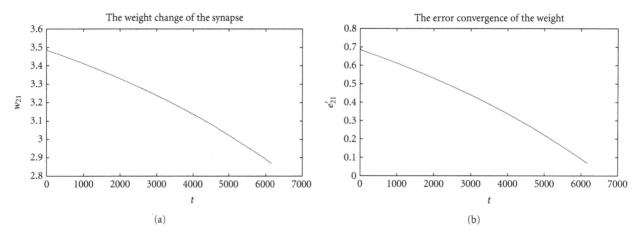

FIGURE 9: Indirect weight changes brought about by STDP and corresponding deviation from $w^* = 2.8$, for the SNN in Figure 3 stimulated using the input spike train in Figure 7.

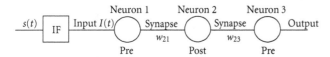

FIGURE 10: Model of three-node LIF spiking neural network.

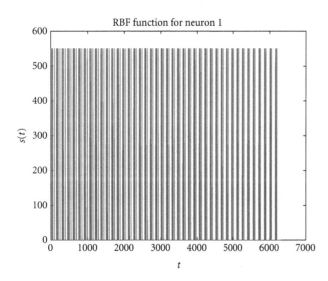

FIGURE 11: Optimized RBF spike model for the SNN in Figure 10.

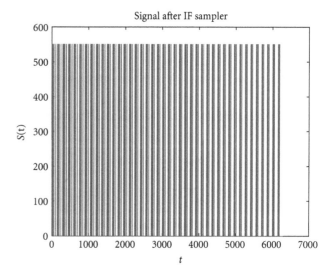

FIGURE 12: Square wave obtained from the LIF sampler, using the optimized RBF spike model in Figure 11.

It can be shown using the LIF SNN model in Section 2 that, under the aforementioned assumptions, the firing times of the first neuron satisfy the constraints,

$$t_{1,k} \le c_k + \frac{\beta}{2},$$

$$t_{1,k} + \Delta^{\text{abs}} \ge c_k + \frac{\beta}{2}, \qquad (28)$$

where Δ^{abs} is an absolute refractory time of the neuron. Then, the firing times of the first neuron can be written as a function of the RBF centers, c_k. By design, the first neuron fires after the same time interval, relative to each square pulse

(Figure 4), due to the chosen RBF heights and widths. Then, the firing times of the first neuron can be written as,

$$t_{1,k} = c_k - \frac{\beta}{2} + T, \qquad (29)$$

where $t_{1,k}$ denotes the firing times of the first neuron, c_k are the centers of the RBF, β is the constant width of the RBF, and T is given by (21).

The RBF spike model is demonstrated in Figure 5, where an example of RBF output obtained from (20) is plotted and, after being fed to the LIF sampler, produces a corresponding square wave which can be used as controlled pulse. It can be seen that the centers of the RBFs precisely determine the times at which a pulse occurs in the square wave and that the square wave maintains the desired constant width and magnitude for all k. The next subsection illustrates how, by adapting the continuous RBF spike model in (20), it is

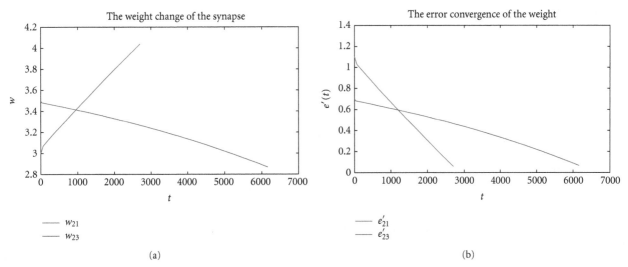

FIGURE 13: Indirect weight changes brought about by STDP and corresponding error functions, for the SNN in Figure 10 stimulated using the input spike train in Figure 12.

possible to minimize a desired error function and train the synaptic weight of the SNN without directly manipulating it.

4.2. Indirect Training Equations.

As explained in Section 2.2, it is assumed that the synaptic weight w_{21} can only be modified by controlling the activity of the SNN input neuron(s), with $i = 1$, and that it obeys the nearest-spike STDP model in (8). Over time, the synaptic weight can change repeatedly, and therefore its final value can be written as the sum of all incremental changes that have occurred over the time interval $[t_i, t_{i+1}]$,

$$w_{21}(t) = \prod_{i=1}^{M} w_0(1 + \Delta w_i), \qquad (30)$$

where, for the two-neuron SNN in Figure 3, $\Delta w_1, \ldots, \Delta w_M$ are due to M pairs of pre- and postsynaptic spikes that occur at any time $t \in [t_i, t_{i+1}]$. Every weight increment Δw_i is induced via STDP and, thus, obeys equation (8). Since the firing times in (8) depend on the centers of the RBF input through (21)–(29), it follows that every weight increment Δw_i is a function of the RBF centers. In this example, the constraints (28) can be written as,

$$\frac{\beta}{2} < c_1, \qquad c_N + \frac{\beta}{2} < t_f, \qquad c_k + \beta < c_{k+1}, \quad \text{for } k = 1, \ldots, N, \qquad (31)$$

where, from Figure 5, $N = 5$.

A training-error function is defined in terms of the desired synaptic weight w^* and the actual value of the synaptic weight $w_{21}(t)$. While different forms of error function may be used, the chosen form determines the complexity of the derivation of the training gradients. It was found that the most convenient form of training-error function can be derived from the ratio of the actual weight over the desired weight,

$$e(t) = \frac{w_{21}(t)}{w^*}, \qquad (32)$$

where $w_{21}(t)$ is the weight value at time $t \in [t_i, t_{i+1}]$, obtained from all previous spikes. As explained in Section 3, w^* can be viewed as the weight that leads to desired output $\hat{y}$ for a given input ξ. It can be seen that when w_{21} is equal to w^*, e is equal to one. Plugging (30) into (36), the weight ratio can be rewritten as,

$$e(t) = \frac{1}{w^*} \prod_{i=1}^{M} w_0(1 + \Delta w_i), \qquad (33)$$

and the error between w_{21} and w^* can be minimized by minimizing the natural logarithm of the ratio (33):

$$E(t) \triangleq \ln[e(t)] = \ln(w_0) + \ln(1 + \Delta w_1) \\ + \cdots + \ln(1 + \Delta w_M) - \ln(w^*). \qquad (34)$$

As is typical of all optimization problems, minimizing a quadratic form presents several advantages [29]. Therefore, at any time $t \in [t_i, t_{i+1}]$, the indirect training algorithm seeks to minimize the quadratic training-error function:

$$J(t) \triangleq E(t)^2 = \{\ln[e(t)]\}^2 = \{\ln(w_0) + \ln(1 + \Delta w_1) \\ + \cdots + \ln(1 + \Delta w_M) \quad (35) \\ - \ln(w^*)\}^2.$$

Then, indirect training can be formulated as an unconstrained optimization problem in which J is to be minimized with respect to the RBF centers, or $P = \{c_k : c_k \in [t_i, t_{i+1}]\}$. Any gradient-based numerical optimization algorithm can be utilized for this purpose. The analytical form of the gradient $\partial J / \partial c_k$ depends on the form of the spike patterns. The following subsection derives this gradient analytically for one example of spike patterns and demonstrates that, using this gradient, the synaptic weight can be trained indirectly to meet the desired value w^* exactly. The same results were derived and demonstrated numerically for all other possible spike patterns, but they are omitted here for brevity. Another representation of error $e'(t)$ is defined below to make the convergence of error more understandable in figures,

$$e'(t) = |w_{21} - w^*|. \tag{36}$$

where, $|\cdot|$ denotes the absolute value.

4.3. Derivation of Gradient Equations for Indirect Training. Consider the case in which $M = 5$, $w^* = 1.72$, and $2a_E > V_{th} - V_0 > a_E$, which results in a two-node SNN (Figure 3) in which neuron $i = 1$ must fire at least two times in order for neuron $i = 2$ to fire. An example of such a spike pattern is shown in Figure 6, where N_1 and N_2 denote spike trains of neuron $i = 1$ and $i = 2$, respectively. In this case, the first neuron fires five times, and the second neuron fires two times. The firing time of the first neuron is controlled by the RBF spike model described in Section 4.1. In Figure 6, $t_{i,k}$ denotes the kth firing time of the ith neuron with $k \in \mathcal{L}_i$, where $\mathcal{L}_i = \{k = 1, \ldots, 5\}$ is an index set for the firing times and i is the index labeling the neurons. In this example, the second neuron fires after $t_{1,3}$ and $t_{1,5}$, because $t_{1,2}$, $t_{1,3}$ and $t_{1,4}$, $t_{1,5}$ are close enough to cause the membrane potential of the second neuron, v_2, to exceed the threshold.

Initially, the synaptic weight is equal to 1.7. The weight change is discontinuous due to the discrete property of spikes. As shown in Figure 6, the weight increases three times at $t_{1,3} + \tau_d$, decreases at $t_{1,4}$, and increases again at $t_{1,5} + \tau_d$. For this example, the synaptic weight changes in five increments:

$$\Delta w_1 = A_+ \exp\left(\frac{t_{1,1}}{\tau_+}\right) \exp\left(\frac{-t_{1,3}}{\tau_+}\right) \exp\left(\frac{-\tau_d}{\tau_+}\right)$$

$$\Delta w_2 = A_+ \exp\left(\frac{t_{1,2}}{\tau_+}\right) \exp\left(\frac{-t_{1,3}}{\tau_+}\right) \exp\left(\frac{-\tau_d}{\tau_+}\right)$$

$$\Delta w_3 = A_+ \exp\left(\frac{-\tau_d}{\tau_+}\right) \tag{37}$$

$$\Delta w_4 = -A_- \exp\left(\frac{t_{1,3}}{\tau_-}\right) \exp\left(\frac{-t_{1,4}}{\tau_-}\right) \exp\left(\frac{\tau_d}{\tau_-}\right)$$

$$\Delta w_5 = A_+ \exp\left(\frac{-\tau_d}{\tau_+}\right).$$

When the equations above are substituted in (35), the training-error function can be written as

$$J = \left\{\ln(w_0) + \ln\left[1 + A_+ \exp\left(\frac{t_{1,1}}{\tau_+}\right) \exp\left(\frac{-t_{1,3}}{\tau_+}\right) \exp\left(\frac{-\tau_d}{\tau_+}\right)\right]\right.$$

$$+ \ln\left[1 + A_+ \exp\left(\frac{t_{1,2}}{\tau_+}\right) \exp\left(\frac{-t_{1,3}}{\tau_+}\right) \exp\left(\frac{-\tau_d}{\tau_+}\right)\right]$$

$$+ \ln\left[1 + A_+ \exp\left(\frac{-\tau_d}{\tau_+}\right)\right]$$

$$+ \ln\left[1 - A_- \exp\left(\frac{t_{1,3}}{\tau_-}\right) \exp\left(\frac{-t_{1,4}}{\tau_-}\right) \exp\left(\frac{\tau_d}{\tau_-}\right)\right]$$

$$\left. + \ln\left[1 + A_+ \exp\left(\frac{-\tau_d}{\tau_+}\right)\right] - \ln(w^*)\right\}^2. \tag{38}$$

Then, the gradients of J with respect to the RBF centers are given by

$$\frac{\partial J}{\partial c_1} = \frac{\partial E^2}{\partial c_1} = \frac{\partial E^2}{\partial t_{1,1}} = 2E\left[\frac{\Delta w_1}{\tau_+(1 + \Delta w_1)}\right]$$

$$\frac{\partial J}{\partial c_2} = \frac{\partial(E^2)}{\partial c_2} = \frac{\partial E^2}{\partial t_{1,2}} = 2E\left[\frac{\Delta w_2}{\tau_+(1 + \Delta w_2)}\right]$$

$$\frac{\partial J}{\partial c_3} = \frac{\partial E^2}{\partial c_3} = \frac{\partial E^2}{\partial t_{1,3}}$$

$$= 2E\left[\frac{-\Delta w_1}{\tau_+(1 + \Delta w_1)} + \frac{-\Delta w_2}{\tau_+(1 + \Delta w_2)} + \frac{\Delta w_4}{\tau_-(1 + \Delta w_4)}\right]$$

$$\frac{\partial J}{\partial c_4} = \frac{\partial E^2}{\partial c_4} = \frac{\partial E^2}{\partial t_{1,4}} = 2E\left[\frac{-\Delta w_4}{\tau_-(1 + \Delta w_4)}\right]$$

$$\frac{\partial J}{\partial c_5} = \frac{\partial E^2}{\partial c_5} = \frac{\partial E^2}{\partial t_{1,5}} = 0. \tag{39}$$

Using the above gradients, the optimal values of $c_1, \ldots, c_5$ can be obtained by minimizing J using a gradient-based numerical algorithm such as Newton's method.

An example of indirect learning algorithm implementation is shown in Figure 6, where the RBF-adjustable parameters (which, in this case, coincide with the firing times of neuron $i = 1$) are optimized to induce a change in the synaptic weight w_{21} from an initial value of 1.704, to a desired value $w^* = 1.72$. Another example, for which the gradient equations are omitted for brevity, is shown in Figures 7–9. In this case, the desired weight value $w^* = 2.8$ is far from the initial weight $w_{21}(t_i) = 3.5$, and thus $N = 43$ spikes are required to train the SNN. The optimal RBF input and corresponding controlled pulse used to stimulate neuron $i = 1$ are shown in Figures 7 and 8, respectively. The time history of the weight w_{21} is plotted in Figure 9(a), along with the corresponding deviation from w^* plotted in Figure 9(b).

5. Generalized Form of Gradient Equations for Indirect Training

A more general form of the gradient equations can be found by rewriting the response of the membrane potential for neuron $i = 2$ in (24), as follows,

$$v(t) = V_0 + \sum_{k=a}^{b} a_E \exp\left[-\frac{t - t_{1,k} - \tau_d}{\tau_m}\right] H(t - t_{1,k} - \tau_d), \tag{40}$$

where $t_{1,k}$ denotes the kth firing time of neuron $i = 1$. Then, the gradients of the training objective function (35) with respect to the centers of the RBF spike model for $M = 5$ are given by the equations in the Appendix, which are obtained in terms of the two functions,

$$g_+\left(t_{1,i}, t_{1,j}\right) = A_+ \exp\left(\frac{t_{1,i}}{\tau_+}\right) \exp\left(\frac{-t_{1,j}}{\tau_+}\right) \exp\left(\frac{-\tau_d}{\tau_+}\right),$$

$$g_-\left(t_{1,i}, t_{1,j}\right) = -A_- \exp\left(\frac{t_{1,i}}{\tau_-}\right) \exp\left(\frac{-t_{1,j}}{\tau_-}\right) \exp\left(\frac{\tau_d}{\tau_-}\right), \tag{41}$$

where $t_{1,i}$, $t_{1,j}$ are two distinct firing times of neuron $i = 1$.

The methodology presented in Section 4 can also be extended to larger SNNs, although in this case it may be more convenient to compute the gradients of the objective function numerically. As an example, consider the three-neuron SNN in Figure 10, modeled by the approach in Section 2 and with two synaptic weights w_{21} and w_{23} that each obey the STDP mechanism in (8). Suppose that the desired values of the synaptic weights are $w_{21}^* = 4.1$ and $w_{23}^* = 2.8$. Using the indirect learning method presented in this paper, and the gradient provided in the Appendix, a training-error function formulated in terms of the deviations of $w_{21}(t)$ and $w_{23}(t)$ from w_{21}^* and w_{23}^*, respectively, can be minimized with respect to the parameters (centers) P of the RBF spike model (20).

Once the optimal RBF spike model, plotted in Figure 11, is fed to the LIF sampler, the controlled pulse plotted in Figure 12 is obtained and implemented via I_{inj}. The controlled pulse is thus used to stimulate neuron $i = 1$ at precise instants in time that corresponds to centers of the optimal RBF spike model. By this approach, $w_{21}(t)$ can be made to converge to the desired value w_{21}^*. The same method is implemented to stimulate neuron $i = 2$ to make the value of $w_{23}(t)$ converge to w_{23}^*. The time histories of the weight values $w_{21}(t)$ and $w_{23}(t)$, obtained by the indirect training algorithm are plotted in Figure 13(a). As is also shown by the corresponding training errors, plotted in Figure 13(b), the SNN weights over time converge to the desired values, that is $w_{21}^* = 4.1$ and $w_{23}^* = 2.8$. These results demonstrate that, even for larger SNNs, the indirect training method presented in this paper is capable of modifying synaptic weights until they meet their desired values, without direct manipulation. Since this indirect training algorithm only relies on modulating the activity of the input neurons via controlled input spike trains, it also has the potential of being realizable *in vitro* and *in silico* to train biological neuronal networks and CMOS/memristor nanoscale chips, respectively.

6. Summary and Conclusion

Recently, several algorithms have been proposed for training spiking neural networks through biologically plausible learning mechanisms, such as spike-timing-dependent synaptic plasticity. These algorithms, however, rely on being able to modify the synaptic weights directly or STDP. In other words, they minimize a desired objective function with respect to weight increments that are assumed to be controllable and,

thus, are decided by a weight update rule, and then are implemented directly by the training algorithm. In several potential applications of spiking neural networks, synaptic weights cannot be manipulated directly but change over time by virtue of pre- and postsynaptic neural activity. In these applications, the activity of selected input neurons can be controlled via programming voltages or pulses of blue light that induce precise spiking of the input neurons, at precise moments in time.

This paper presents an indirect learning method that induces changes in the synaptic weights by modulating spike-timing-dependent plasticity using controlled input spike trains, in lieu of the weight increments. The key difficulty to be overcome is that indirect learning seeks to adapt a pulse signal, such as a square wave or Rademacher function, in place of continuous-valued weights. Pulse signals that can be delivered to stimulate input neurons and cause them to spike, such as blue light patterns or programming voltages, are represented by piece-wise continuous, multi-valued (or many-to-one), and nondifferentiable functions that are not well suited to numerical optimization. Furthermore, stimulation patterns typically are generated by spike models that are stochastic, such as the Poisson spike model. Therefore, even when the spike model is optimized, it does not allow for precise timing of pre- and post-synaptic firings, and as a result, may induce undesirable changes in the synaptic weights. This paper presents a deterministic and adaptive spike model derived from radial basis functions and a leaky integrate-and-fire sampler. This spike model can be easily optimized to determine the sequence of spike timings that minimizes a desired objective function and, then, used to stimulate input neurons. The results demonstrate that this methodology is capable of inducing the desired synaptic plasticity in the network and modify synaptic weights to meet their desired values only by virtue of controlled input spike trains that are realizable both in biological neuronal networks and in CMOS/memristor nanoscale chips.

Appendix

The gradients of the training objective function can be derived as follows. The membrane potential of neuron 2 is denoted by $v_{i,j}(t)$, where the membrane potential can only be affected by presynaptic spikes that occur within the time interval $[t_{1,i}, t_{1,j}]$.

$$\frac{\partial E^2}{\partial c_1} = \begin{cases} 2E\left[\dfrac{g_+(t_{1,1}, t_{1,3})}{\tau_+(1 + g_+(t_{1,1}, t_{1,3}))}\right] & \text{if } v(t_{1,3} + \tau_d)_{1,3} > V_{\text{th}} \\[2ex] 2E\left[\dfrac{g_+(t_{1,1}, t_{1,2})}{\tau_+(1 + g_+(t_{1,1}, t_{1,2}))}\right] & \text{if } v(t_{1,2} + \tau_d)_{1,2} > V_{\text{th}} \\[2ex] 2E\left[\dfrac{g_+(t_{1,1}, t_{1,4})}{\tau_+(1 + g_+(t_{1,1}, t_{1,4}))}\right] & \text{if } v(t_{1,4} + \tau_d)_{1,4} > V_{\text{th}} \\[2ex] 2E\left[\dfrac{g_+(t_{1,1}, t_{1,5})}{\tau_+(1 + g_+(t_{1,1}, t_{1,5}))}\right] & \text{if } v(t_{1,5} + \tau_d)_{1,5} > V_{\text{th}}. \end{cases}$$

$$\frac{\partial E^2}{\partial c_2} = \begin{cases} 2E\left[\dfrac{g_+(t_{1,2},t_{1,3})}{\tau_+(1+g_+(t_{1,2},t_{1,3}))}\right] & \text{if } v(t_{1,3}+\tau_d)_{1,3} > V_{\text{th}} \\[3mm] 2E\left[\dfrac{-g_+(t_{1,1},t_{1,2})}{\tau_+(1+g_+(t_{1,1},t_{1,2}))}\right] & \text{if } v(t_{1,2}+\tau_d)_{1,2} > V_{\text{th}},\ v(t_{1,5}+\tau_d)_{3,5} > V_{\text{th}} \\[3mm] & c_3 > \dfrac{c_5+c_2+2\tau_d}{2} \\[3mm] 2E\left[\dfrac{-g_+(t_{1,1},t_{1,2})}{\tau_+(1+g_+(t_{1,1},t_{1,2}))} + \dfrac{g_-(t_{1,2},t_{1,3})}{\tau_-(1+g_-(t_{1,2},t_{1,3}))}\right] & \text{if } v(t_{1,2}+\tau_d)_{1,2} > V_{\text{th}},\ v(t_{1,4}+\tau_d)_{3,4} > V_{\text{th}}, \\[3mm] & c_3 < \dfrac{c_4+c_2+2\tau_d}{2}\ \text{ or } v(t_{1,2}+\tau_d)_{1,2} > V_{\text{th}}, \\[3mm] & v(t_{1,5}+\tau_d)_{3,5} > V_{\text{th}},\ c_3 < \dfrac{c_5+c_2+2\tau_d}{2} \\[3mm] 2E\left[\dfrac{-g_+(t_{1,1},t_{1,2})}{\tau_+(1+g_+(t_{1,1},t_{1,2}))} + \dfrac{g_-(t_{1,2},t_{1,3})}{\tau_-(1+g_-(t_{1,2},t_{1,3}))}\right. & \\[3mm] \left. + \dfrac{g_-(t_{1,2},t_{1,4})}{\tau_-(1+g_-(t_{1,2},t_{1,4}))} + \dfrac{g_-(t_{1,2},t_{1,5})}{\tau_-(1+g_-(t_{1,2},t_{1,5}))}\right] & \text{if } v(t_{1,2}+\tau_d)_{1,2} > V_{\text{th}},\ v(t_{1,5}+\tau_d)_{3,5} < V_{\text{th}} \\[3mm] 2E\left[\dfrac{g_+(t_{1,2},t_{1,4})}{\tau_+(1+g_+(t_{1,2},t_{1,4}))}\right] & \text{if } v(t_{1,4}+\tau_d)_{1,4} > V_{\text{th}}. \end{cases}$$

$$\frac{\partial E^2}{\partial c_3} = \begin{cases} 2E\left[\dfrac{-g_+(t_{1,1},t_{1,3})}{\tau_+(1+g_+(t_{1,1},t_{1,3}))} + \dfrac{-g_+(t_{1,2},t_{1,3})}{\tau_+(1+g_+(t_{1,2},t_{1,3}))}\right. & \\[3mm] \left. + \dfrac{g_-(t_{1,3},t_{1,4})}{\tau_-(1+g_-(t_{1,3},t_{1,4}))}\right] & \text{if } v(t_{1,3}+\tau_d)_{1,3} > V_{\text{th}}, \\[3mm] & v(t_{1,5}+\tau_d)_{4,5} > V_{\text{th}},\ c_3 > 2c_4-c_5-2\tau_d \\[3mm] 2E\left[\dfrac{-g_+(t_{1,1},t_{1,3})}{\tau_+(1+g_+(t_{1,1},t_{1,3}))} + \dfrac{-g_+(t_{1,2},t_{1,3})}{\tau_+(1+g_+(t_{1,2},t_{1,3}))}\right] & \text{if } v(t_{1,3}+\tau_d)_{1,3} > V_{\text{th}},\ v(t_{1,5}+\tau_d)_{4,5} > V_{\text{th}}, \\[3mm] & c_3 < 2c_4-c_5-2\tau_d \\[3mm] 2E\left[\dfrac{g_+(t_{1,3},t_{1,5})}{\tau_+(1+g_+(t_{1,3},t_{1,5}))}\right] & \text{if } v(t_{1,2}+\tau_d)_{1,2} > V_{\text{th}},\ v(t_{1,5}+\tau_d)_{3,5} > V_{\text{th}}, \\[3mm] & c_3 > \dfrac{c_5+c_2+2\tau_d}{2}\ \text{ or } \\[1mm] & v(t_{1,5}+\tau_d)_{1,5} > V_{\text{th}} \\[3mm] 2E\left[\dfrac{-g_-(t_{1,2},t_{1,3})}{\tau_-(1+g_-(t_{1,2},t_{1,3}))}\right] & \text{if } v(t_{1,2}+\tau_d)_{1,2} > V_{\text{th}},\ v(t_{1,5}+\tau_d)_{3,5} > V_{\text{th}}, \\[3mm] & c_3 < \dfrac{c_5+c_2+2\tau_d}{2}\ \text{ or } \\[1mm] & v(t_{1,2}+\tau_d)_{1,2} > V_{\text{th}},\ v(t_{1,4}+\tau_d)_{3,4} > V_{\text{th}}, \\[3mm] & c_3 < \dfrac{c_4+c_2+2\tau_d}{2}\ \text{ or } \\[1mm] & v(t_{1,2}+\tau_d)_{1,2} > V_{\text{th}},\ v(t_{1,5}+\tau_d)_{3,5} < V_{\text{th}} \\[3mm] 2E\left[\dfrac{g_+(t_{1,3},t_{1,4})}{\tau_+(1+g_+(t_{1,3},t_{1,4}))}\right] & \text{if } v(t_{1,2}+\tau_d)_{1,2} > V_{\text{th}},\ v(t_{1,4}+\tau_d)_{3,4} > V_{\text{th}}, \\[3mm] & c_3 > \dfrac{c_4+c_2+2\tau_d}{2}\ \text{ or } \\[1mm] & v(t_{1,4}+\tau_d)_{1,4} > V_{\text{th}} \\[3mm] 2E\left[\dfrac{-g_+(t_{1,1},t_{1,3})}{\tau_+(1+g_+(t_{1,1},t_{1,3}))} + \dfrac{-g_+(t_{1,2},t_{1,3})}{\tau_+(1+g_+(t_{1,2},t_{1,3}))}\right. & \\[3mm] \left. + \dfrac{g_-(t_{1,3},t_{1,4})}{\tau_-(1+g_-(t_{1,3},t_{1,4}))} + \dfrac{g_-(t_{1,3},t_{1,5})}{\tau_-(1+g_-(t_{1,3},t_{1,5}))}\right] & \text{if } v(t_{1,3}+\tau_d)_{1,3} > V_{\text{th}},\ v(t_{1,5}+\tau_d)_{4,5} < V_{\text{th}}. \end{cases}$$

$$\frac{\partial E^2}{\partial c_4} = \begin{cases} 2E\left[\dfrac{-g_-(t_{1,3},t_{1,4})}{\tau_-(1+g_-(t_{1,3},t_{1,4}))}\right] & \text{if } v(t_{1,3}+\tau_d)_{1,3} > V_{\text{th}},\ v(t_{1,5}+\tau_d)_{4,5} > V_{\text{th}}, \\ & c_4 < \dfrac{c_3+c_5+2\tau_d}{2} \text{ or} \\ & v(t_{1,3}+\tau_d)_{1,3} > V_{\text{th}},\ v(t_{1,5}+\tau_d)_{4,5} < V_{\text{th}} \\[2pt] 2E\left[\dfrac{g_+(t_{1,4},t_{1,5})}{\tau_+(1+g_+(t_{1,4},t_{1,5}))}\right] & \text{if } v(t_{1,3}+\tau_d)_{1,3} > V_{\text{th}},\ v(t_{1,5}+\tau_d)_{4,5} > V_{\text{th}}, \\ & c_4 > \dfrac{c_3+c_5+2\tau_d}{2} \text{ or} \\ & v(t_{1,2}+\tau_d)_{1,2} > V_{\text{th}},\ v(t_{1,5}+\tau_d)_{3,5} > V_{\text{th}}, \\ & c_3 > \dfrac{c_2+c_5+2\tau_d}{2} \text{ or} \\ & v(t_{1,2}+\tau_d)_{1,2} > V_{\text{th}},\ v(t_{1,5}+\tau_d)_{3,5} > V_{\text{th}}, \\ & c_3 < \dfrac{c_2+c_5+2\tau_d}{2} \\[2pt] 2E\left[\dfrac{-g_+(t_{1,3},t_{1,4})}{\tau_+(1+g_+(t_{1,3},t_{1,4}))}+\dfrac{g_-(t_{1,4},t_{1,5})}{\tau_-(1+g_-(t_{1,4},t_{1,5}))}\right] & \text{if } v(t_{1,2}+\tau_d)_{1,2} > V_{\text{th}}, \\ & v(t_{1,4}+\tau_d)_{3,4} > V_{\text{th}},\ c_4 < 2c_3-c_2-2\tau_d \\[2pt] 2E\left[\dfrac{g_-(t_{1,4},t_{1,5})}{\tau_-(1+g_-(t_{1,4},t_{1,5}))}\right] & \text{if } v(t_{1,2}+\tau_d)_{1,2} > V_{\text{th}},\ v(t_{1,4}+\tau_d)_{3,4} > V_{\text{th}}, \\ & c_4 > 2c_3-c_2-2\tau_d \\[2pt] 2E\left[\dfrac{-g_-(t_{1,2},t_{1,4})}{\tau_-(1+g_-(t_{1,2},t_{1,4}))}\right] & \text{if } v(t_{1,2}+\tau_d)_{1,2} > V_{\text{th}},\ v(t_{1,5}+\tau_d)_{3,5} < V_{\text{th}} \\[2pt] 2E\left[\dfrac{-g_+(t_{1,1},t_{1,4})}{\tau_+(1+g_+(t_{1,1},t_{1,4}))}+\dfrac{-g_+(t_{1,2},t_{1,4})}{\tau_+(1+g_+(t_{1,2},t_{1,4}))}\right. & \\ \left.\quad +\dfrac{-g_+(t_{1,3},t_{1,4})}{\tau_+(1+g_+(t_{1,3},t_{1,4}))}+\dfrac{g_-(t_{1,4},t_{1,5})}{\tau_-(1+g_-(t_{1,4},t_{1,5}))}\right] & \text{if } v(t_{1,4}+\tau_d,1,4) > V_{\text{th}} \\[2pt] 2E\left[\dfrac{g_+(t_{1,4},t_{1,5})}{\tau_+(1+g_+(t_{1,4},t_{1,5}))}\right] & \text{if } v(t_{1,5}+\tau_d,1,5) > V_{\text{th}}. \end{cases}$$

$$\frac{\partial E^2}{\partial c_5} = \begin{cases} 0 & \text{if } v(t_{1,3}+\tau_d)_{1,3} > V_{\text{th}}, \\ & v(t_{1,5}+\tau_d)_{4,5} > V_{\text{th}},\ c_5 > 2c_4-c_3-2\tau_d \\[2pt] 2E\left[\dfrac{-g_+(t_{1,4},t_{1,5})}{\tau_+(1+g_+(t_{1,4},t_{1,5}))}\right] & \text{if } v(t_{1,3}+\tau_d)_{1,3} > V_{\text{th}}, \\ & v(t_{1,5}+\tau_d)_{4,5} > V_{\text{th}},\ c_5 < 2c_4-c_3-2\tau_d \\[2pt] 2E\left[\dfrac{-g_+(t_{1,3},t_{1,5})}{\tau_+(1+g_+(t_{1,3},t_{1,5}))}+\dfrac{-g_+(t_{1,4},t_{1,5})}{\tau_+(1+g_+(t_{1,4},t_{1,5}))}\right] & \text{if } v(t_{1,2}+\tau_d)_{1,2} > V_{\text{th}}, \\ & v(t_{1,5}+\tau_d)_{3,5} > V_{\text{th}},\ c_5 < 2c_3-c_2-2\tau_d \\[2pt] 2E\left[\dfrac{-g_+(t_{1,4},t_{1,5})}{\tau_+(1+g_+(t_{1,4},t_{1,5}))}\right] & \text{if } v(t_{1,2}+\tau_d)_{1,2} > V_{\text{th}}, \\ & v(t_{1,5}+\tau_d)_{3,5} > V_{\text{th}}, c_5 > 2c_3-c_2-2\tau_d \\[2pt] 2E\left[\dfrac{-g_-(t_{1,4},t_{1,5})}{\tau_-(1+g_-(t_{1,4},t_{1,5}))}\right] & \text{if } v(t_{1,2}+\tau_d)_{1,2} > V_{\text{th}},\ v(t_{1,4}+\tau_d)_{3,4} > V_{\text{th}} \\[2pt] 2E\left[\dfrac{-g_-(t_{1,2},t_{1,5})}{\tau_-(1+g_-(t_{1,2},t_{1,5}))}\right] & \text{if } v(t_{1,2}+\tau_d)_{1,2} > V_{\text{th}},\ v(t_{1,5}+\tau_d)_{3,5} < V_{\text{th}} \\[2pt] 2E\left[\dfrac{-g_-(t_{1,3},t_{1,5})}{\tau_-(1+g_-(t_{1,3},t_{1,5}))}\right] & \text{if } v(t_{1,3}+\tau_d)_{1,3} > V_{\text{th}},\ v(t_{1,5}+\tau_d)_{4,5} < V_{\text{th}} \\[2pt] 2E\left[\dfrac{-g_-(t_{1,4},t_{1,5})}{\tau_-(1+g_-(t_{1,4},t_{1,5}))}\right] & \text{if } v(t_{1,4}+\tau_d)_{1,4} > V_{\text{th}} \\[2pt] 2E\left[\dfrac{-g_+(t_{1,1},t_{1,5})}{\tau_+(1+g_+(t_{1,1},t_{1,5}))}+\dfrac{-g_+(t_{1,2},t_{1,5})}{\tau_+(1+g_+(t_{1,2},t_{1,5}))}\right. & \\ \left.\quad +\dfrac{-g_+(t_{1,3},t_{1,5})}{\tau_+(1+g_+(t_{1,3},t_{1,5}))}+\dfrac{-g_+(t_{1,4},t_{1,5})}{\tau_+(1+g_+(t_{1,4},t_{1,5}))}\right] & \text{if } v(t_{1,5}+\tau_d)_{1,5} > V_{\text{th}}. \end{cases}$$

$$(A.1)$$

Acknowledgment

This work was supported by the National Science Foundation, under ECCS Grant 0925407.

References

[1] J. J. B. Jack, D. Nobel, and R. Tsien, *Electric Current Flow in Excitable Cells*, Oxford University Press, Oxford, UK, 1st edition, 1975.

[2] A. L. Hodgkin and A. F. Huxley, "A quantitative description of membrane current and its application to conduction and excitation in nerve," *The Journal of Physiology*, vol. 117, no. 4, pp. 500–544, 1952.

[3] W. Maass, "Noisy spiking neurons with temporal coding have more computational power than sigmoidal neurons," *Advances in Neural Information Processing Systems*, vol. 9, pp. 211–217, 1997.

[4] C. M. A. Pennartz, "Reinforcement learning by Hebbian synapses with adaptive thresholds," *Neuroscience*, vol. 81, no. 2, pp. 303–319, 1997.

[5] S. Ferrari, B. Mehta, G. Di Muro, A. M. J. VanDongen, and C. Henriquez, "Biologically realizable reward-modulated hebbian training for spiking neural networks," in *Proceedings of the International Joint Conference on Neural Networks (IJCNN '08)*, pp. 1780–1786, Hong Kong, June 2008.

[6] R. Legenstein, C. Naeger, and W. Maass, "What can a neuron learn with spike-timing-dependent plasticity?" *Neural Computation*, vol. 17, no. 11, pp. 2337–2382, 2005.

[7] J. P. Pfister, T. Toyoizumi, D. Barber, and W. Gerstner, "Optimal spike-timing-dependent plasticity for precise action potential firing in supervised learning," *Neural Computation*, vol. 18, no. 6, pp. 1318–1348, 2006.

[8] R. V. Florian, "Reinforcement learning through modulation of spike-timing-dependent synaptic plasticity," *Neural Computation*, vol. 19, no. 6, pp. 1468–1502, 2007.

[9] S. G. Wysoski, L. Benuskova, and N. Kasabov, "Adaptive learning procedure for a network of spiking neurons and visual pattern recognition," in *Proceedings of the 8th International Conference on Advanced Concepts for Intelligent Vision Systems (ACIVS '06)*, vol. 4179 of *Lecture Notes in Computer Science*, pp. 1133–1142, Antwerp, Belgium, September 2006.

[10] S. H. Jo, T. Chang, I. Ebong, B. B. Bhadviya, P. Mazumder, and W. Lu, "Nanoscale memristor device as synapse in neuromorphic systems," *Nano Letters*, vol. 10, no. 4, pp. 1297–1301, 2010.

[11] A. M. VanDongen, "Vandongen laboratory," http://www.van-dongen-lab.com/.

[12] T. J. Van De Ven, H. M. A. VanDongen, and A. M. J. VanDongen, "The nonkinase phorbol ester receptor $\alpha 1$-chimerin binds the NMDA receptor NR2A subunit and regulates dendritic spine density," *Journal of Neuroscience*, vol. 25, no. 41, pp. 9488–9496, 2005.

[13] P. Dayan and L. F. Abbott, *Theoretical Neuroscience: Computational and Mathematical Modeling of Neural Systems*, MIT Press, Cambridge, Mass, USA, 2001.

[14] W. Gerstner and W. Kistler, *Spiking Neuron Models: Single Neurons, Populations, Plasticity*, Cambridge University Press, Cambridge, UK, 2006.

[15] G. Foderaro, C. Henriquez, and S. Ferrari, "Indirect training of a spiking neural network for flight control via spike-timing-dependent synaptic plasticity," in *Proceedings of the 49th IEEE Conference on Decision and Control (CDC '10)*, pp. 911–917, Atlanta, Ga, USA, December 2010.

[16] A. Aldroubi and K. Gröchenig, "Nonuniform sampling and reconstruction in shift-invariant spaces," *SIAM Review*, vol. 43, no. 4, pp. 585–620, 2001.

[17] A. A. Lazar and L. T. Toth, "A toeplitz formulation of a real-time algorithm for time decoding machines," in *Proceedings of the Telecommunication Systems, Modeling and Analysis Conference*, 2003.

[18] E. M. Izhikevich, "Which model to use for cortical spiking neurons?" *IEEE Transactions on Neural Networks*, vol. 15, no. 5, pp. 1063–1070, 2004.

[19] E. M. Izhikevich, "Simple model of spiking neurons," *IEEE Transactions on Neural Networks*, vol. 14, no. 6, pp. 1569–1572, 2003.

[20] A. N. Burkitt, "A review of the integrate-and-fire neuron model: I. Homogeneous synaptic input," *Biological Cybernetics*, vol. 95, no. 1, pp. 1–19, 2006.

[21] S. Song, K. D. Miller, and L. F. Abbott, "Competitive Hebbian learning through spike-timing-dependent synaptic plasticity," *Nature Neuroscience*, vol. 3, no. 9, pp. 919–926, 2000.

[22] P. Sjostrom, G. Turrigiano, and S. Nelson, "Rate, timing, and cooperativity jointly determine cortical synaptic plasticity," *Neuron*, vol. 32, no. 6, pp. 1149–1164, 2001.

[23] S. Ferrari and R. Stengel, "Model-based adaptive critic designs," in *Learning and Approximate Dynamic Programming*, J. Si, A. Barto, and W. Powell, Eds., John Wiley & Sons, 2004.

[24] R. E. Bellman, *Dynamic Programming*, Princeton University Press, Princeton, NJ, USA, 1957.

[25] R. Howard, *Dynamic Programming and Markov Processes*, MIT Press, Cambridge, Mass, USA, 1960.

[26] A. M. J. VanDongen, J. Codina, J. Olate et al., "Newly identified brain potassium channels gated by the guanine nucleotide binding protein G(o)," *Science*, vol. 242, no. 4884, pp. 1433–1437, 1988.

[27] J. E. Dennis and R. B. Schnabel, *Numerical Methods for Unconstrained Optimization and Nonlinear Equations*, SIAM, Englewood Cliffs, NJ, USA, 1996.

[28] H. G. Feichtinger, J. C. Príncipe, J. L. Romero, A. Singh Alvarado, and G. A. Velasco, "Approximate reconstruction of bandlimited functions for the integrate and fire sampler," *Advances in Computational Mathematics*, vol. 36, no. 1, pp. 67–78, 2012.

[29] R. F. Stengel, *Optimal Control and Estimation*, Dover Publications, Inc., 1986.

12

Analysis of Changes in Market Shares of Commercial Banks Operating in Turkey Using Computational Intelligence Algorithms

M. Fatih Amasyali,[1] Ayse Demırhan,[2] and Mert Bal[3]

[1] Department of Computer Engineering, Yildiz Technical University, Davutpasa Campus, Esenler, 34220 Istanbul, Turkey
[2] Department of Business Administration, Yildiz Technical University, Yildiz Campus, Besiktas, 34349 Istanbul, Turkey
[3] Department of Mathematical Engineering, Yildiz Technical University, Davutpasa Campus A-116, Esenler, 34220 Istanbul, Turkey

Correspondence should be addressed to Mert Bal; mert.bal@gmail.com

Academic Editor: Wolfgang Faber

This paper aims to model the change in market share of 30 domestic and foreign banks, which have been operating between the years 1990 and 2009 in Turkey by taking into consideration 20 financial ratios of those banks. Due to the fragile structure of the banking sector in Turkey, this study plays an important role for determining the changes in market share of banks and taking the necessary measures promptly. For this reason, computational intelligence methods have been used in the study. According to the research results, it is seen that it was not able to properly anticipate the data for the banking sector in the periods of financial crises (2000-2001 and 2008-2009). However, it is seen that, Simple Linear Regression is distinguished as a good algorithm among the computational intelligence algorithms for all periods between the years 1990 and 2009.

1. Introduction

As a natural result of the financial liberalization in the economy and the banking industry in Turkey after 1980s, the competition in the banking industry increased significantly due to the reasons such as many new domestic and foreign players in the banking industry, release of the fund transfers especially from international markets, enabling the banks to make transactions in foreign currencies, advances in the technology, and introducing new services by the banks in the industry. Therefore, a bank, operating in the banking industry, can differentiate itself from the other banks only if it can develop new strategies.

In recent years, because of economic and financial crisis, some of the public and private banks were bankrupted and some of them are merged and therefore they were forced to change how they operate. In this instance, a serious competition occurred among the surviving banks to take the market shares of the banks that have left the industry. The banks, which have evaluated the present circumstances, used cutting edge technology, and improved the scope of their products and services, were able to advance forward significantly. Thus, these advances create a necessary environment for such banks to improve their market shares. Therefore, evaluating their position in the market and developing new strategies in accordance with their positions became much more important.

The presence of a tough competition between the banks besides the fragile structure of the banking sector in Turkey makes it important to determine the change in the market shares of banks and to take the necessary measures. For this reason, goal-oriented estimations that would be made by using computational intelligence methods are of great importance for the industry.

2. General Situation of Turkish Banking Sector

The banks during the period following 1980s are mostly multibranch banks which were financed by public sector and operating in deposit banking field and have oligopolistic structure. In private banking point of view, the banks belonging to holdings have significance in the sector. In the banking sector between 1980 and 1990, with the help of the politics towards financial liberalization and resulting environment, the banks could adapt themselves to meet the international criteria [1]. During this period of financial liberalization process in Turkey, Capital Markets, Istanbul Stock Exchange (ISE), the Interbank Money Market (Interbank), and Foreign Exchange Market were established and Istanbul Gold Exchange started to operate [2]. In addition to this, Savings Deposit Insurance Fund (SDIF) is also established. SDIF is an institution in the banking sector which guarantees the rights of depositors and the regulating system. Gaining functionality of the free economy mechanism and rearrangements towards liberalization of the market have created significant impacts on the banking system [3]. The competition in the market increased due to new foreign/domestic players in the sector and liberating the deposit/credit interest rates [4].

As a result of the new legal and institutional regulations, helping new players to enter the market, compete, and expand in the sector, the number of the banks in Turkish banking sector has experienced a rapid expansion in employment, service diversification, and technological infrastructure points [5].

In 1999, a significant economic contraction in the economic activities and rising real interest rates caused a decline in private sector credit demand, a deterioration of the asset quality, and an increase in the need of liquidity of public banks, in particular banks with weak financial situation. In the late 1990s, macroeconomic instability in the banking sector, financial risks encountered, high costs of the resources, unfair competition conditions, lack of equity capital, oligopolistic structure, the rapid advancements in technology, holdings, and shallow capital market are some of the known basic problems [6, 7].

At the beginning of 2000, a comprehensive economic program has been implemented in order to reduce inflation and restore economic growth environment. In general, since the second half of the year, the conditions such as delays in the structural adjustment arrangements, inflation which did not fall as quickly as expected, and increasing costs of public goods and services were increased at the same level as the inflation; uncontrolled domestic demand caused deterioration of the economic outlook, and as a result of those reasons a serious concussion occurred in November 2000 and February 2001 in the banking sector.

Even though their arising points are quite different from each other, the nature of both crises which occurred in November 2000 and February 2001 is financial [8]. The starting circumstances of the crises affect the duration and depth of the crisis. The circumstances in question usually show the fragility of the economic structure in the country experiencing the crisis [9]. The basis of these two crises experienced in Turkey is due to the fragile nature of the banking sector [10]. November 2000 crisis was due to the liquidity problem in the banking sector. Increasing demand for liquidity during this period could not be met and this caused accelerated increase in the interest rates and exchange rates and the crisis in the financial market was deepened [11].

In addition, if we look at the crisis in February 2001, with the impact of rising financial fragility after November, it was a direct attack on Turkish Lira. This crisis that started in economic and financial system has quickly spread to the real sector.

November 2000 and February 2001 crisis intensified the problems happening in the banking sector further and introduced new problems. The banking sector, which was having serious difficulties due to liquidity and interest risk after the November crisis, faced significant losses arising from foreign exchange risk with the February crisis [12].

The significant increase in the interest rates, as a result of the crisis occurred in the November 2000, the financial structure of the public banks in the need of excessive overnight borrowing and the banks under the coverage of SDIF [13].

In order to solve the problems permanently and increase the competitiveness of the banking sector and after the financial crises in November 2000 and February 2001, a program has been established; a special emphasis was given to financial sector and the measures to be taken in this regard were determined.

The financial sector in Turkey was also affected negatively to a large extent by the global crises that affected all the world economies negatively in 2008. When it is considered from the point of deposit in investment and development banks, particularly in the last quarter of the year 2008 and in the beginning of the year 2009, the balance sheet risks increased rapidly, foreign funding opportunities became fewer, and the need for liquidity increased [14].

In line with the international developments, the income in the Turkish economy decreased, the private sector demand shrank, and the volume of foreign trade decreased whereas the budget deficit and unemployment rate increased and direct investments decreased. Therefore, in order to soften and restrict the negative impacts of the global crisis, many measures were taken by the related institutions in order to expand both the money and the financial politics during that period [15].

Computational intelligence algorithms that we have used in the paper will be described in Section 3.

3. Computational Intelligence Algorithms

In computational intelligence area, the aim is prediction of output values based on input values. If the output values are labels, this problem is named as a classification problem. If the output values are numeric values, it is named as a regression problem. Both of classification and regression problems construct a prediction model from the training set. The model performance is evaluated on the test set. For our problem the outputs are numeric. So, we have used the regression algorithms.

The regression approximation addresses the problem of estimating a function $y = f(x)$ based on a given dataset $G = \{(x_i, d_i)\}_{i=1}^{N}$, where, $x_i = [x_{i1}, x_{i2}, \ldots, x_{im}]$ is input vector, d_i is the real value, y_i is the estimated value, f is the estimation function, N is the number of observations, and m is the number of features.

In litreture, several regression algorithms are proposed for building the estimation function. In this section, the used ones are briefly introduced.

3.1. Zero Rule (ZeroR).

Zero Rule (ZeroR, 0-R) is a trivial classifier, but it gives a lower bound on the performance of a given dataset which should be significantly improved by more complex classifiers. As such it is a reasonable test on how well the class can be predicted without considering the other attributes [16].

3.2. M5 Model Rules (M5R).

Generates a decision list for regression problems using separate-and-conquer. In each iteration it builds a model tree using M5 and makes the "best" leaf into a rule [17].

3.3. Decision Table (DT).

A decision table consists of a hierarchical table in which each entry in a higher level table gets broken down by the values of a pair of additional attributes to form another table. The structure is similar to dimensional stacking. Given a training sample containing labeled instances, an induction algorithm builds a hypothesis in some representation. The representation investigated here is a decision table with a default rule mapping to the majority class, when it is abbreviated as DTM. A DTM has two components:

(1) a *schema*, which is a set of features, and

(2) a *body*, which is a multiset of labeled instances.

Each instance consists of a value for each of the features in the schema and a value for the label. Given an unlabelled instance $\vec{x}$, the label assigned to the instance by a DTM classifier is computed as follows.

Let I be the set of labeled instances in the DTM exactly matching the given instance $\vec{x}$, where only the features in the schema are required to match and all other features are ignored. If $I = \emptyset$, return the majority class in the DTM. Otherwise, return the majority class in I. Unknown values are treated as distinct values in the matching process [18].

3.4. Reduced Error Pruning Tree (REP Tree).

Reduced Error Pruning (REP) was introduced by Quinlan [19] in the context of decision tree learning. It has been subsequently adapted to rule set learning as well [20]. It produces an optimal pruning of a given tree—the smallest tree among those with minimal error with respect to a given set of pruning examples [20, 21]. The REP algorithm works in two phases: first the set of pruning examples S is classified using the given tree T to be pruned. Counters that keep track of the number of examples of each class passing through each node are updated simultaneously. In the second phase—a bottom-up pruning phase—those parts of the tree that can be removed without increasing the error of the remaining hypothesis are pruned away [22]. The pruning decisions are based on the node statistics calculated in the top-down classification phase.

3.5. Conjunctive Rule (CR).

This class implements a single conjunctive rule learner that can predict for numeric and nominal class labels.

A rule consists of antecedents "AND"ed together and the consequent (class value) for the classification/regression. In this case, the consequent is the distribution of the available classes (or mean for a numeric value) in the dataset. If the test instance is not covered by this rule, then it is predicted using the default class distributions/value of the data not covered by the rule in the training data. This learner selects an antecedent by computing the Information Gain of each antecedent and prunes the generated rule using Reduced Error Pruning or simple prepruning based on the number of antecedents. For classification, the information of one antecedent is the weighted average of the entropies of both the data covered and not covered by the rule. For regression, the information is the weighted average of the mean-squared errors of both the data covered and not covered by the rule. In pruning, weighted average of the accuracy rates on the pruning data is used for classification while the weighted average of the mean-squared errors on the pruning data is used for regression [23].

3.6. Gaussian Process Regression (GPR).

Probabilistic regression is usually formulated as follows.

Given a training set $D = \{(\vec{x}_i, y_i), i = 1, 2, \ldots, n\}$ of n pairs of (vectorial) inputs $\vec{x}_i$ and noisy (real, scalar) outputs y_i, compute the predictive distribution of the function values f_* (or noisy y_*) at test locations $\vec{x}_*$. In the simplest case we assume that the noise is additive, independent, and Gaussian, such that the relationship between the (latent) function $f(\vec{x})$ and the observed noisy targets y is given by

$$y_i = f(\vec{x}_i) + \varepsilon_i, \quad \text{where } \varepsilon_i \sim \mathcal{N}\left(0, \sigma_{\text{noise}}^2\right), \quad (1)$$

where σ_{noise}^2 is the variance of the noise, and we use the notation $\mathcal{N}(\vec{a}, A)$ for the Gaussian distribution with mean $\vec{a}$ and covariance A [24].

The GP is a popular nonparametric model for supervised learning problems [25]. A Gaussian Process (GP) is a collection of random variables, any finite number of which have consistent joint Gaussian distributions. Gaussian Process (GP) regression is a Bayesian approach which assumes a GP prior over functions; that is, a priori the function values behave according to

$$p\left(\vec{f} \mid \vec{x}_1, \vec{x}_2, \ldots, \vec{x}_n\right) = \mathcal{N}\left(\vec{0}, K\right), \quad (2)$$

where $\vec{f} = [f_1, f_2, \ldots, f_n]^T$ is a vector of latent function values $f_i = f(\vec{x}_1)$ and K is a covariance matrix, whose entries are given by the covariance function $K_{ij} = k(\vec{x}_i, \vec{x}_j)$. Valid covariance functions give rise to semidefinite covariance matrices. In general, positive semidefinite kernels are valid covariance functions. The covariance function encodes our assumptions about the function we wish to learn by defining a notion of similarity between two function values as a function of the corresponding two inputs.

A very common covariance function is the Gaussian, or squared exponential:

$$K_{ij} = k\left(\vec{x}_i, \vec{x}_j\right) = v^2 \exp\left(-\frac{\left\|\vec{x}_i - \vec{x}_j\right\|^2}{2\lambda^2}\right), \quad (3)$$

where v^2 controls the prior variance, and λ is an isotropic lengthscale parameter that controls the rate of decay of the covariance that determines how far away $\vec{x}_i$ must be from $\vec{x}_j$ for f_i to be unrelated to f_j [24].

3.7. Isotonic Regression (IR). The Isotonic Regression (IR) problem is considered in the following least distance setting. Given a vector $y \in R^n$, a strictly positive vector of weights $w \in R^n$, and a directed acyclic graph $G(N, E)$ with the set of nodes $N = \{1, 2, \ldots, n\}$, we find $x^* \in R^n$ that solves the problem

$$\min \quad \sum_{i=1}^{n} w_i(x_i - y_i)^2 \quad (4)$$

$$\text{s.t.} \quad x_i \leq x_j \quad \forall (i, j) \in E.$$

Since this is a strictly convex quadratic programming problem its solution x^* is unique. The optimality conditions and an analysis of the typical block (or cluster) structure of x^* can be found in [26–28]. The monotonicity constraints defined by the acyclic graph $G(N, E)$ imply a partial order of the components $x_i, i = 1, 2, \ldots, n$.

A special case of Isotonic Regression problem arises when there is a complete order of the components. This problem, referred to as IRC problem, is defined by a directed graph $G(N, E)$ and is formulated as follows:

$$\min \quad \sum_{i=1}^{n} w_i(x_i - y_i)^2 \quad (5)$$

$$\text{s.t.} \quad x_1 \leq x_2 \leq \cdots \leq x_n.$$

IR problem has numerous important applications, for instance, in machine learning, data mining, statistics, operations research, and signal processing. These applications are characterized by a very large value of n. For such large-scale problems, it is of great practical importance to develop algorithms whose complexity does not rise with n too rapidly. The existing optimization-based algorithms [29] and statistical IR algorithms have either high computational complexity or low accuracy of the approximation to the optimal solution they generate.

The most widely used method for solving IRC problem (5) is the so-called Pool-Adjacent-Violator (PAV) algorithm [30–32]. This algorithm is of computational complexity $O(n)$ [11–13]. The PAV algorithm has been extended by Pardalos and Xue [28] to the special case of IR problem (4), in which the partial order of the components is presented by a directed tree [33].

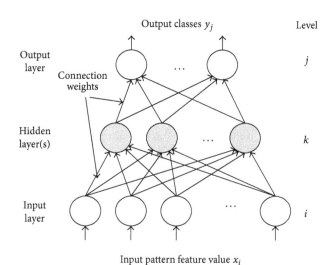

FIGURE 1: Structure of a Multilayer Perceptron [36].

3.8. Linear Regression (LR). The final model is a linear regression of a subsample of the attributes. The subsample is selected by iteratively removing the one with the smallest standardized coefficient until no improvement is observed in the estimate of the error given by the Akaike Information Criterion (AIC) [34]

$$\vec{y} = \vec{w}_0 + \vec{w}_i \cdot \vec{x}_i + \varepsilon. \quad (6)$$

The AIC value, with the assumption of eventual normally distributed errors, is calculated as follows:

$$\text{AIC} = 2k + N \ln\left(\frac{\text{RSS}}{N}\right), \quad (7)$$

where k is the number of parameters in the model, RSS is the residual of sum of the squares, and N is the number of observations [35].

3.9. Multilayer Perceptron (MLP). Multilayer Perceptron (MLP) also referred to as multilayer feedforward neural networks is the most used and popular neural network method. It belongs to the class of supervised neural network. The MLP topology consists of three sequential layers of processing nodes: an input layer, one or more hidden layers, and an output layer which produces the classification results. A MLP structure is shown in Figure 1 [36].

The principle of the network is that when data are presented at the input layer, the network nodes perform calculations in the successive layers until an output value is obtained at each of the output nodes. This output signal should be able to indicate the appropriate class for the input data. A node in MLP can be modeled as one or more artificial neurons, which computes the weighted sum of the inputs at the presence of the bias and passes this sum through the nonlinear activation function. This process is defined as follows [36]:

$$\mu_j = \sum_{i=1}^{N} w_{ji}x_i + \theta_j, \tag{8}$$

$$y_j = \varphi_j\left(\mu_j\right),$$

where μ_j is the linear combination of inputs $x_1, x_2, \ldots, x_N$, θ_j is the bias (adjustable parameter), w_{ji} is the connection synaptic weight between the input x_i and the neuron j, $\varphi(\cdot)$ is the activation function (usually nonlinear function) of the jth neuron, and y_j is the output. Here, hyperbolic tangent and logistic sigmoid function can be used for the nonlinear activation function. But, in most of the application widely used logistic sigmoid function is applied as follows:

$$\varphi\left(\lambda\right) = \frac{1}{1 + e^{-\lambda}}, \tag{9}$$

where λ represents the slope of the sigmoid [37].

The bias term θ_j contributes to the left or right shift of the sigmoid activation function, depending on whether θ_j takes a positive or negative value.

Learning in a MLP is an unconstrained optimization problem, which is subject to the minimization of a global error function depending on the synaptic weights of the network [38].

The first backpropagation learning algorithm for use with MLP structures was presented by Rumelhart et al. [39]. The backpropagation algorithm is one of the simplest and most general methods for the supervised training of MLP. This algorithm uses a gradient descent search method to minimize a mean square error between the desired output and the actual outputs. Backpropagation algorithm is defined as follows [36–40]:

(I) initialize all the connection weights w with small random values from a pseudorandom sequence generator;

(II) repeat until convergence (either when the error J is below a preset value or until the gradient $\partial J/\partial w$ is smaller than a preset value);

    (i) compute the update using $\Delta w(m) = -\xi(\partial J(m)/\partial w)$,

    (ii) iterative algorithm requires taking a weight vector at iteration m and updating it as $(m+1) = w(m) + \Delta w(m)$,

    (iii) compute the error $J(m + 1)$,

where m is the iteration number, w represents all the weights in the network, and ξ is the learning rate and merely indicates the relative size of the change in weights. The error J can be chosen as the mean square error function between the actual output y_j and the desired output d_j and d and y are the desired and the network output vector of length N:

$$J\left(w\right) = \frac{1}{2}\sum_{j=1}^{N}\left(d_j - y_j\right)^2 = \frac{1}{2}(d - y)^2. \tag{10}$$

3.10. Simple Linear Regression (SLR). It is the process of fitting straight lines (models) between each attribute and output. In (11), the values of $\vec{w}$ and $\vec{w}_0$ are estimated by the method of least squares. Consider

$$\vec{y} = \vec{w} \cdot \vec{x} + \vec{w}_0 . \tag{11}$$

The model having lowest squared error is selected as the final model among each parameter model [35].

3.11. Support Vector Machines (SVMs). The Support Vector Machines (SVMs) [41] are types of learning machines based on statistical learning theory. SVMs are supervised learning methods that have been widely and successfully used for pattern recognition in different areas [42]. Especially in recent years SMVs with linear or nonlinear kernels have become one of the most promising learning algorithms for classification as well as regression [43]. The problem that SVMs try to solve is to find an optimal hyperplane that correctly classifies data points by separating the points of two classes as much as possible [44].

Let x_i (for $1 \leq i \leq N_x$) be the input vectors in input space, with corresponding binary labels $y_i \in \{-1, 1\}$. Let $\vec{X}_i = \Phi(x_i)$ be the corresponding vectors in feature space, where $\Phi(x_i)$ is the implicit kernel mapping, and let $K(x_i, x_j) = \Phi(x_i) . \Phi(x_j)$ be the kernel function, implying a dot product in the feature space [45]. $K(x, y)$ represents the desired notion of similarity between data x and y. $K(x, y)$ needs to satisfy Mercer's condition in order for Φ to exist [44]. There are a number of kernel functions which have been found to provide good generalization capabilities [46]. The kernel function that has been used in SVM is a linear function and the details of the function are given below

Linear Kernel: $K(x_i, x_j) = x_i^T x_j$.

The optimization problem for a soft-margin SVM is

$$\min_{\vec{w},b} \left\{\frac{1}{2}\|\vec{w}\|^2 + C\sum_i \xi_i\right\}, \tag{12}$$

subject to the constraints $y_i(\vec{w}_i x + b) = 1 - \xi_i$ and $\xi_i \geq 0$, where $\vec{w}$ is the normal vector of the separating hyperplane in feature space, and $C > 0$ is a regularization parameter controlling the penalty for misclassification. Equation (12) is referred to as the primal equation. From the Lagrangian form of (12), we derive the dual problem:

$$\max_{\alpha} \left\{\sum_i \alpha_i - \frac{1}{2}\sum_{i,j}\alpha_i\alpha_j y_i y_j K\left(x_i, x_j\right)\right\} \tag{13}$$

subject to $0 \leq \alpha_i \leq C$. This is a quadratic optimization problem that can be solved efficiently using algorithms such as Sequential Minimal Optimization (SMO) [47]. Typically, many α_i go to zero during optimization, and the remaining x_i corresponding to those $\alpha_i > 0$ are called support vectors. To simplify notation, from here on we assume that all nonsupport vectors have been removed, so that N_x is now the number of support vectors, and $\alpha_i > 0$ for all i. With this formulation, the normal vector of the separating plane $\vec{w}$ is calculated as

$$\vec{w} = \sum_{i=1}^{N_x} \alpha_i y_i \, \vec{x}_i. \tag{14}$$

Note that because $\vec{X}_i = \Phi(x_i)$ is defined implicitly, $\vec{w}$ exists only in feature space and cannot be computed directly. Instead, the classification $f(\vec{q})$ of a new query vector $\vec{q}$ can only be determined by computing the kernel function of $\vec{q}$ with every support vector

$$f(\vec{q}) = \text{sign}\left(\sum_{i=1}^{N_x} \alpha_i y_i K(\vec{q}, x_i) + b\right), \tag{15}$$

where the bias term b is the offset of the hyperplane along its normal vector, determined during SVM training [45].

3.12. IB1 (One Nearest Neighbor). IB1 [33] is an implementation of the simplest similarity based learner, known as nearest neighbor. IB1 simply finds the stored instance closest (according to Eucklidean distance metric) to the instance to be classified. The new instance is assigned to the retrieved instance's class. Equation (16) shows the distance metric employed by IB1. Consider

$$D(x, y) = \sqrt{\sum_{i=1}^{n} f(x_i, y_i)}. \tag{16}$$

Equation (16) gives the distance between two instances x and y; x_i and y_i refer to the ith feature value of instances x and y, respectively. For numeric valued attributes $f(x_i, y_i) = (x_i - y_i)^2$, for symbolic valued attributes $f(x, y) = 0$, if the feature values x_i and y_i are the same, and 1 if they differ [48].

3.13. K-Star. K-star [49] can be considered as a variation of instance based learning which uses an entropic distance measure. To compute the distance between two samples, the concept of "complexity of transforming from one sample into another sample" is introduced. A K-star distance is then defined by summing over all possible transformation paths between two distances. This approach can be applied on real valued attributes, as well as symbolic attributes [50].

3.14. Additive Regression (AR). It is initially focused on the regression problem where the response y is quantitative, and it is aimed to model the mean $E(y \mid x) = F(x)$. The additive model has the following form:

$$F(x) = \sum_{i=1}^{N} f_i(x_i). \tag{17}$$

Here there is a separate function $f_i(x_i)$ for each of the N input variables x_i. More generally, each component f_i is a function of a small prespecified subset of the input variables. The "backfitting algorithm" is a convenient modular algorithm for fitting additive models. A backfitting update is

$$f_i(x_i) \longleftarrow E\left[y - \sum_{k \neq i} f_k(x_k) \mid x_i\right] \tag{18}$$

Any method or algorithm for estimating a function of x_i can be used to obtain an estimate of the conditional expectation in (18). In particular, this can include nonparametric smoothing algorithms, such as local regression or smoothing splines. In the right hand side, all the latest versions of the functions f_i are used in forming the partial residuals. The backfitting cycles are repeated until convergence [51]. Under fairly general conditions, backfitting can be shown to converge to the minimizer of $E(y - F(x))^2$ [52].

3.15. Bagging. Bagging [53] predictors is a method for generating multiple versions of a predictor and using these to get on aggregated predictor. The aggregation averages over the versions when predicting a numerical outcome and does a plurality vote when predicting a class. The multiple versions are formed by making bootstrap replicates of the learning set and using these as new learning sets. Tests on real and simulated data sets using classification and regression trees and subset selection in linear regression show that bagging can give substantial gains in accuracy. The vital element is the instability of the prediction method. If perturbing the learning set can cause significant changes in the predictor constructed, then bagging can improve accuracy [53].

4. Purpose of Study

The study aims to determine which parameters (factors) affect the change in the market shares of the public and private commercial banks and the foreign banks established in Turkey and have branches operating in Turkey between 1990 and 2009, in parallel with the economic and social developments that occurred during this period in the country.

Three market shares, which can be considered as the indicator of all market shares, are taken into account in the study. These figures (*Y1*, *Y2*, and *Y3*) are the market shares as an indicator of the market share in total deposits (*Y3*), as an indicator of the success of the bank in deposit collection, the market share in total credits (*Y3*), as an indicator of the contribution to the total credits, and finally the market share in the total assets (*Y1*) as an indicator of the change in the reliability and soundness of the bank.

Because of the long-term effects of the Russian and Asian crises encountered in 1997 and 1998, November 2000 and February 2001 crises were experienced successively with deeper financial strength in Turkey. These crises affected mostly the banks which do not have solid financial structures and cannot act according to the conditions experienced. Therefore, 2001 crisis with regard to the banking sector should not only be considered economically. After 2001, the banking sector has been renewed with new regulations. Therefore, another purpose of the study is to determine if the crises affect the market shares of the banks.

TABLE 1: The data of the banks for the period of 1990–2009.

Number	Bank name
1	Z. Bankası
2	H. Bankası
3	Vakıfbank
4	İş Bankası
5	Akbank
6	Alternatifbank
7	Şekerbank
8	G. Bankası
9	Citibank
10	Credit Agricole Indosuez
11	T.E. Bankası
12	Finansbank
13	Anadolu
14	Adabank
15	Oyakbank (ING Bank)
16	Arap-Türk
17	Tekstilbank
18	Turkish Bank
19	Türk Dış Ticaret (FORTIS)
20	H. Bank
21	Bank M.
22	HSBC
23	Banca Di Roma
24	ABN-Amro
25	West LB AG
26	Y. K. Bankası
27	Societe Generale (S.A)
28	Bayındırbank
29	Bank Europa (Sitebank)
30	Pamukbank (BFB)

Resource: The Banks Association of Turkey, Banks in Turkey 1990–2009
http://www.tbb.org.tr/.

5. Dataset and Parameters Used in Study

5.1. Scope of Study. The public and private commercial banks and the foreign banks established in Turkey between 1990 and 2009 are included in the study. The bankrupted banks, the banks that were transferred to SDIF and the way of operation has been changed and development and investment banks are excluded from the study.

For the period 1990–2009, the data belonging to 30 banks listed in Table 1 are used in the study.

The market shares of the banks can be determined using three different criteria: market shares in total assets, total credits, and total deposits [54]. Total assets, total credits, and total deposits factors, which can be used as indicators of the change in the market share, shall be explained using the following ratios: which is important for banks to continue their operations; capital adequacy ratios, profitability ratios which is important to measure the profitability of the banks, liquidity ratios which show the status of short-term debt

repayment, income-expenditure structure rates, which give information about which items are playing important role in total income and expenditure of the banks and correction of the profit of the bank changing which income and expenditure items, and asset quality and the ratios showing the group shares of the banks. All of those figures show the situation of the banks as well as giving illustrative information about if the banks will face a problem in the future. Therefore, following those ratios will help to take necessary precautions in case of negative developments. The precautions that will be taken immediately will not only prevent the decrease in the market shares but also will help the banks to catch the opportunities that cause their market shares to increase. The ratios showing the market shares of the banks used in the study are dependent variables and capital adequacy, asset quality, liquidity, profitability, and the ratios showing the group shares are explanatory variables. An average value is calculated as a dependent variable that indicates the market shares of banks by using total assets ($Y1$), total credit ($Y2$), and total deposit ($Y3$) rates of all the banks in the sector. In determination of the market shares of the banks in the study during the period 1990 and 2009, analysis will be developed using computational intelligence algorithms and 20 financial ratios relating to capital adequacy, asset quality, liquidity, profitability, and the ratios showing the group shares.

The data used in the study consists of secondary data which were taken from the book "Our Banks" and prepared annually by Banks Association of Turkey. 20 financial ratios prevailing for the period between 1990 and 2009 are shown in Table 2.

The liquidity ratios are defining the power of repayment of the short-term debt of businesses, and the profitability ratios are the indicators for the businesses' ability to provide a satisfactory profit for the invested capital and the effectiveness of management in well-functioning financial markets. To those areas where the profitability is limited, financial investors do not put their money and the entrepreneurs do not make investments. In addition, the credit institutions are reluctant to give credits to the businesses which have low profitability. The ratios relating to capital adequacy, asset quality, liquidity, profitability, and the ratios showing the group shares are important to the businesses and therefore they are crucial to banks. With the calculation of those ratios, the banks can determine both their situation and their position in the sector more efficiently. Therefore, all of the ratios above are included as explanatory variables.

6. Experimental Results

The bank dataset collection includes 20 features/inputs (see Table 2) and an output feature (changes in market shares) for each year (1990–2009). For each year, a dataset is formed including input features and an output feature. Each dataset consists of 30 samples. All features were normalized between 0 and 1.

We have applied 15 machine learning algorithms from WEKA library [16] to predict the output of samples. In Table 3 the algorithms and IDs are given.

TABLE 2: 20 financial ratios that are used between the period of 1990 and 2009.

Code	Ratios
	Capital adequacy ratios (CA)
CA1	(Shareholders' equity + profit)/total assets
CA2	(Shareholders' equity + profit)/(deposit + nondeposit sources)
CA3	(Net working capital)/total assets
CA4	(Shareholders' equity + profit)/(total assets + noncash loans)
	Assets quality ratios (AQ)
AQ1	Total loans/total assets
AQ2	Loans under follow-up/total loans
AQ3	Permanent assets/total assets
	Liquidity ratios (L)
L1	Liquid assets/total assets
L2	Liquid assets/(deposit + nondeposit sources)
L3	TC liquid assets/total assets
	Profitability ratios (P)
P1	Net profit (losses)/total assets (ROA)
P2	Net profit (losses)/total shareholders' equity (ROE)
P3	Profit (losses) before taxes after continuing operations/total assets
	Income-expenditure structure ratios (IE)
IE1	Net interest income after receivable under follow-up/total assets
IE2	Interest income (net)/interest expenses
IE3	Noninterest income (net)/noninterest expenses
IE4	Personnel expenses/other operating income
	Group shares ratios (GS)
GS1	Total assets
GS2	Total loans
GS3	Total deposits
	Market shares ratio (MS)
MS	MS = (Y1 + Y2 + Y3)/3
	Y1: total assets; Y2: total loans; Y3: total deposits

Resource: The Banks Association of Turkey, Banks in Turkey 1990–2009 http://www.tbb.org.tr/

The default design parameters were selected for Zero Rule, M5 rules, decision table, conjunctive rule, REP Tree, Gaussian Processes, Isotonic Regression, linear regression, Multilayer Perceptron, Simple Linear Regression, support vector machine regression, one nearest neighbor, and Kstar algorithms. For the meta algorithms (additive regression and bagging), the ensemble sizes were selected as 100.

The performance of each classification algorithm was evaluated using 5-fold cross-validation. In each 5-fold cross-validation, each dataset is randomly split into 5 equal sized segments and results are averaged over 5 trials. The performance evaluation is based on root mean-squared error (RMSE) defined in (19). Consider

$$\text{RMSE} = \sqrt{\frac{1}{N}\sum_{i=1}^{N}(d_i - y_i)^2}, \qquad (19)$$

TABLE 3: The used algorithms and names.

Algorithm ID	Algorithm name
(1)	ZeroR
(2)	M5 rules
(3)	Decision table
(4)	Conjunctive rule
(5)	REP Tree
(6)	Gaussian Processes
(7)	Isotonic Regression
(8)	Linear regression
(9)	Multilayer Perceptron
(10)	Simple Linear Regression
(11)	SMOreg
(12)	IBk (one nearest neighbor)
(13)	Kstar
(14)	Additive regression
(15)	Bagging

where y^i is the estimated output for ith test sample, d^i is the real output value of ith test sample, and N is the number of the test samples. Table 4 shows the root mean-squared error results.

According to Table 4, the best algorithm (having the most minimum errors) is Simple Linear Regression. This very simple algorithm generally performs better than all the other complicated algorithms.

According to Table 4, the best predicted years are 2006 and 2007. The worst predicted years are 2001, 2002, 2008, and 2009.

Due to the financial crisis experienced in the beginning of 2000s in Turkey and the global crisis that affected our country as well as all the world economies in the period 2008-2009, the estimations for those periods (2001, 2002, 2008, and 2009) did not lead to good results. It is seen that this situation is based on the fact that economic and financial data are much more fluctuating in the crisis periods in comparison to stagnation periods.

Two questions were raised when we want to have more understanding on the dynamics of the datasets.

(1) The datasets includes 20 features. It is known that the irrelevant features can badly affect results. Is it possible to get better results with fewer features?

(2) Which features affected the results the most?

To answer these related questions we applied Correlation Based Feature Selection (CFS) [50] algorithm for each year's dataset separately. CFS method will be explained briefly below.

CFS evaluates the worth of a subset of attributes by considering the individual predictive ability of each future along with the degree of redundancy between them. Correlation coefficients are used to estimate correlation between subset of attributes and class, as well as intercorrelations between the features. Relevance of a group of features grows with the correlation between features and classes and decreases

TABLE 4: The RMSEs of the compared algorithms over 20 bank datasets.

Year/dataset	1	2	3	4	5	6	7	8	9	10	11	12	13	14	15	Min. RMSE	Best algorithm ID
1990	0.19	0.07	0.16	0.16	0.18	0.14	0.1	5.15	0.16	0.05	0.56	0.11	0.11	0.19	0.15	0.05	10
1991	0.2	0.09	0.14	0.18	0.18	0.15	0.11	0.47	0.13	0.06	0.15	0.13	0.14	0.17	0.15	0.06	10
1992	0.18	0.12	0.16	0.16	0.17	0.15	0.11	0.13	0.12	0.07	0.07	0.13	0.12	0.16	0.15	0.07	10
1993	0.19	0.12	0.14	0.18	0.19	0.16	0.12	0.16	0.16	0.07	0.08	0.14	0.14	0.16	0.15	0.07	10
1994	0.2	0.09	0.15	0.17	0.17	0.15	0.1	0.21	0.17	0.06	0.13	0.12	0.12	0.13	0.14	0.06	10
1995	0.19	0.08	0.17	0.18	0.18	0.16	0.11	0.14	0.19	0.07	0.09	0.15	0.17	0.18	0.15	0.07	10
1996	0.18	0.07	0.13	0.16	0.17	0.15	0.11	0.21	0.14	0.07	0.16	0.13	0.12	0.13	0.14	0.07	10
1997	0.2	0.13	0.17	0.17	0.18	0.16	0.13	0.29	0.16	0.08	0.18	0.12	0.13	0.18	0.15	0.08	10
1998	0.22	0.12	0.17	0.17	0.17	0.17	0.1	0.2	0.18	0.09	0.13	0.15	0.12	0.13	0.13	0.09	10
1999	0.22	0.11	0.2	0.19	0.18	0.18	0.14	0.35	0.15	0.09	0.17	0.18	0.13	0.19	0.14	0.09	10
2000	0.23	0.11	0.14	0.19	0.17	0.19	0.09	0.2	0.13	0.09	0.13	0.19	0.16	0.15	0.14	0.09	7
2001	0.27	0.24	0.17	0.24	0.24	0.23	0.21	0.36	0.33	0.26	0.34	0.23	0.17	0.27	0.21	0.17	13
2002	0.28	0.29	0.26	0.23	0.23	0.23	0.21	1.01	0.41	0.24	0.52	0.29	0.23	0.29	0.21	0.21	15
2003	0.27	0.12	0.15	0.18	0.16	0.15	0.1	0.22	0.11	0.11	0.06	0.09	0.18	0.16	0.12	0.06	11
2004	0.26	0.07	0.14	0.13	0.11	0.15	0.1	0.19	0.07	0.08	0.1	0.08	0.18	0.13	0.1	0.07	9
2005	0.3	0.16	0.21	0.16	0.17	0.16	0.11	0.32	0.19	0.1	0.09	0.09	0.17	0.15	0.13	0.09	11
2006	0.31	0.06	0.19	0.13	0.12	0.14	0.07	0.03	0.03	0.04	0.02	0.06	0.15	0.12	0.1	0.02	11
2007	0.33	0.05	0.19	0.16	0.13	0.17	0.05	0.02	0.04	0.06	0.02	0.06	0.14	0.14	0.11	0.02	11
2008	0.37	0.48	0.38	0.41	0.38	0.36	0.4	0.7	0.56	0.43	0.54	0.54	0.47	0.4	0.36	0.36	15
2009	0.34	0.39	0.41	0.37	0.36	0.35	0.46	0.39	0.63	0.37	0.48	0.48	0.44	0.54	0.36	0.34	1

TABLE 5: The selected features according to the years.

Year	Selected features				
1990	P3	IE3	GS3		
1991	L1	P3	GS3		
1992	L2	GS2	GS3		
1993	L2	P3	IE2	GS1	GS3
1994	AQ2	L1	GS1	GS2	GS3
1995	AQ1	AQ2	IE3	GS1	
1996	CA3	GS1	GS2	GS3	
1997	L1	P3	GS1	GS3	
1998	L2	IE1	GS3		
1999	L1	IE2	GS1	GS2	GS3
2000	L1	GS3			
2001	AQ2	L3	GS1		
2002	CA2	L1	IE2	GS1	
2003	L1	P2	GS1	GS2	GS3
2004	P2	GS1	GS2	GS3	
2005	IE3	GS1	GS2	GS3	
2006	GS1	GS2	GS3		
2007	CA3	P2	GS1	GS2	GS3
2008	L3	IE3			
2009	CA3	L2	P2		

TABLE 6: The most selected features and selection frequencies.

Feature name	Selection frequency
GS3	15
GS1	13
GS2	9
L1	7
AQ2	4
IE3	4
P2	4
P3	4
L2	4
IE2	3
CA3	3
L3	2
IE1	1
CA2	1

bidirectional search, best-first search, and genetic search. Equation formalizes the heuristic:

$$r_{zc} = \frac{t\overline{r_{zi}}}{\sqrt{t + t(t-1)\overline{r_{ii}}}}, \qquad (20)$$

where r_{zc} is the correlation between the summed feature subsets and the class variable, t is the number of subset features, $\overline{r_{zi}}$ is the average of the correlations between the

with growing intercorrelation [50]. CFS is used to determine the best feature subset and is usually combined with search strategies such as forward selection, backward elimination,

TABLE 7: The RMSEs of the compared algorithms over 20 dimensionally reduced bank datasets.

Year/data set	1	2	3	4	5	6	7	8	9	10	11	12	13	14	15	Min. RMSE	Best algorithm ID
1990	0.19	0.05	0.12	0.15	0.16	0.13	0.09	0.05	0.09	0.05	0.05	0.09	0.12	0.13	0.14	0.05	10
1991	0.2	0.05	0.12	0.15	0.17	0.13	0.1	0.05	0.09	0.05	0.06	0.12	0.15	0.13	0.13	0.05	10
1992	0.18	0.07	0.13	0.15	0.17	0.13	0.11	0.06	0.1	0.07	0.05	0.1	0.1	0.13	0.14	0.05	11
1993	0.19	0.08	0.13	0.18	0.18	0.14	0.12	0.08	0.11	0.07	0.06	0.12	0.08	0.13	0.14	0.06	11
1994	0.2	0.06	0.13	0.17	0.17	0.13	0.1	0.06	0.11	0.06	0.06	0.11	0.11	0.12	0.13	0.06	10
1995	0.19	0.07	0.16	0.17	0.18	0.14	0.11	0.07	0.12	0.06	0.08	0.15	0.16	0.13	0.14	0.06	10
1996	0.18	0.07	0.11	0.16	0.16	0.13	0.11	0.07	0.12	0.07	0.07	0.1	0.1	0.11	0.13	0.07	10
1997	0.2	0.1	0.14	0.16	0.18	0.14	0.13	0.09	0.12	0.08	0.08	0.1	0.09	0.14	0.15	0.08	10
1998	0.22	0.1	0.14	0.16	0.16	0.15	0.1	0.1	0.15	0.09	0.09	0.11	0.11	0.11	0.12	0.09	10
1999	0.22	0.13	0.17	0.19	0.18	0.14	0.14	0.09	0.13	0.09	0.08	0.09	0.1	0.16	0.14	0.08	11
2000	0.23	0.08	0.1	0.14	0.13	0.13	0.09	0.08	0.1	0.09	0.09	0.08	0.09	0.09	0.1	0.08	8
2001	0.27	0.23	0.14	0.22	0.22	0.21	0.2	0.2	0.26	0.23	0.2	0.25	0.2	0.26	0.19	0.14	3
2002	0.28	0.24	0.25	0.22	0.23	0.23	0.22	0.24	0.38	0.23	0.23	0.3	0.27	0.24	0.2	0.2	15
2003	0.27	0.06	0.14	0.17	0.15	0.11	0.1	0.07	0.06	0.11	0.04	0.08	0.1	0.12	0.11	0.04	11
2004	0.26	0.05	0.13	0.11	0.1	0.11	0.1	0.05	0.06	0.08	0.03	0.06	0.09	0.09	0.08	0.03	11
2005	0.3	0.06	0.2	0.16	0.14	0.11	0.11	0.07	0.07	0.1	0.04	0.06	0.08	0.11	0.11	0.04	11
2006	0.31	0.03	0.19	0.12	0.11	0.08	0.07	0.01	0.02	0.04	0.01	0.05	0.05	0.08	0.09	0.01	8
2007	0.33	0.04	0.19	0.15	0.11	0.11	0.05	0.02	0.02	0.06	0.01	0.04	0.08	0.1	0.09	0.01	11
2008	0.37	0.39	0.33	0.36	0.38	0.36	0.33	0.38	0.44	0.37	0.42	0.45	0.36	0.42	0.35	0.33	3
2009	0.34	0.37	0.37	0.35	0.35	0.34	0.4	0.37	0.44	0.35	0.37	0.42	0.4	0.52	0.36	0.34	1

subset features and the class variable, and $\overline{r_{ii}}$ is the average intercorrelation between subset features [48–55]. Equation (20) is, in fact, Pearson's correlation, where all variables have been standardized. In Table 5, the selected features are given.

In Table 6, the selection frequencies of the fetures are given.

According to Table 6 the most selected features are among GS groups. In our study, domestic and foreign banks other than development and investment banks operating in Turkey are examined. According to our study, the share of each single bank within its own group has an influence on its share in the whole banking sector to a certain extent. As it may be derived from the analysis results, the variable representing the group shares had mostly a priority and was effective for the forecasts made with regard to the market shares of banks. Therefore, it is seen that such situation may have a positive impact on the banks, which are able to come to the fore in terms of technological developments, wide product range, and competitive advantage and increase their shares within their own groups, towards increasing their shares throughout the whole industry banks.

With the dimensionally reduced datasets, the same experiments are repeated with the same 15 algorithms in Table 7. The results are given at Table 7.

According to Table 7, the best algorithms (having the most minimum errors) are Simple Linear Regression and Support Vector Regression.

The best and the worst predicted years are the same with all featured datasets.

To determine the effect of feature selection Figure 2 was drawn. In Figure 2, x-axis shows the years and y-axis shows the minimum error of the 15 algorithms. The solid line shows the minimum errors of all featured datasets. The dotted line shows the minimum errors of dimensionally reduced datasets.

According to Figure 2, the feature selection process has positive effects over almost all years. Because of the fact that the obtained errors with dimensionally reduced datasets are lower than all featured datasets, the generated rules by the best algorithms over dimensionally reduced datasets are given at Table 8.

When Tables 8 and 5 are investigated together, it can be seen that the selected features by the feature selection algorithm and the used features in the rules are very similar.

The performance differences among algorithms were also investigated with t-test. t-test says whether there is a significant difference between two distributions or not. In our experiments, each algorithm produces 5 RMSEs for each dataset, because we used 5-fold cross-validation. The distributions which are compared are these errors of algorithms. In Table 9, the number of datasets where there is significant difference between the algorithms at the rows and columns is given. The most successful 4 algorithms (decision table, linear

TABLE 8: The rules generated by the best algorithm for each year (dataset).

Year	Algorithm ID	Rule
1990	10	MS = 0.97 ∗ GS3 − 0.02
1991	10	MS = 0.99 ∗ GS3 − 0.02
1992	11	MS = −0.0292 ∗ (normalized) $L2$ + 0.3947 ∗ (normalized) GS2 + 0.5996 ∗ (normalized) GS3 + 0.0068
1993	11	MS = −0.1056 ∗ (normalized) $L2$ + 0.0094 ∗ (normalized) $P3$ + 0.0052 ∗ (normalized) IE2 + 0.4708 ∗ (normalized) GS1 + 0.523 ∗ (normalized) GS3 + 0.0044
1994	10	MS = 1.04 ∗ GS1 − 0.02
1995	10	MS = 0.99 ∗ GS1 − 0.02
1996	10	MS = 1 ∗ GS1 − 0.01
1997	10	MS = 0.97 ∗ GS3 + 0
1998	10	MS = 1.06 ∗ GS3 + 0.01
1999	11	MS = −0.0237 ∗ (normalized) $L1$ − 0.0225 ∗ (normalized) IE2 + 0.296 ∗ (normalized) GS1 + 0.3055 ∗ (normalized) GS2 + 0.3722 ∗ (normalized) GS3 + 0.0272
2000	8	MS = −0.1229 ∗ $L1$ + 0.9571 ∗ GS3 + 0.0769
2001	3	If GS1 in (−inf−0.1] then MS = 0.03137 If GS1 in (0.3–0.4] then MS = 0.59189 If GS1 in (0.4–0.5] then MS = 0.041797 If GS1 in (0.5–0.6] then MS = 0.441048 If GS1 in (0.8–0.9] then MS = 0.093575 If GS1 in (0.9–inf) then MS = 1.0
2002	15, 11	The best performed algorithm is bagging. But the rules generated by bagging are very long. Instead of giving these long rules, a rule generated by the second best algorithm (SMOreg) is given. MS = −0.2014 ∗ (normalized) CA2 − 0.0089 ∗ (normalized) $L1$ − 0.0859 ∗ (normalized) IE2 + 0.7895 ∗ (normalized) GS1 + 0.1961
2003	11	MS = −0.0024 ∗ (normalized) $L1$ + 0.0009 ∗ (normalized) $P2$ + 0.3401 ∗ (normalized) GS1 + 0.2689 ∗ (normalized) GS2 + 0.4899 ∗ (normalized) GS3 − 0.0007
2004	11	MS = −0.0015 ∗ (normalized) $P2$ + 0.342 ∗ (normalized) GS1 + 0.2547 ∗ (normalized) GS2 + 0.4802 ∗ (normalized) GS3 − 0.0001

TABLE 8: Continued.

Year	Algorithm ID	Rule
2005	11	MS = −0.0028 ∗ (normalized) IE3 + 0.3304 ∗ (normalized) GS1 + 0.3268 ∗ (normalized) GS2 + 0.4712 ∗ (normalized) GS3 + 0.0002
2006	8	MS = 0.1241 ∗ GS1 + 0.3862 ∗ GS2 + 0.6142 ∗ GS3 + −0.0026
2007	11	MS = 0.0049 ∗ (normalized) CA3 + 0.0012 ∗ (normalized) $P2$ + 0.3388 ∗ (normalized) GS1 + 0.3281 ∗ (normalized) GS2 + 0.471 ∗ (normalized) GS3 − 0.0056
2008	3	If $L3$ in (−inf–0.1] then MS = 0.1942307 If $L3$ in (0.1–0.2] then MS = 0.479808 If $L3$ in (0.2–0.3] then MS = 0.073077 If $L3$ in (0.3–0.4] then MS = 0.019231 If $L3$ in (0.4–0.5] then MS = 0.980769 If $L3$ in (0.5–0.6] then MS = 0.2230765 If $L3$ in (0.6–0.7] then MS = 0.0826925 If $L3$ in (0.7–0.8] then MS = 0.042308 If $L3$ in (0.9–inf) then MS = 0.242308
2009	1	MS = 0.403535

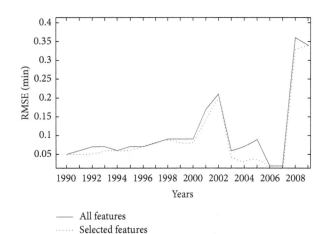

FIGURE 2: The effect of feature selection.

regression, Simple Linear Regression, and Support Vector Regression) were compared with all the other algorithms.

In Table 9, the values in the cells has the $(X/Y/Z)$ format. X shows that the number of datasets of the algorithm at the column has statistically significant lower error than the algorithm at the row. Z shows that the number of datasets of the algorithm at the column has statistically significant higher error than the algorithm at the row. Y shows the number of datasets the algorithm at the column has no statistically significant difference error than the algorithm at the row.

According to Table 9, decision table algorithm has no better performance than the other 3 compared algorithms (see third row). There is not any significant difference between

TABLE 9: Comparison of the best 4 algorithms with all the other algorithms by t-test.

Algorithm ID	3—Decision table	8—Linear regression	10—Simple linear regression	11—Support vector regression
1	(12/8/0)	(16/4/0)	(15/5/0)	(16/4/0)
2	(0/17/3)	(0/20/0)	(0/20/0)	(1/19/0)
3		(4/16/0)	(4/16/0)	(5/15/0)
4	(1/19/0)	(10/10/0)	(6/14/0)	(11/9/0)
5	(0/20/0)	(11/9/0)	(9/11/0)	(14/6/0)
6	(0/18/2)	(2/18/0)	(1/19/0)	(2/18/0)
7	(0/18/2)	(2/18/0)	(1/19/0)	(4/16/0)
8	(0/16/4)	—	(0/20/0)	(0/20/0)
9	(0/17/3)	(0/20/0)	(0/20/0)	(2/18/0)
10	**(0/16/4)**	**(0/20/0)**	—	**(2/17/1)**
11	(0/15/5)	(0/20/0)	(1/17/2)	—
12	(1/15/4)	(3/17/0)	(2/18/0)	(4/16/0)
13	(0/16/4)	(2/18/0)	(0/20/0)	(2/18/0)
14	(2/18/0)	(4/16/0)	(3/17/0)	(8/12/0)
15	(0/20/0)	(2/18/0)	(0/20/0)	(4/16/0)

Simple Linear Regression and linear regression. Support Vector Regression has 2 better and one lower performance than linear regression.

In other words, there are very small differences between the best performed 4 algorithms over 20 datasets. Simple Linear Regression generates very simple and understandable rules. It has very good performance among other 14 algorithms. Because of its simplicity, the prediction process time is very fast. Because of these reasons we can say that Simple Linear Regression is the best solution to predict market shares values in bank datasets.

7. Conclusion

The study uses the data of 30 domestic and foreign banks other than development and investment banks, which have been operating between the years 1990 and 2009 in Turkey. 20 financial ratios of those banks, which are gathered by the Banks Association of Turkey, were taken into consideration in order to model and anticipate the change in their market shares.

This study would serve to determine the changes in market share of banks and to take measures quickly when it is necessary due to the fragile structure of the banking sector in Turkey. For this reason, computational intelligence algorithms were used in the study so that the algorithm that leads to the best estimation could be determined. As a result of the analysis, it is seen that Simple Linear Regression is the best algorithm for all periods. However, due to the financial crisis experienced in the beginning of 2000s in Turkey and the global crisis that had big impacts on our country as well as all the world economies in the period 2008-2009, the estimations for those periods (2001, 2002, 2008, and 2009) did not lead to good results.

As a result of the analysis, it is seen that the share of each bank within its own group was more effective with regard to the estimations for the market shares of banks throughout the whole sector. For this reason, it is seen that such situation may have a positive impact on the banks, which are able to come to the fore in terms of technological developments, wide product range, and competitive advantage and increase their shares within their own groups, towards increasing their shares throughout the whole industry banks.

It is seen that using some specific features rather than all features leads to better results in the analysis. During the selection of features, it is seen that the specified features are in line with the features of the rules created.

Conflict of Interests

The authors declare that there is no conflict of interests regarding the publication of this paper.

References

[1] F. Çolak and A. Yigidim, *Türk Bankacılık Sektöründe Kriz*, Nobel Yayın Dağıtım, Ankara, Turkey, 2001 (Turkish).

[2] S. Oksay, "Finansal piyasalarda yeni yasal düzenlemeler ihtiyacı ve türk finans sistemi," *Sosyal Bilimler Enstitüsü Öneri Dergisi*, 2000 (Turkish).

[3] M. Ural, "bankacılık sistemimizde verimlilik," *D.E.Ü.İ.İ.B.F. Dergisi*, vol. 2, pp. 147–157, 1999 (Turkish).

[4] Türkiye Bankalar Birliği, "50. Yılında Türkiye Bankalar Birliği ve Türkiye'de Bankacılık Sistemi (1958–2007)," İstanbul, Turkey, 2008 (Turkish).

[5] Bankacılık Düzenleme ve Denetleme Kurumu, "Yıllık Rapor 2001," 2002 (Turkish).

[6] H. Seyidoğlu, *Uluslar Arası İktisat, Geliştirilmiş*, Güzem Yayıncılık, İstanbul, Turkey, 13th edition, 1999 (Turkish).

[7] B. Tunay, *Finans Sisteminde Yeni Yönelimler: Türk Finans Piyasalarının Bugünü ve Geleceği*, Beta Basım yayım Dağıtım, İstanbul, Turkey, 2001 (Turkish).

[8] H. Tunç, "Finansal Kriz ve Türkiye Ekonomisi," İSO Dergisi 421, 2001 (Turkish).

[9] K. Duman, "Finansal kriz ve bankacılık sektörünün yeniden yapılandırılması," *Akdeniz Üniversitesi İ.İ.B.F. Dergisi*, vol. 4, 2002 (Turkish).

[10] I. Sayım, K. Duman, and A. Korkmaz, "Türkiye ekonomisinde finansal krizler: bir faktör analizi uygulaması," *D.E.Ü.İ.İ.B.F. Dergisi*, vol. 1, pp. 45–69, 2004 (Turkish).

[11] R. Karluk, *Türkiye Ekonomisi: Tarihsel Gelişim Yapısal ve Sosyal Değişim*, Beta Basım, İstanbul, Turkey, 2004 (Turkish).

[12] S. Uyar, *Bankacılık Krizleri*, Ziraat Matbaacılık, Ankara, Turkey, 2003 (Turkish).

[13] Bankacılık Düzenleme ve Denetleme Kurumu, "Bankacılık Sektörü Yeniden Değerlendirme Programı," 2001 (Turkish).

[14] Türkiye Bankalar Birliği, "Bankalarımız 2009," İstanbul, Turkey, 2010, (Turkish).

[15] Türkiye Bankalar Birliği, "Bankalarımız 2010," İstanbul, Turkey, 2011, (Turkish).

[16] Weka Manual for Version 3-6-3.

[17] M. Hall, G. Holmes, and E. Frank, "Generating rule sets from model trees," in *Proceedings of the 12th Australian Joint Conference on Artificial Intelligence*, pp. 1–12, Springer, Sydney, Australia, 1999.

[18] R. Kohavi, "The power of decision tables," in *Proceedings of the European Conference on Machine Learning (ECML '95)*, N. Lavrac and S. Wrobel, Eds., pp. 174–189, Springer, Berlin, Germany, 1995.

[19] J. R. Quinlan, "Simplifying decision trees," *International Journal of Man-Machine Studies*, vol. 27, no. 3, pp. 221–234, 1987.

[20] T. Elomaa and M. Kääriäinen, "An analysis of reduced error pruning," *Journal of Artificial Intelligence Research*, vol. 15, pp. 163–187, 2001.

[21] F. Esposito, D. Malerba, and G. Semeraro, "A comparative analysis of methods for pruning decision trees," *IEEE Transactions on Pattern Analysis and Machine Intelligence*, vol. 19, no. 5, pp. 476–491, 1997.

[22] M. Kääriäinen, T. Malinen, and T. Elomaa, "Selective rademacher penalization and reduced error pruning of decision trees," *Journal of Machine Learning Research*, vol. 5, pp. 1107–1126, 2004.

[23] I. H. Witten and E. Frank, *Data Mining: Practical Machine Learning Tools and Techniques with Java Implementations*, Morgan Kaufmann, San Francisco, Calif, USA, 1999.

[24] J. Q. Candela, C. E. Rasmussen, and C. K. I. Williams, "Approximation methods for Gaussian process regression," Tech. Rep., http://research.microsoft.com/pubs/70486/tr-2007-124.pdf.

[25] C. Walder, K. I. Kim, and B. Schölkopf, "Sparse multiscale Gaussian process regression," in *Proceedings of the 25th International Conference on Machine Learning (ICML '08)*, W. W. Cohen, A. McCallum, and S. T. Roweis, Eds., pp. 1112–1119, ACM Press, Helsinki, Finland.

[26] M. J. Best and N. Chakravarti, "Active set algorithms for isotonic regression; a unifying framework," *Mathematical Programming*, vol. 47, no. 3, pp. 425–439, 1990.

[27] C. I. C. Lee, "The min-max algorithm and isotonic regression," *The Annals of Statistics*, vol. 11, no. 2, pp. 467–477, 1983.

[28] P. M. Pardalos and G. Xue, "Algorithms for a class of isotonic regression problems," *Algorithmica*, vol. 23, no. 3, pp. 211–222, 1999.

[29] V. de Simone, M. Marina, and G. Toraldo, "Isotonic regression problems," in *Encyclopedia of Optimization*, C. A. Floudas and P. M. Pardalos, Eds., Kluwer Academic, Dordrecht, The Netherlands, 2001.

[30] M. Ayer, H. D. Brunk, G. M. Ewing, W. T. Reid, and E. Silverman, "An empirical distribution function for sampling with incomplete information," *The Annals of Mathematical Statistics*, vol. 26, no. 4, pp. 641–647, 1955.

[31] R. E. Barlow, D. J. Bartholomew, J. M. Bremner, and H. D. Brunk, *Statistical Inference under Order Restrictions*, Wiley, New York, NY, USA, 1972.

[32] D. L. Hanson, G. Pledger, and F. T. Wright, "On consistency in monotonic regression," *The Annals of Statistics*, vol. 1, no. 3, pp. 401–421, 1973.

[33] O. Burdakov, O. Sysoev, A. Grimvall, and M. Hussian, "An $O(n^2)$ algorithm for isotonic regression," in *Nonconvex Optimization and Its Applications*, G. di Pillo and M. Roma, Eds., vol. 83 of *Large-Scale Nonlinear Optimization Series*, pp. 25–33, Springer, 2006.

[34] H. Akaike, "A new look at the statistical model identification," *IEEE Transactions on Automatic Control*, vol. 19, no. 6, pp. 716–723, 1974.

[35] S. Ekinci, U. B. Celebi, M. Bal, M. F. Amasyali, and U. K. Boyaci, "Predictions of oil/chemical tanker main design parameters using computational intelligence techniques," *Applied Soft Computing Journal*, vol. 11, no. 2, pp. 2356–2366, 2011.

[36] H. Yan, Y. Jiang, J. Zheng, C. Peng, and Q. Li, "A multilayer perceptron-based medical decision support system for heart disease diagnosis," *Expert Systems with Applications*, vol. 30, no. 2, pp. 272–281, 2006.

[37] V. Havel, J. Martinovic, and V. Snasel, "Creating of conceptual lattices using multilayer perceptron," in *Proceedings of the International Workshop on Concept Lattices and Their Applications (CLA '05)*, R. Belohlavek and V. Snasel, Eds., pp. 149–157, Olomouc, Czech Republic, 2005.

[38] A. B. Goktepe, E. Agar, and A. H. Lav, "Role of learning algorithm in neural network-based backcalculation of flexible pavements," *Journal of Computing in Civil Engineering*, vol. 20, no. 5, pp. 370–373, 2006.

[39] D. E. Rumelhart, G. E. Hinton, and R. J. Williams, "Learning representations by back-propagating errors," *Nature*, vol. 323, no. 6088, pp. 533–536, 1986.

[40] R. O. Duda, P. E. Hart, and D. G. Stork, *Pattern Classification*, John Wiley & Sons, New York, NY, USA, 2001.

[41] V. N. Vapnik, *The Nature of Statistical Learning Theory*, Springer, New York, NY, USA, 1995.

[42] B. Keshari and S. M. Watt, "Hybrid mathematical symbol recognition using support vector machines," in *Proceedings of the 9th International Conference on Document Analysis and Recognition (ICDAR '07)*, pp. 859–863, IEEE Computer Society, Curutiba, Brazil, September 2007.

[43] C.-M. Huang, Y.-J. Lee, D. K. J. Lin, and S.-Y. Huang, "Model selection for support vector machines via uniform design," *Computational Statistics and Data Analysis*, vol. 52, no. 1, pp. 335–346, 2007.

[44] E. Frias-Martinez, A. Sanchez, and J. Velez, "Support vector machines versus multi-layer perceptrons for efficient off-line signature recognition," *Engineering Applications of Artificial Intelligence*, vol. 19, no. 6, pp. 693–704, 2006.

[45] T. Benyang and D. Mazzoni, "Multiclass reduced-set support vector machines," in *Proceedings of the 23rd International Conference on Machine Learning (ICML '06)*, pp. 921–928, ACM, Pittsburgh, Pa, USA, June 2006.

[46] J. N. S. Kwong and S. Gong, "Learning support vector machines for a multi-view face model," in *Proceedings of the British*

Machine Vision Conference (BMVC '99), T. P. Pridmore and D. Elliman, Eds., pp. 503–512, British Machine Vision Association, Nottingham, UK, 1999.

[47] J. Platt, "Fast training of support vector machines using sequential minimal optimization," in *Advances in Kernel Methods-Support Vector Learning*, B. Schölkopf, C. Burges, and A. Smola, Eds., MIT Press, 1999.

[48] M. A. Hall, *Correlation-based feature selection for machine learning [Ph.D. thesis]*, The University of Waikato, Hamilton, New Zealand, 1999.

[49] J. G. Cleary and L. E. Trigg, "K*: an instance-based learner using on entropic distance measure," in *Proceedings of the 12th International Conference on Machine Learning (ICML '95)*, A. Prieditis and S. J. Russell, Eds., pp. 108–114, Morgan Kaufmann, Tahoe City, Calif, USA, 1995.

[50] Y. Zhao, "Learning user keystroke patterns for authentication," *International Journal of Mathematics and Computer Science*, vol. 1, pp. 149–154, 2005.

[51] J. Friedman, T. Hastie, and R. Tibshirani, "Additive logistic regression: a statistical view of boosting," *The Annals of Statistics*, vol. 28, no. 2, pp. 337–407, 2000.

[52] A. Buja, T. Hastie, and R. Tibshirani, "Linear smoothers and additive models," *The Annals of Statistics*, vol. 17, no. 2, pp. 453–555, 1989.

[53] L. Breiman, "Bagging predictors," *Machine Learning*, vol. 24, no. 2, pp. 123–140, 1996.

[54] Türkiye Bankalar Birliği, "Bankalarımız 2005," Türkiye Bankalar Birliği Yayınları, İstanbul, Turkey, 2006, (Turkish).

[55] A. G. Karegowda, A. S. Manjunath, and M. A. Jayaram, "Comparative study of attribute selection using gain ratio and correlation based feature selection," *International Journal of Information Technology and Knowledge Management*, vol. 2, pp. 271–277, 2010.

13

Downscaling Statistical Model Techniques for Climate Change Analysis Applied to the Amazon Region

David Mendes,[1] **José Antonio Marengo,**[2] **Sidney Rodrigues,**[3] **and Magaly Oliveira**[3]

[1] *Climate Science Program, Federal University of Rio Grande do Norte, 59082-200 Natal, RN, Brazil*
[2] *Instituto Nacional de Pesquisas Espaciais (INPE), Avenida dos Astronautas, 1.758 Jardim da Granja, 12227-010 São José dos Campos, SP, Brazil*
[3] *World Wild Life Fund Brazil (WWF), SHIS EQ QL 6/8 Conjunto, 71620-430 Brasilia, DF, Brazil*

Correspondence should be addressed to David Mendes; davidmendes@ect.ufrn.br

Academic Editor: Ozgur Kisi

The Amazon is an area covered predominantly by dense tropical rainforest with relatively small inclusions of several other types of vegetation. In the last decades, scientific research has suggested a strong link between the health of the Amazon and the integrity of the global climate: tropical forests and woodlands (e.g., savannas) exchange vast amounts of water and energy with the atmosphere and are thought to be important in controlling local and regional climates. Consider the importance of the Amazon biome to the global climate changes impacts and the role of the protected area in the conservation of biodiversity and state-of-art of downscaling model techniques based on ANN Calibrate and run a downscaling model technique based on the Artificial Neural Network (ANN) that is applied to the Amazon region in order to obtain regional and local climate predicted data (e.g., precipitation). Considering the importance of the Amazon biome to the global climate changes impacts and the state-of-art of downscaling techniques for climate models, the shower of this work is presented as follows: the use of ANNs good similarity with the observation in the cities of Belém and Manaus, with correlations of approximately 88.9% and 91.3%, respectively, and spatial distribution, especially in the correction process, representing a good fit.

1. Introduction

The Amazon is an area covered predominantly by dense tropical rainforest with relatively small inclusions of several other types of vegetation (e.g., Bromeliad, Heliconia, Orchids, water lily, and others). In the last decades, scientific research has suggested a strong link between the health of the Amazon and the integrity of the global climate: tropical forests and woodlands (e.g., Cerrado) exchange vast amounts of water and energy with the atmosphere and are thought to be important in controlling local and regional climates [1]. The same authors showed that the assessment of future cerrado land use scenarios is also necessary to understand the future climate and ecosystem health of the Amazon. The Amazon Biome is an area covered predominantly by dense tropical rainforest with relatively small inclusions of several other types of vegetation. It encompasses 6.7 million km^2 (twice the size of India) and is shared by eight countries (Brazil, Bolivia, Peru, Ecuador, Colombia, Venezuela, Guyana, and Suriname), as well as the overseas territory of French Guiana.

The Amazon Biome houses at least 11% of the world's known biodiversity, including endemic and endangered flora and fauna, and its river accounts for 15-16% of the world's total river discharge into the oceans. The Amazon River flows for more than 6,600 km and with its hundreds of tributaries and streams contains the largest number of freshwater fish species in the world. Equally impressive are the unfathomable numbers of mammals, birds, amphibians, and reptiles found across the biome.

1.1. The Importance of the Amazon Rainforest for Local and Global Climate. Tropical forests and woodlands (e.g., savannas) exchange vast amounts of water and energy with the atmosphere and are thought to be important in controlling local and regional climates.

Water released by plants into the atmosphere through evapotranspiration (evaporation and plant transpiration) and to the ocean by the rivers influences world climate and the circulation of ocean currents. This process works as a feedback mechanism, as the process also sustains the regional climate on which it depends.

Marengo et al. [2] say that Amazonian rainforest plays a crucial role in the climate system, helping to drive atmospheric circulations in the tropics by absorbing energy and recycling about half of the rainfall that falls on it. Amazonia can be categorized as a region at great risk due to climate variability and change. The risk is not only due to projected climate change but also through synergistic interactions with existing threats not related to climate change, such as land clearance, forest fragmentation, and fire [2].

Several papers on deforestation quote the following.

(1) Baidya Roy and Avissar [3] simulated the impact of deforestation on Rondônia State. They found that vegetation breezes formed and converged above deforested areas, resulting in strong updrafts carrying the moisture that had transpired from the forest and generating shallow-convection clouds.

(2) Gandu et al. [4] showed and evaluated the impact of deforestation on the climate of the eastern portion of the Amazon Basin. This region is primarily an area of native tropical rainforest but also contains several other natural 86 ecosystems such as mangroves and savanna.

(3) Avissar et al. [5] have summarized possible changes in rainfall accumulation due to a progressive expansion of deforestation in three scenarios.

(a) Rainfall will first decrease rapidly then more slowly as the deforested area expands.

(b) Given the abovementioned finding, it could be anticipated that rainfall will first remain unaffected (or possibly even increase) because of initial deforestation, but it will then fall rapidly as the deforested area crosses some threshold estimated at 30–50% of deforestation.

(c) Rainfall will decrease linearly with deforested area.

Oyama and Nobre [6] findings performed with General Circulation Model (GCM) suggest that deforestation may establish a permanent savanna in Amazonia, mostly over the east, but Ramos da Silva et al. [7] the rainfall toward the west and with stronger impacts during extreme events (e.g., El Niño). Thus, the combination of the large-scale effects on the drying of the eastern part of the basin and local mesoscale systems cause a much stronger effect over region.

Another important factor is increase of temperature, wind speed, and latent heat flux, causing a decrease because of expanding deforestation in the Amazon forest.

1.2. Extreme Tendency and the Precipitation over Amazon Basin. The climate change over Amazon Basin detected an observed warming of +0.57°C/100 year until 1997 [8]. Marengo et al. [9, 10] cited magnitude and size of the records and uncertainty is high since studies have found trends that vary in direction when different length periods are used.

An analysis of extreme rainfall over Amazon Basin has been hampered by the degree of spatial coherence and uncertainty due to reduced number of station distribution in region [9–11]. Several studies in the Amazon Basin, based on time series of rainfall data (e.g., [12, 13]), have produced conflicting results, principally in relation to trend rainfall; Marengo [14] identifies a weak positive rainfall trend in the whole Amazon Basin, with negative rainfall over northern and positive rainfall over southern section of the basin. Valverde and Marengo [15] show the annual variability of extreme precipitation indices, such as, maximum lengths of dry spell which were sensitive to identification periods of droughts. Similarly, it verified that extreme rains (>50 mm/day) occur with or without events El-Niño. In 2005, severe drought in the past 40 years and one of the most intense of the last 100 years affected Amazon Basin. Marengo et al. [9, 10] suggest that drought was not caused by El Niño, but by (1) the anomalously warm tropical North Atlantic, (2) the reduced intensity in northeast trade wind moisture transport into southern Amazonia during the peak summertime season, and (3) the weakened upward motion over this section of Amazonia, resulting in reduced convective development and rainfall. Marengo et al. [9, 10] showed that drought of 2005 affected western Amazon Basin, unlike El Niño-induced drought, which affects central and eastern Amazon Basin. In October 2006, rainfall began again and alleviated the situation, and, by February 2006, rainfall was above the normal. This rapid change in rainfall patterns directly linked to the change in the pattern of SST in the North Atlantic.

Cox et al. [16] examine the possible links of the drought of Amazon Basin in 2005 to climate change, verifying that the reduction of dry season (July to October) rainfall in western Amazon Basin is well-correlated with an index of north-south SST gradient across the equatorial Atlantic related to the Atlantic Multidecadal Oscillation (AMO). More recent study linking statistical downscaling were used (e.g., [17]) to identify extremes of Amazon climate. Mendes and Marengo [17] used neural network for downscaling with IPCCR-AR4 models, the authors find that model test results indicate that the neural network model significantly outperforms the statistical models for the downscaling of daily precipitation variability; based on experience of Mendes and Marengo [17], this paper uses neural network model to correct climate extremes over Amazon Basin. Nobre et al. [18] showed and indicated that both this fraction of the deforested area and the spatial continuity of the vegetated area might be important for modulation of global climate change, principally significant remote atmospheric responses to Amazon deforestation scenarios. Cox et al. [16] showed the climate change simulation over the Amazon Basin and identified a link between the Atlantic Ocean that exerts an influence on the climate of Amazonia, which presents strong tendency for the sea surface temperature condition associated with drought to become much more common owing to continuing reduction in reflective aerosol pollution in the Northern Hemisphere.

1.3. Downscaling and Artificial Neural Network for Amazon Basin. There are few studies that make the ANN compared to the Amazon Basin that cited; Mendes and Marengo [17], showed that the downscaling models were developed and validated using IPCC AR4 model output and observed daily precipitation. In this paper, five AOGCMs for the twentieth century (20C3M) and future, the performance in downscaling of the temporal neural network was compared to that of an autocorrelation statistical downscaling model with emphasis on its ability to reproduce the observed climate variability and tendency for the period 1970–1999. The test results indicate that the neural network model significantly outperforms the statistical models for the downscaling of daily precipitation variability.

Espinoza et al. [19] describes the main circulation patterns (CP) in the Amazonian Basin over the 1975–2002 period and their relationship with rainfall variability, using an approach combining artificial neural network (Self-Organizing Maps) and Hierarchical Ascendant Classification. These results demonstrate the potential of using ANN to better understand local rainfall variability in the Amazon Basin. Particularly, this work supplies important information about large-scale atmospheric circulation and extreme rainfall relationship in the Amazon.

Other studies relate future climate in South America; for example, Boulanger et al. [20] developed a statistical method based on neural networks and Bayesian statistics to evaluate the models' skills in simulating late twentieth century temperature over continental areas. As the study demonstrates, the use of neural networks, optimized by Bayesian statistics, leads to two major results. First, the model weight indices can be interpreted as optimal weights for a linear combination of the climate models. Second, the comparison between the neural network projection of twenty-first century conditions and a linear combination of such conditions allows the identification of the regions, which will most probably change, according to model biases and model ensemble variance.

As there are few studies that use ANN to identify climatic extremes over the Amazon Basin, we believe that this study presented here can be an initial way related to extreme rain conditions and other variables using an artificial technique.

2. Neural Network Model (ANN)

An ANN is a system based on the operation of biological neural network and in other works it is an emulation of biological neural system.

Advantages of ANN are the following.

(a) An ANN can perform tasks that a linear program cannot.

(b) When an element of the ANN fails, it can continue without any problem by their parallel nature.

(c) An ANN learns and does 161 not to be reprogrammed.

(d) It can be implemented without any problem.

Disadvantages of ANN are the following.

(a) It is necessary for the ANN training to operate.

(b) The architecture of ANN is different from the architecture of microprocessors therefore it needs to be emulated.

(c) It requires high processing time for large ANN.

ANN is among the newest signal-processing technologies in the engineer's toolbox. The field is highly interdisciplinary, but our approach will restrict the view to the engineering perspective. Definitions and style of computation an ANN is on adaptive, most after nonlinear system that learns to perform a function from data (input and output). An input presented to the ANN and a corresponding desired or target response set at the output (in this case the training is called supervised).

The ability to identify a relationship from given patterns makes it possible for ANNs to solve large-scale complex problems such as pattern recognition, nonlinear modelling, classification, association, and control.

Before its application to any problem, the network first trained whereby the target output at each output neuron is compared with the network output and the difference or error is minimized by adjusting the weights and biases through some training algorithm. Training in ANNs consists of three elements: (1) weights between neurons that define the relative importance of the inputs, (2) a transfer function that controls the generation of the output from a neuron, and (3) learning laws that describe how the adjustments of the weights are made during training. During training, a neuron receives inputs from a previous layer, weights each input with a prearranged value, and combines these weighted inputs.

In this study sigmoid function was employed as an activation function in the training of the network. The sigmoid function is a bounded, monotonic, nondecreasing function that provides a graded, nonlinear response.

The ANN diagram (Figure 1) is a full-connected two layers, feed-forward, perception ANN. "Fully connected" means that the output from each input and hidden neuron is distributed to all of the neurons in the following layer. "Feed-forward" means that the values only move from input to hidden to output layer; no values are feedback to earlier layer.

The learning of ANNs was accomplished by a back-propagation algorithm. Back-propagation is the most commonly used supervised training algorithm in the multilayered feed-forward networks. In back-propagation networks, information is processed in the forward direction from the input layer to the hidden layer and then to the output layer (Figure 1).

We use in this work the same argument as Mendes and Marengo [17], where the goal of the training process is to find the set of weight values that will cause the output from the ANN to match the actual target values as closely as possible.

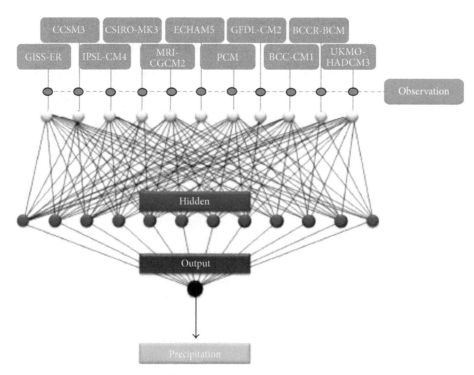

FIGURE 1: Structure of the artificial neural network.

There are several issues involved in designing and training a multilayer perceptron network:

(1) deciding how many neurons to use on each hidden layer,

(2) selecting how many hidden layers to use in the network,

(3) finding a globally optimal solution that avoids local minima,

(4) validating the neural network to test for overfitting,

(5) converging to on optimal solution in a reasonable period.

Training of the ANN is accomplished by providing inputs to the model, computing the output, and adjusting the interconnection weight until the desired output is reached. The error back-propagation algorithm is used to train the network, using the mean square error (MSE) over the training samples as the objective function. One part is used for training, the second is used for cross-validation, and the third part is used for testing.

2.1. Procedure for Training the Network. In this paper, we used the training of the ANN by providing inputs to the model, computing the output, and adjusting the interconnection weight until the desired output is reached. The back-propagation algorithm error is used to train the network, using the mean square error over the training samples as the objective function. One part is used for training, the second is used for cross-validation, and the third part is used for testing.

The number of intermediate units was obtained through a trial-and-error procedure. The error between the value predicted by the ANN and the value actually observed was then measured and propagated backward along the feed-forward connection.

Another important factor in training was a sensitivity analysis to determine the most relevant predictors, which need to be selected for further retraining. Sensitivity analysis provides a measure of the relative importance among the predictors (input of the ANN) by calculating how the model output varies in response to variation of an input.

3. Observed and Model Datasets

The data used in this paper were from rain gauges located within the Amazon Basin, which are part of the Brazilian national hydrometeorological network. They were provided by the National Water and Electric Energy Agency of Brazil (ANEEL), whose sources include the ANEEL network. Precipitation (P) is computed from rainfall observations in the Amazon Basin and is derived for the entire basin. Stations were also used in other countries of South America, Instituto de Hidrología, Meteorología y Estudos ambientales (IDEAM) da Colombia; Instituto Nacional de Meteorología y Hidrologia do Equador (INAMHI); Servicio Nacional de Meteorología e Hidrología del Peru (SENAMHI); Servicio Nacional de Meteorología e Hidrología de Bolivia (SENAMHI); Instituto Nacional de Meteorología y Hidrología de Venezuela (INAMEH).

Vincent et al. [21] cited that data quality assessment is an important requirement before the calculation of indices since

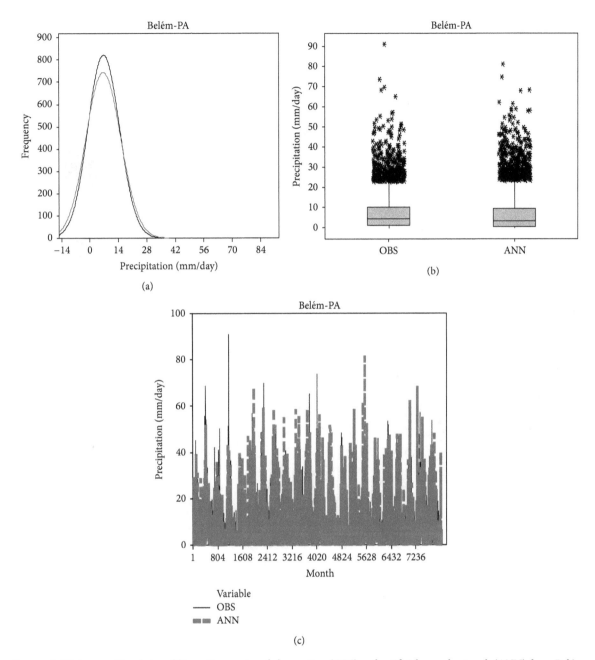

FIGURE 2: Histogram, Boxplot, and linear time series of observation (OBS) and artificial neural network (ANN) from Belém.

any erroneous outlier can have a serious impact on the trends in extremes.

The coupled atmosphere-ocean GCMs (AOGCMs) outputs are 208 interpolated over the 2.5° × 2.5° grid defined for the observation. The period used for present conditions (20C3M run scenario) is 1970–1999, and the future is 2011–2040, 2041–2070, and 2071–2100 as derived from ten IPCC AR4 models. The ten models (Table 1) represent state of-the-art AOGCMs. It is important to note, however, that the 20c3m simulation is intended to represent the same historical total-forcing scenarios, including both natural variability and the effect of human emissions on climate.

4. Application and Result

Initially, we apply the technique of validating the ANN for two towns in the Amazon Basin, Belém and Manaus (Figures 2 and 3). Figures 2 and 3 show an excellent correlation between observation and ANNs, both in Belém (Figure 2(b)) and Manaus (Figure 3(b)) showing the reduced uncertainty observed data.

Comparison of results obtained using the ANNs compared with observation indicates that the network is a potential competitive alternative tool for the analysis of multivariate time series (Figures 2 and 3).

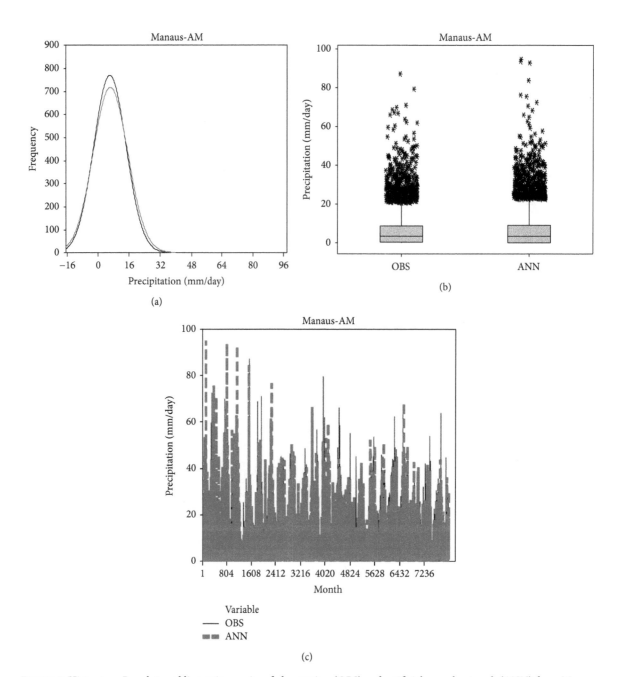

FIGURE 3: Histogram, Boxplot, and linear time series of observation (OBS) and artificial neural network (ANN) from Manaus.

For most indices, the regionally averaged series are expressed in the index units, but several of the precipitation indices have millimeter units. Thus at the regional-wide scale, there is a consistency between indices that average daily rainfall. In this paper, four indexes are used for the precipitation climate extremes as follows:

(a) PRCPTOT: annual total wet-day precipitation (precipitation ≥1 mm),

(b) CDII: annual total precipitation divided by the number of wet days (precipitation ≥1 mm),

(c) CDD: maximum number of consecutive days with daily rainfall <1 mm,

(d) R25mm: annual count of days when precipitation ≥25 mm.

The results for all indices (Figure 4) are summarized over all stations over the Amazon Basin, including the fraction of station with trends that are significant at the 5% level, in the 6–9% range, and that are not significant (statistical) by Kendall's tau.

We use a nonparametric trend statistic Kendall's tau for monotonic trends, which makes no assumption about the distribution of the data or the linearity of any trend (e.g.,

TABLE 1: Climate models with daily data for precipitation available from PCMDI.

Models data		Spatial resolution	
Models	Font	Resolution	Km
CCSR	NCAR/USA	$1.4° \times 1.4°$	$154 \times 154 \, km$
CSIRO-MK3.0	CSIRO/Australia	$1.9° \times 1.9°$	$209 \times 209 \, km$
ECHAM5/MPI-OM	MAX-PLACK/Germany	$1.9° \times 1.9°$	$209 \times 209 \, km$
GFDL-CM2.0	NOAA/GFCL/USA	$2.0° \times 2.5°$	$220 \times 275 \, km$
BCCR-BCM2.0	BCCR/Norway	$1.9° \times 1.9°$	$209 \times 209 \, km$
GISS-ER	NASA/GISS/USA	$4.0° \times 5.0°$	$440 \times 440 \, km$
IPSL-CM4	IPSL/France	$2.5° \times 3.7°$	$275 \times 413 \, km$
MRI-CGCM2.3.2	MRI/Japan	$2.8° \times 2.8°$	$308 \times 308 \, km$
PCM	NCAR/USA	$2.8° \times 2.8°$	$308 \times 308 \, km$
BCC-CM1	BCC/China	$1.9° \times 1.9°$	$209 \times 209 \, km$
HADCM3	Hadley Centre/UK	$3.75° \times 2.5°$	$370 \times 250 \, km$

TABLE 2: Trend analysis for 1979–2000 for regional time series 507 of anomalies from the Amazon Basin.

Index	Units	Trend, units/period Observation	Trend, units/period ANN
PRECPTOT	mm	4.89	4.66
SDII	mm	0.34	0.43
CDD	Number of days	0.77	0.72
R25mm	Number of days	1.20	1.01

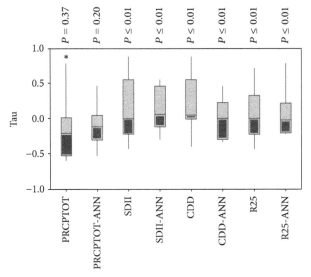

FIGURE 4: Trends of Kendall's Tau for all indices.

Regional time series of several precipitation indices can be seen in Table 2. Most stations show no significant trends for the different indices, due to the relatively short period of data, both for observation and for ANNs.

Checked is a small difference between observation and ANNs; this small difference is related to the homogeneity of the time series of precipitation. This is due to the fact that data quality assessment is an important requirement before the calculation of indices since any erroneous outlier can have a serious impact on the trends in extremes. There is a small trend more positive in all four indices (Table 2).

In the present study, we aim at evaluating the evolution of large-scale patterns rather than regionally averaged indices. A solution to the present problem is the use of an artificial neural network interpolation approach which should lead to determine optimal combination of models.

Figure 5(a) shows the difference between models (Table 1) versus observation data. The difference is normalized. The great difference is located over north, west, and southwest Amazon Basin, with values in 1 mm/day (Figure 5(a)). After application of Ann's correction, the results are very good, principally over the central and east Amazon Basin. In the north, west and southwest improvement occurred, reducing the value of difference.

Figure 6 shows the trend for the R25mm. In this figure, we have elected, for ease of interpretation, to show just the sign of the trend as well as flag interpolation with trends significant at $P < 0.05$, using the ANN as calibration models. This figure shows significant high value over northeast and northwest Amazon Basin, with proximally 52 days with rainfall >25 mm. These two areas have very high annual rainfall value, above 3000 mm [14]. These results show that the calibration gets the signal variability of rainfall over the Amazon Basin.

Hollander and Wolfe [22]). Kendall's tau also standardizes the trend between 1.0 and 1.0, enabling comparison of trends across different parts of the region, where the absolute values of trends can vary. New et al. [23] cited, "as Kendall's tau does not give an indication of the magnitude of trend, we also calculate the least squares linear trends."

Figure 4 showed fraction of station with positive and negative trends by observation data and Ann's application, where the indices for the ANNs subtract the uncertainties in the observed data.

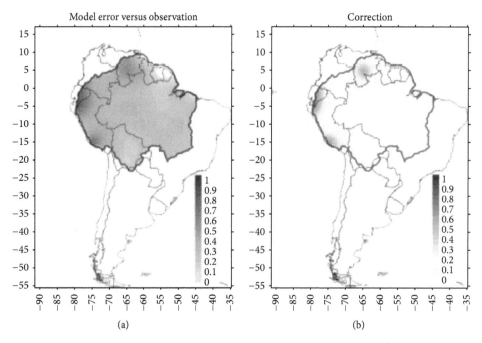

FIGURE 5: Difference between models and observation data (mm/day) (a) and correction from artificial neural network (mm/day) (b). Period between 1979 and 2000.

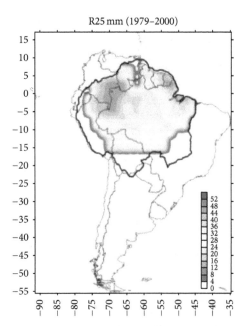

FIGURE 6: Sign of the linear trend in rainfall indices. Very heavy precipitation days (annual count of days when precipitation ≥25 mm).

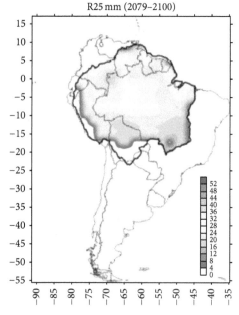

FIGURE 7: Sign of the linear trend in rainfall indices. Very heavy precipitation days (annual count of days when precipitation ≥25 mm) for 2079–2100 period and A2 scenarios.

This result is relatively coherent with observation data. Such values are beyond the range of the dataset used for training. The artificial neural network makes its extrapolation skill not questionable. Figure 7 shows a significant decrease in extreme rainfall across the Amazon Basin, decreasing by almost 50% days with rainfall exceeding 25 mm. In the areas where the 20th 277 century (Figure 6) had many days

with rainfall exceeding 25 mm, especially in the northwest Amazon Basin, this reduction was decreased of up to 30%.

Finally, a comparison between the outputs of the models and ANNs was very good. This technique of using ANN in the identification and correction of meteorological data is new and effective.

5. Discussion

This study is an examination of the trends in indices of rainfall extreme over the Amazon Basin during 1979 to 2000 and future scenarios A2 (IPCC, 2007) for 2071–2100. Fundamentally, it is necessary to use new techniques to identify extreme events. In this paper, we use artificial neural network as a tool for identification and calibration output model.

Amazon basin can be categorized as a region at great risk due to climate variability and change. Marengo et al. [2] cited that the risk is not only due to projected climate change but also through synergistic interaction with existing threats not to climate change. The Amazon Basin is affected by large climate variability and extreme events, with the strongest increase in 2005.

Marengo et al. [2] shows that large section of the western Amazon Basin experienced the most severe drought in the 40 years and also one of the most intense of the last 100 years; the authors suggest that the drought was not caused by El-Niño but by (a) the anomalously warm tropical North Atlantic, (b) the reduced intensity in northeast trade wind moisture transport into southern Amazon Basin during the summertime season, and (c) the weakened upward motion over this section of the Amazon Basin, resulting in reduced convection development and rainfall.

We have described the results of an analysis of extreme in climate data for output models and output from ANN. Regionally average dry spell length, average rainfall intensity, and annual 1 day maximum rainfall all show statistically significant increasing trends.

A synthesis of the results is as follows.

(i) Eleven models (11) were very good at detecting extreme rainfall indices.

(ii) The use of ANNs showed good similarity with the observation (Figures 2 and 3), in the cities of Belém and Manaus, with correlations of approximately 88.9% and 91.3%, respectively.

(iii) The method of trends of Kendall's tau of the ANNs showed a "shortening" in the variability in all indices calculated (Figure 4).

(iv) The spatial distribution, especially in the correction process (Figure 5), represents a decrease in the differences of up to 50%.

(v) The index of extreme R25mm can be spatially well represented (Figure 6).

(vi) In projection of the 21st century, a decrease of days with rainfall above 25 mm up to 35% for the A2 scenario (IPCC, 2007).

Conflict of Interests

The authors declare that there is no conflict of interests regarding the publication of this paper.

Acknowledgments

The authors wish to thank the World Wildlife Fund (WWF) for their financial support in the development of this study. They thank the IPCC for facilitating the access to the simulation output and thank the international modeling group for providing their data for analysis, the Program for Climate Model Diagnosis and Intercomparison (PCMDI).

References

[1] M. H. Costa and G. F. Pires, "Effects of Amazon and Central Brazil deforestation scenarios on the duration of the dry season in the arc of deforestation," *International Journal of Climatology*, vol. 30, no. 13, pp. 1970–1979, 2010.

[2] J. Marengo, C. A. Nobre, R. A. Betts, P. M. Cox, G. Sampaio, and L. Salazar, "Global warming and climate change in Amazonia: climate-vegetation feedback and impacts on water resources," in *Amazonia and Global Change*, M. Keller, M. Bustamante, J. Gash et al., Eds., vol. 186 of *Geophysical Monograph Series*, pp. 273–292, AGU, Washington, DC, USA, 2009.

[3] S. Baidya Roy and R. Avissar, "Impact of land use/land cover change on regional hydrometeorology in Amazonia," *Journal of Geophysical Research D*, vol. 107, no. 20, pp. 4–12, 2002.

[4] A. W. Gandu, J. C. P. Cohen, and J. R. S. de Souza, "Simulation of deforestation in eastern Amazonia using a high-resolution model," *Theoretical and Applied Climatology*, vol. 78, no. 1–3, pp. 123–135, 2004.

[5] R. Avissar, P. L. Silva Dias, M. A. Silva Dias, and C. A. Nobre, "The Large Scale Biosphere Atmosphere Experiment in Amazonia (LBA). Insights and future research needs," *Journal of Geophysical Research*, vol. 107, no. 20, pp. 1–6, 2002.

[6] M. D. Oyama and C. A. Nobre, "A new climate-vegetation equilibrium state for Tropical South America," *Geophysical Research Letters*, vol. 30, no. 23, p. 2199, 2003.

[7] R. R. da Silva, D. Werth, and R. Avissar, "Regional impacts of future land-cover changes on the Amazon basin wet-season climate," *Journal of Climate*, vol. 21, no. 6, pp. 1153–1170, 2008.

[8] R. Victoria, L. Matinelli, J. Moraes et al., "Surface air temperature variations in the Amazon region and its border during this century," *Journal of Climate*, vol. 11, pp. 1105–1110, 1998.

[9] J. A. Marengo, C. A. Nobre, J. Tomasella, M. F. Cardoso, and M. D. Oyama, "Hydro-climatic and ecological behaviour of the drought of Amazonia in 2005," *Philosophical Transactions of the Royal Society B: Biological Sciences*, vol. 363, no. 1498, pp. 1773–1778, 2008.

[10] J. A. Marengo, C. A. Nobre, J. Tomasella et al., "The drought of Amazonia in 2005," *Journal of Climate*, vol. 21, no. 3, pp. 495–516, 2008.

[11] M. R. Haylock, G. C. Cawley, C. Harpham, R. L. Wilby, and C. M. Goodess, "Downscaling heavy precipitation over the United Kingdom: a comparison of dynamical and statistical methods and their future scenarios," *International Journal of Climatology*, vol. 26, no. 10, pp. 1397–1415, 2006.

[12] J. A. Marengo, W. R. Soares, C. Saulo, and M. Nicolini, "Climatology of the low-level jet east of the Andes as derived from the NCEP-NCAR reanalyses: characteristics and temporal variability," *Journal of Climate*, vol. 17, pp. 2261–2280, 2004.

[13] H. Matsuyama, J. A. Marengo, G. O. Obregon, and C. A. Nobre, "Spatial and temporal variabilities of rainfall in tropical South America as derived from climate prediction Center merged

analysis of precipitation," *International Journal of Climatology*, vol. 22, no. 2, pp. 175–195, 2002.

[14] J. A. Marengo, "Interdecadal variability and trends of rainfall across the Amazon basin," *Theoretical and Applied Climatology*, vol. 78, no. 1-3, pp. 79–96, 2004.

[15] M. Valverde and J. A. Marengo, "Mudanças na Circulação Atmosférica sobre a América do Sul para cenários futuros de clima projetados pelos modelos globais do IPCC AR4," *Revista Brasileira de Meteorologia*, vol. 25, pp. 125–145, 2010.

[16] P. M. Cox, P. P. Harris, C. Huntingford et al., "Increasing risk of Amazonian drought due to decreasing aerosol pollution," *Nature*, vol. 453, no. 7192, pp. 212–215, 2008.

[17] D. Mendes and J. A. Marengo, "Temporal downscaling: a comparison between artificial neural network and autocorrelation techniques over the Amazon Basin in present and future climate change scenarios," *Theoretical and Applied Climatology*, vol. 100, no. 3, pp. 413–421, 2010.

[18] P. Nobre, M. Malagutti, D. F. Urbano, R. A. F. de Almeida, and E. Giarolla, "Amazon deforestation and climate change in a coupled model simulation," *Journal of Climate*, vol. 22, no. 21, pp. 5686–5697, 2009.

[19] J. C. Espinoza, J. Ronchail, M. Lengaigne et al., "Revisiting wintertime cold air intrusions at the east of the Andes: propagating features from subtropical Argentina to Peruvian Amazon and relationship with large-scale circulation patterns," *Climate Dynamics*, vol. 41, no. 7-8, pp. 1983–2002, 2012.

[20] J. P. Boulanger, F. Martinez, and E. C. Segura, "Projection of future climate change conditions using IPCC simulations, neural networks and bayesian statistics—part 1: temperature mean state and seasonal cycle in South America," *Climate Dynamics*, vol. 27, no. 2-3, pp. 233–259, 2006.

[21] L. A. Vincent, T. C. Peterson, V. R. Barros et al., "Observed trends in indices of daily temperature extremes in South America 1960–2000," *Journal of Climate*, vol. 18, no. 23, pp. 5011–5023, 2005.

[22] M. Hollander and D. A. Wolfe, *Nonparametric Statistical Methods*, John Wiley & Sons, New York, NY, USA, 1973.

[23] M. New, B. Hewitson, D. B. Stephenson et al., "Evidence of trends in daily climate extremes over southern and west Africa," *Journal of Geophysical Research D: Atmospheres*, vol. 111, no. 14, Article ID D14102, 2006.

14

Genetic Algorithm-Based Artificial Neural Network for Voltage Stability Assessment

Garima Singh and Laxmi Srivastava

Electrical Engineering Department, Madhav Institute of Technology and Science, Gwalior 474 005, India

Correspondence should be addressed to Laxmi Srivastava, srivastaval@hotmail.com

Academic Editor: Ping Feng Pai

With the emerging trend of restructuring in the electric power industry, many transmission lines have been forced to operate at almost their full capacities worldwide. Due to this, more incidents of voltage instability and collapse are being observed throughout the world leading to major system breakdowns. To avoid these undesirable incidents, a fast and accurate estimation of voltage stability margin is required. In this paper, genetic algorithm based back propagation neural network (GABPNN) has been proposed for voltage stability margin estimation which is an indication of the power system's proximity to voltage collapse. The proposed approach utilizes a hybrid algorithm that integrates genetic algorithm and the back propagation neural network. The proposed algorithm aims to combine the capacity of GAs in avoiding local minima and at the same time fast execution of the BP algorithm. Input features for GABPNN are selected on the basis of angular distance-based clustering technique. The performance of the proposed GABPNN approach has been compared with the most commonly used gradient based BP neural network by estimating the voltage stability margin at different loading conditions in 6-bus and IEEE 30-bus system. GA based neural network learns faster, at the same time it provides more accurate voltage stability margin estimation as compared to that based on BP algorithm. It is found to be suitable for online applications in energy management systems.

1. Introduction

Voltage stability is concerned with the ability of the power system to maintain acceptable voltages at all the system buses under normal conditions as well as after being subjected to a disturbance. Thus, the analysis of voltage stability deals with finding the voltage levels at all buses in the system under different loading conditions to ascertain the stability limit and margin. A power system enters a state of voltage instability when a disturbance, increase in load demand or change in system conditions causes a progressive and uncontrollable decline of bus voltages.

The main factor causing voltage instability is the inability of the power system to meet the reactive power demand. In most of the cases, voltage profiles show no abnormality prior to undergoing voltage collapse because of the load variation. Voltage stability margin (VSM) is a static voltage stability index which is used to quantify how "close" a particular operating point is to the point of voltage collapse [1]. Thus, VSM may be used to estimate the steady-state voltage stability limit of a power system. Knowledge of the voltage stability margin is of vital importance to utilities in order to operate their system with appropriate security and reliability

During the last few years, several methodologies for detecting the voltage collapse points (saddle-node bifurcations) in power systems using steady-state analysis techniques have been modified and applied for the determination of analyzing voltage stability of power systems for example PV and QV curves, sensitivity-based indices [2] and continuation power flow methods [3, 4]. Other methods, such as bifurcation theory [5], energy function [6], singular value decomposition [7], and so forth, have been also reported in the literature.

These analytical methods involve considerable computational effort and require significantly large computational time and, hence, cannot be used directly for online monitoring and initiation of preventive control actions to enhance system voltage stability. For online applications, there is a need for quick detection of the potentially dangerous situations of voltage instability so that necessary actions may be taken to avoid the occurrence of voltage collapse in a power system.

Recently, artificial neural networks (ANNs) have been proposed for voltage stability evaluation [1, 8–16] as they have the ability to properly classify a highly nonlinear relationship, and, once trained, they can classify new data much faster than it would be possible by solving the model analytically. However, most of the published work in the area of voltage stability employed either multi-layer perceptron networks trained by back propagation algorithm [8–14]. In reference [13], the energy function-based voltage stability indicator is predicted using the multi-layer perception (MLP) with a second-order learning rule and the radial basis function (RBF) network. The input to the neural network consists of real and reactive power injections at all load buses in the system for a particular loading condition, while the output of the network is the energy margin. In [14], an approach based on artificial feed-forward neural network (FFNN) is presented for assessing power system voltage stability. The approach uses real and reactive power, as well as voltage vectors for generators and load buses to train the neural net (NN). The input properties of the NN are generated from offline training data with various simulated loading conditions using a conventional voltage stability algorithm-based on the L-index. In reference [1] parallel self-organizing hierarchical neural network is developed for assessing power system voltage stability while in [15, 16], Kohonen's self-organizing feature map (SOFM) has been proposed for quantifying stability margins.

In typical power systems, there are voluminous amount of input data. Then, the success of ANN applications also depends on the systematic approach of selecting highly important features which will result in a compact and efficient ANN. Different feature reduction methods for voltage stability assessment are compared in [17]. Feature reduction is crucial for the success of ANN application, although each has its own merit and demerit. Feature selection based on clustering technique can identify important parameters directly measurable from the power system.

Voltage instability is, in general, caused by either of two types of system disturbances: increase in load demand and contingencies. In the present paper, voltage instability due to increase in load demand is considered. A genetic algorithm-based back propagation neural network [18–23] has been proposed for voltage stability margin estimation which evaluates system stability from static viewpoint. Input features for GABPNN are selected by applying angular distance-based clustering technique in the real and reactive loads [24, 25].

These conventional methods of voltage stability assessment are computationally intensive and data sensitive. On the other hand, artificial neural network-based approach is fast and provides result even with partially missing/noisy data. Back propagation (BP) searches on the error surface by means of the gradient descent technique in order to minimize the error. It is therefore likely to get struck in a local minimum [18]. On the other hand in GABPNN,

there exist genetic algorithms (GA) which are adaptive search and optimization algorithms that mimic the principles of natural genetics. Genetic algorithms are quite different from traditional search and optimization techniques used in engineering design problems but at the same time exhibit simplicity, ease of operation, minimal requirements, and global perspective.

2. Genetic Algorithm-Based BP Neural Network

The idea to hybridize the two approaches, namely, GA and BPN follows naturally. Rajasekaran and Pai [20] used GAs to guide back propagation network in finding the necessary connections instead of full connections in order to enhance the speed of training. The general schematic of the genetic algorithm (GA) is considered to be a stochastic heuristic (or metaheuristic) method. Genetic algorithms are inspired by adaptive and evolutionary mechanisms of live organisms.

Genetic algorithm is an adaptive search technique used for solving mathematical problems and engineering optimization problems that emulates Darwin's evolutionary theory that is fittest is likely to survive. Genetic algorithm attempts to find a good (or best) solution to the problem by genetically breeding a population of individuals over a series of generations. In genetic algorithm, each individual in the population represents a candidate solution to the given problem. The GA transforms a population (set) of individuals, each with an associated fitness value, into a new generation of the population using reproduction, crossover and mutation. Core of the GA is genetic recombination of strings. Generally, a population of strings is randomly generated at the beginning of the process.

An important characteristic of GA is that global feature of search is related to the diversity of the initial population: the more diverse the population, the more global the search. From the initial population, selection strategy based on fitness proportion is adopted to select individuals in current population. Higher selective pressure often leads to the loss of diversity in the population, which causes premature convergence but at the same time improves convergence speed. Therefore, a balance is required between population diversity and convergence speed for obtaining the good performance of GA. Then reproduction, cross-over, and mutation operators are randomly applied to produce next generation population until genetic stopping condition is satisfied.

When the GA is correctly implemented for solving any problem, the population evolves over successive iterations with the fitness value increasing towards global optimum. Several features of GAs like no dependency on gradient information, less likely to be trapped in local minima, ability to deal with the problems where no explicit/exact objective function is available, ability to deal with the concave objective function-based optimization problems, and make them much more robust than many other search algorithms. Moreover GAs are much superior to conventional search and optimization techniques in high-dimensional problem space due to their inherent parallelism and directed stochastic search implemented by recombination operators.

TABLE 1: Genetic algorithm operations.

(A) Generate randomly an initial population of individuals.

(B) Carry out the following substeps iteratively for each generation until a termination condition is fulfilled.

(i) Evaluate fitness of each individual to check its ability to solve the specific problem and save the best individual of all preceding population.

(ii) Select pair of individuals to be parents for reproduction on the basis of their fitness.

(iii) Generate offsprings from parents by implementing genetic search operators such as cross-over/mutation. Add them to the population.

TABLE 2: General framework of GAs for neural network training.

(i) Decode each individual in the current population into a set of connection weights and construct a corresponding ANN with the weights.

(ii) Evaluate the ANN by computing its total mean square error between actual and target outputs.

(iii) Determine fitness of individual as inverse of error. The higher is the error, the lower is the fitness.

(iv) Store the weights for mating pool formation.

(v) Implement search operators such as cross-over/mutation to parents to generate offsprings.

(vi) Calculate fitness for new population.

(vii) Repeat steps (iii) to (vi) until the solution converge.

(viii) Extract optimized weights.

GA operates[18] through a simple cycle of three stages, which are described in Table 1.

As shown in Table 1, in substep (ii), *selection* is based on fitness, that is, the fitter an individual the greater the chance for this individual to get selected for reproduction and contribute offspring for the next generation. *Cross-over* operator takes two chromosomes and swaps part of their genetic information to produce new chromosomes. *Mutation* is implemented by occasionally altering a random bit in a string before the offsprings are inserted into the new population. The performance of GA is achieved by having a balanced combination of three control parameters. These control parameters are crossover probability, mutation probability, and population size. Some important observations related to GA are the following:

(i) Increasing the crossover probability increases the recombination of building blocks. But it also increases the disruption of good strings.

(ii) Increasing the mutation probability tends to transform the genetic search into random search, but it also helps reintroduce lost genetic material.

(iii) Increasing the population size increases the diversity and reduces the probability of premature convergence to a local optimum, but it also increases the time required for the population to converge to the optimal region in the search space.

2.1. Weight Optimization Using GA for ANN Training. Artificial neural networks and genetic algorithms are both abstractions of natural processes. They are formulated into a computational model so that the learning power of neural networks and adaptive capabilities of evolutionary processes can be combined [18]. Genetic algorithms can help to determine optimized neural network interconnection weights, as well as, to provide faster mechanism for training of the neural network. Training a given neural network generally means to determine an optimal set of connection weights. This is formulated as the minimization of some network error functions, over the training data set, by iteratively adjusting the weights. The mean square error between the target and actual output averaged over all output nodes serves as a good estimate of the fitness of the network configuration corresponding to the current input. Conventionally a back-propagation neural network (BPNN) updates its weights

through a gradient descent technique with backward error propagation. This gradient search technique sometimes gets stuck into local minima. Gas, on the other hand, though not guaranteed to find global optimum solution, have been found to be good at finding "acceptably good" solutions "acceptably quickly" [18].

The GA-based weight optimization during training of an ANN follows two steps. The first step is encoding strings for the representation of connection weights. The second step is the evolutionary process simulated by GA, in which search operators have to be implemented in conjunction with the representation scheme. The evolution stops when the population has converged. A population is said to have converged when 95% of the individuals constituting the population share the same fitness value [20]. The whole process for neural network training using a genetic algorithm is shown in Table 2.

Obstacles to the success of GA in evolving the weights for a fixed network structure include the manner in which weights are encoded to the chromosomes and the definition of the "fitness function" that allows the preferential reproduction of good offsprings and prevents premature convergence to a poor solution [18, 20]. Although GA offers an attractive way to optimize ANN weights, it is relatively slow in local fine tuning in comparison to gradient methods. A desirable approach in this case would be to integrate a local gradient search with the GA.

2.2. Weight Extraction. To determine the fitness value for each of the chromosomes, we extract weight from each of chromosomes.

Let $x_1, x_2, \ldots, x_d, \ldots, x_L$ represent a chromosome and $x_{kd+1}, x_{kd+2}, \ldots, x_{(k+1)d}$ represent the kth gene ($k \geq 0$) in the chromosome. The actual weight is given by

$$w_k = \begin{cases} +\dfrac{x_{kd+2}10^{d-2} + x_{kd+3}10^{d-3} + \cdots x_{(k+1)d}}{10^{d-2}}, \\ \qquad\qquad \text{if } 5 \leq x_{kd+1} \leq 9, \\ -\dfrac{x_{kd+2}10^{d-2} + x_{kd+3}10^{d-3} + \cdots x_{(k+1)d}}{10^{d-2}}, \\ \qquad\qquad \text{if } 0 \leq x_{kd+1} \leq 5. \end{cases} \tag{1}$$

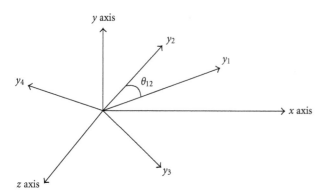

FIGURE 1: Vectors y shown in 3-dimensional space.

2.3. Feature Selection. In any neural network application, if a large number of input variables are used, the number of interconnection weights will increase and the training of neural network will be extremely slow. To overcome this problem, those variables are selected as input to a neural network that has significant effect on its output, that is, on voltage stability margin. Performance of any neural network mainly depends upon the input features selected for its training. It is essential to reduce the number of inputs to a neural network and to select its optimum number.

To select the input features, angular distance base-clustering method is used. The basic principle for clustering is to group the total N system variables ($S_1, S_2, \ldots, S_N$) into G clusters such that the variables in a cluster have similar characteristics and then pick out one representative variable from a cluster as the feature for that cluster. This will reduce the number of system variables from N to G. For the purpose of feature selection using the clustering technique, let M training patterns are created.

With the state vector $X'' = [x'_{i1}, x'_{i2}, \ldots, x'_{iN}]$ ($i = 1, 2, \ldots, M$) at hand, From the matrix X'

$$
X' = \begin{bmatrix} x'_{11} & x'_{12} & \ldots & x'_{1N} \\ x'_{21} & x'_{22} & \ldots & x'_{2N} \\ \vdots & \vdots & \ldots & \vdots \\ x'_{M1} & x'_{M2} & \ldots & x'_{MN} \end{bmatrix} \begin{matrix} \leftarrow & \text{operating point} & 1 \\ \leftarrow & \text{operating point} & 2 \\ \vdots & \vdots & \vdots \\ \leftarrow & \text{operating point} & M \end{matrix} \quad (2)
$$

It is observed that row i of matrix X' contains the value for N-system variables ($S_1, S_2, \ldots, S_N$) at operating point i while column j of matrix X' consists of the S_j variable in the M training patterns. Define the column vector $Y_j = [X'_{lj}, \ldots, X'_{Mj}]^T = [Y'_{lj}, \ldots, Y'_{Mj}]^T$. Then the variables S_j can be clustered based on these vectors Y_j.

Those system variables with similar vector Y will be grouped in a cluster. As shown in Figure 1, two vectors $y1$ and $y2$ which are similar to each other will have a small angle between them. We can, therefore, put a group of these similar vectors in a cluster. To do this, define the cosine value of the angle θ_{jk} between two vector Y_j and Y_k as

$$
\cos(\varphi_{jk}) = \frac{(Y_j Y_k)}{(|Y_j| |Y_k|)}. \quad (3)
$$

This cosine value can be used to evaluate the degree of similarity between two vectors. If $\cos(\theta_{jk})$ is greater than a specified threshold ρ_t, the two vectors Y_j and Y_k are regarded as two similar vectors and are put in the same cluster. Details of clustering algorithm are described as follows.

Step 1. Let the system variable S_l belong to cluster 1 and the cluster vector for cluster 1 be equal to column $C_l = [c_{l1}, \ldots, c_{Ml}]^T$ vector Y_l, that is,

$$
c_{il} = y_{il} \quad \text{for } l = 1, 2, \ldots, M. \quad (4)
$$

Set initial count $j = 0$, $G = 1$.

Step 2. Increase j by one.

Step 3. Compute the cosine value D_g between vector Y_j and C_g ($g = 1, 2, \ldots, G$)

$$
D_g = \frac{\left(\sum_{i=1}^{M} y_{ij} c_{ig}\right)}{\left(\sum_{i=1}^{M} y_{ij}^2 \sum_{i=1}^{M} c_{ig}^2\right)^{1/2}}, \quad g = 1, 2, \ldots, G. \quad (5)
$$

Let $D_{gm} = \max(D_g)$.

If $D_{gm} < \rho_t$ (a specified threshold), the present vector Y_j is far from any existing cluster vectors, and we have to create a new cluster for system variable S_j.

Step 4. If $D_{gm} > \rho_t$, the present vector Y_j is close to cluster vector C_{gm} of cluster g_m, and system variable S_j should be assigned g_m. Proceed to Step 4.

If vector Y_j has not been presented before, let system variable S_j be grouped in cluster g_m, then update the cluster vector $C_{gm} = [c_{1gm}, c_{2gm}, \ldots, c_{Mgm}]^T$ as follows:

$$
c_{igm} = y_{il} + c_{igm} k_{gm} \quad i = 1, 2, \ldots, M, \quad (6)
$$

where k_{gm} is the number of system variable in cluster g_m. Go to Step 6. If the vector Y_j has been presented before and variable S_j has been grouped in cluster g_m, go to Step 6.

If vector Y_j has been presented before and variable S_j has been grouped in a different cluster $g_{m'}$, move system variable S_j to cluster g_m and execute the update formulae.

$$
C_{igm} = y_{ij} + C_{igm} k_{gm}, \quad i = 1, 2, \ldots, M,
$$
$$
C_{igm'} = -y_{ij} + C_{igm'} k_{gm'}, \quad i = 1, 2, \ldots, M, \quad (7)
$$

where k_{gm} is the number of system variable in cluster vector g_m. In this case, this is a move in cluster elements. Go to Step 6.

Step 5. Create a new cluster g_n for system variable S_j with the cluster vector

$$
C_{gm} = [c_{1gm}, c_{2gm}, \ldots, c_{Mgm}]^T, \quad (8)
$$

where $c_{igm} = y_{ij}$, $i = 1, 2, \ldots, M$.

Increase G by one and go to Step 6.

Step 6. If $j = N$, proceed to Step 7; otherwise, go to Step 2.

Step 7. If there is any move in cluster elements in the preceding N iterations, reset j to zero and proceed to Step 2. Otherwise, go to Step 8.

Step 8. For each cluster g, find a system variable S_g whose column vector y_g is closest to the cluster vector C_g, that is,

$$\frac{\left(\sum_{i=1}^{M} y_{gj}c_{ig}\right)}{\left(\sum_{i=1}^{M} y_{gj}^2 \sum_{i=1}^{M} c_{ig}^2\right)^{1/2}} \geq \frac{\left(\sum_{i=1}^{M} y_{ij}c_{ig}\right)}{\left(\sum_{i=1}^{M} y_{ij}^2 \sum_{i=1}^{M} c_{ig}^2\right)^{1/2}}. \quad (9)$$

For any S_j in cluster g, let system variable S_g be the feature for cluster g. Store the system variables and feature variable for each cluster and stop.

2.4. Data Normalization. During training of a neural network, the higher valued input variables may tend to suppress the influence of smaller ones. To overcome this problem, the neural networks are trained with normalized input data, leaving the network to learn weights associated with the connections emanating from these inputs. The raw data are scaled in the range 0.1–0.9 for use by neural networks to minimize the effect of magnitude between input [18]. In case of output variable, if it assumes values close to unity (≥ 1) or (0), it causes difficulty in training as the value unity or zero are practically never realized by the activation or threshold function. A way to overcome this difficulty is to normalize the variables ($\times$) to keep its values between some suitable range (say 0.1 and 0.9). In the present application, each input parameter ($\times$) is normalized as $\times_n$ before being applied to the neural network according to the following equation:

$$x_n = \frac{0.8 \times (x - x_{\min})}{x_{\max} - x_{\min}} + 0.1, \quad (10)$$

where $x_{\max}$ and $x_{\min}$ are the maximum and minimum value of data parameter X. The input data are normalized between 0.9 and 0.1. Similarly, output data (VSM) are normalized between 0.9 and 0.1. During testing phase, the output of the neural network is demoralized to obtain the actual value of voltage stability margin.

3. Solution Algorithm

Sequential steps (flowchart) for developing GABPNN proposed for voltage stability margin estimation are illustrated in Figure 2. The algorithm for VSM estimation has been summarized as follows.

Step 1. Generate a large number of load patterns by perturbing the loads at all the buses in wide range randomly.

Step 2. Normalize input data as selected from the angular distance base-clustering method and the output, that is, voltage stability margin λ_0 to train the GABPNN.

Step 3. Set numbers of generations for genetic optimization of weights.

Step 4. Initialize structure for the neural network, that is, input-hidden-output nodes for determining the number of weights.

Step 5. Set generation count as $g = 0$.

Step 6. Generate randomly the initial population p_g of real coded chromosomes C_g^G, where G is population size.

Step 7. Extract weights for each of the population P_g.

Step 8. Calculate the fitness value for each individual in the population as,

$$\text{Fitness} = \frac{1}{(\text{RMS error})}. \quad (11)$$

Step 9. Get the mating pool ready by replacing worst fit individuals with high-fit individuals.

Step 10. Using cross-over mechanism, reproduce offsprings from the parent chromosomes.

Step 11. Next generation population is achieved. Increase generation count by 1, that is,

$$g = g + 1. \quad (12)$$

Step 12. Check, if $g < G$, then go to Step 7, otherwise go to next step.

Step 13. Training is complete. Extract optimized weights from converged population P_G.

Step 14. Test the developed GABPNN for unseen load patterns.

In the proposed GABPNN, GA performs the weight adaptation for acquiring the minimized error during the training. Before executing certain task, GA requires several parameters to be devised for its proper functioning. Some of them are gene encoding, population initialization, selection, reproduction, fitness evaluation, and so forth. The basic computing elements in GAs are *genes*, which are joined together to form a string of values referred to as a *chromosome*. *Genes* encoding is required to represent weights. To carry out efficient weight optimization in ANN, it is important to have a proper encoding scheme.

There is no definite view in the literature about suitability of encoding schemes for chromosomes. Too complicated scheme provides high flexibility in problem representation but may reduce GA's efficiency due to complicated operations. On the other hand, too simple representation may suffer from slow or premature convergence. This requires a careful selection of an encoding scheme such that GA operations are not compromised but still provides enough flexibility to support dynamic weight adaptation. In the present work, real value coding is adopted for *gene* encoding.

Size of the population of individuals (chromosomes) is generated randomly to start the genetic search procedure. The size of population depends upon number of weights

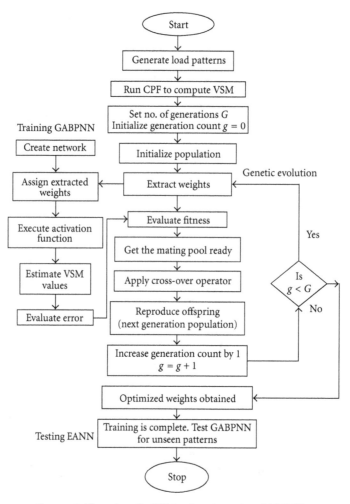

FIGURE 2: Flow chart for VSM estimation using GABPNN.

to be optimized multiplied by *gene length*. The number of weights to be optimized is determined from neural network configuration. In this work, artificial neural network architecture is assumed to be fixed. If the artificial neural network architecture is *x-y-z*, that is, *x* input neurons, *y* hidden neurons and *z* output neurons, then

$$\text{Number of weights (genes)} = (x + z) * y, \quad (13)$$

$$\text{Population size (chromosome length)} = (x + z) * y * d, \quad (14)$$

where *d = gene length*. Choosing a population size of $(x + z) * y * d$, an initial population of P_i chromosomes is to be randomly generated.

Thus, population size depends upon the number of digits to be used to represent each weight. An appropriate gene length is required for an adequate population size. This way selection of digits to represent a weight is of great importance. Too few digits may result in poor convergence, while a large number of digits per weight will lead to slow convergence due to very long chromosomal string. In the present work, each weight is encoded as a fixed 5-digit string

(i.e., $d = 5$), representing weights in the range $[-5,5]$. After deciding the encoding scheme and generating an initial population of *chromosomes*, the program for GABPNN was implemented, as explained above.

Convergence is the progress towards increasing uniformity in fitness values, as each time lowest fitness is replaced with maximum fitness value. Fitness function is taken as inverse of root mean square error (RMS) function. For the converged population, that is, group of individuals comprising minimum RMS, final optimized weights are extracted and decoded. These optimized weights belong to the trained GABPNN, which is ready for testing on unseen load patterns.

4. System Studies

The GA-based back propagation neural network approach has been implemented for voltage stability margin estimation for standard 6-bus system [18] and IEEE 30-bus system [26]. Though the GABPNN-based approach performed well in both the test systems, but due to limited space, the results of only one test system, that is, IEEE 30-bus system

TABLE 3: Output and error during testing of GABPNN (10-4-1).

TP	Voltage stability margin		Error (p.u.)	Error (% age)	TP	Voltage stability margin		Error (p.u.)	Error (% age)
	Actual	By GABPNN				Actual	By GABPNN		
1	1.45935	1.4304	0.029	1.9849	2	1.62284	1.6169	0.0059	0.3612
3	1.57712	1.5733	0.0038	0.2397	4	1.41375	1.3865	0.0272	1.9244
5	1.64237	1.6341	0.0083	0.5061	6	1.52868	1.5105	0.0182	1.1905
7	1.55574	1.5763	−0.0206	−1.3238	8	1.43946	1.4307	0.0088	0.6145
9	1.5849	1.584	0.0009	0.0561	10	1.47208	1.5002	−0.0281	−1.9118
11	1.41474	1.4116	0.0031	0.2221	12	1.52114	1.5229	−0.0018	−0.1206
13	1.48234	1.5262	−0.0439	−2.9627	14	1.49136	1.4847	0.0067	0.4479
15	1.51966	1.5246	−0.0049	−0.3213	16	1.52114	1.5486	−0.0275	−1.8086
17	1.71256	1.7131	−0.0006	−0.0356	18	1.58577	1.6148	−0.029	−1.8276
19	1.65003	1.6502	−0.0002	−0.011	20	1.59516	1.595	0.0001	0.0048
21	1.45626	1.4538	0.0025	0.1718	22	1.52262	1.5097	0.0129	0.8503
23	1.5655	1.5485	0.017	1.0834	24	1.47739	1.4733	0.0041	0.276
25	1.55784	1.5675	−0.0096	−0.6174	26	1.82254	1.8215	0.0011	0.0619
27	1.43748	1.4152	0.0223	1.5501	28	1.44526	1.4396	0.0057	0.394
29	1.61876	1.5927	0.0261	1.6113	30	1.68389	1.6946	−0.0107	−0.6365

TP: Testing Pattern.

are given in this paper. The IEEE 30-bus system consists of 30 buses and 41 lines. The GABPNN is trained in order to estimate the voltage stability margin λ_o under changing load in normal system operation. For voltage stability margin estimation, 250 load patterns were generated by varying loads randomly at all the buses in the range of 50 to 160% of their base case values and utilizing the corresponding voltage stability margin value as obtained from continuation power flow method (UWPFLOW) [27]. As voltage stability problem usually occurs due to loading condition of a power system, the real and reactive power injections are considered as possible inputs for the GA-based neural network. Input features are selected by applying angular distance-based clustering technique. Using this feature selection method, 8 no. of power injections (P2, P8, P9, P11, P12, Q8, Q11, Q12) were selected with the threshold ρ_t as 0.936. In addition to these features, total real and reactive loads of the power system were selected as input features making the total number of input variable equal to 10.

Out of 250 patterns, 200 patterns are selected randomly for training and the remaining 50 for testing the performance of the trained GABPNN model. During training, it has been found that the number of hidden nodes has affected the convergence rate by increasing or decreasing the complexity of the neural network architecture. Hence, hidden nodes are selected on the "trial and error" basis for obtaining fitness convergence in the minimum number of generations with high convergence rate. In VSM estimation problem, the optimum size of the GABPNN has been found to be 10-4-1. The optimal training for GABPNN was achieved in 15 iterations only.

During testing phase, the 50 testing patterns were tested for evaluating the performance of the trained GABPNN. The testing results of all the 30 patterns are shown in Table 3 and

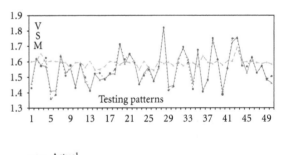

FIGURE 3: Testing performance of the trained GABPNN and BPNN.

in Figure 3. As can be observed from the table and figure, the trained GABPNN provided good results during testing phase.

4.1. Comparison of GABPNN and BPNN. As the BP neural network is the most popular ANN model and has been implemented in almost every area of engineering, in this paper the performance of GABPNN model has been compared with BPNN model. To compare the effectiveness of the proposed GABPNN approach, a BP model with the same structure that is 10-4-1 was trained for 2500 iterations. The testing results of the trained BPNN are given in Table 4. As can be observed from Table 4, the testing performance of BP model was not satisfactory. This model provided maximum error as 15.71% with rms error of 0.113 pu. On the other hand, the developed GABPNN provided the maximum error of 3.51% and rms error 0.021 pu. However, the training time for both the models was almost same (approximately 13.5 seconds).

TABLE 4: Output and error during testing of BPNN (10-4-1).

TP	Voltage stability margin		Error (p.u.)	Error (% age)	TP	Voltage stability margin		Error (p.u.)	Error (% age)
	Actual	By BPNN				Actual	By BPNN		
1	1.45935	1.6012	−0.1419	9.72028	2	1.62284	1.60577	0.01707	1.05201
3	1.57712	1.6534	−0.0763	4.83691	4	1.41375	1.59554	−0.1818	12.8586
5	1.64237	1.6064	0.03596	2.18981	6	1.52868	1.60288	−0.0742	4.85421
7	1.55574	1.59965	−0.0439	2.82266	8	1.43946	1.59497	−0.1555	10.8038
9	1.5849	1.55658	0.02833	1.78727	10	1.47208	1.59467	−0.1226	8.32796
11	1.41474	1.595	−0.1803	12.7416	12	1.52114	1.56406	−0.0429	2.82164
13	1.48234	1.60372	−0.1214	8.18847	14	1.49136	1.54934	−0.058	3.88758
15	1.51966	1.55096	−0.0313	2.06016	16	1.52114	1.57032	−0.0492	3.23347
17	1.71256	1.60263	0.10993	6.41887	18	1.58577	1.59772	−0.012	0.75347
19	1.65003	1.58203	0.068	4.1212	20	1.59516	1.60209	−0.0069	0.43449
21	1.45626	1.59506	−0.1388	9.53137	22	1.52262	1.60296	−0.0803	5.27643
23	1.5655	1.54795	0.01755	1.12097	24	1.47739	1.60231	−0.1249	8.45509
25	1.55784	1.56032	−0.0025	0.15901	26	1.82254	1.54385	0.27869	15.2913
27	1.43748	1.60245	−0.165	11.4763	28	1.44526	1.58866	−0.1434	9.92211
29	1.61876	1.59693	0.02184	1.34888	30	1.68389	1.57389	0.11	6.53222

5. Conclusion

In this paper, a hybrid intelligent approach involving genetic algorithm for artificial neural network development has been proposed for voltage stability margin estimation in power system. The fast and accurate estimation of VSM has been considered as an effective way for assessing the stability of a power system from viewpoint of voltage. Implementation of GA makes it possible to achieve effective input-output mapping in artificial neural network with considerable speed-up in its training.

The proposed GABPNN approach sums up the goodness of evolutionary computing and artificial neural networks both. The value of this hybrid approach is that GA requires no gradient information so less susceptible than back-propagation to local variations in the error surface. Another advantageous aspect is that they operate in a population of possible solution candidates in parallel, instead of starting with a single candidate and iteratively operate on it using some sort of heuristics. The proposed approach provides acceptably good generalization ability during testing and found computationally efficient in VSM estimation. Successful application of GABPNN establishes the suitability of the proposed ANN model for online assessment of voltage stability.

Acknowledgments

The authors sincerely acknowledge the financial support provided by Department of Science and Technology (D.S.T), New Delhi, India under Research Grant no F.No.SR/S3/EECE/0064/2009 dated 22-01-10 and Director, Madhav Institute of Technology and Science, Gwalior, India for carrying out this research work.

References

[1] L. Srivastava, S. N. Singh, and J. Sharma, "Estimation of loadability margin using parallel self-organizing hierarchical neural network," Computers and Electrical Engineering, vol. 26, no. 2, pp. 151–167, 2000.

[2] P. Kundur, Power System Stability and Control, McGraw-Hill, New York, NY, USA, 1994.

[3] V. Ajjarapu and C. Christy, "The continuation power flow: a tool for steady state voltage stability analysis," IEEE Transactions on Power Systems, vol. 7, no. 1, pp. 416–423, 1992.

[4] C. A. Canizares and F. L. Alvarado, "Point of collapse and continuation methods for large AC/DC systems," IEEE Transactions on Power Systems, vol. 8, no. 1, pp. 1–8, 1993.

[5] C. A. Canizares, "On bifurcations, voltage collapse and load modeling," IEEE Transactions on Power Systems, vol. 10, no. 1, pp. 512–522, 1995.

[6] T. J. Overbye and C. L. DeMarco, "Improved techniques for power system voltage stability assessment using energy methods," IEEE Transactions on Power Systems, vol. 6, no. 4, pp. 1446–1452, 1991.

[7] P. A. Löf, T. Smed, G. Andersson, and D. J. Hill, "Fast calculation of a voltage stability index," IEEE Transactions on Power Systems, vol. 7, no. 1, pp. 54–64, 1992.

[8] B. Jeyasurya, "Artificial neural networks for power system steady-state voltage instability evaluation," Electric Power Systems Research, vol. 29, no. 2, pp. 85–90, 1994.

[9] D. Salatino, R. Sbrizzai, M. Trovato, and M. La Scala, "Online voltage stability assessment of load centers by using neural networks," Electric Power Systems Research, vol. 32, no. 3, pp. 165–173, 1995.

[10] A. A. El-Keib and X. Ma, "Application of artificial neural networks in voltage stability assessment," IEEE Transactions on Power Systems, vol. 10, no. 4, pp. 1890–1896, 1995.

[11] H. P. Schmidt, "Application of artificial neural networks to the dynamic analysis of the voltage stability problem," IEE Proceedings: Generation, Transmission & Distribution, vol. 144, pp. 371–376, 1997.

[12] A. Mohamed and G. B. Jasmon, "Neural network approach to dynamic voltage stability prediction," *Electric Machines and Power Systems*, vol. 25, no. 5, pp. 509–523, 1996.

[13] V. R. Dinavahi and S. C. Srivastava, "ANN based voltage stability margin prediction," in *Proceedings of the IEEE Power Engineering Society Summer Meeting*, vol. 2, pp. 1275–1279, Vancouver, Canada, July 2001.

[14] S. Kamalasadan, D. Thukaram, and A. K. Srivastava, "A new intelligent algorithm for online voltage stability assessment and monitoring," *International Journal of Electrical Power & Energy Systems*, vol. 31, no. 2-3, pp. 100–110, 2009.

[15] S. Chauhan and M. P. Dave, "Kohonen neural network classifier for voltage collapse margin estimation," *Electric Machines and Power Systems*, vol. 25, no. 6, pp. 607–619, 1996.

[16] Y. H. Song, H. B. Wan, and A. T. Johns, "Kohonen neural network based approach to voltage weak buses/areas identification," *IEE Proceedings: Generation, Transmission & Distribution*, vol. 144, pp. 340–344, 1997.

[17] W. Nakawiro and I. Erlich, "Online voltage stability monitoring using artificial neural network," in *Proceedings of the 3rd International Conference on Deregulation and Restructuring and Power Technologies (DRPT '08)*, pp. 941–947, Nanjing, China, April 2008.

[18] S. N. Pandey, S. Tapaswi, and L. Srivastava, "Integrated evolutionary neural network approach with distributed computing for congestion management," *Applied Soft Computing Journal*, vol. 10, no. 1, pp. 251–260, 2010.

[19] P. P. Palmes, T. Hayasaka, and S. Usui, "Mutation-based genetic neural network," *IEEE Transactions on Neural Networks*, vol. 16, no. 3, pp. 587–600, 2005.

[20] S. Rajasekaran and G. A. V. Pai, *Neural Networks, Fuzzy Logic and Genetic Algorithms—Synthesis and Applications*, Prentice-Hall Press, New Delhi, India, 2006.

[21] P. Ramasubramanian and A. Kannan, "A genetic-algorithm based neural network short-term forecasting framework for database intrusion prediction system," *Soft Computing*, vol. 10, no. 8, pp. 699–714, 2006.

[22] S. K. Oh and W. Pedrycz, "Multi-layer self-organizing polynomial neural networks and their development with the use of genetic algorithms," *Journal of the Franklin Institute*, vol. 343, no. 2, pp. 125–136, 2006.

[23] S. K. Oh, W. Pedrycz, and S. B. Roh, "Genetically optimized hybrid fuzzy set-based polynomial neural networks," *Journal of the Franklin Institute*, vol. 348, pp. 415–425, 2011.

[24] Y.-Y. Hsu, C.-R. Chen, and C.-C. Su, "Analysis of electromechanical modes using an artificial neural network," *IEE Proceedings: Generation, Transmission & Distribution*, vol. 141, no. 3, pp. 198–204, 1994.

[25] S. Sharma and L. Srivastava, "Prediction of transmission line overloading using intelligent technique," *Applied Soft Computing Journal*, vol. 8, no. 1, pp. 626–633, 2008.

[26] L. L. Freris and A. M. Sasson, "Investigation of the load-flow problem," *Proceedings of the Institution of Electrical Engineers*, vol. 115, no. 10, pp. 1459–1470, 1968.

[27] C. A. Canizares and F. L. Alvarado, "UWPFLOW Program," University of Waterloo, 2000, http://www.power.uwaterloo.ca/.

15

Multilayer Perceptron for Prediction of 2006 World Cup Football Game

Kou-Yuan Huang and Kai-Ju Chen

Department of Computer Science, National Chiao Tung University, 1001 University Road, Hsinchu 30010, Taiwan

Correspondence should be addressed to Kou-Yuan Huang, kyhuang@cs.nctu.edu.tw

Academic Editor: Mohamed A. Zohdy

Multilayer perceptron (MLP) with back-propagation learning rule is adopted to predict the winning rates of two teams according to their official statistical data of 2006 World Cup Football Game at the previous stages. There are training samples from three classes: win, draw, and loss. At the new stage, new training samples are selected from the previous stages and are added to the training samples, then we retrain the neural network. It is a type of on-line learning. The 8 features are selected with ad hoc choice. We use the theorem of Mirchandani and Cao to determine the number of hidden nodes. And after the testing in the learning convergence, the MLP is determined as 8-2-3 model. The learning rate and momentum coefficient are determined in the cross-learning. The prediction accuracy achieves 75% if the draw games are excluded.

1. Introduction

Neural network methods had been used in the analysis of sport data and had good performance. Purucker employed the supervised and unsupervised neural networks to analyze and predict the winning rate of National Football League (NFL), and found that multilayer perceptron neural network (MLP) with supervised learning performed better than Kohonen's self-organizing map network with unsupervised learning [1]. Condon et al. used MPL to predict the score of a country which participated in the 1996 Summer Olympic Games [2]. And the result outperformed that of regression model. Rotshtein et al. used the fuzzy model with genetic algorithm and neural network to predict the football game of Finland [3]. Silva et al. used MLP to build the non-linear relationship between factors and swimming performance to estimate the performance of swimmers, and the difference between the true and the estimated result was low [4]. However, there are few discussions on the parameter determination of MLP in different applications. Here, we adopt the supervised multilayer perceptron neural network with error back-propagation learning rule (BP) to predict the winning rate of 2006 World Cup Football Game (WCFG). We use the theorem to determine the number of hidden

nodes. Also we determine the learning rate and momentum coefficient by the less average time and deviation time in the cross-learning.

According to the schedule of 2006 WCFG, shown in Figure 1, there are 32 teams in this competition and overall 64 matches at 5 stages in this tournament from the beginning to the end. The competition rules in each stage are explained as follows.

(1) Stage 1 is the group match, also known as round robin tournament. There is no extending time after 90 minutes regular time. In this stage, there are 32 teams in 8 groups (Group A–H), each group has 4 teams, and each team plays 3 matches. There are 6 matches in each group and there are 8 groups, so totally it has 48 matches (Match 1–48) in stage 1. The criterion of gaining points is that winning one game has 3 points, drawing one game has 1 point, and losing one game has 0 point. After stage 1, two teams that have the higher points in each group enter the next stage. Table 1 lists the score table for 32 teams in 8 groups after 48 matches finished at stage 1.

(2) The competition rule of stages 2–5 is single elimination tournament. It is necessary to have penalty

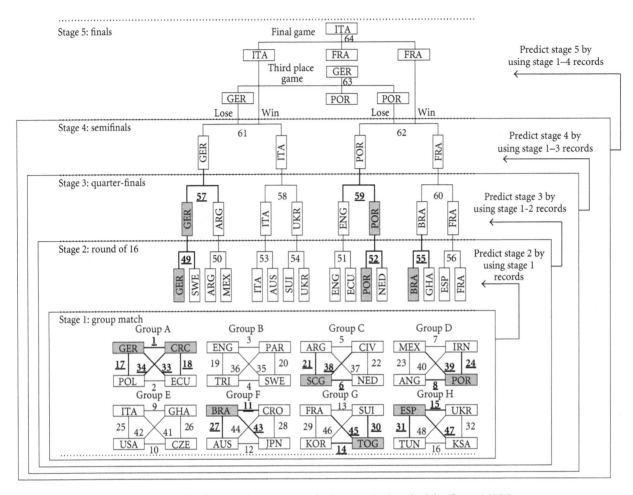

FIGURE 1: Total 64 matches at 5 stages for 32 teams in the schedule of 2006 WCFG.

kick if two teams tie after regular time (90 minutes) and additional time (30 minutes). The winner enters the next stage and the loser is eliminated from the competition. Stage 2 is the round of 16, and there are 8 matches (Match 49–56) for 16 teams. Stage 3 is the quarter-finals, and there are 4 matches (Match 57–60) for 8 teams. Stage 4 is the semifinals, and there are 2 matches (Match 61-62) for 4 teams. Stage 5 is the final-game, and there are 4 teams (the same teams as in stage 4) for 2 games. One is the third place game (Match 63), and the other is the final game (Match 64).

From the website of 2006 WCFG held in Germany [5], we can obtain the official 64 matches' statistical records provided by FIFA [6]. From the report of each match, there are 17 statistical items: goals for, goal against, shots, shot on goal, penalty kicks, fouls suffered, yellow cards, red cards, corner kicks, direct free kicks to goal, indirect free kicks to goal, offside, own goals, cautions, expulsions, ball possession, and foul committed, which represent the ability index to win the game. From these statistical data, we apply an MLP neural network to predict the winning rate of two teams at the next stage games (stage 2 to 5) by means of their statistic data from previous games. Figure 2 shows the supervised

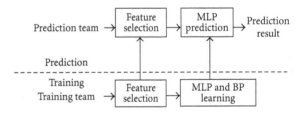

FIGURE 2: Supervised prediction system.

prediction system, which is composed of two parts: training part and prediction part. There are training samples from three classes: win, draw, and loss.

2. Feature Selection and Normalization

2.1. Feature Selection. We get 64 match reports from [5], and there are 17 statistical items in each match report. We select 8 items by an ad hoc choice, and they effectively represent the significant capability to win the game as the input features. Ad hoc choice is a common process to the real application of an algorithm. These 8 features are marked as x_1 = goals for (GF), x_2 = shots (S), x_3 = shots on goal (SOG), x_4 = corner

TABLE 1: Score table after finished 48 matches at stage 1.

Group (team)		Win	Draw	Loss	Play	Point
				Keys		
A	*Germany*	3	0	0	3	**9**
	Ecuador	2	0	1	3	6
	Poland	1	0	2	3	3
	Costa Rica	0	0	3	3	**0**
B	England	2	1	0	3	7
	Sweden	1	2	0	3	5
	Paraguay	1	0	2	3	3
	Trinidad and Tobago	0	1	2	3	1
C	Argentina	2	1	0	3	7
	Netherlands	2	1	0	3	7
	Côte d'Ivoire	1	0	2	3	3
	Serbia and Montenegro	0	0	3	3	**0**
D	*Portugal*	3	0	0	3	**9**
	Mexico	1	1	1	3	4
	Angola	0	2	1	3	2
	Iran	0	1	2	3	1
E	Italy	2	1	0	3	7
	Ghana	2	0	1	3	6
	Czech Republic	1	0	2	3	3
	USA	0	1	2	3	1
F	*Brazil*	3	0	0	3	**9**
	Australia	1	1	1	3	4
	Croatia	0	2	1	3	2
	Japan	0	1	2	3	1
G	Switzerland	2	1	0	3	7
	France	1	2	0	3	5
	Korea Republic	1	1	1	3	4
	Togo	0	0	3	3	**0**
H	*Spain*	3	0	0	3	**9**
	Ukraine	2	0	1	3	6
	Tunisia	0	1	2	3	1
	Saudi Arabia	0	1	2	3	1

kicks (CK), x_5 = direct free kicks to goal (DFKG), x_6 = indirect free kicks to goal (IDFKG), x_7 = ball possession (BP), and x_8 = fouls suffered (FS).

2.2. Normalization: Relative Ratio As Input Feature. We consider relative ratio as input feature. Training samples and prediction samples are normalized by relative ratio as follows:

$$\text{If } x_{iA} = x_{iB}, \quad \text{then } y_{iA} = y_{iB} = 0.5$$
$$\text{else } y_{iA} = \frac{x_{iA}}{x_{iA} + x_{iB}}, \quad y_{iB} = \frac{x_{iB}}{x_{iA} + x_{iB}}, \quad i = 1, \dots, 8. \tag{1}$$

The input features of $x_1 - x_8$ are converted into $y_1 - y_8$ by (1), and then the $y_1 - y_8$ are fed into the neural network model for training or prediction. In (1), the symbol "A" indicates team A and the symbol "B" indicates team B. The symbol "i" is the index of 8 features. The input values of $y_1 - y_8$ are between 0–1 after normalization. We set "If $x_{iA} = x_{iB}$, then $y_{iA} = y_{iB} = 0.5$" that includes "if $x_{iA} = x_{iB} = 0$, then $y_{iA} = y_{iB} = 0.5$." The example of normalization result of Germany (GER) versus Costa Rica (CRC) is listed in Table 2.

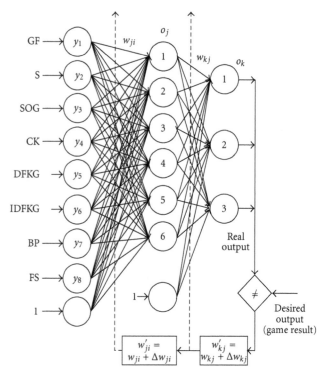

FIGURE 3: MLP network used in predicting the winning rate of 2006 WCFG.

3. Multilayer Perception with Back-Propagation Learning Algorithm

MLP model with BP learning algorithm is important since 1986 [7, 8]. The weighting coefficient adjustment can be referred to in [7–9]. Figure 3 shows the 8-6-3 MLP with one hidden layer used in this study to predict the winning rate of the football games. There are 8 inputs, 6 hidden nodes, and 3 outputs. Each symbol is explained as below: **y** is the input data vector with 8 features that have been normalized, w is the connection weights between nodes of two layers, net is the value which is the sum of the product of inputs and weighting coefficients, f(net) is the transfer function and the value is in $0 \sim 1$, o is the output value, d is the desired output, and e is the error value. The transfer function used in hidden layer and output layer is a log-sigmoid function, shown in (2). Using the least-squared error and with gradient descent method, we can get (3) and (4) for weighting coefficient adjustment. Considering the momentum term in the inertia effect of the previous step adjustment, the final adjustment equations are modified as (5) and (6), where η is the learning rate, t is the index of iteration, and β is the momentum coefficient:

$$f(\text{net}) = \frac{1}{1 + e^{-\text{net}}} \qquad (f \text{ is in } 0 \sim 1), \tag{2}$$

$$\Delta w_{kj} = \eta(d_k - o_k) f_k'(\text{net}_k) o_j, \tag{3}$$

TABLE 2: Data normalization of GER versus CRC.

Feature name	Features	Before Normalization		After Normalization	
		Team A (GER)	Team B (CRC)	Team A (GER)	Team B (CRC)
GF	x_1	4	2	0.6666	0.3333
S	x_2	21	4	0.84	0.16
SOG	x_3	10	2	0.8333	0.1666
CK	x_4	7	3	0.7	0.3
DFKG	x_5	1	0	1	0
IDFKG	x_6	0	0	0.5	0.5
BP	x_7	63%	37%	0.63	0.37
FS	x_8	12	11	0.5217	0.4782

$$\Delta w_{ji} = \eta \left[\sum_{k=1}^{K} (d_k - o_k) f_k'(\text{net}_k) w_{kj} \right] f_j'\left(\text{net}_j\right) o_i, \quad (4)$$

$$\Delta w_{kj}(t) = \eta(d_k - o_k) f_k'(\text{net}_k) o_j + \beta \Delta w_{kj}(t-1), \quad (5)$$

$$\Delta w_{ji}(t) = \eta \left[\sum_{k=1}^{K} (d_k - o_k) f_k'(\text{net}_k) w_{kj} \right] f_j'\left(\text{net}_j\right) o_i \\ + \beta \Delta w_{ji}(t-1). \quad (6)$$

4. Training, MLP Model, and Prediction

4.1. Training Samples. At stage 1, we select the teams which win or lose all the three games as the training samples. The data are representative samples of the win or loss. But the selection is ad hoc also. They are italicized in Table 1. Also we select the teams which have the draw games. We set the desired output to 1-0-0 for winning the game, 0-1-0 is for the draw game, and set to 0-0-1 for losing the game.

From stage 2, the winning team's record will be added to training samples for all subsequent stages' training process only if the team had won three games at stage 1.

The selected training teams (background color is gray in Figure 1) and training matches (the bold line and bold number with under line in Figure 1) from stage 1 to stage 4 are as follows. Also, the draw games are selected as training samples (Match 4, 13, 16, 23, 25, 28, 29, 35, 37, 40, and 44). Games that end in penalty shoot-out after stage 2 are considered as draw games. Only the record of the regular 90 minutes and extension 30 minutes is calculated.

(1) The selected training samples for predicting the games in round of 16 (stage 2)—we select the teams whose score is either 9 (win 3 games) or 0 (lose 3 games) at stage 1 as the representatives of winning team or losing teams. Also, teams in draw games are selected as training samples. Then those game's records are normalized to relative ratios as the training data. Consequently, we can find 21 samples from the 20 matches of 7 teams as the training data. We have 4 teams with 3 wins: GER, POR, BRA, and ESP, and 3 teams with 3 losses: CRC, SCG, and TOG. GER and CRC have one match and their records are selected as two training samples. Besides, there are 11 draw games (Match 4, 13, 16, 23, 25, 28, 29, 35,

37, 40, and 44) in group matches. So there are 22 training samples for draw games. Totally, there are 43 (21 + 22 = 43) training samples.

(2) The selected training samples for predicting the games in quarter-finals (stage 3)—besides the 43 training data at the stage 1, we add the match data of stage 2 from those teams, which are not only the winner at stage 2, but also have all 3 wins at stage 1, as the training samples. We can find 3 teams' records (GER, POR, and BRA) as the training samples at stage 2. Also, there is a game (SUI versus UKR), which ends in penalty kick, and we consider it as a draw game. Therefore, currently we have 48 (43 + 3 + 2 = 48) training samples for the training to predict at stage 3. Although ITA is the winner at stage 2, it is not selected as the training sample. It is because ITA did not win 3 games at stage 1.

(3) The selected training samples for predicting the games in the semifinals (stage 4)—besides the above 48 training samples, we add 4 samples (GER, ARG, ENG, and POR) from 2 draw games which need penalty kick at stage 3 as the training samples. Therefore, we totally have 52 (48 + 4 = 52) training samples. ITA is the winner at stage 3, but it is also not selected as the training sample. It is because ITA did not win 3 games at stage 1.

(4) The training samples for predicting the games in the finals (stage 5)—because the two teams (ITA and FRA) do not have all 3 wins at stage 1, they are not selected as the training samples. The training samples at stage 5 are the same as that at stage 4 (52 training samples).

4.2. Input Team Data for Predicting. We do not have to predict the game result at stage 1, but records at stage 1 are extracted in order to predict the game results at the next stages. Therefore, the input data used to predict game results at stages 2–5 are described as follows:

(1) The input data for predicting round of 16 (stage 2)— we respectively take the *average* value from the 3 match records of each winning team that enters stage 2 as the input data. Totally, we get 16 input team data for the 8 games that we want to predict at stage 2. For

example, the input team data to predict the winner of GER versus SWE are listed in Table 3.

(2) The input data for predicting the quarter-finals (stage 3)—the input data are taken from the records of stages 1-2. We respectively take the average value from the 4 match records (3 games from stage 1 and 1 game from stage 2) of each team as the input data. Totally, there are 8 input team data for the 4 games that we want to predict in quarter-finals.

(3) The input data for predicting the semifinals (stage 4)—the input data are got from stage 1~3. We respectively take the average value from the 5 match records of each team as the input data. Therefore, we totally get 4 input team data for the two games to predict result of semifinals.

(4) The input data for predicting the finals (stage 5)— the input data are got from stage 1~4. We respectively take the average value from the 6 match records of each team, which have entered the final stage, as the input data. Therefore, totally 4 input team data are ready for the last two final games we want to predict.

4.3. Determination of the Number of Hidden Nodes by Theorem. Mirchandani and Cao [10] proposed a theorem that maximum number of separable regions (M) is a function of the number of hidden nodes (H), and input space dimension (d).

$$M(H, d) = \sum_{k=0}^{d} C(H, k), \quad \text{where } C(H, k) = 0, \ H < k. \quad (7)$$

There are total 52 training samples at stage 4 and the input dimension d is 8. Based on formula (7), when the network has 6 hidden nodes, it makes the maximum 64 separable regions:

$$M(6, 8) = C(6, 0) + C(6, 1) + \cdots + C(6, 8) = 2^6 = 64. \quad (8)$$

Therefore, 6 hidden nodes are sufficient. So from the theorem we adopt the 8-6-3 MLP model.

4.4. Cross Determination of Parameters for the Back-Propagation Learning. Kecman ever recommended the ranges of learning rate η and momentum coefficient β for BP learning [11]. Here we use cross-learning. We use the 43 training team samples selected from stage 1 in the training set. The cross procedures of determining the parameter settings for BP are listed in Table 4.

To determine the momentum coefficient β, we set hidden nodes = 6, mean square error (MSE) = 0.01, and fixed learning rate η = 0.1, then test five different momentum coefficients β (β = 0.5, 0.6, 0.7, 0.8, and 0.9). Each β setting is tested for 40 tests. Testing results are listed in Table 5. From Table 5, it shows that the standard deviation of convergent iterations at β = 0.8 is the smallest, which means the training process is more stable. Therefore, we decide to set momentum coefficient β to be 0.8 in the MLP model.

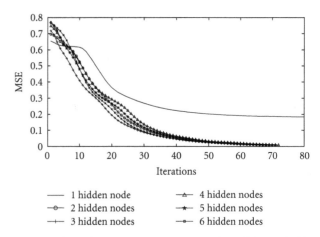

FIGURE 4: Plots of MSE versus iterations under 6 different hidden node MLP models. Set β = 0.8 and η = 0.9.

After setting the β = 0.8, we find the learning rate η next in this kind of cross-learning. We set hidden nodes = 6, MSE = 0.01, fixed β = 0.8, and then test five different learning rate η (η = 0.1, 0.3, 0.5, 0.7, and 0.9). Each η setting is tested for 40 tests. The testing result is listed in Table 6. From Table 6, we find out that when η is set as 0.9, the learning can have a less average convergent time than other η settings. Finally, using this systematic analysis, we decide to set the learning rate η = 0.9 and momentum coefficient β = 0.8 in the MLP model.

4.5. Refine the Number of Hidden Nodes. From a previous theorem, it needs 6 hidden nodes to converge for 52 training samples with 8 input dimensions. However, in practice, the number of required hidden nodes may be less than that in theory due to data distributions. It is worth checking the number of hidden nodes for MLP to converge in this application. Tests are made from 6 hidden nodes to 1 hidden node with total 52 training samples at stage 4. We decrease one hidden node at each time for learning convergent test. Figure 4 shows the plots of MSE versus iterations for 1–6 hidden nodes. The result shows that MLP converges in 80 iterations when 6, 5, 4, 3, and 2 hidden nodes are given. But it cannot converge with only one hidden node even after 10,000 iterations. For clear view, Figure 4 only shows first 80 iterations. According to this test, we conclude that it needs only two hidden nodes for MLP to train samples. We can infer that some training samples are grouped together, and we do not need the 6 hidden nodes.

5. Prediction Results

From previous analysis, the final prediction model used in this study is 8-2-3 MLP with BP learning. The parameter settings for BP learning are η = 0.9, β = 0.8, and MSE = 0.01. The prediction method is explained as follows.

We input the average data of each team into the well-trained MLP. Then we compare the output values of the first output node if two teams in a game to determine the win or

TABLE 3: Input data used to predict the winning rate of GER versus SWE at stage 2.

Features	Team A (GRE)				Team B (SWE)			
	Rec. 1	Rec. 2	Rec. 3	Average	Rec. 1	Rec. 2	Rec. 3	Average
GF	0.6664	1	1	0.8889	0.5	1	0.5	0.6667
S	0.84	0.7619	0.6818	0.7929	0.75	0.7692	0.4286	0.6493
SOG	0.8333	0.7619	0.8182	0.7612	0.75	0.5152	0.3913	0.5522
CK	0.7	0.7143	0.45	0.6214	0.4737	0.6667	0.6667	0.6023
DFKG	1	0.5	0	0.5	1	0.5	0.5	0.6667
IDFKG	0.5	0.5	0	0.3333	0.5	0.5	0.5	0.5
BP	0.63	0.58	0.43	0.5467	0.6	0.57	0.37	0.54
FS	0.5217	0.5526	0.538	0.5374	0	0.4412	0.4194	0.2868

TABLE 4: Procedures of determining the parameters for BP learning rule.

To determine parameters	Fixed conditions	Variable conditions	Observation items
Momentum coefficient β	(1) Hidden nodes = 6 (2) MSE = 0.01 (3) $\eta = 0.1$	(1) $\beta = 0.5, 0.6, 0.7, 0.8, 0.9$ (2) Testing times = 40	Average convergent iterations and standard deviation of convergent iterations
Learning rate η	(1) Hidden nodes = 6 (2) MSE = 0.01 (3) $\beta = 0.8$	(1) $\eta = 0.1, 0.3, 0.5, 0.7, 0.9$ (2) Testing times = 40	Average convergent iterations

TABLE 5: Average iterations and standard deviation of 40 tests under different settings of β. Set MSE = 0.01, hidden nodes = 6, $\eta = 0.1$.

β	0.5	0.6	0.7	0.8	0.9
Average convergent iterations	821.3	758.4	702.9	667.5	629.7
Standard deviation of convergent iterations	51.27	42.58	35.28	27.24	35.79

TABLE 6: Set MSE = 0.01, hidden nodes = 6, $\beta = 0.8$, then test average iterations of 40 tests with five different η settings.

η	0.1	0.3	0.5	0.7	0.9
Average convergent iterations	667	219	133.97	97.9	77.9

loss. The team with bigger output value of the first output node, meaning the greater ability to win the game, is the winner. The winning rate prediction results of two teams at each game from stage 2 to stage 5 are listed in Table 7. The symbol "W" means the team is the winner whose real output value of the first output node is bigger. The symbol "L" means that the team is the loser whose real output value of the first output node is smaller.

The prediction results must compare with the real game results. The symbol "Y" means that the prediction result is correct, and the symbol "N" means that the prediction result is wrong. The symbol "N/A" means that the prediction result is not counted because two teams draw.

From Table 7, we can see the percentage of prediction accuracy at stage 2 is 85.7% (6/7), and the percentages at the following stages are 50% (1/2), 50% (1/2), and 100% (1/1). Totally, there are nine correct predictions, three error

predictions (N), and four noncounted real draw games (N/A) in 16 games.

The prediction for football games is not easy because the players use feet to control the ball. Too many factors and situations are sometimes changeable, and thus the game results are usually unpredictable. Scoring is not easy in football games, so there are many draw games in the records. Most of the time neural network can only predict the winner and loser. In fact, it is not easy to get an equal winning rate from the output value of the first output node of MLP for two teams, and to predict the draw game. So we exclude the draw games in the calculation of prediction accuracy. If we exclude four draw games (Match 54, 57, 59, 64) and calculate the average prediction accuracy of other 12 games from stage 2 to stage 5, the percentage of the prediction accuracy is 75% (9/12).

The odds can be calculated from the MLP for betting reference and its formula is defined as follows:

$$\text{Odd(Team\_A versus Team\_B)} = \frac{O_B}{O_A}, \qquad (9)$$

where O_A and O_B are the real outputs from the first output node of MLP for team A and team B. The odds for team B versus team A are reversed. The results of odds are also shown in Table 7.

6. Conclusions and Discussions

In this study, we adopt multilayer perceptron with back-propagation learning to predict the winning rate of 2006 WCFG. We select 8 significant statistical records from 17 official records of 2006 WCFG. The 8 records of each team are transformed into relative ratio values with another team. Then the average ratio values of each team at previous stages

TABLE 7: Prediction results of winning rates from stage 2 to stage 5.

Stage	Match	Team	Outputs from MLP			Prediction result	Game result	Prediction correct	Prediction accuracy	Odds
			Node 1 (win)	Node 2 (draw)	Node 3 (lose)					
2	49	GRE	0.9914	0.2010	0	W	W	Y		0.79
		SWE	0.7866	0.3230	0.0001	L	L			1.26
	50	ARG	0.9604	0.0799	0	W	W	Y		0.04
		MEX	0.0338	0.9631	0.0102	L	L			28.4
	51	ENG	0.8325	0.2620	0.0001	W	W	Y		0.88
		ECU	0.7348	0.3779	0.0001	L	L			1.13
	52	POR	0.9909	0.0221	0	W	W	Y		0.97
		NED	0.9570	0.0864	0	L	L		85.7% (6/7)	1.04
	53	ITA	0.9856	0.0330	0	W	W	Y		0.01
		AUS	0.0129	0.9786	0.0329	L	L			76.5
	54	SUI	0.9843	0.0353	0	W	D	N/A		0.79
		UKR	0.7823	0.3176	0.0001	L	D			1.26
	55	BRA	0.9912	0.0212	0	W	W	Y		0.22
		GHA	0.2219	0.8161	0.0013	L	L			4.47
	56	ESP	0.9914	0.0209	0	W	L	N		0.89
		FRA	0.8848	0.1954	0.0001	L	W			1.12
3	57	GER	0.9878	0.0169	0.0001	W	D	N/A		0.91
		ARG	0.9017	0.1382	0.0003	L	D			1.10
	58	ITA	0.9841	0.0220	0.0001	W	W	Y		0.33
		UKR	0.3225	0.7406	0.0031	L	L		50% (1/2)	3.05
	59	ENG	0.9546	0.0639	0.0002	L	D	N/A		1.03
		POR	0.9868	0.0182	0.0001	W	D			0.97
	60	BRA	0.9874	0.0175	0.0001	W	L	N		0.88
		FRA	0.8703	0.1784	0.0005	L	W			1.13
4	61	GER	0.9864	0.0252	0	L	L	Y		1.0008
		ITA	0.9872	0.0238	0	W	W		50% (1/2)	0.9992
	62	POR	0.9843	0.0289	0	W	L	N		0.98
		FRA	0.9653	0.0608	0	L	W			1.02
5	63	GER	0.9372	0.1354	0	W	W	Y		0.98
		POR	0.9221	0.1628	0	L	L		100% (1/1)	1.02
	64	ITA	0.9917	0.0257	0	W	D	N/A		0.99
		FRA	0.9846	0.0433	0	L	D			1.01

are fed into 8-2-3 MLP for predicting the win and loss. The teams of 3 wins, 3 losses, and draws at stage 1 are selected as the training samples. The 8 records and training samples are selected by ad hoc choice. It is a common process to the real application of an algorithm. New training samples are added to the training set of the previous stages, and then we retrain the neural network. It is a type of on-line learning. The learning rate and the momentum coefficient are determined by the less average and deviation time in the cross-learning.

We use the theorem of Mirchandani and Cao to determine the number of hidden nodes. It is 6, and the MLP model is 8-6-3. After the testing in the learning convergence, the MLP is determined as 8-2-3 model. We can infer that some training samples are grouped together and we do not need the 6 hidden nodes.

If the draw games are excluded, the prediction accuracy can achieve 75% (9/12).

The 8 features are selected in ad hoc choice. But if we want to select 8 best features, we must work on C(17,8) combinations in analysis. We can select the feature set such that the error is the smallest or the distance measure is the maximum. Usually we may use divergence computation, Bhattacharyya distance, Matusita distance, and Kolmogorov distance in the use of distance measures for feature selection [12]. Also we can use entropy in the feature selection [12].

There are other methods: conjugate gradient method, Levenberg-Mardquardt method, simulated annealing, and genetic algorithm that can be used in the learning [13–17]. But MLP with BP learning is simpler in the determination of hidden node number, parameter setting, and the observation of learning convergence in this application. Other pattern classification methods may be used for comparison in prediction accuracy [12, 18].

From pattern recognition point of view, compared with the two class training sets (win and loss), the three class training sets (win, draw, and loss) can have the more reliable prediction accuracy, because the decision regions or boundaries after training can be more precise.

Acknowledgments

The authors would like to thank the reviewer for his suggestion of selecting draw teams into the training sets to improve the prediction accuracy. The authors also thank Mr. Wen-Lung Chang for his collection of data.

References

[1] M. C. Purucker, "Neural network quarterbacking," *IEEE Potentials*, vol. 15, no. 3, pp. 9–15, 1996.

[2] E. M. Condon, B. L. Golden, and E. A. Wasil, "Predicting the success of nations at the Summer Olympics using neural networks," *Computers and Operations Research*, vol. 26, no. 13, pp. 1243–1265, 1999.

[3] A. P. Rotshtein, M. Posner, and A. B. Rakityanskaya, "Football predictions based on a fuzzy model with genetic and neural tuning," *Cybernetics and Systems Analysis*, vol. 41, no. 4, pp. 619–630, 2005.

[4] A. J. Silva, A. M. Costa, P. M. Oliveira et al., "The use of neural network technology to model swimming performance," *Journal of Sports Science and Medicine*, vol. 6, no. 1, pp. 117–125, 2007.

[5] "FIFA World Cup Germany—match schedule, matches and results, and statistics reports," 2006, http://fifaworldcup.yahoo.com.

[6] Official website of FIFA, http://www.fifa.com .

[7] D. E. Rumelhart, G. E. Hinton, and R. J. Williams, "Learning representations by back-propagating errors," *Nature*, vol. 323, no. 6088, pp. 533–536, 1986.

[8] D. E. Rumelhart and J. L. McClelland, *Parallel Distributed Processing: Explorations in the Microstructure of Cognition*, vol. 1, MIT Press, Cambridge, Mass, USA, 1986.

[9] K.-Y. Huang, *Neural Networks and Pattern Recognition*, Weikeg Publishing Co., Taipei, Taiwan, 2003.

[10] G. Mirchandani and W. Cao, "On hidden nodes for neural nets," *IEEE Transactions on Circuits and Systems*, vol. 36, no. 5, pp. 661–664, 1989.

[11] V. Kecman, *Learning and Soft Computing: Support Vector Machines, Neural Networks, and Fuzzy Logic Models*, MIT Press, Cambridge, Mass, USA, 2001.

[12] K. Fukunaga, *Statistical Pattern Recognition*, Academic Press, New York, NY, USA, 2nd edition, 1990.

[13] F. Møller, "A scaled conjugate gradient algorithm for fast supervised learning," *Neural Networks*, vol. 6, no. 4, pp. 525–533, 1993.

[14] M. T. Hagan, H. B. Demuth, and M. Beale, *Neural Network Design*, PWS Publishing Company, Boston, Mass, USA, 1996.

[15] S. Haykin, *Neural Networks and Learning Machine*, Pearson Education, 3rd edition, 2009.

[16] S. Kirkpatrick, C. D. Gelatt, and M. P. Vecchi, "Optimization by simulated annealing," *Science*, vol. 220, no. 4598, pp. 671–680, 1983.

[17] J. H. Holland, *Adaptation in Natural and Artificial Systems*, University of Michigan Press, 1975.

[18] S. Theodoridis and K. Koutroumbas, *Pattern Recognition*, Elsevier, New York, NY, USA, 4th edition, 2009.

16

Using Artificial Neural Networks to Predict Direct Solar Irradiation

James Mubiru

Department of Physics, Makerere University, P.O. Box 7062, Kampala, Uganda

Correspondence should be addressed to James Mubiru, jwm_mubiru@yahoo.com

Academic Editor: Matt Aitkenhead

This paper explores the possibility of developing a prediction model using artificial neural networks (ANNs), which could be used to estimate monthly average daily direct solar radiation for locations in Uganda. Direct solar radiation is a component of the global solar radiation and is quite significant in the performance assessment of various solar energy applications. Results from the paper have shown good agreement between the estimated and measured values of direct solar irradiation. A correlation coefficient of 0.998 was obtained with mean bias error of 0.005 MJ/m^2 and root mean square error of 0.197 MJ/m^2. The comparison between the ANN and empirical model emphasized the superiority of the proposed ANN prediction model. The application of the proposed ANN model can be extended to other locations with similar climate and terrain.

1. Introduction

Much of the work of the prediction of solar radiation has been the estimation of global solar radiation, yet data of the two main components (direct and diffuse) of global solar radiation are equally important. These components are required in a variety of applications such as in thermal analyses and crop models. There is need to estimate these components in the absence of measured values. Some authors such as Davies and McKay [1] and Gueymard [2] have used radiative transfer models in the estimation of direct solar irradiance. Such models take into account interactions between the direct solar irradiance and terrestrial atmosphere. The problem with the use of such models is the unavailability of some of the atmospheric information needed. Simpler models that relate direct solar irradiance with global irradiance have been developed by Vignola and McDaniels [3] and Louche et al. [4]. Other empirical models have been used to predict solar radiation by Majumdar et al. [5] in relation to surface humidity and absolute air mass; accuracy of prediction has been found to be ±10% with 95% confidence limits. Al-Mohamad [6] has calculated empirically direct solar radiation as one of the solar radiation components giving a relative percentage error in the range of ±3% between the calculated and actual

values. Benson et al. [7] have derived daily and monthly regressions for direct solar radiation as one of the solar radiation components, which relate to sunshine duration. However, the empirical approach has tended to assume linearity in the prediction process.

The uncertain nature of solar radiation and the modeling abilities of artificial neural networks (ANNs) have inspired the application of ANN techniques to predict solar radiation [8]. ANN is an intelligent system that has the capacity to learn, memorize, and create relationships among data [9]. They simulate a human brain and are ideal for modeling nonlinear, dynamic, noise-ridden, and complex systems. According to Haykin [10], an ANN is a massively parallel distributed processor that has a natural propensity for storing experiential knowledge and making it available for use. ANNs have been used by Tymvios et al. [11] and Sözen et al. [12] to predict global solar radiation.

Generally, neural networks have been applied successfully in a number of application areas such as mathematics, engineering, medicine, economics, meteorology, psychology, and neurology. In particular, they have been used in a broad range of applications including pattern recognition and classification, function approximation and prediction, optimization, automatic control, constraint satisfaction, associative memory, data compression, diagnostics, multisensor data fusion, identification, fault detection, signal processing, and tracking [8, 13–15].

Neural networks have been used in climate modeling by Krasnopolsky and Fox-Rabinovitz [16] and Dibike and Coulibaly [17], and forecasting sea surface temperature by Wu et al. [18]. ANNs have also been used in generating "loss of load probability" curves for sizing PV standalone systems [19] and prediction of performance parameters of flat-plate solar collectors [20].

This study explores the application of artificial neural networks in predicting monthly average daily direct solar radiation. The developed ANN prediction model is compared with an empirical model.

2. Literature Review of Estimation of Direct Solar Radiation

Using measured data from three Canadian stations, Iqbal [21] developed an empirical model represented by the following equation, which correlates monthly average daily beam transmittance $\overline{H}_b/\overline{H}_0$ with relative sunshine duration $(\overline{S}/\overline{S}_0)$:

$$\frac{\overline{H}_b}{\overline{H}_0} = a_1 + b_1\left(\frac{\overline{S}}{\overline{S}_0}\right) + c_1\left(\frac{\overline{S}}{\overline{S}_0}\right)^2, \tag{1}$$

where $\overline{H}_b$ is the monthly average daily direct solar radiation, $\overline{H}_0$ is the monthly average daily extraterrestrial solar radiation, $\overline{S}$ monthly average daily sunshine hours, and $\overline{S}_0$ is the average day length. The corresponding empirical coefficients a_1, b_1, and c_1 were −0.18, 1.45, and −1.12, respectively. A standard error of estimate of 0.025 was obtained.

Ideriah [22] developed a model for computing two solar radiation components, one of which was direct solar radiation, at Ibadan, Nigeria. Deviations were within 15%, when the estimates were compared with the experimental data. Hussain [23] obtained a prediction relation by correlating monthly average daily direct solar irradiation with bright sunshine hours using data from seven locations in north and central India. Monthly estimates of direct solar irradiation were calculated and compared with measured values. Root mean square errors were within 3% and 6%, for the seven locations and other sites in India.

Nonnormalized measured data from two sites with dissimilar radiation climate was fitted by regression. The quadratic form of the regression gave the lowest standard error of estimate, 10.6% of the mean value of the direct solar irradiance. The two sites were Valentia, in Ireland (51°56′N, 10°15′W) and Bet Dagan, in Israel (32°00′N, 34°49′E) [24]. Mubiru et al. [25] correlated monthly average daily beam transmittance $\overline{H}_b/\overline{H}_0$ with monthly average daily clearness index $(\overline{H}/\overline{H}_0)$ on a horizontal surface at a site in Kampala, Uganda (0.32°N, 32.58°E), giving a correlation coefficient of 0.967. The correlation is represented by the following equation

$$\frac{\overline{H}_b}{\overline{H}_0} = a_2 + b_2\left(\frac{\overline{H}}{\overline{H}_0}\right), \tag{2}$$

TABLE 1: The four study sites with their location parameters.

Station	Latitude	Longitude (degree east)	Altitude (m)
Mbarara	−0.62	30.65	1413
Lira	2.28	32.93	1189
Tororo	0.68	34.17	1170
Kampala	0.32	32.58	1220

Positive north latitude

where $\overline{H}$ is the monthly average daily global solar radiation and a_2, b_2 are empirical coefficients. The estimates from the resulting empirical model were compared with measured values giving a root mean square error of 0.359 and a mean bias error of −0.010.

Zhandire [26] attempted to predict hourly direct solar radiation using artificial neural networks at a location in South Africa. A feedforward neural network was used where inputs to the network included the clearness index and the ratio $1/\cos\theta_z$ where θ_z is the zenith angle. The experimental data used was for a period from March to May. The error analysis showed the mean bias error varied between −21 and 89 W/m^2 and root mean square error between 21 and 147 W/m^2. A small time series was used in this study and therefore the results may not be quite conclusive.

3. Test Area and Data

Table 1 shows four locations that have been selected and used for the study. The direct solar radiation was measured as an additional parameter from a Kipp and Zonen CSD-1 sensor with an accuracy of ±50 W/m^2. Global solar irradiation data was measured using a Kipp and Zonen CM6B Pyranometer. The direct and global solar irradiation was measured from 2003 to 2005. Sunshine hours' were obtained using a Kipp and Zonen CSD 1 sunshine duration sensors and covers the same period as the solar irradiation data. The maximum temperature data was obtained from the Uganda Meteorological Department and covers a period from 1993 to 2005. Monthly average daily values of these parameters were computed and used in this study. The monthly average daily extraterrestrial solar irradiation $\overline{H}_0$ and average day length $\overline{S}_0$ were calculated from expressions defined by Duffie and Beckmann [27].

4. Feedforward Neural Network

This study employed a feedforward neural network. A typical neural network consists of an input, a hidden, and output layer. Other components include a neuron, weight, and a transfer function. Figure 1 shows a typical neuron in a feedforward network. An input x_j is transmitted through a connection that multiplies its strength by a weight $w_{i,j}$ to give a product $x_j w_{i,j}$. This product is an argument to a transfer function f which yields an output y_i represented by the

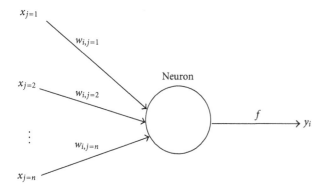

FIGURE 1: Typical neuron in a feedforward network.

following equation this kind of interaction is reflected in a process referred to as training:

$$y_i = f\left(\sum_{j=1}^{n} x_j w_{i,j}\right), \qquad (3)$$

where i is an index of neuron in hidden layer and j is an index of an input to the network.

A training process requires an algorithm which directs learning within an artificial neural network. Backpropagation is one of the existing training algorithms. The former minimizes the mean square difference between the network output and the desired output. The associated error function is expressed as follows; minimizing this error function results in an updating rule to adjust the weights of the connections between neurons:

$$E = \left(\frac{1}{P}\right) \sum_{p} \sum_{k} \left(d_{pk} - o_{pk}\right)^2, \qquad (4)$$

where p is a pattern index, k is an index of elements in the output vector, d_{pk} is the kth element in the target vector in the pth pattern, o_{pk} is the kth element in the output vector in the pth pattern, and P is the total number of training patterns.

The process of presenting an input-output pair, computing the error function and updating the weights continues until the error function reaches a prespecified value or the weights no longer change. At this point the training process stops, then testing and operation of the new network is pursued [28, 29].

5. Experimental Procedure

The data from the four study sites was split into two such that the dataset (36 sets) from three stations, that is, Mbarara, Lira and Tororo, was used for *training* the ANN and building the empirical model. The dataset (12 sets) from the Kampala station was reserved for *validating* both the ANN and empirical models. The training dataset is used to adjust the neural network so that a best fitting of the nonlinear function representing the phenomenon under investigation is reached. The validation dataset is used to evaluate the generalization of the neural network [30].

Figure 2 shows a proposed artificial neural network model. It is a feedforward backpropagation network with the following six input variables: latitude Lat, longitude Lon, altitude Alt, monthly average daily values of global solar irradiation $\overline{H}$, sunshine hours $\overline{S}$, and maximum temperature $\overline{T}_{\max}$. The output variable is monthly average daily direct solar irradiation $\overline{H}_b$. Three transfer functions were investigated, which included the tangent sigmoid, log sigmoid, and linear functions. One-hidden and two-hidden layer architectures were tested in which the number of neurons was varied. Twelve backpropagation training algorithms were tested in order to obtain the most suitable for the training process. A description of these algorithms can be found in the MATLAB manual by Demuth and Beale [31]. Overall, the following is an outline of the procedure used in the development of the ANN model [32].

(i) Normalize input and target values, in the range 1 to −1.

(ii) Define matrix size of the dataset.

(iii) Partition and create training and validation subdatasets.

(iv) Create a feedforward neural network.

(v) Train the feedforward neural network.

(vi) Generate output values.

(vii) Unnormalize the output values.

(viii) Check performance of the neural network by comparing the output values with target values.

The MATLAB version 6.5 program was utilized in this study.

Estimated values were compared with measured values through correlation and error analysis. The latter was carried out through computation of mean bias error (MBE) and root mean square error (RMSE), represented by the following equations

$$\text{MBE} = \frac{\left(\sum_{i=1}^{N} (y_i - x_i)\right)}{N},$$

$$\text{RMSE} = \sqrt{\frac{\left(\sum_{i=1}^{N} (y_i - x_i)^2\right)}{N}}, \qquad (5)$$

where y_i is an estimated value, x_i is a measured value, and N is equal to the number of observations.

6. Results and Discussions

6.1. Modeling Using Artificial Neural Networks. The linear transfer function was fixed at the output layer while the sigmoid tangent and log sigmoid functions were tested in the hidden layer. Results in usage of either sigmoid transfer functions in the hidden layer did not show a significant difference. The tangent sigmoid transfer function was chosen, though. Similarly, there was no significant difference when two hidden layers were used as compared to one hidden layer. One-hidden layer was used in order to minimize the

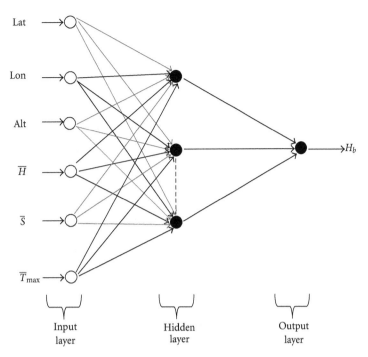

FIGURE 2: Artificial neural network structure.

complexity of the proposed ANN model. Among the twelve training algorithms investigated, the Levenberg-Marquardt gave a correlation coefficient r of over 0.96 when the measured values were correlated with the estimated values. After several trials, *six* neurons were found to be the most appropriate for the training process.

The estimates obtained from the proposed ANN model were correlated with the measured values, giving a correlation coefficient r of 0.998. The corresponding MBE was 0.005 MJ/m^2 and the RMSE was 0.197 MJ/m^2. These results indicate a good fitting between the estimated and measured monthly average daily direct solar irradiation values.

6.2. Modeling Using Empirical Method. The monthly average daily beam transmittance was correlated with monthly average daily relative sunshine duration and with monthly average daily clearness index, transforming (1) and (2), respectively, into

$$\frac{\overline{H}_b}{\overline{H}_0} = -0.370 + 1.741\left(\frac{\overline{S}}{\overline{S}_0}\right) - 0.900\left(\frac{\overline{S}}{\overline{S}_0}\right)^2, \quad (6)$$

$$\frac{\overline{H}_b}{\overline{H}_0} = -0.232 + 0.964\left(\frac{\overline{H}}{\overline{H}_0}\right). \quad (7)$$

Estimates of monthly average daily direct solar irradiation were computed using both (6) and (7) and then compared with the measured values. Results showed correlation coefficient r equal to 0.892 and 0.907, respectively; the MBE was 0.088 and −0.177, respectively, and RMSE was equal to 1.275 and 1.196, respectively. Overall results showed (7) as a better empirical formulation than (6).

TABLE 2: Results of correlation and error analysis.

Model	r	MBE (MJ/m^2)	RMSE (MJ/m^2)
ANN	0.998	0.005	0.197
Equation (6)	0.892	0.088	1.275
Equation (7)	0.907	−0.177	1.196

6.3. Comparison between the ANN and Empirical Model. Table 2 shows results of correlation and error analysis for the ANN and empirical models. The estimates from (7) were compared with those from the proposed ANN model and the results showed the superiority of the ANN model. Further still, Figures 3, 4, 5, and 6 show a similar trend for the measured, neural network (NN) and empirically estimated values of direct solar irradiation, at all the four stations. However, the empirical model overestimates the direct solar irradiation in Mbarara and Lira and underestimates in Tororo and Kampala stations, throughout the year. The over- and underestimation tendencies of the empirical model are due to the fact that such a model does not ably capture all the radiative complexities typical of direct solar radiation. The ANN model does this more appropriately.

7. Conclusions

An artificial neural network model has been developed, which could be used to estimate monthly average daily direct solar radiation at four locations in Uganda, and at locations with similar climate. The ANN architecture designed is a feedforward backpropagation with one hidden layer containing six neurons with tangent sigmoid as the transfer

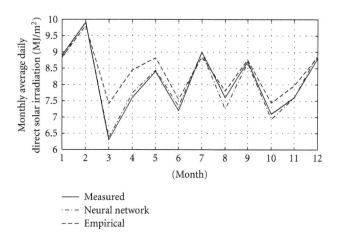

Figure 3: Comparison of neural networks and empirical models for Mbarara site.

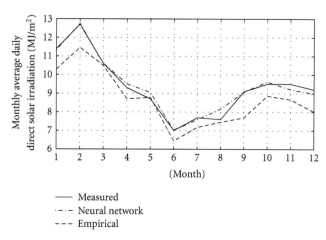

Figure 6: Comparison of neural networks and empirical models for Kampala site.

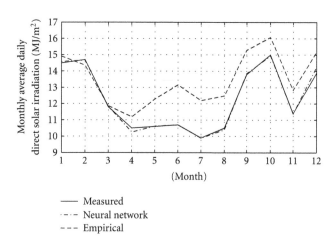

Figure 4: Comparison of neural networks and empirical models for Lira site.

function. The output layer utilized a linear transfer function. The training algorithm used was the Levenverg-Marquardt. The input variables to the ANN model are monthly average daily values of global solar irradiation, sunshine hours, and maximum temperature together with latitude, longitude, and altitude of the location. The proposed ANN model proved to be superior over the empirical model in the prediction process. The ANN model is capable of capturing the nonlinear nature of solar radiation more reliably.

Nomenclature

$\overline{H}_b$:   Monthly average daily direct solar radiation
$\overline{H}_0$:   Monthly average daily extraterrestrial solar radiation
$\overline{S}$:   Monthly average daily sunshine hours
$\overline{S}_0$:   Average day length
$\overline{H}$:   Monthly average daily global solar radiation
$\overline{T}_{max}$:   Monthly average daily maximum temperature
ANN: Artificial neural networks
NN: Neural networks
Lat: Latitude
Lon: Longitude
Alt: Altitude
r: Correlation coefficient
MBE: Mean bias error
RMSE: Root mean square error.

References

[1] J. A. Davies and D. C. McKay, "Estimating solar irradiance and components," *Solar Energy*, vol. 29, no. 1, pp. 55–64, 1982.

[2] C. Gueymard, "Critical analysis and performance assessment of clear sky solar irradiance models using theoretical and measured data," *Solar Energy*, vol. 51, no. 2, pp. 121–138, 1993.

[3] F. Vignola and D. K. McDaniels, "Beam-global correlations in the Pacific Northwest," *Solar Energy*, vol. 36, no. 5, pp. 409–418, 1986.

[4] A. Louche, G. Notton, P. Poggy, and G. Simonnot, "Correlations for direct normal and global horizontal irradiation on

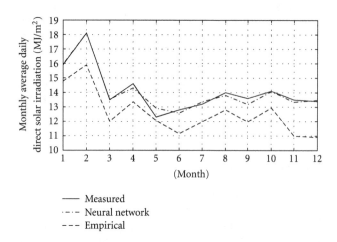

Figure 5: Comparison of neural networks and empirical models for Tororo site.

a French Mediterranean site," *Solar Energy*, vol. 46, no. 4, pp. 261–266, 1991.

[5] N. C. Majumdar, B. L. Mathur, and S. B. Kaushik, "Prediction of direct solar radiation for low atmospheric turbidity," *Solar Energy*, vol. 13, no. 4, pp. 383–394, 1972.

[6] A. Al-Mohamad, "Global, direct and diffuse solar-radiation in Syria," *Applied Energy*, vol. 79, no. 2, pp. 191–200, 2004.

[7] R. B. Benson, M. V. Paris, J. E. Sherry, and C. G. Justus, "Estimation of daily and monthly direct, diffuse and global solar radiation from sunshine duration measurements," *Solar Energy*, vol. 32, no. 4, pp. 523–535, 1984.

[8] K. S. Reddy and M. Ranjan, "Solar resource estimation using artificial neural networks and comparison with other correlation models," *Energy Conversion & Management*, vol. 44, no. 15, pp. 2519–2530, 2003.

[9] W. Huang and C. Murray, "Application of an artificial neural network to predict tidal currents in an inlet," Tech. Rep. ERDC/CHL CHETN-IV-58, US Army Corps of Engineers, 2003.

[10] Haykin, *Neural Networks: A Comprehensive Foundation*, Macmillan, New York, NY, USA, 1994.

[11] F. S. Tymvios, C. P. Jacovides, S. C. Michaelides, and C. Scouteli, "Comparative study of Ångström's and artificial neural networks' methodologies in estimating global solar radiation," *Solar Energy*, vol. 78, no. 6, pp. 752–762, 2005.

[12] A. Sözen, E. Arcaklioglu, and M. Özalp, "Estimation of solar potential in Turkey by artificial neural networks using meteorological and geographical data," *Energy Conversion & Management*, vol. 45, no. 18-19, pp. 3033–3052, 2004.

[13] S. Trajkovic, B. Todorovic, and M. Stankovic, "Estimation of FAO Penman C factor by RBF networks," *Facta Universitatis*, vol. 2, no. 3, pp. 185–191, 2001.

[14] M. Mohandes, S. Rehman, and T. O. Halawani, "Estimation of global solar radiation using artificial neural networks," *Renewable Energy*, vol. 14, no. 1–4, pp. 179–184, 1998.

[15] R. Knutti, T. F. Stocker, F. Joos, and G. K. Plattner, "Probabilistic climate change projections using neural networks," *Climate Dynamics*, vol. 21, no. 3-4, pp. 257–272, 2003.

[16] V. M. Krasnopolsky and M. S. Fox-Rabinovitz, "Complex hybrid models combining deterministic and machine learning components for numerical climate modeling and weather prediction," *Neural Networks*, vol. 19, no. 2, pp. 122–134, 2006.

[17] Y. B. Dibike and P. Coulibaly, "Temporal neural networks for downscaling climate variability and extremes," *Neural Networks*, vol. 19, no. 2, pp. 135–144, 2006.

[18] A. Wu, W. W. Hsieh, and B. Tang, "Neural network forecasts of the tropical Pacific sea surface temperatures," *Neural Networks*, vol. 19, no. 2, pp. 145–154, 2006.

[19] L. Hontoria, J. Aguilera, and P. Zufiria, "A new approach for sizing stand alone photovoltaic systems based in neural networks," *Solar Energy*, vol. 78, no. 2, pp. 313–319, 2005.

[20] S. A. Kalogirou, "Prediction of flat-plate collector performance parameters using artificial neural networks," *Solar Energy*, vol. 80, no. 3, pp. 248–259, 2006.

[21] M. Iqbal, "Correlation of average diffuse and beam radiation with hours of bright sunshine," *Solar Energy*, vol. 23, no. 2, pp. 169–173, 1979.

[22] F. J. K. Ideriah, "A model for calculating direct and diffuse solar radiation," *Solar Energy*, vol. 26, no. 5, pp. 447–452, 1981.

[23] M. Hussain, "Correlating beam radiation with sunshine duration," *Solar Energy*, vol. 48, no. 3, pp. 145–149, 1992.

[24] G. Stanhill, "Estimation of direct solar beam irradiance from measurements of the duration of bright sunshine," *International Journal of Climatology*, vol. 18, no. 3, pp. 347–354, 1998.

[25] J. Mubiru, E. J. K. B. Banda, and T. Otiti, "Empirical equations for the estimation of monthly average daily diffuse and beam solar irradiance on a horizontal surface," *Discovery and Innovation*, vol. 16, no. 3-4, pp. 157–164, 2004.

[26] E. Zhandire, "Artificial neural networks model for estimating beam solar radiation from hemispherical solar radiation," in *Proceedings of the 8th College on Thin Films Technology*, vol. 8.7, pp. 62–67, Dar es salaam, Tanzania, 2004.

[27] J. A. Duffie and W. A. Beckmann, *Solar Engineering of Thermal Processes*, chapter 1–3, Wiley-Interscience Publication, New York, NY, USA, 1980.

[28] M. Mohandes, A. Balghonaim, M. Kassas, S. Rehman, and T. O. Halawani, "Use of radial basis functions for estimating monthly mean daily solar radiation," *Solar Energy*, vol. 68, no. 2, pp. 161–168, 2000.

[29] M. Ghiassi, H. Saidane, and D. K. Zimbra, "A dynamic artificial neural network model for forecasting time series events," *International Journal of Forecasting*, vol. 21, no. 2, pp. 341–362, 2005.

[30] H. K. Elminir, F. F. Areed, and T. S. Elsayed, "Estimation of solar radiation components incident on Helwan site using neural networks," *Solar Energy*, vol. 79, no. 3, pp. 270–279, 2005.

[31] H. Demuth and M. Beale, *Neural Network Toolbox: User's Guide Version 3.0*, MathWorks, 1998.

[32] J. Mubiru and E. J. K. B. Banda, "Estimation of monthly average daily global solar irradiation using artificial neural networks," *Solar Energy*, vol. 82, no. 2, pp. 181–187, 2008.

17

The Generalized Dahlquist Constant with Applications in Synchronization Analysis of Typical Neural Networks via General Intermittent Control

Zhang Qunli

Department of Mathematics, Heze University, Heze 274015, Shandong, China

Correspondence should be addressed to Zhang Qunli, qunli-zhang@126.com

Academic Editor: Tomasz G. Smolinski

A novel and effective approach to synchronization analysis of neural networks is investigated by using the nonlinear operator named the generalized Dahlquist constant and the general intermittent control. The proposed approach offers a design procedure for synchronization of a large class of neural networks. The numerical simulations whose theoretical results are applied to typical neural networks with and without delayed item demonstrate the effectiveness and feasibility of the proposed technique.

1. Introduction

Since its introduction by Pecora and Carrol in 1990, synchronization of chaotic systems [1–10] is of great practical significance and has received great interest in recent years. In the above literature, the approach applied to stability analysis is basically Lyapunov's method. As we all know, the construction of a proper Lyapunov function becomes usually very skillful, and Lyapunov's method does not specifically describe the convergence rate near the equilibrium of the system. Hence, there is little compatibility among all of the stability criteria obtained so far.

The concept named the generalized Dahlquist constant [11] has been applied to the investigation of impulsive synchronization [12, 13] analysis.

Intermittent control [14–18] has been used for a variety of purposes in engineering fields such as manufacturing, transportation, air-quality control, and communication. Synchronization using an intermittent control method has been discussed [15–18]. Compared with continuous control methods [2–10], intermittent control is more efficient when the system output is measured intermittently rather than continuously. Our interest focuses on the class of intermittent control with time duration, wherein the control is activated in certain nonzero time intervals and is off in other

time intervals. A special case of such a control law is of the form

$$
U(t) = \begin{cases} -k(y(t) - x(t)), & (nT \le t < nT + \delta), \\ 0, & (nT + \delta \le t < (n+1)T), \end{cases}
$$

(1)

where k denotes the control strength, $\delta > 0$ denotes the switching width, and T denotes the control period. In this paper, based on the generalized Dahlquist constant and the Gronwall inequality, a general intermittent controller

$$
U(t) = \begin{cases} -k(y(t) - x(t)), & (h(n)T \le t < h(n)T + \delta), \\ 0, & (h(n)T + \delta \le t < h(n+1)T), \end{cases}
$$

(2)

is designed, where $h(n)$ is a strictly monotone increasing function on n with $h(0) = 0$ then sufficient yet generic criteria for synchronization of typical neural networks with and without delayed item are obtained.

This paper is organized as follows. In Section 2, some necessary background materials are presented, and a simple configuration of coupled neural networks is formulated. Section 3 deals with synchronization. The theoretical results

The Generalized Dahlquist Constant with Applications in Synchronization Analysis of Typical Neural Networks via
General Intermittent Control

163

are applied to typical chaotic neural networks, and numerical simulations are shown in this section. Finally, some concluding remarks are given in Section 4.

2. Formulations

Let X be a Banach space endowed with the Euclidean norm $\| \cdot \|$, that is, $\|x\| = \sqrt{x^T x} = \sqrt{\langle x, x \rangle}$, where $\langle \cdot, \cdot \rangle$ is inner product, and, let Ω be a open subset of X. We consider the following system:

$$\frac{dx(t)}{dt} = F(x(t)) + G(x(t - \tau)), \qquad (3)$$

where F, G are nonlinear operators defined on Ω, $x(t), x(t - \tau) \in \Omega$, τ is a time-delayed positive constant, and $F(0) = 0, G(0) = 0$.

Definition 1. System (3) is called to be exponentially stable on a neighborhood Ω of the equilibrium point if there exist constants $\mu > 0, M > 0$, such that

$$\|x(t)\| \le M e^{-\mu t} \|x_0\| \quad (t \ge 0), \qquad (4)$$

where $x(t)$ is any solution of (3) initiated from $x(t_0) = x_0$.

Definition 2 (see [11]). Suppose Ω is an open subset of Banach space X, and $F : \Omega \to X$ is an operator.

The constant

$$\alpha(F) = \sup_{x,y \in \Omega, x \ne y} \frac{1}{\|x - y\|} \lim_{r \to +\infty} f(r) \qquad (5)$$

is called to be the generalized Dahlquist constant of F on Ω, where $f(r) = \|(F + rI)x - (F + rI)y\| - r\|x - y\|$; here, denote by $F + rI$ the operator mapping every point $x \in \Omega$ onto $F(x) + rx$.

For $r \ge 0$,

$$f(r) = \|(F + rI)x - (F + rI)y\| - r\|x - y\|$$

$$= \sqrt{(k(r))^T k(r)} - r\sqrt{(x - y)^T (x - y)} \qquad (6)$$

$$= f_1(r) - f_2(r),$$

where $k(r) = F(x) - F(y) + r(x - y)$, $f_1(r) = \sqrt{(k(r))^T k(r)}$, $f_2(r) = r\sqrt{(x - y)^T (x - y)}$

$$\frac{df_1(r)}{dr} = \frac{(F(x) - F(y))^T (x - y) + r\|x - y\|^2}{f_1(r)}$$

$$= \frac{f_3(r)}{f_1(r)}, \qquad (7)$$

$$\frac{df_2(r)}{dr} = \sqrt{(x - y)^T (x - y)},$$

where $f_3(r) = (F(x) - F(y))^T (x - y) + r\|x - y\|^2$. According to the Cauchy-Bunie Khodorkovsky inequality, we obtain

$$\left(f_1(r) \sqrt{(x - y)^T (x - y)} \right)^2 - (f_3(r))^2$$

$$= \|F(x) - F(y)\|^2 \|x - y\|^2 - \left((F(x) - F(y))^T (x - y) \right)^2$$

$$= \langle F(x) - F(y), F(x) - F(y) \rangle \langle x - y, x - y \rangle$$

$$- (\langle F(x) - F(y), x - y \rangle)^2 \ge 0. \qquad (8)$$

Therefore,

$$\left| f_1(r) \sqrt{(x - y)^T (x - y)} \right| \ge |f_3(r)| \ge f_3(r). \qquad (9)$$

That is

$$f_1(r) \sqrt{(x - y)^T (x - y)} \ge f_3(r),$$

$$\frac{df_1(r)}{dr} - \frac{df_2(r)}{dr} \le 0, \qquad (10)$$

$$\frac{df(r)}{dr} \le 0.$$

So the function $f(r), r \ge 0$, is monotone decreasing; thus, the limit

$$\lim_{r \to +\infty} f(r) \qquad (11)$$

exists.

3. Synchronization Analysis and Examples

Theorem 3. *If the operator G in the system (3) satisfies*

$$\|G(x) - G(y)\| \le l\|x - y\| \qquad (12)$$

for any $x, y \in \Omega$, where l is a positive constant, then two solutions, $x(t)$ and $y(t)$, respectively, initiated from $x(t_0) = x_0 \in \Omega, y(t_0) = y_0 \in \Omega$ satisfy

$$\|x - y\| \le \|x_0 - y_0\| \exp\{\lambda(t - t_0)\}, \quad \forall t \ge 0, \qquad (13)$$

where $\lambda = \alpha(F) + \exp\{-\alpha(F)\tau\}l$.

Proof. Assume $x(t)$ and $y(t)$ are the solutions of (3), respectively, under the initial conditions $x(t_0) = x_0 \in \Omega$, $y(t_0) = y_0 \in \Omega$. We have

$$(e^{rt} x(t))'_t = r e^{rt} x(t) + e^{rt} F(x(t)) + e^{rt} G(x(t - \tau))$$

$$= e^{rt}(F + rI)x(t) + e^{rt} G(x(t - \tau)) \qquad (14)$$

for all $t \ge 0$ and $r > 0$. $\qquad \square$

For all $x_0, y_0 \in \Omega, t > s \ge 0$,

$$e^{rt}[x(t) - y(t)] = e^{rs}[x(s) - y(s)] + \int_s^t k(r, u) du, \qquad (15)$$

where $k(r, u) = e^{ru}[(F + rI)x(u) - (F + rI)y(u) + (G(x(u - \tau)) - G(y(u - \tau)))]$.

So

$$e^{rt}\|x(t) - y(t)\| - e^{rs}\|x(s) - y(s)\| \leq \int_s^t h(r, u)du, \quad (16)$$

where $h(r, u) = e^{ru}(\|(F + rI)x(u) - (F + rI)y(u)\| + \|G(x(u - \tau)) - G(y(u - \tau))\|)$.

Then for all $t \geq 0$, we infer that

$$e^{rt}(\|x(t) - y(t)\|)'_t \leq h(r, t). \quad (17)$$

Therefore, we obtain

$$e^{rt}(\|x(t) - y(t)\|)'_t \leq h(r, t) - re^{rt}\|x(t) - y(t)\|. \quad (18)$$

Letting $r \to +\infty$, then

$$\begin{aligned}
(\|x(t) - y(t)\|)'_t &\leq \alpha(F)\|x(t) - y(t)\| \\
&\quad + \|G(x(t - \tau)) - G(y(t - \tau))\| \\
&\leq \alpha(F)\|x(t) - y(t)\| \\
&\quad + l\|x(t - \tau) - y(t - \tau)\|. \quad (19)
\end{aligned}$$

Integrating inequality (19) over $[t_0, t]$, we have

$$\begin{aligned}
\|x(t) - y(t)\| &\leq e^{\alpha(F)(t - t_0)}\|x_0 - y_0\| \\
&\quad + \int_{t_0}^t e^{\alpha(F)(t - s)}l\|x(s - \tau) - y(s - \tau)\|ds. \quad (20)
\end{aligned}$$

That is

$$\begin{aligned}
e^{-\alpha(F)(t - t_0)}\|x(t) - y(t)\| &\leq \|x_0 - y_0\| \\
&\quad + \int_{t_0}^t e^{-\alpha(F)(s - t_0)}l\|x(s - \tau) - y(s - \tau)\|ds, \\
&\leq \|x_0 - y_0\| \\
&\quad + e^{-\alpha(F)\tau}l\int_{t_0 - \tau}^{t - \tau} e^{-\alpha(F)(s - t_0)}\|x(s) - y(s)\|ds. \quad (21)
\end{aligned}$$

Using the Gronwall inequality [19, 20], we have

$$e^{-\alpha(F)(t - t_0)}\|x(t) - y(t)\| \leq \|x_0 - y_0\|\exp\{e^{-\alpha(F)\tau}l(t - t_0)\}. \quad (22)$$

Then

$$\|x(t) - y(t)\| \leq \|x_0 - y_0\|\exp\{(\alpha(F) + e^{-\alpha(F)\tau}l)(t - t_0)\}. \quad (23)$$

Let system (3) be the drive system, and we consider the response system

$$\frac{dy(t)}{dt} = F(y(t)) + G(y(t - \tau)) + U(t), \quad (24)$$

where $x, y \in R^n$ are the state variables, $F(\cdot), G(\cdot)$ are nonlinear operators, $U(t)$ is a feedback control term, and

$$U(t) = \begin{cases} -k(y(t) - x(t)), & (h(n)T \leq t < h(n)T + \delta), \\ 0, & (h(n)T + \delta \leq t < h(n + 1)T), \end{cases} \quad (25)$$

where k denotes the control strength, T is the control period, δ is called the control width, and $h(n)$ is a strictly monotone increasing function on n with $h(0) = 0$.

In this paper, our goal is to design suitable function, $h(n)$ and suitable parameters, δ, T, and k such that system (24) synchronizes to system (3).

Subtract (3) from (24), the error system is obtained

$$\frac{de(t)}{dt} = \begin{cases} F(y(t)) - F(x(t)) \\ +G(y(t - \tau)) - G(x(t - \tau)) - ke(t), \\ \qquad (h(n)T \leq t < h(n)T + \delta), \\ F(y(t)) - F(x(t)) \\ +G(y(t - \tau)) - G(x(t - \tau)), \\ \qquad (h(n)T + \delta \leq t < h(n + 1)T), \end{cases} \quad (26)$$

where $e = y - x$. Then we have the following result.

Theorem 4. *Suppose that the operator G in the systems (3) and (24) satisfies condition (12), and $\alpha(F)$ is defined as in Definition 2, and $\lambda = \alpha(F) + \exp\{-\alpha(F)\tau\}l$. Then the synchronization of (3) and (24), given in (26), is asymptotically stable if the parameters δ, T, and k are such that*

$$\inf\left((r + \lambda)\delta\frac{h^{-1}(t - \delta/T)}{t} - \lambda\right) > 0, \quad (27)$$

where $r = k - \lambda > 0$, $h^{-1}(\cdot)$ is inverse function of the function $h(\cdot)$.

Proof. From Theorem 3, we can get the conclusion as follows:

$$\|e(t)\| \leq \|e(h(n)T)\|\exp\{-r(t - h(n)T)\} \quad (28)$$

for any $h(n)T \leq t < h(n)T + \delta$,

$$\|e(t)\| \leq \|e(h(n)T + \delta)\|\exp\{\lambda(t - h(n)T - \delta)\} \quad (29)$$

for any $h(n)T + \delta \leq t < h(n + 1)T$.

The Generalized Dahlquist Constant with Applications in Synchronization Analysis of Typical Neural Networks via General Intermittent Control

165

Consider conditions (28) and (29), and we can get the conclusion that

$$\|e(t)\| \leq \begin{cases} \|e(0)\| \exp\{-rt + (r+\lambda)h(n)T - n(r+\lambda)\delta\}, \\ \qquad (h(n)T \leq t < h(n)T + \delta), \\ \|e(0)\| \exp\{\lambda t - (n+1)(r+\lambda)\delta\} \\ \qquad (h(n)T + \delta \leq t < h(n+1)T), \end{cases}$$

$$\leq \begin{cases} \|e(0)\| \exp\left\{-\left((r+\lambda)\delta \dfrac{h^{-1}(t-\delta/T)}{t} - \lambda\right)t\right\}, \\ \qquad (h(n)nT \leq t < h(n)T + \delta), \\ \|e(0)\| \exp\left\{-\left((r+\lambda)\delta \dfrac{h^{-1}(t/T)}{t} - \lambda\right)t\right\}, \\ \qquad (h(n)T + \delta \leq t < h(n+1)T). \end{cases}$$

$$(30)$$

When $t \to \infty$, $\|e(t)\| \to 0$ is obtained under condition (27) and (26) becomes asymptotically stable. $\square$

Corollary 5. *Letting* $G(x(t-\tau)) = 0$, $\lambda = \alpha(F)$ *be defined as in Definition 2, and condition (27) is satisfied, then result similar to Theorem 4 is obtained.*

Corollary 6. *Supposing that* $h(n) = pn, p > 0$, *the operator* G *in the systems (3) and (24) satisfies condition (12), and* $\alpha(F)$ *is defined as in Definition 2, and* $\lambda = \alpha(F) + \exp\{-\alpha(F)\tau\}l$ *then; the synchronization of (3) and (24), given in (26), is asymptotically stable if the parameters* δ, T, *and* k *are such that*

$$(r+\lambda)\delta \frac{1}{pT} - \lambda > 0, \qquad (31)$$

where $r = k - \lambda > 0$.

In the simulations of the following examples, we always choose $T = 5$, $k = 10$ and make use of the norm $\|x\| = \sqrt{x^T x}$, where $x \in R^n$.

Example 7. Consider a typical delayed Hopfield neural network [21–23] with two neurons:

$$\dot{x}(t) = -Cx(t) + Af(x(t)) + Bf(x(t-\tau)), \qquad (32)$$

where $x(t) = (x_1(t), x_2(t))^T$, $f(x(t)) = (\tanh(x_1(t)), \tanh(x_2(t)))^T$, $\tau = (1)$, and $C = \left(\begin{smallmatrix} 1 & 0 \\ 0 & 1 \end{smallmatrix}\right)$, $A = \left(\begin{smallmatrix} 2.0 & -0.1 \\ -5.0 & 3.0 \end{smallmatrix}\right)$, with $B = \left(\begin{smallmatrix} -1.5 & -0.1 \\ -0.2 & -2.5 \end{smallmatrix}\right)$.

It should be noted that the network is actually a chaotic delayed Hopfield neural network.

Equation (32) is considered as the drive system, and the response system is defined as follows:

$$\dot{y}(t) = -Cy(t) + Af(y(t)) + Bf(y(t-\tau)) + U(t), \\ y(t_0) = y_0. \qquad (33)$$

We calculate and get the value $l < 9.15$, $\alpha(F) \leq 0.7993$, where $F(x(t)) = -Cx(t) + Af(x(t))$, $G(x(t-\tau)) = Bf(x(t-\tau))$. Choose $h(n) = n, \delta = 4$, and it is easy to verify that condition (31) is satisfied. Let the initial condition be

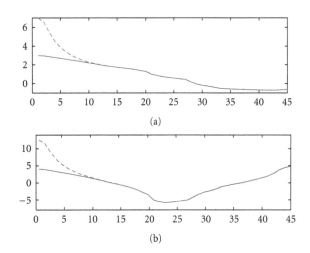

FIGURE 1: (a) Synchronization of $x_1(t)$ and $y_1(t)$. (b) Synchronization of $x_2(t)$ and $y_2(t)$.

$(x_1\ x_2\ y_1\ y_2)^T = (3\ 4\ 7\ 12.5)^T$. Then it can be clearly seen in Figure 1 that the drive system (32) synchronizes with the response system (33).

Example 8. Considering a typical delayed chaotic neural network (29) with two neurons [24, 25] as the drive system, (31) as the response system, where $x(t) = (x_1(t), x_2(t))^T$, $f(x(t)) = (f_1(x_1(t)), f_2(x_2(t)))^T$, $f_i(x_i(t)) = 0.5(|x_i(t) + 1| - |x_i(t) - 1|)$, $i = 1, 2$, $\tau = (1)$, $C = \left(\begin{smallmatrix} 1 & 0 \\ 0 & 1 \end{smallmatrix}\right)$, $A = \left(\begin{smallmatrix} 1+\pi/4 & 20 \\ 0.1 & 1+\pi/4 \end{smallmatrix}\right)$, with $B = \left(\begin{smallmatrix} -1.3\sqrt{2}\pi/4 & 0.1 \\ 0.1 & -1.3\sqrt{2}\pi/4 \end{smallmatrix}\right)$.

It is easily seen that the operator $f(x(t))$ is differential on x in Example 7, but the operator $f(x(t))$ is not so in this example.

We calculate and get the value $l < 1.3\sqrt{2}\pi/2 + 0.2$, $\alpha(F) \leq 1.0855$, where $F(x(t)) = -Cx(t) + Af(x(t))$, $G(x(t-\tau)) = Bf(x(t-\tau))$. Choose $h(n) = 2n, \delta = 4$, and it is easy to verify that condition (31) is satisfied. Let the initial condition be $(x_1\ x_2\ y_1\ y_2)^T = (3\ 4\ 17\ 12.8)^T$. Then the synchronization property of this example can be clearly seen in Figure 2.

Example 9. Consider an autonomous Hopfield neural network with four neurons [26, 27]:

$$\dot{x}(t) = -Cx(t) + Af(x(t)), \qquad (34)$$

where $x(t) = (x_1(t), x_2(t), x_3(t), x_4(t))^T$, $f(x(t)) = (\tanh(x_1(t)), \tanh(x_2(t)), \tanh(x_3(t)), \tanh(x_4(t)))^T$, and

$$C = \begin{pmatrix} 1 & 0 & 0 & 0 \\ 0 & 1 & 0 & 0 \\ 0 & 0 & 1 & 0 \\ 0 & 0 & 0 & 1 \end{pmatrix},$$

$$(35)$$

$$A = \begin{pmatrix} 0.85 & -2 & -0.5 & 0.5 \\ 1.8 & 1.15 & 0.6 & 0.3 \\ 1.1 & 1.21 & 2.5 & 0.05 \\ 0.1 & -0.4 & -1.5 & 1.45 \end{pmatrix}.$$

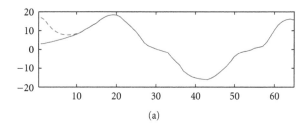

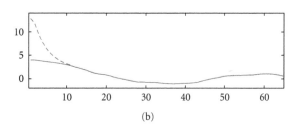

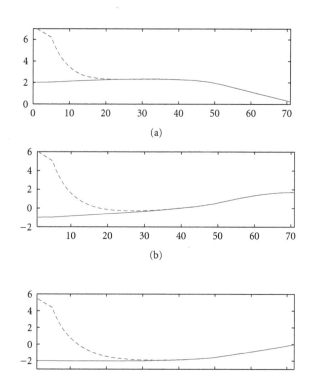

FIGURE 2: (a) Synchronization of $x_1(t)$ and $y_1(t)$. (b) Synchronization of $x_2(t)$ and $y_2(t)$.

Das II et al. [26] have reported that the system (34) posses a chaotic behavior.

Equation (34) is considered as the drive system, and the response system is defined as follows:

$$\dot{y}(t) = -Cy(t) + Af(y(t)) + U(t),$$
$$y(t_0) = y_0. \tag{36}$$

We calculate and get the value $\alpha(F) \leq 1.4369$, where $F(x(t)) = -Cx(t) + Af(x(t))$ and choose $h(n) = n/2, \delta = 2$. It is easy to verify that condition (31) is satisfied. Let the initial condition be $(x_1\ x_2\ x_3\ x_4\ y_1\ y_2\ y_3\ y_4)^T = (2\ -1\ -2\ 1\ 7\ 6\ 5.4\ 9)^T$. Then it can be clearly seen in Figure 3 that the drive system (34) synchronizes with the response system (36).

Example 10. Consider a typical hyperchaotic neural network (32) with two neurons [28] as the drive system, (33) as the response system, where $x(t) = (x_1(t), x_2(t), x_3(t), x_4(t))^T$, $f(x(t)) = (0, 0, 0, |x_4 + 1| - |x_4 - 1|)^T$, and

$$C = \begin{pmatrix} 0 & 0 & 1 & 1 \\ 0 & -2 & -1 & 0 \\ -14 & 14 & 0 & 0 \\ -100 & 0 & 0 & 100 \end{pmatrix},$$
$$A = \begin{pmatrix} 0 & 0 & 0 & 0 \\ 0 & 0 & 0 & 0 \\ 0 & 0 & 0 & 0 \\ 0 & 0 & 0 & 100 \end{pmatrix}. \tag{37}$$

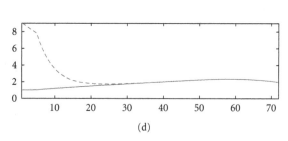

FIGURE 3: (a) Synchronization of $x_1(t)$ and $y_1(t)$. (b) Synchronization of $x_2(t)$ and $y_2(t)$. (c) Synchronization of $x_3(t)$ and $y_3(t)$. (d) Synchronization of $x_4(t)$ and $y_4(t)$.

We calculate and get the value $\alpha(F) \leq 14.8559$, where $F(x(t)) = -Cx(t) + Af(x(t))$ and choose $h(n) = n^2/(n+1), \delta = 2$. It is easy to verify that the condition (27) is satisfied. Letting the initial condition be $(x_1\ x_2\ x_3\ x_4\ y_1\ y_2\ y_3\ y_4)^T = (2\ -1\ -2\ 1\ 7\ 6\ 5.4\ 9)^T$. Then the synchronization property of this example can be clearly seen in Figure 4.

4. Conclusion

Approaches for synchronization of two coupled neural networks which use the nonlinear operator named the generalized Dahlquist constant and the general intermittent control have been presented in this paper. Strong properties of global and asymptotic synchronization have been achieved in a finite number of steps. The techniques have been successfully applied to typical neural networks. Numerical simulations have verified the effectiveness of the method.

The Generalized Dahlquist Constant with Applications in Synchronization Analysis of Typical Neural Networks via General Intermittent Control

167

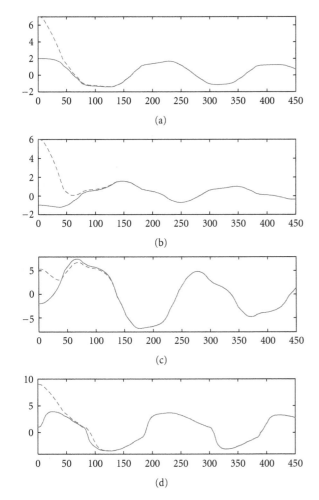

FIGURE 4: (a) Synchronization of $x_1(t)$ and $y_1(t)$. (b) Synchronization of $x_2(t)$ and $y_2(t)$. (c) Synchronization of $x_3(t)$ and $y_3(t)$. (d) Synchronization of $x_4(t)$ and $y_4(t)$.

Acknowledgment

This work is supported by Research Fund Project of the Heze University under Grant: XY10KZ01.

References

[1] W. Deng, J. Lü, and C. Li, "Stability of N-dimensional linear systems with multiple delays and application to synchronization," *Journal of Systems Science and Complexity*, vol. 19, no. 2, pp. 149–156, 2006.

[2] E. M. Elabbasy, H. N. Agiza, and M. M. El-Dessoky, "Global synchronization criterion and adaptive synchronization for new chaotic system," *Chaos, Solitons and Fractals*, vol. 23, no. 4, pp. 1299–1309, 2005.

[3] Q. Zhang, J. Zhou, and G. Zhang, "Stability concerning partial variables for a class of time-varying systems and its applications in chaos synchronization," in *Proceedings of the 24th Chinese Control Conference*, pp. 135–139, South China University of Technology Press, 2005.

[4] Q. Zhang and G. Jia, "Chaos synchronization of Morse oscillator via backstepping design," *Annals of Differential Equations*, vol. 22, no. 3, pp. 456–460, 2006.

[5] Q. L. Zhang, "Synchronization of multi-chaotic systems via ring impulsive control," *Control Theory and Applications*, vol. 27, no. 2, pp. 226–232, 2010.

[6] J. Cao, Z. Wang, and Y. Sun, "Synchronization in an array of linearly stochastically coupled networks with time delays," *Physica A*, vol. 385, no. 2, pp. 718–728, 2007.

[7] J. Cao and L. Li, "Cluster synchronization in an array of hybrid coupled neural networks with delay," *Neural Networks*, vol. 22, no. 4, pp. 335–342, 2009.

[8] L. Li and J. Cao, "Cluster synchronization in an array of coupled stochastic delayed neural networks via pinning control," *Neurocomputing*, vol. 74, no. 5, pp. 846–856, 2011.

[9] H. R. Karimi and P. Maass, "Delay-range-dependent exponential H∞ synchronization of a class of delayed neural networks," *Chaos, Solitons and Fractals*, vol. 41, no. 3, pp. 1125–1135, 2009.

[10] J. Cao, D. W. C. Ho, and Y. Yang, "Projective synchronization of a class of delayed chaotic systems via impulsive control," *Physics Letters A*, vol. 373, no. 35, pp. 3128–3133, 2009.

[11] J. G. Peng and Z. B. Xu, "On asymptotic behaviours of nonlinear semigroup of Lipschitz operators with applications," *Acta Mathematica Sinica. Chinese Series*, vol. 45, no. 6, pp. 1099–1106, 2002.

[12] Q. L. Zhang, "Generalized Dahlquist constant with application in impulsive synchronization analysis," in *the International Conference on Logistics Systems and Intelligent Management (ICLSIM '10)*, pp. 1896–1900, January 2010.

[13] G. Jia and Q. Zhang, "Impulsive synchronization of hyperchaotic Chen system," in *Proceeding of the 20th Chinese Control and Decision Conference*, pp. 123–127, 2008.

[14] J. Huang, C. Li, and Q. Han, "Stabilization of delayed chaotic neural networks by periodically intermittent control," *Circuits, Systems, and Signal Processing*, vol. 28, no. 4, pp. 567–579, 2009.

[15] J. Yu, H. Jiang, and Z. Teng, "Synchronization of nonlinear systems with delay via periodically intermittent control," *Journal of Xinjiang University*, vol. 28, no. 3, pp. 310–315, 2010.

[16] Z. Dong, Y. Wang, M. Bai, and Z. Zuo, "Exponential synchronization of uncertain master-slave Lur'e systems via intermittent control," *Journal of Dynamics and Control*, vol. 7, no. 4, pp. 328–333, 2009.

[17] W. Xia and J. Cao, "Pinning synchronization of delayed dynamical networks via periodically intermittent control," *Chaos*, vol. 19, no. 1, Article ID 013120, 2009.

[18] J. Huang, C. Li, and Q. Han, "Stabilization of delayed chaotic neural networks by periodically intermittent control," *Circuits, Systems, and Signal Processing*, vol. 28, no. 4, pp. 567–579, 2009.

[19] B. Shi, D. Zhang, and M. Gai, *Theory and Applications of Differential Equations*, National Defense Industry Press, 2005.

[20] J. Kuang, *Applied Inequalities*, Shandong Science and Technology Press, 2004.

[21] L. Xiang, J. Zhou, Z. R. Liu, and S. Sun, "On the asymptotic behavior of Hopfield neural network with periodic inputs," *Applied Mathematics and Mechanics*, vol. 23, no. 12, pp. 1220–1226, 2002.

[22] K. Gopalsamy and X. Z. He, "Stability in asymmetric Hopfield nets with transmission delays," *Physica D*, vol. 76, no. 4, pp. 344–358, 1994.

[23] H. Lu, "Chaotic attractors in delayed neural networks," *Physics Letters A*, vol. 298, no. 2-3, pp. 109–116, 2002.

[24] M. Gilli, "Strange attractors in delayed cellular neural networks," *IEEE Transactions on Circuits and Systems I*, vol. 40, no. 11, pp. 849–853, 1993.

[25] Z.-S. Wang, H.-G. Zhang, and Z.-L. Wang, "Global synchronization of a class of chaotic neural networks," *Acta Physica Sinica*, vol. 55, no. 6, pp. 2687–2693, 2006.

[26] P. K. Das II, W. C. Schieve, and Z. Zeng, "Chaos in an effective four-neuron neural network," *Physics Letters A*, vol. 161, no. 1, pp. 60–66, 1991.

[27] C.-J. Cheng, T.-L. Liao, J.-J. Yan, and C.-C. Hwang, "Synchronization of neural networks by decentralized feedback control," *Physics Letters A*, vol. 338, no. 1, pp. 28–35, 2005.

[28] Z. Q. Wu, F. X. Tan, and S. X. Wang, "Synchronization of the hyper-chaotic system of cellular neural network based on passivity," *Acta Physica Sinica*, vol. 55, no. 4, pp. 1651–1658, 2006.

18

A Novel Learning Scheme for Chebyshev Functional Link Neural Networks

Satchidananda Dehuri

Department of Information and Communication Technology, Fakir Mohan University, Vyasa Vihar, Balasore, Orissa 756019, India

Correspondence should be addressed to Satchidananda Dehuri, satchi.lapa@gmail.com

Academic Editor: Giacomo Indiveri

A hybrid learning scheme (ePSO-BP) to train Chebyshev Functional Link Neural Network (CFLNN) for classification is presented. The proposed method is referred as hybrid CFLNN (HCFLNN). The HCFLNN is a type of feed-forward neural networks which have the ability to transform the nonlinear input space into higher dimensional-space where linear separability is possible. Moreover, the proposed HCFLNN combines the best attribute of particle swarm optimization (PSO), back propagation learning (BP learning), and functional link neural networks (FLNNs). The proposed method eliminates the need of hidden layer by expanding the input patterns using Chebyshev orthogonal polynomials. We have shown its effectiveness of classifying the unknown pattern using the publicly available datasets obtained from UCI repository. The computational results are then compared with functional link neural network (FLNN) with a generic basis functions, PSO-based FLNN, and EFLN. From the comparative study, we observed that the performance of the HCFLNN outperforms FLNN, PSO-based FLNN, and EFLN in terms of classification accuracy.

1. Introduction

In recent years, higher-order neural networks [1], particularly FLNN, have been widely used to classify nonlinearly separable patterns and can be viewed as a problem of approximating an arbitrary decision boundary. Broadly, artificial neural networks have become one of the most acceptable soft computing tools for approximating the decision boundaries of a classification problem [2, 3]. In fact, a multilayer perceptron (MLP) with a suitable architecture is capable of approximating virtually any function of interest [4]. This does not mean that finding such a network is easy. On the contrary, problems, such as local minima trapping, saturation, weight interference, initial weight dependence, and overfitting, make neural network training difficult.

An easy way to avoid these problems consists in removing the hidden layers. This may sound a little inconsiderate at first, since it is due to them that nonlinear input-output relationships can be captured. Encouragingly enough, the removing procedure can be executed without giving up nonlinearity, provided that the input layer is endowed with additional higher-order units [5, 6]. This is the idea behind higher-order neural networks (HONNs) [7] like functional link neural networks (FLNNs) [8], ridge polynomial neural networks (RPNNs) [1, 7], and so on. HONNs are simple in their architectures and require fewer number of weights to learn the underlying approximating polynomials. This potentially reduces the number of required training parameters. As a result, they can learn faster since each iteration of the training procedure takes less time. This makes them suitable for complex problem solving where the ability to retrain or adopt new data in real time is critical. Currently, there have been many algorithms used to train the functional link neural networks, such as back-propagation learning algorithm [2], genetic algorithm [9], particle swarm optimization [10], and so on. Back-propagation learning algorithms have their own limitations. However, we can advocate that if the search for the BP learning algorithms starts from the near optimum with a small tuning of the learning parameters, the searching results can be improved.

Genetic algorithms and particle swarm optimization can be used for training the FLNN to reduce the local optimality and speed up the convergence. But training using genetic algorithm is discouraging because of the following limitations: in the training process, it requires encoding and decoding operator which is commonly treated as a long-standing barrier of neural networks researchers. The important problem of applying genetic algorithms to train neural networks may be unsatisfactory because recombination operators incur several problems, such as competing conventions [11] and the epistasis effect [12]. For better performance, real coded genetic algorithms [13, 14] have been introduced. However, they generally employ random mutations, and, hence, still require lengthy local searches near a local optima. On the other hand, PSO has some attractive properties. It retains previous useful information, whereas GAs destroy the previous knowledge of the problems once the population changes. PSO encourages constructive cooperation and information sharing among particles, which enhances the search for a global optimal solution. Successful applications of PSO to some optimization problems such as function minimization [15, 16] and neural networks design [17, 18] have demonstrated its potential. It is considered to be capable to reduce the ill effect of the BP learning algorithm of neural networks, because it does not require gradient and differentiable information.

Unlike the GA, the PSO algorithm has no complicated operators such as cross-over and mutation. In the PSO algorithm, the potential solutions, called as particles, are obtained by flowing through the problem space by following the current optimum particles. Generally speaking, the PSO algorithm has a strong ability to find the most optimistic result, but it has a disadvantage of easily getting into a local optimum. After suitably modulating the parameters for the PSO algorithm, the rate of convergence can be speeded up, and the ability to find the global optimistic result can be enhanced. The PSO algorithm search is based on the orientation by tracing *pbest*, that is, each particle's best position in its history, and tracing *gbest* that is all particles best position in their history, it can rapidly arrive around the global optimum. However, because the PSO algorithm has several parameters to be adjusted by empirical approach, if these parameters are not appropriately set, search will proceed very slow near the global optimum. Hence, to cope up with this problem, we suggested a novel evolvable PSO (ePSO) and back propagation (BP) algorithm as a learning method of Chebyshev functional link neural network (CFLNN) for fine tuning of the connection weights.

1.1. Outline. The remainder of this paper is organized as follows. Some the recently proposed functional link neural networks (FLNNs) are reviewed in Section 2. Section 3 provides the detailed algorithm of HCFLNN for classification. In Section 4, we have presented experimental results with a comparative study. Section 5 concludes the article with a future research scope.

2. Functional Link Neural Networks

FLNNs are higher order neural networks without hidden units introduced by Klassen et al. [19] in 1988. Despite their linear nature, FLNNs can capture nonlinearly input-output relationships, provided that they are fed with an adequate set of polynomial inputs, or the functions might be a subset of a complete set of orthonormal basis functions spanning an n-dimensional representation space, which are constructed out of the original input attributes [20].

In contrast to the linear weights of the input patterns produced by the linear links of artificial neural network, the functional link acts on an element of a pattern or on the entire pattern itself by generating a set of linearly independent functions, then evaluating these functions with the pattern as an argument. Thus, class separability is possible in the enhanced feature space. For a D-dimensional classification problem, there are $((D + r)!/D! \cdots r!)$ possible polynomials up to degree r that can be constructed. For most of the real life problems, this is too big number, even for degree 2, which obviously discourages us from achieving our goal. However, we can still resort to constructive and pruning algorithms in order to address this problem. In fact, Sierra et al. [21] have proposed a new algorithm for the evolution of functional link networks which makes use of a standard GAs [9] to evolve near minimal linear architectures. Moreover, the complexity of the algorithm still needs to be investigated.

However, the dimensionality of many problems is itself very high and further increasing the dimensionality to a very large extent that may not be an appropriate choice. So, it is advisable and also a new research direction to choose a small set of alternative functions, which can map the function to the desired extent with an output of significant improvement. FLNN with a trigonometric basis functions for classification, as proposed in [8], is obviously an example. Chebyshev FLNN is also another improvement in this direction, the detailed is discussed in Section 3. Some of the potential contributions in FLNNs and their success for application in variety of problems are given below.

Haring and Kok [22], has proposed an algorithm that uses evolutionary computation (specifically genetic algorithm and genetic programming) for the determination of functional links (one based on polynomials and another based on expression tree) in neural network. Patra and Pal [23] have proposed a FLNN and applied to the problem of channel equalization in a digital communication channel. It relies on BP-learning algorithm. Haring et al. [24] were presenting a different ways to select and transform features using evolutionary computation and show that this kind of selection of features is a special case of so-called functional links.

Dash et al. [25] have proposed a FLNN with trigonometric basis functions to forecast the short-term electric load. Panagiotopoulos et al. [26] have reported better results by applying FLNN for planning in an interactive environment between two systems: the challenger and the responder. Patra et al. [27] have proposed a FLNN with back-propagation learning for the identification of nonlinearly dynamic systems.

With the encouraging performance of FLNN [23, 27], Patra and van den Bos [28] further motivated and came up with another FLNN with three sets of basis functions such as Chebyshev, Legendre, and power series to develop an intelligent model of the CPS involving less computational complexity. In the sequel, its implementation can be economical and robust.

In [21], a genetic algorithm for selecting an appropriate number of polynomials as a functional input to the network has been proposed by Sierra et al. and applied to the classification problem. However, their main concern was the selection of optimal set of functional links to construct the classifier. In contrast, the proposed method gives much emphasis on how to develop the learning skill of the classifier.

A Chebyshev functional link artificial neural networks have been proposed by Patra and Kot [29] for nonlinearly dynamic system identification. This is obviously another improvement in this direction and also a source of inspiration to further validate this method in other application domain. The proposed method is clearly an example. Singh and Srivastava [30] have estimated the degree of insecurity in a power system with a set of orthonormal trigonometric basis functions.

In [31], an evolutionary search of genetic type and multiobjective optimization such as accuracy and complexity of the FLNN in the Pareto sense is used to design a generalized FLNN with internal dynamics and applied to system identification.

Majhi and Shalabi [32] have applied FLNN for digital watermarking, their results show that FLNN has better performance than other algorithms in this line. In [33], a comparative performance of three artificial neural networks has been given for the detection and classification of gear faults. Authors reported that FLNN is comparatively better than others.

Misra and Dehuri [8] have used a FLNN for classification problem in data mining with a hope to get a compact classifier with less computational complexity and faster learning. Purwar et al. [34] have proposed a Chebyshev functional link neural network for system identification of unknown dynamic nonlinearly discrete-time systems. Weng et al. [35] have proposed a reduced decision feedback Chebyshev functional link artificial neural networks (RDF-CFLANN) for channel equalization.

Two simple modified FLANNs are proposed by Krishnaiah et al. [36] for estimation of carrageenan concentration. In the first model, a hidden layer is introduced and trained by EBP. In the second model, functional links are introduced to the neurons in the hidden layer, and it is trained by EBP. In [37], a FLANN with trigonometric polynomial functions is used in intelligent sensors for harsh environment that effectively linearizes the response characteristics, compensates for nonidealities, and calibrates automatically. Dehuri et al. [38] have proposed a novel strategy for feature selection using genetic algorithm and then used as the input in FLANN for classification.

With this discussion, we can conclude that a very few applications of HONNs have so far been made in classification task. Although theoretically this area is rich, but application specifically in classification is poor. Therefore, the proposed contribution can be another improvement in this direction.

3. Hybrid Chebyshev FLNN

3.1. Chebyshev Functional Link Neural Network. It is well known that the nonlinearly approximation of the Chebyshev orthogonal polynomial is very powerful by the approximation theory. Combining the characteristics of the FLNN and Chebyshev orthogonal polynomial the Chebyshev functional link neural network what we named as CFLNN is resulted. The proposed method utilizes the FLNN input-output pattern, the nonlinearly approximation capabilities of Chebyshev orthogonal polynomial, and the evolvable particle swarm optimization(ePSO)-BP learning scheme for classification.

The Chebyshev FLNN used in this paper is a single-layer neural network. The architecture consists of two parts, namely transformation part (i.e., from a low-dimensional feature space to high-dimensional feature space) and learning part. The transformation deals with the input feature vector to the hidden layer by approximate transformable method. The transformation is the functional expansion (FE) of the input pattern comprising of a finite set of Chebyshev polynomial. As a result, the Chebyshev polynomial basis can be viewed as a new input vector. The learning part uses the newly proposed ePSO-BP learning.

Alternatively, we can approximate a function by a polynomial of truncated power series. The power series expansion represents the function with a very small error near the point of expansion, but the error increases rapidly as we employ it at points farther away. The computational economy to be gained by Chebyshev series increases when the power series is slowly convergent. Therefore, Chebyshev series are frequently used for approximations to functions and are much more efficient than other power series of the same degree. Among orthogonal polynomials, the Chebyshev polynomials converge rapidly than expansion in other set of polynomials [8]. Moreover, Chebyshev polynomials are easier to compute than trigonometric polynomials. These interesting properties of Chebyshev polynomial motivated us to use CFLNN for approximation of decision boundaries in the feature space.

3.2. Evolvable Particle Swarm Optimization (ePSO). Evolvable particle swarm optimization (ePSO) is an improvement over the PSO [10]. PSO is a kind of stochastic algorithm to search for the best solution by simulating the movement and flocking of birds. The algorithm works by initializing a flock of birds randomly over the searching space, where every bird is called as a particle. These particles fly with a certain velocity and find the global best position after some iteration. At each iteration k, the ith particle is represented by a vector x_i^k in multidimensional space to characterize its position. The velocity v_i^k is used to characterize its velocity. Thus, PSO maintains a set of positions:

$$S = \left\{ x_1^k, x_2^k, \ldots, x_N^k \right\} \tag{1}$$

and a set of corresponding velocities

$$V = \left\{ v_1^k, v_2^k, \ldots, v_N^k \right\}. \tag{2}$$

Initially, the iteration counter $k = 0$, and the positions x_i^0 and their corresponding velocities v_i^0 ($i = 1, 2, \ldots, N$) are generated randomly from the search space Ω. Each particle changes its position x_i^k per iteration. The new position x_i^{k+1} of the ith particle ($i = 1, 2, \ldots, N$) is biased towards its best position p_i^k with minimized functional value $f(\cdot)$ referred to as personal best or *pbest*, found by the particle so far, and the very best position p_g^k, referred to as the global best or *gbest*, found by its companions. The *gbest* is the best position in the set

$$P = \left\{ p_1^k, p_2^k, \ldots, p_N^k \right\}, \quad \text{where } p_i^0 = x_i^0, \; \forall i. \tag{3}$$

We can say a particle in P as good or bad depending on its personal best being a good or bad point in P. Consequently, we call the ith particle (jth particle) in P the worst (the best) if $p_i^k (p_j^k)$ is the least (best) fitted, with respect to function value in P. The *pbest* and *gbest* is denoted as p_i^k and p_g^k, respectively.

At each iteration k, the position x_i^k of the ith particle is updated by a velocity v_i^{k+1} which depends on three components: its current velocity v_i^k, the cognition term (i.e., the weighted difference vectors $(p_i^k - x_i^k)$), and the social term (i.e., the weighted difference vector $(p_g^k - x_i^k)$).

Specifically, the set P is updated for the next iteration using

$$x_i^{k+1} = x_i^k + v_i^{k+1}, \tag{4}$$

where $v_i^{k+1} = v_i^k + r_1 \cdot c_1 \cdot (p_i^k - x_i^k) + r_2 \cdot c_2 \cdot (p_g^k - x_i^k)$.

The parameters r_1 and r_2 are uniformly distributed in random numbers in $[0, 1]$ and c_1 and c_2, known as the cognitive and social parameters, respectively, and are popularly chosen to be $c_1 = c_2 = 2.0$ [40]. Thus, the values $r_1 \cdot c_1$ and $r_2 \cdot c_2$ introduce some stochastic weighting in the difference vectors $(p_i^k - x_i^k)$ and $(p_g^k - x_i^k)$, respectively. The set P is updated as the new positions x_i^{k+1} that are created using the following rules with a minimization of the cost function:

$$p_i^{k+1} = x_i^{k+1} \quad \text{if } f\left(x_i^{k+1}\right) < f\left(p_i^k\right), \text{ otherwise } p_i^{k+1} = p_i^k. \tag{5}$$

This process of updating the velocities v_i^k, positions x_i^k, *pbest* p_i^k, and the *gbest* p_g^k is repeated until a user-defined stopping condition is met.

We now briefly present a number of improved versions of PSO and then show where our modified PSO can stand.

Shi and Eberhart [39] have done the first modification by introducing a constant inertia ω, which controls how much a particle tends to follow its current directions compared to the memorized *pbest* p_i^k and the *gbest* p_g^k. Hence, the velocity update is given by

$$v_i^{k+1} = \omega \cdot v_i^k + r_1 \cdot c_1 \cdot \left(p_i^k - x_i^k \right) + r_2 \cdot c_2 \cdot \left(p_g^k - x_i^k \right), \tag{6}$$

where the values of r_1 and r_2 are realized component wise.

Again Shi and Eberhart [40] proposed a linearly varying inertia weight during the search. the inertia weight is linearly reduced during the search. This entails a more globally search

during the initial stages and a more locally search during the final stages. They also proposed a limitation of each particle's velocity to a specified maximum velocity $v^{\max}$. The maximum velocity was calculated as a fraction $\tau (0 < \tau \leq 1)$ of the distance between the bounds of the search space, that is, $v^{\max} = \tau \cdot (x^u - x^l)$.

Fourie and Groenwold [41] suggested a dynamic inertia weight and maximum velocity reduction. In this modification, an inertia weight and maximum velocity are then reduced by fractions α and β, respectively, if no improvement in p_g^k occur after a prespecified number of iterations h, that is,

$$\text{if } f\left(p_g^k\right) = f\left(p_g^{k-1}\right) \quad \text{then } w_{k+1} = \alpha w_k \text{ and } v_k^{\max} = \beta v_k^{\max}, \tag{7}$$

where α and β are such that $0 < \alpha$, $\beta < 1$.

Clerc and Kennedy [42] introduced another interesting modification to PSO in the form of a constriction coefficient χ, which controls all the three components in velocity update rule. This has an effect of reducing the velocity as the search progress. In this modification, the velocity update is given by

$$v_i^{k+1} = \chi \left(v_i^k + r_1 c_1 \left(p_i^k \right) + r_2 c_2 \left(p_g^k - x_i^k \right) \right),$$
$$\text{where } \chi = \frac{2}{\left| 2 - \phi - \sqrt{\phi^2 - 4\phi} \right|}, \quad \phi = c_1 + c_2 > 4. \tag{8}$$

Da and Ge [18] also modified PSO by introducing a temperature like control parameter as in the simulated annealing algorithm. Zhang et al. [43] have modified the PSO by introducing a new inertia weight during the velocity update. Generally in the beginning stages of their algorithm, the inertial weight ω should be reduced rapidly, when around optimum, the inertial weight ω should be reduced slowly. They adopted the following rule:

$$\omega = \omega_0 - \left(\frac{\omega_1}{\text{MAXITER1}} \right) * t, \quad \text{if } 1 \leq t \leq \text{MAXITER1},$$
$$\omega = (\omega_0 - \omega_1) * \exp\left(\frac{(\text{MAXITER1} - k)}{\nu} \right),$$
$$\text{if MAXITER1} < k \leq \text{MAXITER}, \tag{9}$$

where ω_0 is the initial inertia weight, ω_1 is the inertial weight of linear section ending, MAXITER is the total searching generations, MAXITER1 is the used generations that inertia weight is reduced linearly, and k is a variable whose range is $[1, \text{MAXITER}]$. By adjusting k, they are getting different ending values of inertial weight.

In this work, the inertial weight is evolved as a part of searching the optimal sets of weights. However, the evolution of inertial weight is restricted between an upper limit (ω^u) and lower limit ω^l. If it exceeds the boundary during the course of training the network, then the following rule is adopted for restricting the value of ω:

$$\omega = \omega^l + \frac{c\_\text{value}}{3\omega^u} \left(\omega^u - \omega^l \right), \tag{10}$$

where $c\_$value is the exceeded value.

In addition, the proposed method also uses the adaptive cognitive acceleration coefficient (c_1) and the social acceleration coefficients (c_2). c_1 has been allowed to decrease from its initial value of c_{1i} to c_{1f} while c_2 has been increased from c_{2i} to c_{2f} using the following equations as in [44]:

$$c_1^k = \left(c_{1f} - c_{1i}\right) \frac{k}{\text{MAXITER}} + c_{1i},$$
$$c_2^k = \left(c_{2f} - c_{2i}\right) \frac{k}{\text{MAXITER}} + c_{2i}. \tag{11}$$

3.3. ePSO-BP Learning Algorithm. The ePSO-BP is an learning algorithm which combines the ePSO global searching capability with the BP algorithm local searching capability. Similar to the GA [9], the ePSO algorithm is a global algorithm, which has a strong ability to find global optimistic result, and this ePSO algorithm, however, has a disadvantage that the search around global optimum is very slow. The BP algorithm, on the contrary, has a strong ability to find local optimistic result, but its ability to find the global optimistic result is weak. By combining the ePSO with the BP, a new algorithm referred to as ePSO BP hybrid learning algorithm is formulated in this paper. The fundamental idea for this hybrid algorithm is that at the beginning stage of searching for the optimum, the PSO is employed to accelerate the training speed. When the fitness function value has not changed for some generations, or value changed is smaller than a predefined number, the searching process is switched to gradient descending searching according to this heuristic knowledge. Similar to the ePSO algorithm, the ePSO BP algorithm's searching process is also started from initializing a group of random particles. First, all the particles are updated according to (4), until a new generation set of particles are generated, and then those new particles are used to search the global best (*gbest*) position in the solution space. Finally, the BP algorithm is used to search around the global optimum. In this way, this hybrid algorithm may find an optimum more quickly. The procedure for this ePSO BP algorithm can be summarized by the following computational steps.

(1) Initialize the positions and velocities of a group of particles randomly in the range of [0, 1]. Initialize the cognitive and social acceleration initial and final coefficients (i.e., c_{1i}, c_{1f}, c_{2i}, and c_{2f}).

(2) Evaluate each initialized particle's fitness value, and p_i is set as the positions of the current particles, while p_g is set as the best position of the initialized particles.

(3) If the maximal iterative generations are arrived, go to Step 10, else, go to Step 4.

(4) The best particle of the current particles is stored. The positions and velocities of all the particles are updated according to (4) and (6), then a group of new particles are generated.

(5) Adjust the value of c_1 and c_2 by using (11).

(6) Adjust the inertia weights ω according to equation (10) if it flies beyond the boundary of ω.

(7) Evaluate each new particle's fitness value, and the worst particle is replaced with the stored best particle. If the ith particle's new position is better than p_i, p_i is set as the new position of the ith particle. If the best position of all new particles is better than p_g, then p_g is updated.

(8) If the current p_g is unchanged for 15 consecutive generations, then go to Step 9; else, go to Step 3.

(9) Use the BP algorithm to search around p_g for some epochs, if the search result is better than p_g, output the current search result, or else, output p_g.

(10) Output the global optimum p_g.

The parameter ω, in the above ePSO BP algorithm, evolves simultaneously with the weights of the CFLANN during the course of training. The parameter MAXITER1 is generally adjusted to an appropriate value by many repeated experiments, then an adaptive gradient descending method is used to search around the global optimum p_g. The BP algorithm based on gradient descending has parameter called learning rate which controls the convergence of the algorithm to an optimal local solution. In practical applications, users usually employed theoretical, empirical, or heuristic methods to set a good value for this learning rate. In this paper, we adopted the following strategy for learning rate:

$$\mu = k * \exp(-v * \text{epoch}), \tag{12}$$

where μ is learning rate, k and v are constants, epoch is a variable that represents iterative times, through adjusting k and v and we can control the reducing speed of learning rate.

3.4. ePSO-BP Learning Algorithm for CFLNN. Learning of a CFLNN may be considered as approximating or interpolating a continuous multivariate function $\phi(X)$ by an approximating function $\phi_W(X)$. In CFLNN architecture, a set of basis functions φ and a fixed number of weight parameters W are used to represent $\phi_W(X)$. With a specific choice of a set of basis functions ψ, the problem is then to find the weight parameters W that provide the best possible approximation of φ on the set of input-output samples. This can be achieved by iteratively updating W. The interested reader about the detailed theory of FLNN can refer to [21].

Let k training patterns be applied to the FLNN and can be denoted by $\langle X_i, Y_i \rangle$, $i = 1, 2, \ldots, k$ and let the weight matrix be W. At the ith instant $i = 1, 2, \ldots, k$, the D-dimensional input pattern and the CFLNN output are given by $X_i = \langle x_{i1}, x_{i2}, \ldots, x_{iD} \rangle$, $i = 1, 2, \ldots, k$, and $\hat{Y}_i = [\hat{y}_i]$, respectively. Its corresponding target pattern is represented by $Y_i = [y_i]$, $i = 1, 2, \ldots, k$. Hence $\forall i, X = [X_1, X_2, \ldots, X_k]^T$. The augmented matrix of D-dimensional input pattern and the CFLNN output are given by

$$\left\langle X : \widehat{Y} \right\rangle = \begin{pmatrix} x_{11} & x_{12} & . & x_{1D} & : & \widehat{y_1} \\ x_{21} & x_{22} & . & x_{2D} & : & \widehat{y_2} \\ . & . & . & . & : & . \\ . & . & . & . & : & . \\ x_{k1} & x_{k2} & . & x_{kD} & : & \widehat{y_k} \end{pmatrix}. \quad (13)$$

As the dimension of the input pattern is increased from D to D' by a set of basis functions φ, given by $\varphi(X_i) = [Ch_1(x_{i1}), Ch_2(x_{i1}),\ldots, Ch_1(x_{i2}), Ch_2(x_{i2})\ldots, Ch_1(x_{iD}), Ch_2(x_{iD}),\ldots]$. The $k \times D'$ dimensional weight matrix is given by $W = [W_1, W_2,\ldots, W_k]^T$, where W_i is the weight vector associated with the ith output and is given by $W_i = [w_{i1}, w_{i2}, w_{i3},\ldots, w_{iD'}]$. The ith output of the CFLNN is given by $\widehat{y}_i(t) = \rho(\Sigma_{j=1}^{D'}\psi_j(x_{ij}) \cdot w_{ij})\forall i$. The error associated with the ith output is given by $e_i(t) = y_i(t) - \widehat{y}_i(t)$. Using the ePSO back-propagation (BP) learning, the weights of the CFLNN can be optimized. The high-level algorithms then can be summarized as follows.

(1) Input the set of given k training patterns.

(2) Choose the set of orthonormal basis functions.

(3) For $i = 1 : k$

(4) Expand the feature values using the chosen basis functions.

(5) Calculated the weighted sum and then fed to the output node.

(6) error = error + $e(k)$

(7) End for

(8) If the error is tolerable then stop otherwise go to (9).

(9) Update the weights using ePSO BP learning rules and go to step (3).

4. Empirical Study

This section is divided into five subsections. Section 4.1 describes the datasets taken from UCI [45] repository of machine learning databases. The parameters required for the proposed method are given in Section 4.2. The performance of the hybrid CFLNN using some of the datasets especially considered by Sierra et al. [21] compared with the model proposed by Sierra et al. in Section 4.3. In Section 4.4, the classification accuracy of hybrid CFLNN is compared with FLNN [8]. In Section 4.5, we compared the performance of hybrid CFLNN with FLNN proposed in [8] using the cost matrix analysis and then compared with the results obtained by StatLog project [46].

4.1. Description of the Datasets. The availability of results, with previous evolutionary and constructive algorithms (e.g., Sierra et al. [21], Preshelt [47]) has guided us the selection of the following varied datasets taken from the UCI repository of machine learning databases for the addressed neural network learning. Table 1 presents a summary of the main features of each database that has been used in this study.

TABLE 1: Summary of the datasets.

Dataset	Patterns	Attrib.	Clas.	Patterns in class 1	Patterns in class 2	Patterns in class 3
IRIS	150	4	3	50	50	50
WINE	178	13	3	71	59	48
PIMA	768	8	2	500	268	—
BUPA	345	6	2	145	200	—
HEART	270	13	2	150	120	—
CANCER	699	9	2	458	241	—

TABLE 2: Description of the parameters.

Symbol	Purpose of the symbol
N	Size of the swarm
ω	Inertia weight
ω^u	Upper limit of the inertia
ω^l	Lower limit of the inertia
c_1	Cognitive parameter
c_{1i}	Left boundary value of cognitive parameter
c_{1f}	Right boundary value of cognitive parameter
c_2	Social parameter
c_{2i}	Left boundary value of social parameter
c_{2f}	Right boundary value of social parameter
MAXITER	Maximum iterations for stopping an algorithm

4.2. Parameters. All the algorithms have some parameters that have to be provided by the user. The parameters for the proposed hybrid CFLNN are listed in Table 2. However, the parameters for other algorithms are set based on the suggestion. The parameters for EFLN were adopted as suggested in [21]. Similarly, the parameters for FLNN were set as suggested in [8].

The values of the parameters used in this paper are as follows. We set $N = 20 * d$, where d is the dimension of the problem under consideration. The upper limit (ω^u) and lower limit (ω^l) of the inertia are set to $[0.2, 1.8]$. Similarly, the initial and final value of cognitive acceleration coefficients are set to $c_{1i} = 2.5$ and $c_{1f} = 0.5$. The initial and final value of social acceleration coefficients are set to $c_{2i} = 0.5$ and $c_{2f} = 2.5$. the maximum number of iteration is fixed to MAXITER = 500.

In the case of BP learning, the learning parameter μ and the momentum factor ν in hybrid CFLNN was chosen after a several runs to obtain the best results. In the similar manner, the functional expansion of the hybrid CFLNN was carried out.

4.3. Hybrid CFLNN versus EFLN. In this subsection, we will compare the results of hybrid CFLNN with the results of EFLN with polynomial basis functions of degree 1, 2, and 3. The choice of the polynomial degree is obviously a key question in FLNN with polynomial basis functions. However, Sierra et al. [21] have given some guidance to

TABLE 3: Possible number of expanded inputs of degrees ONE, TWO, and THREE.

Dataset	Attributes	Degree 1	Degree 2	Degree 3
IRIS	4	5	15	35
WINE	13	14	105	560
PIMA	8	9	45	165
BUPA	6	7	28	84
HEART	13	14	105	560
CANCER	9	10	55	220

TABLE 4: Comparative results of HCFLNN with EFLN for the cancer and PIMA dataset by considering the average training error (MTre), average validation error (MVe), and average test error (MTe).

Dataset	HCFLNN			EFLN		
	MTre	MVe	MTe	MTre	MVe	MTe
Cancer 1	4.01	2.76	2.57	4.27	1.89	2.09
Cancer 2	3.95	3.97	4.66	4.37	2.96	3.96
cancer 3	4.13	3.51	4.43	3.29	3.01	4.65
BUPA 1	16.26	21.98	22.62	19.07	22.44	23.29
BUPA 2	17.90	24.12	22.35	19.84	18.63	20.37
BUPA 3	15.34	19.92	21.96	16.68	17.81	24.44

TABLE 5: Comparative average performance of HCFLNN and FLNN [21] based on the confidence level ($\alpha = 95\%$).

Dataset	HCFLNN	FLNN
IRIS train	0.9964 ± 0.0136	0.9866 ± 0.0260
Test set	0.9864 ± 0.0262	0.9866 ± 0.0260
WINE train	0.9842 ± 0.0259	0.9605 ± 0.0405
Test set	0.9708 ± 0.0350	0.9550 ± 0.0431
PIMA train	0.8064 ± 0.0395	0.7877 ± 0.0409
Test set	0.7928 ± 0.0405	0.7812 ± 0.0414

TABLE 6: Comparative Average Performance of HCFLNN and FLNN [8] based on the Confidence Level ($\alpha = 98\%$).

Dataset	HCFLNN	FLNN
IRIS Train	0.9964 ± 0.0161	0.9866 ± 0.0309
Test set	0.9864 ± 0.0312	0.9866 ± 0.0309
WINE Train	0.9842 ± 0.0308	0.9605 ± 0.0481
Test set	0.9708 ± 0.0416	0.9550 ± 0.0512
PIMA Train	0.8064 ± 0.0470	0.7877 ± 0.0486
Test set	0.7928 ± 0.0482	0.7812 ± 0.0492

TABLE 7: Weight Matrix of classes to Penalize.

Real Classification	Model Classification	
	Class 1	Class 2
Class 1	0	ω_2
Class 2	ω_1	0

optimize the polynomial degree that can best suit to the architecture. Considering degrees of the polynomial 1, 2, and 3, the possible number of expanded inputs of the above datasets are given in Table 3.

For the sake of convenience, we report the results of the experiments conducted on CANCER and BUPA and then compared with the methods EFLN [21]. We partitioned both datasets into three sets: training, validation, and test sets. Both the networks are trained for 1500 epochs (it should be carefully examined) on the training set, and the error on the validation set was measured after every 10 epochs. Training was stopped when a maximum of 1500 epochs had been trained. The test set performance was then computed for that state of the network which had minimum validation set error during the training process. This method called early stopping is a good way to avoid overfitting of the network to the particular training examples used, which would reduce the generalization performance. The average error rate corresponding to HCFLNN, and EFLN w.r.t. training, validation, and testing of CANCER, and BUPA datasets are shown in Table 4.

4.4. Hybrid CFLNN versus FLNN.

Here, we will discuss the comparative performance of hybrid CFLNN with FLNN using three datasets IRIS, WINE, and PIMA. In this case, the total set of samples are randomly divided into two equal folds. Each of these two folds are alternatively used either as a training set or as a test set. As the proposed learning method ePSO BP learning is a stochastic algorithm, so 10 independent runs were performed for every single fold. The training results obtained in the case of HCFLNN, averaged over 10 runs, are compared with the single run of FLNN.

Similarly, the performance of both classifiers in test set is illustrated herein.

The plotted results clearly indicate that the performance of HCFLNN is competitive with FLNN, whereas in other classification problems like WINE and PIMA, the HCFLNN is showing a clear boundary.

The comparative performance of HCFLNN with FLNN [8] is given in Tables 5 and 6 w.r.t to the different confidence level (α) of 95% and 98%, respectively.

4.5. Performance of Hybrid CFLNN versus FLNN Based on Heart Data.

In this subsection, we will explicitly examine the performance of the HCFLNN model by considering the heart dataset with the use of the 9-fold cross validation methodology. The reason for using 9-fold cross validation is that to compare the performance with the performance of few of the representative algorithms considered in StatLog Project [46]. In 9-fold cross validation, we partition the database into nine subsets (heart1.dat, heart2.dat,..., heart9.dat), where eight subsets are used for training, and the remaining one is used for testing. The process is repeated nine times in such a way that each time a different subset of data is used for testing. Thus, the dataset was randomly segmented into nine subsets with 30 elements each. Each subset contains about 56% of samples from class 1 (without heart disease) and 44% of samples from class 2 (with heart disease).

The procedure makes use of a weight matrix, which is described in Table 7.

TABLE 8: Heart disease classification performance of FLANN models.

Data subset	Error in training set		Error in test set		C_{train}	C_{test}
	Class 1	Class 2	Class 1	Class 2		
Heart1	13/133	14/107	1/17	1/13	0.35	0.2
Heart2	14/133	12/107	2/17	1/13	0.31	0.23
Heart3	13/134	15/106	4/16	2/14	0.37	0.47
Heart4	13/133	10/107	1/17	4/13	0.26	0.7
Heart5	13/133	16/107	3/17	2/13	0.39	0.43
Heart6	13/134	14/106	6/16	0/14	0.35	0.2
Heart7	15/133	13/107	0/17	3/13	0.33	0.5
Heart8	18/133	17/107	1/17	0/13	0.43	0.03
Heart9	20/134	9/106	2/16	1/14	0.27	0.23
Mean					0.34	0.33

TABLE 9: Heart disease classification performance of HCFLANN models.

Data subset	Error in training set		Error in test set		C_{train}	C_{test}
	Class 1	Class 2	Class 1	Class 2		
Heart1	13/133	14/107	1/17	1/13	0.35	0.2
Heart2	13/133	12/107	1/17	2/13	0.30	0.36
Heart3	12/134	13/106	5/16	1/14	0.32	0.33
Heart4	13/133	10/107	4/17	1/13	0.26	0.30
Heart5	13/133	15/107	3/17	2/13	0.37	0.43
Heart6	13/134	12/106	5/16	1/14	0.30	0.30
Heart7	14/133	13/107	1/17	2/13	0.33	0.37
Heart8	16/133	16/107	0/17	2/13	0.40	0.33
Heart9	18/134	10/106	2/16	1/14	0.28	0.23
Mean					0.32	0.31

The purpose of such a matrix is to penalize wrongly classified samples based on the weight of the penalty of the class. In general, the weight of the penalty for class 2 samples that are classified as class 1 samples is ω_1, while the weight of the penalty for class 1 records that are classified as class 2 samples is ω_2. Therefore, the metric used for measuring the cost of the wrongly classifying patterns in the training and test dataset is given by (14).

$$C_{train} = \frac{(S_1 \times \omega_1 + S_2 \times \omega_2)}{S_{train}},$$

$$C_{test} = \frac{(S_1 \times \omega_1 + S_2 \times \omega_2)}{S_{test}}, \tag{14}$$

where C_{train} is the cost of the training set; C_{test} is the cost of test set; S_1 and S_2 denote the patterns that are wrongly classified as belong to class 1 and 2, respectively; S_{train} and S_{test} are the total number of training and test patterns, respectively.

Table 8 presents the errors and costs of the training and test sets for the FLANN model with a weight value of $\omega_1 = 5$ and $\omega_2 = 1$.

Table 9 illustrates the performance of HCFLANN based on the above definition of cost matrix. The errors in training and test set are explicitly given.

The classification results found by the HCFLNN for the heart disease dataset were compared with the results found in the StatLog project [46]. According to [46], comparison consists of calculating the average cost produced by the nine data subsets used for validation. Table 10 presents the average cost for the nine training and test subsets. The result of the HCFLNN is highlighted in bold.

5. Conclusions and Research Directions

In this paper, we developed a new hybrid Chebyshev functional link neural network (HCFLNN). The hybrid model is constructed using the newly proposed ePSO- back propagation learning algorithm and functional link artificial neural network with the orthogonal Chebyshev polynomials. The model was designed for the task of classification in

TABLE 10: Comparative classification performance of HCFLNN, FLNN with the algorithms considered in [46] using the heart disease bench mark datset.

Methods	C_{test}	C_{train}
HCFLNN	0.31	0.32
FLNN	0.33	0.34
HNFB^{-1}	0.37	0.59
Bayes	0.37	0.35

data mining. The method was experimentally tested on various benchmark datasets obtained from publicly available UCI repository. The performance of the proposed method demonstrated that the classification task is quite well in WINE and PIMA whereas showing a competitive performance with FLNN in IRIS. Further, we compared this model with EFLN and FLNN, respectively. The comparative results of the developed model is showing a clear edge over FLNN. Compared with EFLN, the proposed method has been shown to yield state-of-the-art recognition error rate for the classification problems such as CANCER and BUPA.

With this encouraging results of HCFLNN, our future research includes: (i) testing the proposed method on a more number of real life bench mark classification problems with highly nonlinearly boundaries, (ii) mapping the input features with other polynomials such as Legendre, Gaussian, Sigmoid, power series, and so forth, for better approximation of the decision boundaries, (iii) the stability and convergence analysis of the proposed method, and (iv) the evolution of optimal FLNN using particle swarm optimization.

The HCFLNN architecture, because of its simple architecture and computational efficiency, may be conveniently employed in other tasks of data mining and knowledge discovery in databases [4, 8] such as clustering, feature selection, feature extraction, association rule mining, regression, and so on. The extra calculation generated by the higher-order units can be eliminated, provided that these polynomial terms are stored in memory instead of being recalculated each time the HCFLNN trained.

References

[1] J. Ghosh and Y. Shin, "Efficient higher-order neural networks for classification and function approximation," *International Journal of Neural Systems*, vol. 3, pp. 323–350, 1992.

[2] S. Haykin, *Neural Networks: A Comprehensive Foundation*, Prentice Hall, Englewood Cliffs, NJ, USA, 1999.

[3] O. L. Mangasarian and E. W. Wild, "Nonlinear knowledge-based classification," *IEEE Transactions on Neural Networks*, vol. 19, no. 10, pp. 1826–1832, 2008.

[4] K. Hornik, "Approximation capabilities of multilayer feedforward networks," *Neural Networks*, vol. 4, no. 2, pp. 251–257, 1991.

[5] C. L. Giles and T. Maxwell, "Learning, invariance, and generalization in high-order neural networks," *Applied Optics*, vol. 26, no. 23, pp. 4972–4978, 1987.

[6] Y. H. Pao, *Adaptive Pattern Recognition and Neural Network*, Addison-Wesley, Reading, Mass, USA, 1989.

[7] E. Artyomov and O. Yadid-Pecht, "Modified high-order neural network for invariant pattern recognition," *Pattern Recognition Letters*, vol. 26, no. 6, pp. 843–851, 2005.

[8] B. B. Misra and S. Dehuri, "Functional link neural network for classification task in data mining," *Journal of Computer Science*, vol. 3, no. 12, pp. 948–955, 2007.

[9] D. E. Goldberg, *Genetic Algorithms in Search, Optimization and Machine Learning*, Morgan Kaufmann, 1989.

[10] J. Kennedy and R. Eberhart, "Particle swarm optimization," in *Proceedings of the IEEE International Conference on Neural Networks*, pp. 1942–1948, Pisacataway, NJ, USA, December 1995.

[11] J. D. Schaffer, D. Whitley, and L. J. Eshelman, "Combinations of genetic algorithms and neural networks: a survey of the state of the art," in *Proceedings of International Workshop on Combinations of Genetic Algorithms and Neural Networks*, pp. 1–37, 1992.

[12] Y. Davidor, "Epistasis variance: suitability of a representation to genetic algorithms," *Complex Systems*, vol. 4, pp. 368–383, 1990.

[13] L. J. Eshelman and J. D. Schaffer, "Real coded genetic algorithms and interval schemata," in *Foundation of Genetic Algorithms*, L. D. Whitley, Ed., pp. 187–202, Morgan Kaufmann, 1993.

[14] H. Muhlenbein and D. Schlierkamp-Voosen, "Predictive models for the breeder genetic algorithm I. Continuous parameters optimization," *Evolutionary Computation*, vol. 1, no. 1, pp. 24–49, 1993.

[15] J. F. Schutte and A. A. Groenwold, "A study of global optimization using particle swarms," *Journal of Global Optimization*, vol. 31, no. 1, pp. 93–108, 2005.

[16] M. M. Ali and P. Kaelo, "Improved particle swarm algorithms for global optimization," *Applied Mathematics and Computation*, vol. 196, no. 2, pp. 578–593, 2008.

[17] J. Yu, S. Wang, and L. Xi, "Evolving artificial neural networks using an improved PSO and DPSO," *Neurocomputing*, vol. 71, no. 4–6, pp. 1054–1060, 2008.

[18] Y. Da and X. R. Ge, "An improved PSO-based ANN with simulated annealing technique," *Neurocomputing*, vol. 63, pp. 527–533, 2005.

[19] M. S. Klassen, Y. H. Pao, and V. Chen, "Characteristics of the functional link net: a higher order delta rule net," in *Proceedings of the 2nd Annual International Conference on Neural Networks*, vol. 1, pp. 507–513, San Diago, Calif, USA, 1988.

[20] Y. H. Pao and Y. Takefuji, "Functional-link net computing: theory, system architecture, and functionalities," *Computer*, vol. 25, no. 5, pp. 76–79, 1992.

[21] A. Sierra, J. A. Macías, and F. Corbacho, "Evolution of functional link networks," *IEEE Transactions on Evolutionary Computation*, vol. 5, no. 1, pp. 54–65, 2001.

[22] B. Haring and J. N. Kok, "Finding functional links for neural networks by evolutionary computation," in *Proceedings of the 5th Belgian-Dutch Conference on Machine Learning (BENELEARN '95)*, T. Van de Merckt et al., Ed., pp. 71–78, Brussels, Belgium, 1995.

[23] J. C. Patra and R. N. Pal, "A functional link artificial neural network for adaptive channel equalization," *Signal Processing*, vol. 43, no. 2, pp. 181–195, 1995.

[24] S. Haring, J. N. Kok, and M. C. van Wezel, "Feature selection for neural networks through functional links found by evolutionary computation," in *Proceedings of the 2nd International Symposium on Advances in Intelligent Data Analysis, Reasoning about Data*, X. Liu et al., Ed., vol. 1280 of *Lecture Notes in Computer Science*, pp. 199–210, 1997.

[25] P. K. Dash, A. C. Liew, and H. P. Satpathy, "A functional-link-neural network for short-term electric load forecasting," *Journal of Intelligent and Fuzzy Systems*, vol. 7, no. 3, pp. 209–221, 1999.

[26] D. A. Panagiotopoulos, R. W. Newcomb, and S. K. Singh, "Planning with a functional neural-network architecture," *IEEE Transactions on Neural Networks*, vol. 10, no. 1, pp. 115–127, 1999.

[27] J. C. Patra, R. N. Pal, B. N. Chatterji, and G. Panda, "Identification of nonlinear dynamic systems using functional link artificial neural networks," *IEEE Transactions on Systems, Man, and Cybernetics, Part B*, vol. 29, no. 2, pp. 254–262, 1999.

[28] J. C. Patra and A. van den Bos, "Modeling of an intelligent pressure sensor using functional link artificial neural networks," *ISA Transactions*, vol. 39, no. 1, pp. 15–27, 2000.

[29] J. C. Patra and A. C. Kot, "Nonlinear dynamic system identification using Chebyshev functional link artificial neural networks," *IEEE Transactions on Systems, Man, and Cybernetics, Part B*, vol. 32, no. 4, pp. 505–511, 2002.

[30] S. N. Singh and K. N. Srivastava, "Degree of insecurity estimation in a power system using functional link neural network," *European Transactions on Electrical Power*, vol. 12, no. 5, pp. 353–358, 2002.

[31] T. Marcu and B. Koppen-Seliger, "Dynamic functional link neural networks genetically evolved applied to system identification," in *Proceedings of European Symposium on Artificial Neural Networks (ESANN '04)*, pp. 115–120, Bruges, Belgium, 2004.

[32] B. Majhi and H. Shalabi, "An improved scheme for digital watermarking using functional link artificial neural network," *Journal of Computer Science*, vol. 1, no. 2, pp. 169–174, 2005.

[33] I. A. Abu-Mahfouz, "A comparative study of three artificial neural networks for the detection and classification of gear faults," *International Journal of General Systems*, vol. 34, no. 3, pp. 261–277, 2005.

[34] S. Purwar, I. N. Kar, and A. N. Jha, "On-line system identification of complex systems using Chebyshev neural networks," *Applied Soft Computing Journal*, vol. 7, no. 1, pp. 364–372, 2007.

[35] W. D. Weng, C. S. Yang, and R. C. Lin, "A channel equalizer using reduced decision feedback Chebyshev functional link artificial neural networks," *Information Sciences*, vol. 177, no. 13, pp. 2642–2654, 2007.

[36] D. Krishnaiah, D. M. R. Prasad, A. Bono, P. M. Pandiyan, and R. Sarbatly, "Application of ultrasonic waves coupled with functional link neural network for estimation of carrageenan concentration," *International Journal of Physical Sciences*, vol. 3, no. 4, pp. 90–96, 2008.

[37] J. C. Patra, G. Chakraborty, and S. Mukhopadhyay, "Functional link neural network-based intelligent sensors for harsh environments," *Sensors & Transducers Journal*, vol. 90, pp. 209–220, 2008.

[38] S. Dehuri, B. B. Mishra, and S.-B. Cho, "Genetic feature selection for optimal functional link artificial neural network in classification," in *Proceedings of the 9th International Conference on Intelligent Data Engineering and Automated Learning (IDEAL '08)*, C. Fyfe et al., Ed., vol. 5326 of *Lecture Notes in Computer Science*, pp. 156–163, 2008.

[39] Y. Shi and R. Eberhart, "A modified particle swarm optimizer," in *Proceedings of the IEEE International Conference on Evolutionary Computation (ICEC '98)*, pp. 69–73, IEEE Press, Pisacataway, NJ, USA, May 1998.

[40] Y. Shi and R. C. Eberhart, "Parameter selection in particle swarm optimization," in *Evolutionary Programming VII*, vol. 1447 of *Lecture Notes in Computer Science*, pp. 591–600, Springer, Berlin, Germany, 1998.

[41] P. C. Fourie and A. A. Groenwold, "The particle swarm optimization algorithm in size and shape optimization," *Structural and Multidisciplinary Optimization*, vol. 23, no. 4, pp. 259–267, 2002.

[42] M. Clerc and J. Kennedy, "The particle swarm-explosion, stability, and convergence in a multidimensional complex space," *IEEE Transactions on Evolutionary Computation*, vol. 6, no. 1, pp. 58–73, 2002.

[43] J. R. Zhang, J. Zhang, T. M. Lok, and M. R. Lyu, "A hybrid particle swarm optimization-back-propagation algorithm for feedforward neural network training," *Applied Mathematics and Computation*, vol. 185, no. 2, pp. 1026–1037, 2007.

[44] A. Ratnaweera, S. K. Halgamuge, and H. C. Watson, "Self-organizing hierarchical particle swarm optimizer with time-varying acceleration coefficients," *IEEE Transactions on Evolutionary Computation*, vol. 8, no. 3, pp. 240–255, 2004.

[45] C. L. Blake and C. J. Merz, "UCI repository of machine learning databases," http://www.ics.uci.edu/mlearn/MLRepository.html.

[46] R. P. Lippmann, "An introduction to computing with neural networks," *IEEE ASSP Magazine*, vol. 4, no. 2, pp. 4–22, 1987.

[47] L. Preshelt, "Proben1-a set of neural network benchmark problems and benchmarking rules," Tech. Rep. 21/94, Universitat Karlsruhe, Karlsruhe, Germany, 1994.

19

Early FDI Based on Residuals Design According to the Analysis of Models of Faults: Application to DAMADICS

Yahia Kourd,[1] Dimitri Lefebvre,[2] and Noureddine Guersi[3]

[1] Department of Control Engineering, University of Mohamed Khider, Biskra 07000, Algeria
[2] Electrical Engineering and Automatic Control Research Group (GREAH), University of Le Havre, 25 rue Philippe Lebon, 76058 Le Havre, France
[3] Department of Electronics, University of Badji Mokhtar, Annaba 23000, Algeria

Correspondence should be addressed to Dimitri Lefebvre, dimitri.lefebvre@univ-lehavre.fr

Academic Editor: Paolo Gastaldo

The increased complexity of plants and the development of sophisticated control systems have encouraged the parallel development of efficient rapid fault detection and isolation (FDI) systems. FDI in industrial system has lately become of great significance. This paper proposes a new technique for short time fault detection and diagnosis in nonlinear dynamic systems with multi inputs and multi outputs. The main contribution of this paper is to develop a FDI schema according to reference models of fault-free and faulty behaviors designed with neural networks. Fault detection is obtained according to residuals that result from the comparison of measured signals with the outputs of the fault free reference model. Then, Euclidean distance from the outputs of models of faults to the measurements leads to fault isolation. The advantage of this method is to provide not only early detection but also early diagnosis thanks to the parallel computation of the models of faults and to the proposed decision algorithm. The effectiveness of this approach is illustrated with simulations on DAMADICS benchmark.

1. Introduction

Fault tolerant control and reliability issues for industrial systems and technological processes require the development of advanced fault detection and isolation (FDI) approaches. The main objective of fault detection and isolation is to provide early warnings to operators, such that appropriate actions can be taken to prevent the breakdowns of the system after the occurrence of faults. As a consequence, FDI methods help to avoid system breakdowns and material damages. During the last decades many investigations have been made using analytical approaches for FDI, based on mathematical models. Among the model-based methods, parameter estimation, parity relation, and observers design are the most often applied techniques [1–5]. Unfortunately these approaches require a mathematical description that is often not available in engineering practice. In order to solve this problem, system identification strategies can be applied [6, 7]. One of the most popular nonlinear systems identification approaches is based on the application of artificial neural networks (ANNs) [8–14]. ANNs are computational models with particular properties such as ability to learn, simplicity of implementation, generalization, and good approximation properties.

The aim of fault detection is to deliver alarms when faults occur. The aim of fault diagnosis is to determine the type, magnitude, and location of faults. Detection and diagnosis procedures are based on the observed system and knowledge about the process. So, the inputs of a knowledge-based fault diagnosis system are observed measurements and fault-relevant knowledge about the process [15, 16]. Then, diagnosis of actuators, sensors, and system components can be achieved either via a remote and supervisory diagnosis system or using local intelligence and self-validation methods [17–20]. Such self-validation techniques and condition monitoring are popular for numerous applications in various domains. The usual difficulty with FDI is to provide early diagnosis. Even if detection is generally obtained with short delays algorithms, diagnosis requires more time in order to collect data and process history [21–23]. So, diagnosis needs generally the observation of the fault consequence over a quite long time window and is achieved a posteriori.

This paper focuses on the problem of early fault detection and diagnosis using nonlinear models that are designed with neural networks. Fault detection is based on residuals design and analysis that also estimate the time of fault occurrence. Fault isolation results from the analysis of a bank of additional residuals. These residuals are obtained according to models of faults designed from the faults candidate database. Such models run simultaneously and are updated with the estimated time of occurrence of the faults. The idea to start several models of faults simultaneously once a fault is detected leads to parallel computation that accelerates the diagnosis. Each model behaves according to a single expected fault and is compared using the Euclidean distance with the collected data to provide a rapid diagnosis. The effectiveness of this approach is illustrated according to simulation results obtained with DAMADICS benchmark.

2. FDI Method

The potential of ANNs for FDI problems has been demonstrated in recent years. The neural network approach is applicable to systems for which mathematical models are difficult to obtain. Adaptive ANNs are used to differentiate various faults from the normal conditions, and from one another, according to different fault patterns. Such patterns are extracted from the measured input-output system data, either by offline training or by online learning. In addition ANNs are also helpful to model the nonlinear dynamics according to nonlinear autoregressive structures with exogenous inputs (NARX) [24]. In this section, a FDI method is proposed, that is based on the design of neural models that represent fault-free behaviors as well as faulty behaviors.

2.1. Fault-Free Model Design. In what follows we consider dynamic systems with q inputs $u_i(t)$ and n outputs $y_k(t)$, and we assume that the state variables are not measurable. Such systems often exhibit complex nonlinear dynamics. As a consequence, knowledge-based models are not easy to obtain. Another approach lies in the data-based models. Artificial neural networks are often used for that purpose [25, 26]. The goal is to design models for fault-free and faulty behaviors that will be used for the design of residuals (Figure 1).

In order to get the best ANN architecture, several configurations are tested according to a trial-error processing that uses pruning methods to eliminate useless nodes. The learning of the ANN is obtained according to Levenberg-Marquardt algorithm with early stopping. This algorithm is known for its rapid convergence. During learning stage, the ANN is trained with data collected during the normal functioning (fault-free model). Then the ANN reference models are validated with another set of data. Details about the sizing and training of ANN can be found in [25–27].

2.2. Fault Detection. During monitoring, the direct comparison of the system outputs $y_k(t)$ and fault-free model outputs $y'_k(t)$ leads to n residuals $r_{k0}(t)$:

$$r_{k0}(t) = y_k(t) - y'_k(t), \quad k = 1,\dots,n. \quad (1)$$

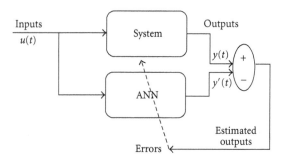

FIGURE 1: Data-based model design.

The residuals $r_{k0}(t)$ provide a source of information about faults for further processing. Fault detection is based on the evaluation of residuals magnitude. It is assumed that each residual $r_{k0}(t)$, $k = 1,\dots,n$ should normally be close to zero in the fault-free case, and it should be far from zero in the case of a fault. Thus, faults are detected by setting threshold S_{k0} on the residual signals (Figure 2, a single residual and a single fault are considered for simplicity). The analysis of residuals $r_{k0}(t)$ also provides an estimate τ_k of the time of occurrence t_f used for diagnosis issue. When several residuals are used, the estimate τ of the time of occurrence of faults is given by

$$\tau = \min\{\tau_k, \ k = 1,\dots,n\}. \quad (2)$$

The faults are detected when the absolute value of one residual $|r_{k0}(t)|$ becomes larger than the threshold S_{k0}:

$$|r_{k0}(t)| \le S_{k0} : \text{ no fault is detected at time } t,$$

$$|r_{k0}(t)| > S_{k0} : \text{ a fault is detected at time } t. \quad (3)$$

The main difficulty with this evaluation is that the measurement of the system outputs $y_k(t)$ is usually corrupted by disturbances (e. g., measurement noise). In practice, due to the modeling uncertainties and disturbances, it is necessary to assign large thresholds S_{k0} in order to avoid false alarms. Such thresholds usually imply a reduction of the fault detection sensitivity and can lead to nondetections.

2.3. Design of the Models of Faults. When multiple faults are considered, the isolation of the detected faults is no longer trivial, and early diagnosis becomes a difficult task. One can multiply the measurements and use some analysis tools (residuals analysis) in order to isolate the faults. But the number of sensors limits the use of such approach. Another approach is to use a history of collected data to improve the knowledge about the faulty behaviors and then to use this knowledge to design models of faults and additional residuals. We design and use such models to estimate each fault candidate and compare with measurements to provide the most probable fault according to the Euclidean distance between estimated and measured signals [28]. This approach is developed in the following: p faults candidates are considered. For each fault candidate, a model FM(j), $j = 1,\dots,p$ based on ANNs is designed (Figure 3). These models are trained according to a procedure similar to

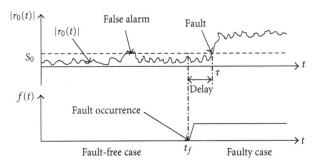

FIGURE 2: Residual-based fault detection.

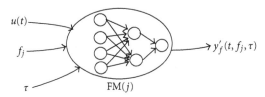

FIGURE 3: Model of fault f_j.

the one used for fault-free reference models design. Each model of fault is trained with data that result from the observation of the faulty behavior corresponding to a single fault f_j. Such data can be founded in history collected for the considered systems or with specific study where faults are enforced in order to investigate the consequences on the system safety, and availability.

Once the model of fault is trained and validated, it produces estimates $y'_k(t, f_j, \tau)$ of the signals $y_k(t)$, $k = 1,\ldots,n$, under the assumption that the fault f_j occurs at time τ. The comparison of this estimates with the actual measurements $y_k(t)$ is used to isolate the fault.

The inputs of network $FM(j)$ are the input signals $u_i(t)$, the fault candidate f_j, and the estimation τ of the time of occurrence for the fault provided by the detection stage. The outputs of network $FM(j)$ are the estimated faulty outputs $y'_k(t, f_j, \tau)$ $k = 1,\ldots,n$, $j = 1,\ldots,p$ obtained assuming that fault f_j disturbs the system from time τ. The models design and learning are obtained with a method similar to the one used for fault-free model.

2.4. Early Fault Diagnosis. The models of faults run simultaneously once a fault is detected according to the estimate τ of the time of occurrence of the fault. Each model will behave according to a single fault candidate, and the resulting behaviors will be compared with the collected data to provide a rapid diagnosis. In case of numerous fault candidates f_j, $j = 1,\ldots,p$, the outputs $y'_k(t, f_j, \tau)$ of the model $FM(j)$ are compared with the measurements $y_k(t)$ to compute additive residuals. The most probable fault candidate is determined according to the comparison of all residuals $r_{kj}(t, \tau)$, $k = 1,\ldots,n$, $j = 1,\ldots,p$ resulting from the n outputs and p models of faults:

$$r_{kj}(t, \tau) = y_k(t) - y'_{kj}\left(t, f_j, \tau\right), \qquad (4)$$

The proposed method uses a time window that can be sized according to the time requirement. Multistep diagnosis with a large window includes a diagnosis delay but will lead to a decision with a high confidence index. On the contrary single step diagnosis leads to immediate diagnosis but with a lower confidence index. To evaluate the probability of each fault candidate, let us define $R_{kj}(t, T, \tau)$ as the cumulative residuals over the sliding time interval $[\max(0, t - T), t]$ of maximal size T:

$$R_{kj}(t, T, \tau) = \sqrt{\int_{\max(0,\, t-T)}^{t} \left(r_{kj}(u,\, \tau)\right)^2 \cdot du}. \qquad (5)$$

Then, $D_j(t, T, \tau)$ is the Euclidean norm of the vector $R_j(t, T, \tau) = (R_{kj}(t, T, \tau))$ of dimension n:

$$D_j(t, T, \tau) = \sqrt{\sum_{k=1}^{k=n} \left(R_{kj}(t, T, \tau)\right)^2}. \qquad (6)$$

$D_j(t, T, \tau)$ is used to decide the most probable fault according to single or Multistep (i.e., immediate or delayed) diagnosis.

Multistep diagnosis at time t results from the a posteriori analysis of $D_j(t, T, \tau)$ computed for the time interval $[0, t]$ (i.e., $T = t$). The most probable fault at time t is given by

$$j^*(0, t) = \arg\min_j\left\{D_j(t, t, \tau), j = 1,\ldots,p\right\}. \qquad (7)$$

A confidence factor $CF_j(t, t, \tau)$ that the current fault is f_j will be given by

$$CF_j(t, t, \tau) = \frac{\sum_{k=1, k \neq j}^{k=p}(D_k(t, t, \tau))}{\sum_{k=1}^{k=p}(D_k(t, t, \tau))}. \qquad (8)$$

$CF_j(t, t, \tau)$ is near 1 when $D_j(t, t, \tau)$ is near 0 and $CF_j(t, t, \tau)$ is far from 1 when $D_j(t, t, \tau)$ is far from 0.

Immediate diagnosis results from the analysis of $D_j(t, 0, \tau)$ computed at time t according to

$$j^*(t, t) = \arg\min_j\left\{D_j(t, 0, \tau), j = 1,\ldots,p\right\}. \qquad (9)$$

In order to attenuate the effects of noise and outlaw values, the most probable fault candidate is determined according to the comparison of the cumulative residuals over a sliding time interval $[\max(0, t - T), t]$ of maximal size T. Single-step diagnosis results as a consequence:

$$j^*(t - T, t) = \arg\min_j\left\{D_j(t, T, \tau), j = 1,\ldots,p\right\} \qquad (10)$$

and the confidence factor $CF_j(t, T, \tau)$ that the current fault is f_j will be given by

$$CF_j(t, T, \tau) = \frac{\sum_{k=1, k \neq j}^{k=p}(D_k(t, T, \tau))}{\sum_{k=1}^{k=p}(D_k(t, T, \tau))}. \qquad (11)$$

The window width T (i.e., number of steps) is selected in order to satisfy real time requirements for rapid diagnosis.

3. Application to the DAMADICS Benchmark

The proposed method is applied on signals obtained with the DAMADICS simulator. Such system has been used to validate and discuss several FDI systems [29–31]. In [30], binary-valued evaluation of the fault symptoms is explored, and the authors focus on the optimization of the neural network architecture according to Akaike Information Criteria and Final Prediction Error. Both criteria include the learning error and also a term that depends on the complexity (size of the network in number of nodes) and on the dimension of the learning set in order to optimize the ratio complexity/performance. The authors provide interesting performances with small networks for detection but some faults are not isolable. In comparison, our approach requires a larger number of networks, and the networks have more nodes but all faults are detected and isolated. In [31], multiple-valued evaluation of the fault symptoms is introduced to improve the distinguishability of faults. Such a method requires a heuristic knowledge about influence of faults on residuals. In comparison, our approach uses binary-valued evaluation of the residuals but needs analytical models of faults of the actuator including the faults candidates that are not used in [31].

3.1. DAMADICS Description. The DAMADICS benchmark is an engineering research case study that can be used to evaluate detection and isolation methods. The benchmark is an electropneumatic valve actuator in the Lublin sugar factory in Poland [32]. The actuator consists of a control valve, a pneumatic servomotor, and a positioner (Figure 4).

In Figure 4, D/A is the data acquisition unit, PC is the positioner processing unit, E/P is the electropneumatic transducer, *V1, V2, V3* are bypass valves, DT stands for displacement, PT for pressure, FT for value flow transducer, and TT for temperature.

In the actuator, faults can appear in control valve, servomotor, electropneumatic transducer, piston rod travel transducer, pressure transmitter, or microprocessor control unit. 19 types of faults are considered ($p = 19$, Table 1). The faults are emulated under carefully monitored conditions, keeping the process operation within acceptable quality limits.

Five available measurements and 1 control value signal have been considered for benchmarking purposes: process control external signal CV, values of liquid pressure on the valve inlet *P1* and outlet *P2*, liquid flow rate *F*, liquid temperature *T1*, and stem displacement *X* (Table 2) [32].

3.2. Residuals Design for Detection. The positioner and control valve are modeled with two multilayer ANNs: netX and netF (Figure 5) that represent the interaction between $q = 4$ inputs and the $n = 2$ outputs in fault-free case according to

$$X' = \text{net}X(\text{CV}, P1, P2, T),$$
$$F' = \text{net}F(X, P1, P2, T). \tag{12}$$

To select the structure of the neural networks netX and netF, numerous tests have been carried out to obtain the

TABLE 1: Faults to be detected and isolated.

Fault	Description
f1	Valve clogging
f2	Valve or valve seat sedimentation
f3	Valve or valve seat erosion
f4	Increasing of valve or bushing friction
f5	External leakage
f6	Internal leakage (valve tightness)
f7	Medium evaporation or critical flow
f8	Twisted servomotor's piston rod
f9	Servomotor's housing or terminals tightness
f10	Servomotor's diaphragm perforation
f11	Servomotor's spring fault
f12	Electropneumatic transducer fault
f13	Rod displacement sensor fault
f14	Pressure sensor fault
f15	Positioner feedback fault
f16	Positioner supply pressure drop
f17	Unexpected pressure change across the valve
f18	Fully or partly opened bypass valves
f19	Flow rate sensor fault

TABLE 2: Input and output variables.

Input	Range	Unit	Description
CV	[0,1]	—	control signal from external PI controller
P1	[2000, 4e + 6]	Pa	Inlet liquid pressure
P2	[2000, 4e + 6]	Pa	Outlet liquid pressure
T1	[30, 110]	°C	Liquid temperature
Output	Range	Unit	Description
X	[0,1]	—	Position of the rod
F	[0,1]	—	Average flow

best architectures (i.e., number of hidden layers and number of neurons by layer) in order to model the operation of the actuator. The training and test data were generated by simulation using Matlab-Simulink models [27]. The selected structures are ANNs with 6 nodes in layer 1, 3 nodes in layer 2, and a single output neuron. The Table 3 sums some results obtained during the training stage in order to select the best architecture [25, 27]. For this purpose, the mean square error (MSE) is worked out over the set of training data and for a training of 1000 epochs.

When the training is over, netF provides estimates of the outputs, and MSE over the training data is about $3.3 \cdot e - 4$ for netX and about $2 \cdot e - 4$ for netF according to a training of 1000 epochs.

Validation is done with the measured data provided by the Lublin Sugar Factory in 2001 [32]. Validation is illustrated in Figure 6.

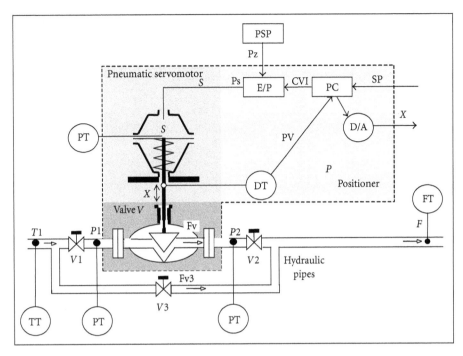

FIGURE 4: DAMADICS actuator.

TABLE 3: Design of the reference models netX and netF.

NetX	Layer 1	Layer 2	Output layer	MSE
Structure 1	6	3	1	0.00033
Structure 2	10	8	1	0.00149
Structure 3	21	12	1	0.00491
NetF	Layer 1	Layer 2	Output layer	MSE
Structure 1	6	3	1	0.000199
Structure 2	4	2	1	0.000849
Structure 3	8	4	1	0.00949

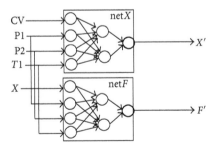

FIGURE 5: ANN fault-free model.

Two residuals are designed according to

$$r_{10}(t) = X(t) - X'(t),$$
$$r_{20}(t) = F(t) - F'(t). \quad (13)$$

3.3. Fault Detection. Fault detection is obtained according to the comparison of the current residuals value with some thresholds. The thresholds are determined according to the standard deviation of the residual for fault-free case. For

output X, $\sigma_1 = 0.0259$ and $S_{10} = 5\sigma_1 = 0.1295$. For output F, $\sigma_2 = 0.0040$ and $S_{20} = 5\sigma_2 = 0.0199$. During normal operation the residuals remain near zero. In Figure 7, the residuals r_{10} and r_{20} are depicted when the fault $f1$ is simulated during interval [20 s 80 s] time units (time units are in seconds). A fault is detected by r_{10} and by r_{20} at time $t = 22$ s when the residuals reach the threshold. From this figure one can also evaluate the delay to detection that is about 2 s for fault f_1. Such information will be used further for diagnosis issue.

The residuals r_{10} and r_{20} are binary valued according to the detection threshold. The Table 4 sums up the residual signatures for the 19 types of faults ($p = 19$). r_{i0^+} means that residual r_{i0} is large positive (according to the previous thresholds) and r_{i0^-} means that residual r_{i0} is large negative. To conclude, all faults are detected according to residual r_{10} and r_{20}.

The residuals analysis is an essential step in FDI systems. The choice of constant or adaptive detection thresholds strongly influences the quality and performance of the FDI. The problem of the threshold selection is closely linked to the behavior of residuals and also to constraints that may be imposed such as security margins tolerance [29]. For this reason, we study the variation of the delay to detection $t_f - \tau$ according to the magnitude of detection thresholds S_{10} and S_{20}. The results are summarized in the Table 5.

According to Table 5 one notices that if the detection thresholds increase, the delay of detection also increases in exponential manner and may lead to nondetections (ND). On the contrary small thresholds may lead to false alarms (FA). So, the thresholds must be thoroughly selected. For the continuation of our work we select the thresholds $S_{10} = 5\sigma_1$ and $S_{20} = 5\sigma_2$.

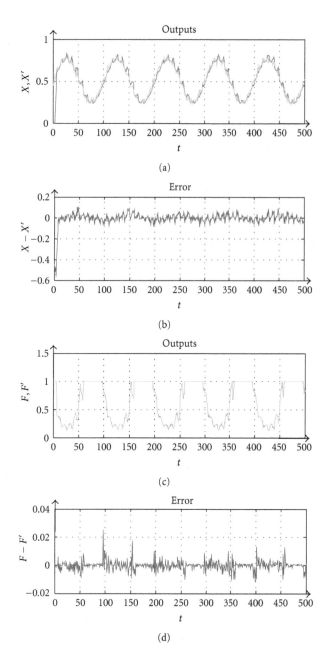

FIGURE 6: Actual output X and estimated output X' (a); residual r_{10} (b); actual output F, and estimated output F' (c); residual r_{20} (d).

TABLE 4: Fault detection and isolation with residuals r_{10} and r_{20}.

Faults	residuals			
	r_{10^+}	r_{10^-}	r_{20^+}	r_{20^-}
Fault free	0	0	0	0
$f1$	1	1	1	1
$f2$	0	0	1	0
$f3$	0	0	0	1
$f4$	0	0	1	1
$f5$	0	0	0	0
$f6$	0	0	0	1
$f7$	1	1	1	1
$f8$	0	0	0	0
$f9$	0	0	0	1
$f10$	1	1	1	1
$f11$	1	1	1	0
$f12$	0	0	0	1
$f13$	0	1	0	1
$f14$	0	0	0	0
$f15$	1	1	1	1
$f16$	1	0	0	1
$f17$	1	1	1	1
$f18$	0	0	0	1
$f19$	0	0	0	1

TABLE 5: Delays to detection.

	Res.	σ	2σ	3σ	4σ	5σ	6σ	7σ
$f12$	r_{10}	2 s	3 s	12 s	39 s	40 s	60 s	ND
$t_f = 500$ s	r_{20}	2 s	2 s	2 s	2 s	2 s	2 s	2 s
$f18$	r_{10}	FA	ND	ND	ND	ND	ND	ND
$t_f = 231$ s	r_{20}	1	2 s	2 s	2 s	2 s	2 s	2 s
$f11$	r_{10}	FA	2 s	2 s	2 s	2 s	3s	ND
$t_f = 485$ s	r_{20}	FA	2 s	2 s	2 s	2 s	2 s	2 s
$f15$	r_{10}	7 s	7 s	8 s	8 s	9 s	17 s	51 s
$t_f = 444$ s	r_{20}	FA	FA	7 s	7 s	7 s	8 s	8 s
$f3$	r_{10}	FA	ND	ND	ND	ND	ND	ND
$t_f = 405$ s	r_{20}	FA	FA	29 s	29 s	35 s	45 s	47 s

3.4. *Fault Diagnosis.* According to Table 4, three groups of faults with similar symptoms can be separated:

group 1 = {$f3$, $f6$, $f9$, $f12$, $f18$, $f19$},

group 2 = {$f1$, $f7$, $f10$, $f15$, $f17$},

group 3 = {Fault-free, $f5$, $f8$, $f14$}.

Within each group, faults are not isolable. For this reason we propose to use the method described in Sections 2.3 and 2.4 in order to improve the isolability of faults and to perform the complete early diagnosis. For this purpose, 19 models of faults FM(j) $j = 1,\ldots,19$ are designed according to the history of data available with DAMADICS benchmark. Each model FM(j) computes two estimated outputs $X'(t, fj, \tau)$, and $F'(t, f_j, \tau)$ and comparisons with measured data lead to the residuals $r_{1j}(t, f_j, \tau)$ and $r_{2j}(t, f_j, \tau)$:

$$r_{1j}\left(t, f_j, \tau\right) = X(t) - X'\left(t, f_j, \tau\right),$$
$$r_{2j}\left(t, f_j, \tau\right) = F(t) - F'\left(t, f_j, \tau\right). \tag{14}$$

The application of diagnosis stage leads to the results in Table 6 and Figures 9 to 11. Let us define the cumulative residuals $R_{1j}(t, T, \tau)$, $R_{2j}(t, T, \tau)$, and the distance $D_j(t, T, \tau)$, according to (5) and (6). Single- and Multistep diagnoses are obtained according to (7) and (10).

For example, $f15$ is simulated within time interval [444 s 1000 s] (Figure 8). The residuals r_{10} and r_{20} are also depicted as the detection thresholds $S_{10} = 5\sigma_1$ and $S_{20} = 5\sigma_2$. According to the detection stage, a fault is detected

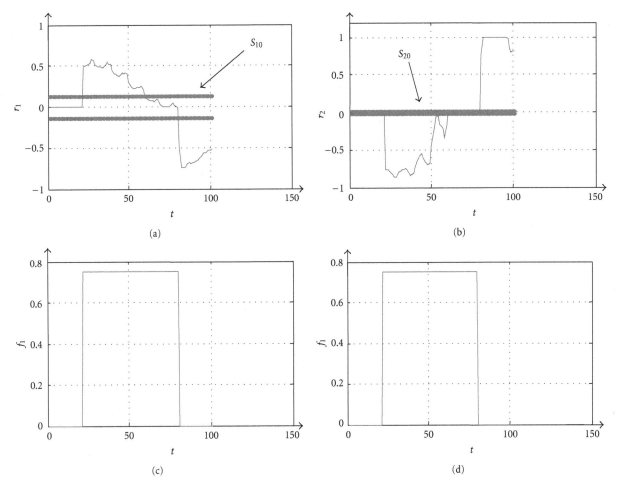

FIGURE 7: Residuals r_{10}, r_{20} when $f1$ is simulated within time interval [20 s 80 s].

at time $\tau = 451$ s with a delay of 7 s, and the group 2 $= \{f1, f7, f10, f15, f17\}$ is isolated (Figure 8). Multistep diagnosis is illustrated with a large time interval $T = t = 1000$ s (Figure 9).

For Multistep diagnosis, Figure 9 and Table 6 report the location of each model FM(j) in plan (R_1, R_2) and also the distance $D_j(t, t, 451)$ at time $t = 1000$ s. The model FM(15) corresponding to the fault candidate f_{15} provides the estimated outputs with the smallest Euclidean distance from the measured outputs. To conclude f_{15} is the most probable fault when residuals are analyzed within time interval [0, 1000 s]. Similar conclusions have been obtained for numerous other simulations.

Another example is provided when fault $f12$ is simulated within time interval [500 s, 1000 s]. According to the detection stage, a fault is detected at time $\tau = 502$ s, and the group 1 $= \{f3, f6, f9, f12, f18, f19\}$ is isolated. Early diagnosis is illustrated with a small time interval $T = 50$ s. Figures 10 and 11 plot the location of each model FM(j) in plan (R_1, R_2) for $t \in [0, 700]$. For any $t \in [0, 700]$, the trajectory with minimal distance to the origin (i.e., minimal value of $D_j(t, 50, \tau)$) corresponds to the most probable fault. In Figures 10 and 11, the most probable fault f_{12} is highlighted. Figure 11 plots details about the trajectory for model FM(12).

One can notice that the trajectories start near the origin (i.e., the effects of the expected faults on residuals are weak) and then go far from origin (i.e., the effects of the expected faults increase). The trajectory corresponding to FM(12) (i.e., the expected fault is the actual one) remains near origin in comparison to the other trajectories. One can conclude that the fault candidate $f12$ is the most probable fault because the distance to the origin is the smallest one. One can also notice that cumulative residuals $R_{1j}(t, T, \tau)$ and $R_{2j}(t, T, \tau)$ cover the positive part of plan (R_1, R_2). The repartition of the cumulative residuals in plan (R_1, R_2) confirms the significance of both outputs $X(t)$ and $F(t)$ to design residuals. Thus, Figures 10 and 11 are also useful to check if the considered outputs are helpful for diagnosis issues. Similar conclusions have been obtained for numerous other simulations.

3.5. Discussion. Kościelny et al. [31] have introduced the distinguishability factor Γ that depends on the cardinal of the set of distinguishable faults. As long as all faults are isolable with our approach, we obtain $\Gamma = 1$. In comparison, $\Gamma = 0.54$ has been obtained in [31]. In [30], Patan et al. just consider 3 faults and mention that f1 is not isolable with his contribution, so that $\Gamma < 1$ for sure. In addition, the delay to

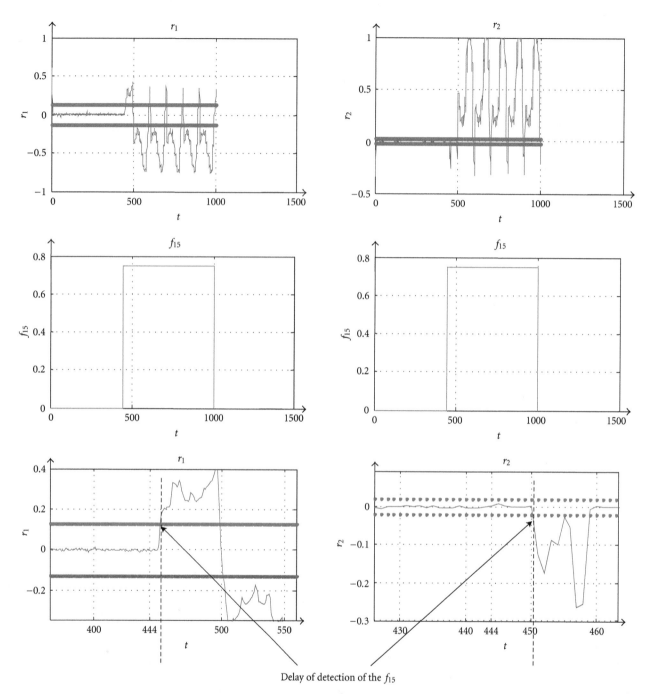

Figure 8: Residual r_{10}, r_{20} when f_{15} is simulated within time interval [444 s 1000 s].

detection is already not discussed in [30, 31]. From our point of view, delay to detection is quite important to consider as long as this delay will also influence the rapidity (and efficiency) of the diagnosis.

It is important to notice that the good performances of our approach are due to a large computation effort: 20 models with 2 outputs each of them are required to compute 40 residuals. In comparison [30] uses only 4 models with 2 outputs for each of them and [31] uses 10 residuals. The Akaike Information Criterion (AIC) and Final Prediction Error (FPE) [30] that measure the ratio complexity/performances remain quite good: FPE (netF) = 0.15

and IAC (netF) = −1.85, but these criteria do not include the complexity due to the number of networks working in parallel. Anyway, in our work, we do not consider the optimization of the ratio complexity/performance as introduced in [30], and we just use NNs of appropriate dimensions so that the training error will be small enough.

4. Conclusion

The method proposed in this work for early detection and diagnosis of faults combines the computing power and the robustness of neural networks with simple real time decision

TABLE 6: Multistep diagnosis according to the bank of models of faults.

Fault Cand. f_j	Model of faults FM(j)		
	R_{1j} (1000, 1000, 451)	R_{1j} (1000, 1000, 451)	D_j (1000, 1000, 451)
f1	14.96	20.02	25.00
f2	9.94	11.23	15.00
f3	10.03	14.79	17.88
f4	9.99	14.29	17.44
f5	10.01	13.47	16.78
f6	10.01	18.13	20.71
f7	14.15	20.02	24.52
f8	10.01	13.57	16.86
f9	10.08	13.65	16.97
f10	11.33	16.65	20.14
f11	9.93	13.59	16.83
f12	8.12	11.01	13.68
f13	10.09	20.01	22.41
f14	10.01	13.57	16.86
f15	*0.53*	*0.24*	*0.58*
f16	11.30	16.42	19.93
f17	10.19	15.29	18.37
f18	10.01	20.02	22.38
f19	10.01	8.65	13.23
Fault free	10.01	13.57	16.86

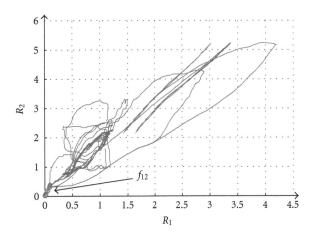

FIGURE 10: Early diagnosis: location of the models FM(j) in plan (R_1, R_2) for fault candidates $f1$ to $f19$.

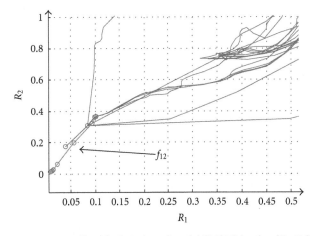

FIGURE 11: Details of the location of model FM(12) in plan (R_1, R_2).

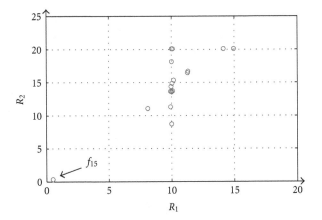

FIGURE 9: Multistep diagnosis: location of the models FM(j) in plan in plan (R_1, R_2) for fault candidates $f1$ to $f19$.

according to the Euclidean distance of cumulative residuals in residual space. The method leads to fault detection, time to failure estimation, and most probable fault evaluation. The results obtained with DAMADICS benchmark illustrate the performance of the method. But it is important to notice that the good performances of our approach are due to a large computation effort. Twenty models with two outputs each of them are required, and these networks work in parallel.

The hardest limitation of the proposed method is the necessity to design models of faults according to each fault candidate. Such design requires time, computational resources, and large history of data. We will consider systematic design of models of faulty behaviors in our future works. Another perspective is to take benefit from the correlation of diagnosis performances with the selection of estimated outputs for residuals design. The analysis of cumulative residuals in the residual space provides an interesting point of view to continue this investigation, and the covering of the residual space will be used to select appropriate residuals. Our next works will also include a deeper interpretation of the distance as a probability or likelihood]

Acknowledgment

The work was supported in part by Ministry of Higher Education and Scientific Research in Algeria.

References

[1] J. Korbicz, J. M. Koscielny, Z. Kowalczuk, and W. Cholewa, *Fault Diagnosis. Models, Artificial Intelligence, Applications*, Springer, Berlin, Germany, 2004.

[2] R. J. Patton and J. Chen, "On eigenstructure assignment for robust fault diagnosis," *International Journal of Robust and Nonlinear Control*, vol. 10, no. 14, pp. 1193–1208, 2000.

[3] H. R. Scola, R. Nikoukah, and F. Delebecque, "Test signal design for failure detection: a linear programming approach," *International Journal of Applied Mathematics and Computer Science*, vol. 13, no. 4, pp. 515–526, 2003.

[4] M. Witczak, *Modeling and Estimation Strategies for Fault Diagnosis of Non-Linear Systems. From Analytical to Soft Computing Approaches*, Springer, Berlin, Germany, 2007.

[5] E. Delaleau, J. P. Louis, and R. Ortega, "Modeling and control of induction motors," *International Journal of Applied Mathematics and Computer Science*, vol. 11, no. 1, pp. 105–129, 2001.

[6] T. Soderstrom et al., *System Identification*, Prentice-Hall International, Hemel Hempstead, Hertfordshire, UK, 1989.

[7] T. Bouthiba, "Fault location in ehv transmission lines using artificial neural networks," *International Journal of Applied Mathematics and Computer Science*, vol. 14, no. 1, pp. 69–78, 2004.

[8] M. Mrugalski, M. Witczak, and J. Korbicz, "Confidence estimation of the multi-layer perceptron and its application in fault detection systems," *Engineering Applications of Artificial Intelligence*, vol. 21, no. 6, pp. 895–906, 2008.

[9] M. M. Gupta, *Static and Dynamic Neural Networks*, John Wiley & Sons, Hoboken, NJ, USA, 2003.

[10] O. Nelles, *Non-Linear Systems Identification. From Classical Approaches to Neural Networks and Fuzzy Models*, Springer, Berlin, Germany, 2001.

[11] S. C. Tan, C. P. Lim, and M. V. C. Rao, "A hybrid neural network model for rule generation and its application to process fault detection and diagnosis," *Engineering Applications of Artificial Intelligence*, vol. 20, no. 2, pp. 203–213, 2007.

[12] V. Uraikul, C. W. Chan, and P. Tontiwachwuthikul, "Artificial intelligence for monitoring and supervisory control of process systems," *Engineering Applications of Artificial Intelligence*, vol. 20, no. 2, pp. 115–131, 2007.

[13] J. Vieira, F. M. Dias, and A. Mota, "Artificial neural networks and neuro-fuzzy systems for modelling and controlling real systems: a comparative study," *Engineering Applications of Artificial Intelligence*, vol. 17, no. 3, pp. 265–273, 2004.

[14] B. Michal, R. Patton, M. Syfert, S. de las Heras, and J. Quevedo, "Introduction to the DAMADICS actuator FDI benchmark study," *Control Engineering Practice*, vol. 14, no. 6, pp. 577–596, 2006.

[15] R. Isermann, "Model-based fault-detection and diagnosis—status and applications," *Annual Reviews in Control*, vol. 29, no. 1, pp. 71–85, 2005.

[16] R. Isermann, *Fault-Diagnosis Systems. An Introduction from Fault Detection to Fault Tolerance*, Springer, Berlin, Germany, 2006.

[17] J. C. Yang and D. W. Clarke, "The self-validating actuator," *Control Engineering Practice*, vol. 7, no. 2, pp. 249–260, 1999.

[18] M. Henry, "Plant asset management via intelligent sensors digital, distributed and for free," *Computing and Control Engineering Journal*, vol. 11, no. 5, pp. 211–213, 2000.

[19] M. Tombs, "Intelligent and self-validating sensors and actuators," *Computing and Control Engineering Journal*, vol. 13, no. 5, pp. 218–220, 2002.

[20] J. B. Gomm, D. L. Yu, and D. Williams, "Sensor fault diagnosis in a chemical process via RBF neural networks," *Control Engineering Practice*, vol. 7, no. 1, pp. 49–55, 1999.

[21] L. Yaguol, H. Zhengjia, and Z. Yahyang, "A new approach to intelligent fault diagnosis of rotating machinery," *Expert Systems with Applications*, vol. 35, no. 4, pp. 1593–1600, 2008.

[22] H. T. Mok and C. W. Chan, "Online fault detection and isolation of nonlinear systems based on neurofuzzy networks," *Engineering Applications of Artificial Intelligence*, vol. 21, no. 2, pp. 171–181, 2008.

[23] J. Zhao, J. Huang, and W. Sun, "On-line early fault detection and diagnosis of municipal solid waste incinerators," *Waste Management*, vol. 28, no. 11, pp. 2406–2414, 2008.

[24] H. Hjalmarsson, A. Juditsky, J. Sjöberg et al., "Nonlinear black-box modeling in system identification: a unified overview," *Automatica*, vol. 31, no. 12, pp. 1691–1724, 1995.

[25] Y. Kourd, N. Guersi, and D. Lefebvre, "A two stages diagnosis method with neuronal networks," in *Proceedings of the International Conference on Electrical Engineering Design and Technologies (ICEEDT '08)*, Hammamet, Tunisie, 2008.

[26] Y. Kourd, N. Guersi, and D. Lefebvre, "A two stages diagnosis method with Neuro-fuzzy approach," in *Proceedings of the 6th Conférence Internationale Francophone d'Automatique*, Nancy, France, 2010.

[27] Y. Kourd, N. Guersi, and D. Lefebvre, "Neuro-fuzzy approach for fault diagnosis: application to the DAMADICS," in *Proceedings of the 7th international Conference on Informatics in Control, Automation and Robotics (ICINCO '10)*, Funchal, Madeira, Portugal, 2010.

[28] M. Blanke, M. Kinnaert, J. Lunze, and M. Staroswiecki, *Diagnosis and Fault Tolerant Control*, Springer, New York, NY, USA, 2003.

[29] D. Lefebvre, H. Chafouk, and M. Lebbal, *Modélisation et Diagnostic des Systèmes. Une Approche Hybride*, Éditions universitaires européennes, 2010.

[30] K. Patan and T. Parisini, "Identification of neural dynamic models for fault detection and isolation: the case of a real sugar evaporation process," *Journal of Process Control*, vol. 15, no. 1, pp. 67–79, 2005.

[31] J. M. Kościelny, M. Bartyś, P. Rzepiejewski, and J. Sá da Costa, "Actuator fault distinguishability study for the DAMADICS benchmark problem," *Control Engineering Practice*, vol. 14, no. 6, pp. 645–652, 2006.

[32] DAMADICS, 2002, http://diag.mchtr.pw.edu.pl/damadics/.

Permissions

The contributors of this book come from diverse backgrounds, making this book a truly international effort. This book will bring forth new frontiers with its revolutionizing research information and detailed analysis of the nascent developments around the world.

We would like to thank all the contributing authors for lending their expertise to make the book truly unique. They have played a crucial role in the development of this book. Without their invaluable contributions this book wouldn't have been possible. They have made vital efforts to compile up to date information on the varied aspects of this subject to make this book a valuable addition to the collection of many professionals and students.

This book was conceptualized with the vision of imparting up-to-date information and advanced data in this field. To ensure the same, a matchless editorial board was set up. Every individual on the board went through rigorous rounds of assessment to prove their worth. After which they invested a large part of their time researching and compiling the most relevant data for our readers. Conferences and sessions were held from time to time between the editorial board and the contributing authors to present the data in the most comprehensible form. The editorial team has worked tirelessly to provide valuable and valid information to help people across the globe.

Every chapter published in this book has been scrutinized by our experts. Their significance has been extensively debated. The topics covered herein carry significant findings which will fuel the growth of the discipline. They may even be implemented as practical applications or may be referred to as a beginning point for another development. Chapters in this book were first published by Hindawi Publishing Corporation; hereby published with permission under the Creative Commons Attribution License or equivalent.

The editorial board has been involved in producing this book since its inception. They have spent rigorous hours researching and exploring the diverse topics which have resulted in the successful publishing of this book. They have passed on their knowledge of decades through this book. To expedite this challenging task, the publisher supported the team at every step. A small team of assistant editors was also appointed to further simplify the editing procedure and attain best results for the readers.

Our editorial team has been hand-picked from every corner of the world. Their multi-ethnicity adds dynamic inputs to the discussions which result in innovative outcomes. These outcomes are then further discussed with the researchers and contributors who give their valuable feedback and opinion regarding the same. The feedback is then collaborated with the researches and they are edited in a comprehensive manner to aid the understanding of the subject.

Apart from the editorial board, the designing team has also invested a significant amount of their time in understanding the subject and creating the most relevant covers. They scrutinized every image to scout for the most suitable representation of the subject and create an appropriate cover for the book.

The publishing team has been involved in this book since its early stages. They were actively engaged in every process, be it collecting the data, connecting with the contributors or procuring relevant information. The team has been an ardent support to the editorial, designing and production team. Their endless efforts to recruit the best for this project, has resulted in the accomplishment of this book. They are a veteran in the field of academics and their pool of knowledge is as vast as their experience in printing. Their expertise and guidance has proved useful at every step. Their uncompromising quality standards have made this book an exceptional effort. Their encouragement from time to time has been an inspiration for everyone.

The publisher and the editorial board hope that this book will prove to be a valuable piece of knowledge for researchers, students, practitioners and scholars across the globe.

List of Contributors

W. Mansour and R. Velazco
TIMA Laboratory, 46 avenue Felix Viallet, 38031 Grenoble, France

R. Ayoubi
Department of Computer Engineering, University of Balamand, Tripoli, Lebanon

H. Ziade
Electrical and Electronics Department, Faculty of Engineering I, Lebanese University, El Arz Street, El Kobbe, Tripoli, Lebanon

W. EL Falou
Electrical and Electronics Department, Faculty of Engineering I, Lebanese University, El Arz Street, El Kobbe, Tripoli, Lebanon
Lebanese French University of Technology and Applied Sciences, Tripoli, Lebanon

Masaaki Tsujitani and Yusuke Tanaka
Division of Informatics and Computer Sciences, Graduate School of Engineering, Osaka Electro-Communication University, Osaka 572-8530, Japan
Biometrics Department, Statistics Analysis Division, EPS Co., Ltd., 3-4-30 Miyahara, Yodogawa-ku, Osaka 532-0003, Japan

C. Muniraj
Department of Electrical Engineering, K. S. Rangasamy College of Technology, Tiruchengode 637 215, India

S. Chandrasekar
Department of Electrical Engineering, SonaPERT R&D Centre, Sona College of Technology, Salem 636 005, India

Amine Chohra
Images, Signals and Intelligent Systems Laboratory (LISSI/EA 3956), Paris-East University (UPEC), avenue Pierre Point, 77127 Lieusaint, France

Ouahiba Azouaoui
Autonomous Robotic Systems (ARS), Development Center of Advanced Technologies (CDTA), Cite 20 Aout 1956, BP 17 Baba Hassen, 16303 Algiers, Algeria

Chunhua Feng
College of Mathematics and Statistics, Guangxi Normal University, Guilin 541004, China

Massimo La Rosa, Riccardo Rizzo and Alfonso Urso
ICAR-CNR, Consiglio Nazionale delle Ricerche, Viale delle Scienze, Ed.11, 90128 Palermo, Italy

Thai Hoang Le
Department of Computer Science, Ho Chi Minh University of Science, Ho Chi Minh City 70000, Vietnam

Vipul K. Dabhi
Information Technology Department, Dharmsinh Desai University, Nadiad 387001, India

Sanjay Chaudhary
IICT, Ahmedabad University, Ahmedabad 380009, India

Jinxiang Cai, Zhenkun Huang and Honghua Bin
School of Science, Jimei University, Xiamen 361021, China

Shang-Jen Chuang, Chiung-Hsing Chen, Chih-Ming Hong and Guan-Yu Chen
Department of Electronic Communication Engineering, National Kaohsiung Marine University, Kaohsiung 81157, Taiwan

X. Zhang, G. Foderaro and S. Ferrari
Laboratory for Intelligent Systems and Control (LISC), Department of Mechanical Engineering and Materials Science, Duke University, Durham, NC 27708, USA

C. Henriquez
Department of Biomedical Engineering and Department of Computer Science, Duke University Durham, NC 27708, USA

A. M. J. Van Dongen
Program in Neuroscience & Behavioral Disorders, Duke-NUS Graduate Medical School, Singapore, Singapore

M. Fatih Amasyali
Department of Computer Engineering, Yildiz Technical University, Davutpasa Campus, Esenler, 34220 Istanbul, Turkey

Ayse Demirhan
Department of Business Administration, Yildiz Technical University, Yildiz Campus, Besiktas, 34349 Istanbul, Turkey

Mert Bal
Department of Mathematical Engineering, Yildiz Technical University, Davutpasa Campus A-116, Esenler, 34220 Istanbul, Turkey

David Mendes
Climate Science Program, Federal University of Rio Grande do Norte, 59082-200 Natal, RN, Brazil

José Antonio Marengo
Instituto Nacional de Pesquisas Espaciais (INPE), Avenida dos Astronautas, 1.758 Jardim da Granja, 12227-010 Sao Jose dos Campos, SP, Brazil

Sidney Rodrigues and Magaly Oliveira
World Wild Life Fund Brazil (WWF), SHIS EQQL 6/8 Conjunto, 71620-430 Brasilia, DF, Brazil

Garima Singh and Laxmi Srivastava
Electrical Engineering Department, Madhav Institute of Technology and Science, Gwalior 474 005, India

Kou-Yuan Huang and Kai-Ju Chen
Department of Computer Science, National Chiao Tung University, 1001 University Road, Hsinchu 30010, Taiwan

James Mubiru
Department of Physics, Makerere University, P.O. Box 7062, Kampala, Uganda

Zhang Qunli
Department of Mathematics, Heze University, Heze 274015, Shandong, China

Satchidananda Dehuri
Department of Information and Communication Technology, Fakir Mohan University, Vyasa Vihar, Balasore, Orissa 756019, India

Yahia Kourd
Department of Control Engineering, University of Mohamed Khider, Biskra 07000, Algeria

Dimitri Lefebvre
Electrical Engineering and Automatic Control Research Group (GREAH), University of Le Havre, 25 rue Philippe Lebon, 76058 Le Havre, France

Noureddine Guersi
Department of Electronics, University of Badji Mokhtar, Annaba 23000, Algeria

Printed in the USA
CPSIA information can be obtained
at www.ICGtesting.com
JSHW051444221024
72173JS00006B/1571